THE EXPLORATIONS OF Captain James Cook IN THE PACIFIC AS TOLD BY SELECTIONS OF HIS OWN JOURNALS 1768-1779

Edited by

A. GRENFELL PRICE
C.M.G., M.A. (OXON), D.LITT.(ADEL), F.R.G.S

Illustrated by

GEOFFREY C. INGLETON

With a new Introduction by

PERCY G. ADAMS
Professor of English
The University of Tennessee

DOVER PUBLICATIONS, INC.
NEW YORK

This Dover edition, first published in 1971, is an unabridged republication of the work originally published by The Limited Editions Club in 1957. This edition also contains a new Introduction by Percy G. Adams.

International Standard Book Number: 0-486-22766-9
Library of Congress Catalog Card Number: 79-145750

Manufactured in the United States of America
Dover Publications, Inc.
180 Varick Street
New York, N.Y. 10014

INTRODUCTION
to the Dover Edition

EXACTLY TWO HUNDRED YEARS AGO CAPTAIN JAMES COOK was sailing the Pacific Ocean on the first of three voyages that were to make him the greatest of sailor explorers the world has known. The two-hundredth anniversary of his decade of unbelievable accomplishments began in London in late July of 1968, on the day of the month when Cook started the *Endeavour* toward the mouth of the Thames. After an address delivered before hundreds of distinguished guests by R. A. Skelton, the chief student of Cook's charts, the celebration moved to the British Museum for a long look at the most attractive, easily the most valuable, exhibit ever arranged to honor the memory of a restless, curious son of earth: there were original maps and drawings, great natural history collections and artifacts, and manuscripts and first editions of dozens of journals and logs kept by Cook and the men who sailed with him. From England the celebration of Cook's exploits has moved and is moving to Tahiti, to New Zealand, to Australia, to Hawaii, to the northwest coast of North America. One of the most appropriate observances of the anniversary has been held at Wellington, for that city overlooks the strait that bears Cook's name and separates the two islands of New Zealand which he knew so well. And there too works the most noted of Cook scholars, Professor J. C. Beaglehole, whose careful editing of the three journals kept by Cook himself—completed just in time for the anniversary—constitutes not only one of the best monuments to the man himself but, appropriately, the best work ever published by the Hakluyt Society. Since those four volumes contain over 3300 pages of notes, essays, and journals and will probably never be reproduced in an inexpensive edition, Dover Publications is offering as its part in the bi-centennial this handsomely illustrated, one-volume selection of entries from the original journals.

Each of the three voyages was carefully planned, for each the British Admiralty provided a detailed set of general instructions, and each increased knowledge and brought fame for James Cook. On the first voyage (1768–1771), taken in the *Endeavour*, Cook went through the Strait of Le Maire to Tahiti, where he observed the transit of Venus at the same time two other expeditions were observing it at far separated spots and where he and his men fell in love with the South Sea paradise discovered a year before by Samuel Wallis; from there he made his way to New Zealand to chart the coast and show it to be two islands, then to the eastern coast of Australia, and finally home by Batavia and South Africa. On the second voyage

(1772–1775), in the *Resolution* and the *Adventure*, Cook sailed in the opposite direction, first to Cape Town and then south to the ice of Antarctica, which he coasted as he headed east looking for the great continent that maps from the time of the middle ages had shown as *Terra Incognita*. Finding no southern continent he twice turned north on this circumnavigation to make huge exploring sweeps among the islands of the warmer part of the South Pacific before returning to the upper latitudes and other tries for the continent. On voyage three (1776–1780), in the *Resolution* and the *Discovery*, the now famous sailor started out as he had on the second circumnavigation but went by the shortest route to the islands of the South Pacific, by then so well known, before heading due north to discover Hawaii; then he explored the northwest coast of North America well into the Bering and Arctic Seas and proved nonexistent the navigable Northwest or Northeast Passage to India which merchants and rulers had long sought from the Atlantic side and which many mapmakers had confidently sketched in as a reality. But the third proved to be Cook's last voyage; for on a second visit to Hawaii, intended to be a respite from the rigors of the Alaskan winter, his luck ran out and he was killed by savages.

It had taken more than luck, however, to move among the giant ice floes that have since captured and crushed so many ships, to brave the reefs and shores of hundreds of unmapped islands small and large, to keep peace with thousands of savages some of whom were cannibals, to guard the health of his men successfully at a time when a circumnavigation normally meant death to so many, and to keep such helpful journals, draw such fine maps, and see the necessity of aiding the scientists whom he took along. For such successes Cook had to have experience as well as genius, and his experience was of the proper, most practical kind. After a bare minimum of schooling he went to sea and by the age of twenty-one had worked his way up to the position of mate on a small coaling ship, meanwhile learning much about piloting, navigation, mathematics, and charting. When the Seven Years' War began he gave up his career to enlist as a seaman in the British navy. Again he quickly gained the admiration of his superiors and rose in rank, serving on three men-of-war and ending as Master of a sixty-four-gun ship, the *Pembroke*, a position that required not only considerable talents as a leader but great ability as a navigator and pilot. During the fight for Canada he provided important charts and gave helpful advice to General Wolfe. When the war was over his former commanders saw to it that his genius was employed in surveying and charting the newly acquired coasts and waters of Newfoundland and the St. Lawrence, a job that permitted him to spend only four winter months a year for several years with his wife and children in England. By 1768, then, James Cook at age forty was well known in the British Admiralty as a man whose talents and training equipped him to be the leader of a long sailing expedition whose object would be not to fight battles or to sack treasure ships but to bring back scientific information.

One of the first evidences of Cook's judgment and ability was his choice of a ship for the voyage. Instead of a large, heavily armored, comfortable navy vessel like the one he had served on last, he selected one of the small, square-rigged coalers out of Whitby, of the kind he had once known so well. It was a masterful choice, for such an expedition required putting in close to shore in order to land scientists and to chart coasts. The coaler's flat bottom and shallow draft were best for such work. Furthermore, great speed and huge guns were not necessary since the civilized world quickly heard of Cook's peaceful pursuit of knowledge: the only men he would need to fear were those poorly armed ones in the Pacific islands who were not yet aware of the values of science. Even the third voyage, which took place during four years of the war fought between Britain and its American colonies and France, was safe. At that time Benjamin Franklin himself sent an open letter to all American armed ships asking them not to "plunder" or in any way "obstruct" the return home of "that most celebrated Navigator and Discoverer Captain Cook," who was doing so much "to the Benefit of Mankind in general." Cook's first small coaler performed its function so well that he never considered any other kind of ship for either of his later voyages of discovery.

Perhaps the most lasting evidence of Cook's genius has been the journals he kept; for while each of the three voyages ultimately supplied the world with numerous accounts produced by crewmen or supernumeraries on his ships, the most important are of course those written by the commander-in-chief himself. But it has not always been possible to read Cook's own words exactly as he wrote them. It was customary in the eighteenth century to order everyone on an official voyage for the Admiralty to turn over all logs and journals he had kept, the reason being that the Admiralty itself wished to publish its "official" version first. On every well known circumnavigation, however, someone—sometimes several people—managed to hide a journal, perhaps by writing it in the margins of a Bible or on such thin paper that it could be secreted in the lining of a jacket. Such subterfuges were profitable since publishers were always ready to pay well for the surreptitious journals. Hardly, for example, had the *Endeavour* docked when one publisher came out with an anonymous account of its voyage. For the "official," ghost-written, version of that first voyage John Hawkesworth was paid at least £6,000, a munificent sum. (His contemporary Henry Fielding received only £1,000 for *Tom Jones*.) Hawkesworth's assignment was to collate Cook's journal with that of Joseph Banks, who went along as chief scientist, then to rewrite the two accounts as one and publish it in 1773 in three volumes along with the journals of the circumnavigators Philip Carteret, Wallis, and John Byron. But Hawkesworth was not Captain Cook, for not only did he depend heavily on Banks but he often rewrote Cook's words and even inserted comments and opinions of his own. Nevertheless, his edition was enormously successful as a publishing venture and is undoubtedly one of the most important travel books. Not until 1893 would Cook's own journal be published, and not until the Hakluyt Society's edition of 1955 would the copy in Cook's handwriting, now preserved in the Commonwealth National Library at Canberra, be given to the world. By the time he had completed his second circumnavigation the explorer was so important that he was permitted to select his own editor, and so his last two journals—both of which are in the British Museum—were brought out substantially as he would have wanted them.

As a writer Cook was untrained and artless, but he learned fast and had good teachers. Without formal schooling he did not spell or punctuate accurately or consistently. Some of his inconsistencies, such as the confusion of *then* and *than*, can be in part attributed to his times; but he had far more trouble with *ie* and *ei* than did his educated contemporaries, and sometimes he wrote a page or more without inserting any mark of punctuation. On the first voyage he was quite close to Joseph Banks, the rich young scientist, highly educated and cultured, whose own journal contains evidence that he was an important influence on Cook as a writer, especially during the early months when they were together. Professor Beaglehole has shown, for example, that while Cook's description of Tahiti owes something to Banks, his account of New Zealand is his own. On the second voyage the mathematician William Wales seems to have had a similar influence, although to a much smaller degree. The explorer's chief teacher, however, was probably James Cook, for just as he taught himself surveying and navigating he must have worked at improving his method of recording what he experienced. The best evidence for such an opinion is to be found in the fact that he constantly wrote and rewrote his second journal. The last journal is, of course, incomplete and must be supplemented by the records of Clerke and King, who succeeded him after his death. Through all his accounts he remained modest and unobtrusive, preferring not only objectivity but his own observations. And to read him, whether in one volume of selections or in four long volumes, is to arrive at certain definite conclusions about him as a man and about the results of his career.

The most obvious conclusion is that no man ever did more to alter and to correct the map of the earth. After him cartographers abandoned the great southern *Terra Incognita* and the equally mythical Northwest Passage while at the same time they were able to sketch in Australia's east coast and Great Barrier Reef even more correctly than Dampier and others had given them the western coast. After him maps could show Hawaii, the southern ice line, the northwest coast of North America, dozens of previously undiscovered islands in Polynesia, and New Zealand as two islands. And since he drew such splendid, professional charts himself, after him the map of the Pacific was everywhere more trustworthy. Furthermore, that map will show how well his names for islands, points, reefs, and mountains have stood the test of time.

His journals will also show Cook's great importance in the struggle to keep sailors healthy while on long voyages. He constantly experimented with diets that would prevent scurvy—sauerkraut, spruce beer, inspissated beer; he kept his crews and their quarters clean; and at every opportunity he stored up supplies of fresh fruits and vegetables. No doubt his discipline and strength of character were in great measure responsible for the success of his health program, for his crews sometimes had to be forced to eat or drink their daily portions of the unappetizing concoctions devised for their good. At any rate, in a century when other circumnavigators—Admiral Anson, for example—often returned with a remnant of those who set out, James Cook on three long voyages lost not a single man to scurvy on the ships he personally commanded.

One striking fact that appears from a reading of and about Captain Cook is that while he does not always name them in his journals the men who sailed with him often reenlisted for a second or third voyage under his command and often went on to achieve the kind of greatness in naval affairs that would have pleased such a commander. Charles Clerke, for example, went with Cook three times, ending up as Captain of the *Discovery*. James Burney was a midshipman and second lieutenant on the second voyage, was promoted to first lieutenant under Clerke, and finally became an admiral and one of the most renowned collectors and editors of accounts of sea voyages. George Vancouver, who was on the last two voyages, became a commander and continued Cook's northwest explorations, leaving his name in a number of places on the coast of Canada and the United States. William Bligh, to be the most notorious crewman Cook had, was obviously capable; certainly he was admired not only as master of the *Resolution* on the last voyage but as a mapmaker who rivalled his great commander; and while he was later the victim of two of the most famous of mutinies, one while on the *Bounty*, one as Governor of New South Wales, he was as successful with scurvy as Cook and he was to navigate the longest open-boat voyage ever made. Then there were Nathaniel Portlock and George Dixon, also on the third voyage, each of whom returned to the Northwest as captain of a ship that would be involved in the Nootka Sound Controversy. On the third voyage, in fact, some twenty-three of the crew had sailed with Cook before. It is safe to say that no sea-going man ever attracted, kept, or produced better sailors.

The supernumeraries on his ships were less prone to reenlist for the arduous voyages, but they were often as famous. Easily the most celebrated was Joseph Banks, who went along as scientist for the first voyage when the geographer Alexander Dalrymple withdrew in anger because he was not placed in command of the expedition. Although Banks was an experienced young man, having already made a voyage on which he studied and collected plants off the northeast coast of North America, he was probably chosen to accompany Cook because he was rich and offered to pay his own way and that of the eight in his retinue. Among those whom he took were the Swede Dr. Daniel Solander, a medical doctor as well as a distinguished student of Linnaeus; and Sydney Parkinson, a draughtsman who died in Batavia but whose account of the circumnavigation was published in London before Hawkesworth's three volumes appeared. Banks's journal, edited in two beautiful volumes by Professor Beaglehole, supplements Cook's first one and is a major travel book, an accomplishment almost as important as his great collection of Polynesian plants now stored at the British Museum. He was impetuous and sometimes angry at Cook for not taking him ashore in dangerous waters so he could add to his collection, but he willingly underwent all hardships and at times even worked like a common seaman; he was amorous and, like Cook's sailors but not Cook himself, succumbed to the beautiful girls of Tahiti; and while he refused to go on the second voyage because he thought his quarters would be inadequate, he remained a friend to Cook and Cook's crewmen. A Fellow of the Royal Society and a member with Goldsmith, Garrick, Burke, and others of Johnson's Club, he was so well known among the literati and intellectuals of London that all of them, including Dr. Johnson, thought of the *Endeavour* as Banks's ship and of the first expedition as having been planned for his benefit alone.

When he resigned from the second voyage, his place was taken by the German Reinhold Forster and his young son Georg. The father, quite a different type from Banks, was churlish and unable to fraternize with the sailors, whom he found vulgar and dirty mouthed. But his collection of plants and artifacts commendably supplements that of Banks, and the huge two-volume journal of voyage two, which his son published against the wishes of the Admiralty and before Cook could bring out his own, is also a fine supplement to Cook's account. Less famous were the assistants William Wales and Bayley, the botanist Dr. Sparrman, and the surgeon Samwell, each of whom produced a journal to go with his scientific accomplishments while sailing on a voyage with Cook.

The supernumerary who struck the eighteenth-century imagination most was the Tahitian Omai, who was brought back on the *Adventure* in 1774 and made a deep mark on London life before Cook took him home three years later. On the first voyage Cook had tried to bring a Polynesian named Tupia to England; but the friendly, likeable Tupia, who helped so much in translating the languages of the Polynesian islands, died at Batavia. The French circumnavigator Bougainville, in the Pacific during part of the time Cook was on the first voyage, had also brought back a native of Tahiti, named Ahutoru; but while Ahutoru enjoyed opera and was the object of sentimental adulation, he did not take Paris the way Omai conquered London. Fanny Burney was surprised at Omai's grace in receiving a sword from the King, and Dr. Johnson "was struck with the elegance of his behaviour" but being no primitivist attributed Omai's good manners to the genteel London society he frequented. Omai, who learned to dance and play excellent chess, was directly or indirectly the subject of plays, poems, and novels, the poet Cowper putting him in *The Task* as his "gentle savage" and the painter-designer Phillippe deLoutherbourg capping a distinguished career in 1785 with scenery for a speaking pantomime called *Omai, or a Trip around the World*. Although apparently not rating Omai's intelligence very high, Cook went out of his way to take him home and to establish him in a position far above the one he had formerly held in Tahiti. There were, in fact, tears shed aboard the *Resolution* and the *Discovery* as the crew left Omai and sailed north to discover Hawaii.

The scientific advances effected by some of Cook's supernumeraries, notably Banks and the Forsters, and by the three voyages in general are incalculable. Trained European scientists had been sent to distant continents and oceans before. The Jesuits missionaries, such as Father Lobo, had informed the French Academy of Sciences and the Royal Society with their trained reports of plants and people of Canada and the Far East. Sir Hans Sloane, long-time Secretary and then President of the Royal Society, was not only a friend of the traveller William Dampier, influencing him to bring back drawings and samples, but had himself gone to the West Indies and returned with a significant collection and with material for a two-volume study of the natural history of the islands which he published in 1707. And Philibert Commerson, another eminent scientist, was with Bougainville at the time Banks was being escorted and protected by Captain Cook. But no previous collection of botanical and zoological lore rivalled the one Cook's scientists turned over to the British Museum. Their plants, especially, have been primary evidence in the perennial argument over whether the Pacific islands were peopled from the east or from the west. In 1954, at the end of a long career, for example, the botanist and biogeographer Elmer Drew Merrill drew most heavily on Cook's scientists not only to answer critics like O. F. Cook and Thor Heyerdahl but to argue again that the Polynesians came from the west and not from the Americas.

But Cook has been important to natural historians, to anthropologists, and to historians in other ways. His journal and the journals of men on his ships are still carefully studied for their details of life in primitive societies, on Tahiti, on New Zealand, on Hawaii. Cook was the first to describe the marvelous and unique weaving on Tonga; he and his crew first described the kangaroo for Europeans; he offered information on the political structure and the religion of the places he visited; and his observations of the secret society of the Arioris, though naïve by the standards of advanced science, are still read with interest by students of fertility cults and religious infanticide.

Yet another way he helped science was to try out on a long voyage the relatively new Harrison chronometer, the accuracy of which would from Cook's day make it possible to determine longitude at sea. Although sailors had for a long time been able to find their latitude with considerable certainty, their longitude was often hundreds of miles in error if they were away from land for as much as a month. Britain and other maritime nations offered huge rewards for a precise timepiece, and "Boards" were founded for "the discovery of longitude at sea." The sextant was invented in 1731 and Harrison perfected his chronometer shortly afterward, even though he was given the reward only after Cook on the second voyage took his chronometer around the world and proved it far better than any other. The precious timepiece was last heard of in the possession of Cook's astronomer Wales, who told how on July 31, 1775, he "brought the Watch up . . . to London in a Post-Chaise and delivered it to the Revd Mr. Mackelyne" at the Board of Longitude.

Of course it is true that Cook's own journals do not record every result of his explorations, describe every important person who sailed with him, or relate every exciting incident or adventure that he and his men participated in. Lieutenant John Rickman, for example, not only managed to get out his journal of the third voyage three years before the official three volumes of Cook and King, but was able to include a long narrative of an adventure he and other sailors had when sent ashore on an unknown island of the South Pacific. Better still are certain passages only Sir Joseph Banks could write—his narrow escape from death at Tierra del Fuego when he and others went ashore to botanize and lost two Negro servants by freezing, or his exciting experiences on the trip inland at Tahiti to recover a stolen quadrant. Cook could not be everywhere, nor was he willing to repeat everything he must have heard; but not one of the more than a dozen journals published by men under his authority, as significant as they are, can rival in importance the volumes written by the great commander himself. For those volumes, or any selections from them, reveal both history and the genius who made it.

It was a genius for the great as well as the small. Cook could plan and execute a voyage spanning years and taking him thousands of miles from any sort of "home" base. But he could also read the journals of previous circumnavigators and avoid their "little" mistakes, as when he made the hazardous trip through the Strait of Le Maire only after waiting for the perfect time he had carefully calculated and then hoisting anchor, raising sails, and scudding through in a matter of hours whereas others had been blown far off course and delayed for days. He could maintain a calm discipline during trying weeks away from land, or he could cooly oversee a crew frantically extricating his maimed ship from an Australian reef. Not only was he able to guard the health of his men better than any sea captain before him; he was able to face primitive people, man-eating or friendly, and force them to return stolen articles. He was a pragmatist who performed all the duties of seamanship, from taking a bearing to making a chart; but he was a man of vision who obviously realized the meaning of what he did. It is true that Fate was kind, to him and to humanity, by drawing him from the crowd, giving him the opportunity, and protecting him during ten dangerous years. And Fate may have been kind in leaving him dead on one of the most beautiful lands he discovered, for any further voyage made by Captain Cook would have been anticlimactic. The Pacific he loved may have been a better quitting place than a desk—or a bed—at the British Naval Hospital.

PERCY G. ADAMS

Knoxville, Tennessee,
October, 1970.

SUGGESTIONS FOR FURTHER READING

BANKS, SIR JOSEPH. *The "Endeavour" Journal of Joseph Banks*. Ed. J. C. Beaglehole. Two volumes. The Trustees of New South Wales in Association with Angus and Robertson, 1962.

BEAGLEHOLE, J. C. *The Exploration of the Pacific*. London, 1947.

CARRINGTON, A. H. *The Life of Captain Cook*. London, 1967.

COOK, JAMES. *The Journals of Captain James Cook on His Voyages of Discovery*. Ed. J. C. Beaglehole. Cambridge: Published for the Hakluyt Society, 1955–1967. *The Voyage of the Endeavour 1768–1771*. Volume I. 1955. *The Voyage of the Resolution and Adventure 1772–1775*. Volume II. 1962. *The Voyage of the Resolution and Discovery 1776–1780*. Volume III, Parts one and two. 1967.

LLOYD, CHRISTOPHER. *Captain Cook, M.A., F.R.* London, 1952.

RICKMAN, JOHN. *Journal of Captain Cook's Last Voyage to the Pacific Ocean*. Ann Arbor, 1966.

SKELTON, R. A. *Charts and Views Drawn by Cook and His Officers*. Cambridge: Published by the Hakluyt Society, 1955.

SPENCE, SYDNEY A. *Captain James Cook, R.N., A Bibliography of His Voyages*. Mitcham, 1960.

WILLIAMSON, JAMES A. *Cook and the Opening of the Pacific*. London, 1946; 1948.

ACKNOWLEDGEMENTS

THE very numerous journals, logs, letters, maps, charts, books, pamphlets, pictures and portraits which portray Cook and his explorations are being listed and discussed in the definitive edition of Cook now being published in four volumes by the Hakluyt Society under the editorship of Professor J. C. Beaglehole so that no detailed references need be given in the present work.

The Limited Editions Club decided that, of the many manuscripts available, the most attractive for publication were the more important parts of Cook's own journals of the three voyages, the first of which is the outstanding treasure of the Australian National Library at Canberra, and the second and third are in the British Museum.

Although Cook himself prepared these Journals for publication, and they bear tribute to his increasing powers of expression and literary experience, the Hakluyt Society was compelled to devote much editorial time and expense in dealing with questions such as Cook's punctuation, contractions and use of capital letters before the Journals could be published. The Society, however, kindly permitted The Limited Editions Club to utilize their material, so far as it had been prepared, even before publication, while Dr Beaglehole checked our proofs as far as his own researches had proceeded, and Mr R. A. Skelton read the Editor's text and provided valuable comments.

In these circumstances The Limited Editions Club expresses its gratitude to the Hakluyt Society and also to Dr Beaglehole and Mr Skelton, and refers its members and readers to the definitive edition for further and more detailed information on Cook.

A. G. P.

ACKNOWLEDGMENTS

CONTENTS

LIST OF ILLUSTRATIONS AND DECORATIONS

FULL PAGE DRAWINGS

MARGINAL DRAWINGS

THE EXPLORATIONS OF

Captain James Cook

IN THE PACIFIC

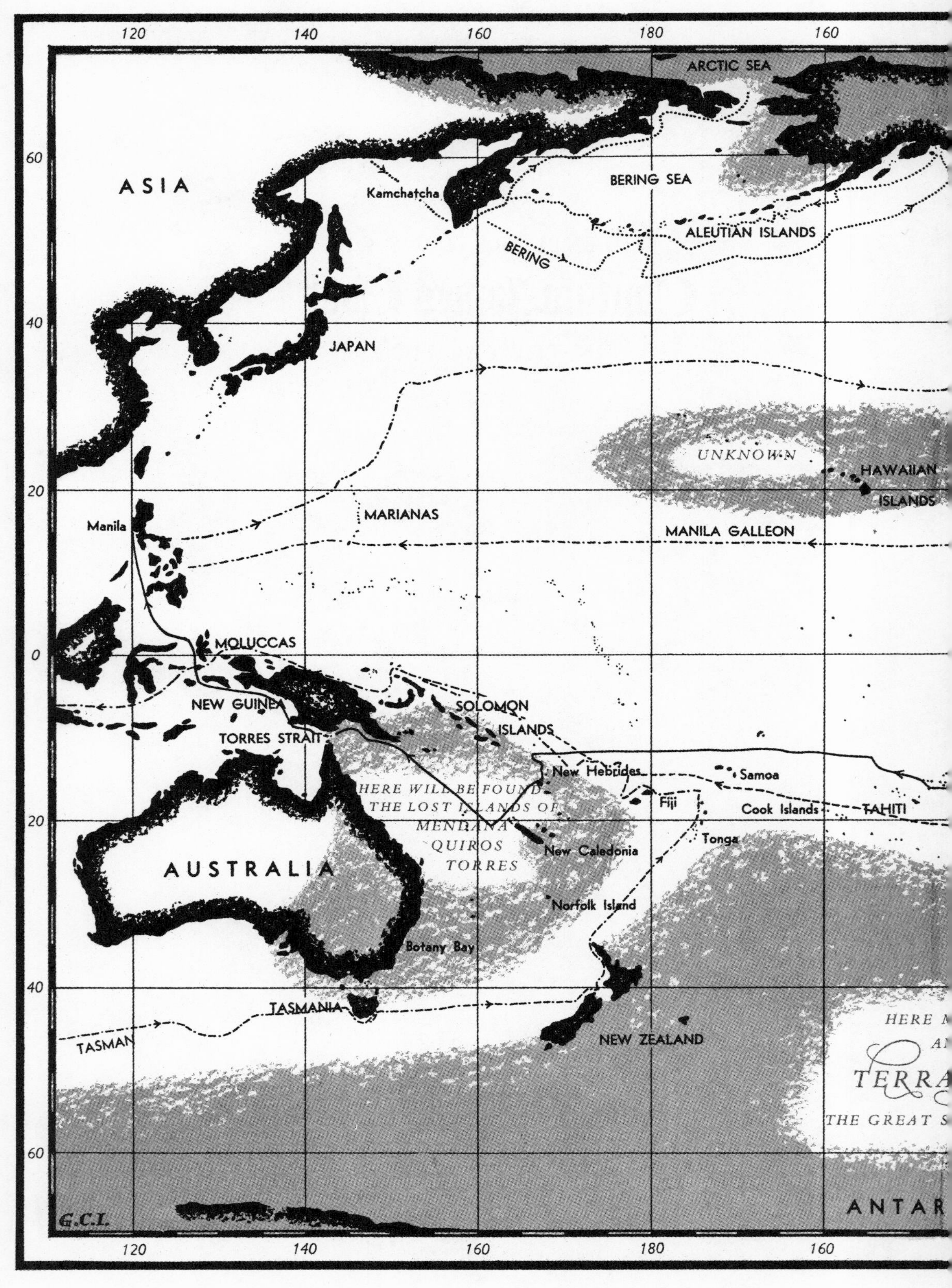

120
140
160
180
160
60
40
20
0
20
40
60
ARCTIC SEA
ASIA
Kamchatcha
BERING SEA
ALEUTIAN ISLANDS
BERING
JAPAN
UNKNOWN
HAWAIIAN
ISLANDS
MARIANAS
Manila
MANILA GALLEON
MOLUCCAS
NEW GUINEA
SOLOMON
ISLANDS
TORRES STRAIT
New Hebrides
Samoa
HERE WILL BE FOUND
THE LOST ISLANDS OF
MENDANA
QUIROS
TORRES
Fiji
Cook Islands
TAHITI
Tonga
New Caledonia
AUSTRALIA
Norfolk Island
Botany Bay
TASMANIA
TASMAN
NEW ZEALAND
THE GREAT S
G.C.I.
ANTAR

THE PACIFIC OCEAN
SHOWING THE KNOWN REGIONS
BEFORE
THE VOYAGES OF CAPTAIN JAMES COOK
HERE MIGHT BE FOUND
THE STRAIT OF ANIAN
AND A ROUTE TO THE
ATLANTIC OCEAN
Nootka Sound
NORTH
AMERICA
Acapulco
Galapagos
Marquesas
TORRES
Juan Fernandez
SOUTH
AMERICA
SCHOUTEN & LE MAIRE
Cape Horn
South Georgia
IT BE FOUND
TENSIVE
USTRALIS
THERN CONTINENT
ICA
TRACKS OF THE NAVIGATORS
TORRES
TASMAN
SCHOUTEN & LE MAIRE
MANILA GALLEON
Outward Voyage
Return Voyage
BERING
140
120
100
80
60
40
60
40
20
0
20
40
60

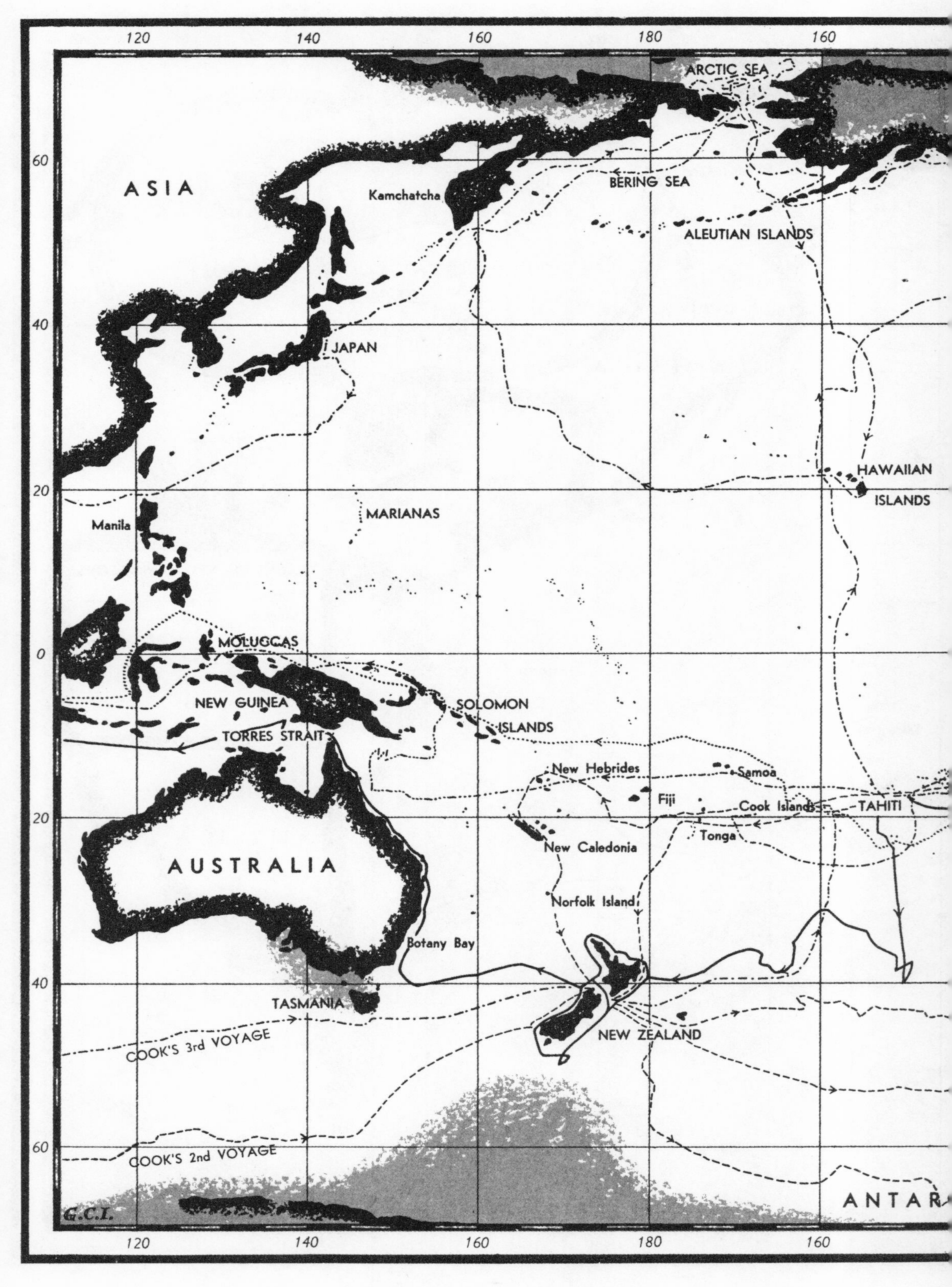

120
140
160
180
160
ARCTIC SEA
ASIA
Kamchatcha
BERING SEA
ALEUTIAN ISLANDS
JAPAN
HAWAIIAN
ISLANDS
MARIANAS
Manila
MOLUCCAS
NEW GUINEA
SOLOMON
ISLANDS
TORRES STRAIT
New Hebrides
Samoa
Fiji
Cook Islands
TAHITI
Tonga
New Caledonia
AUSTRALIA
Norfolk Island
Botany Bay
TASMANIA
NEW ZEALAND
COOK'S 3rd VOYAGE
COOK'S 2nd VOYAGE
ANTAR
G.C.I.
60
40
20
0
20
40
60

THE PACIFIC OCEAN
SHOWING THE KNOWN REGIONS AFTER THE VOYAGES OF CAPTAIN JAMES COOK
TRACKS OF THE NAVIGATORS
CARTERET
BOUGAINVILLE
COOK'S 1st VOYAGE
COOK'S 2nd VOYAGE
COOK'S 3rd VOYAGE
NORTH AMERICA
SOUTH AMERICA
Nootka Sound
Acapulco
Galapagos
Marquesas
CARTERET
Juan Fernandez
BOUGAINVILLE
COOK'S 1st VOYAGE
Cape Horn
South Georgia
ICA
140
120
100
80
60
40
60
40
20
0
20
40
60

Chapter I

OCEAN PROBLEMS OF THE 18*th* CENTURY

"The space unknown from the Tropics to 50° South Latitude must be nearly all land."

ALEXANDER DALRYMPLE, 1767

FEW HISTORIANS WOULD DENY THAT THE SEA-EXPLORATIONS of Bartholomew Diaz, Christopher Columbus, Ferdinand Magellan and James Cook rank with the most fruitful accomplished by Europeans, but few would attempt to compare the merits of seamen who made their discoveries in different regions, times and ships, and with different crews and scientific aids. All made great contributions to man's knowledge of the surface of the Earth; all played leading parts in developments which opened up four new and unknown continents to the people of the Old World, yet no earlier explorer could present the many sided achievements of Cook in solving the ocean problems of his day and generation—the Eighteenth Century. Even if we admit that between Diaz's rounding of the Cape of Good Hope in 1487 and Cook's discovery of Eastern Australia in 1770 European culture in such forms as shipbuilding, navigation and cartography had made considerable progress, it was nevertheless a stupendous contribution to exploration and science that one man should dissolve the age-old myth of a vast southern continent; discover Eastern Australia, together with Hawaii and other Pacific Islands; delineate New Zealand and forecast its value; confirm Bering's discoveries in the Arctic; greatly advance navigation and cartography and build on the work of Lind and others to save the lives of millions of seamen by the use of anti-scorbutics.

¶ The character of the author of these achievements will be to some extent revealed in the extracts which follow from his own simple and straightforward Journals. It is sufficient to say here that, in spite of a very humble origin and early environment, James Cook rose to the heights of supreme achievement by great ability, great courage, great determination, great capacity for hard work, and the power to take infinite pains. These qualities, which probably resulted in part from a Scottish-Yorkshire ancestry, enabled him to develop, with slight assistance and in the face of almost overwhelming disadvantages, a remarkable aptitude for mathematics and a genius for cartography—that extraordinary skill in the charting of unknown coasts which according to Admiral Wharton 'enabled him to originate, as it may be truly said he did, the art of modern marine surveying'. Yet in spite of the fact that his great achievements made him famous in his own lifetime, he remained reserved, unostentatious and modest. When he completed his first expedition, one of the most fruitful explorations in history, he modestly wrote to the British Admiralty, 'I flatter myself that the discoveries we have made, tho' not great, will apologise for the length of the voyage'.

❡ For the understanding of Cook's contribution towards the solution of the ocean problems of the Eighteenth Century consideration must be given to the state of knowledge on at least five great questions at the time of his first expedition in 1768-71. These questions were the existence of a vast Southern Continent; the size and shape of Eastern Australia and New Zealand; the geography of the far north of the Pacific and the adjoining Arctic; navigation and cartography; and the problem of sea disease. The extracts which follow from Cook's own Journals will illustrate, however, many other contributions made by Cook and his co-workers in fields such as anthropology, botany and zoology.

❡ The mystery of a Southern Continent had existed from classical times when the Greeks had believed that southern land masses must exist to balance those in the north. Ptolemy (A.D. 150) and certain medieval geographers had filled the Southern Hemisphere with a vast continent. About A.D. 1500 explorers, such as Columbus and Magellan, showed that the Earth was a globe of immense size, with ample room for new continents, in addition to the Americas, in the huge Pacific and Southern oceans. Almost simultaneously, however, Diaz's rounding of the Cape of Good Hope, and Magellan's discovery of his Straits, followed in 1578 by Drake's discovery of the Cape Horn passage, punched seaways from the eastern and western Atlantic into the newly discovered oceans, and this, with the existing Asian sea knowledge, indicated the separation of the Old World from any Southern land masses. In the years which followed Spanish, Dutch, English and other sea voyages across the Pacific in several locations and directions showed that no great continent could exist in the northern or central parts of that ocean, but these expeditions mainly sailed from east to west with the Trade Winds, and, although they discovered many islands which they immediately lost, through inability to calculate longitude, they left unknown the southern seas, in which, through misinterpretation of the reports of Marco Polo and of Magellan's expedition, certain geographers could still locate an immense continent. From

1606 onwards, however, the Dutch, in developing the spice trade of the East Indies, began to produce concrete evidence that some southern land masses existed. Early in 1606 a very fine Dutch seaman, later Admiral William Jansz, who was to fight with and against the English, discovered Australia, and successive Dutch explorers, sailing eastward towards, or southwards from, the East Indies, filled in the map of the continent from the Great Australian Bight in the south to Jansz' discoveries in the Gulf of Carpentaria in the north east. Yet the Dutch did not discover or explore the fertile east coast, possibly because they failed to penetrate from the west the strait between Australia and New Guinea which a Spanish expedition under Torres and Prado navigated from the east in late 1606, probably without sighting the southern continent.

❡ In 1642-3 Anthony Van Diemen, an outstanding Dutch Governor of the East Indies, made a highly important contribution to the solution of the problem, when, at the suggestion of the far-sighted pilot Visscher, he despatched Abel Tasman and Visscher to sail from Mauritius with the westerly winds in order to find a commercial route to South America. Keeping far south of the tracks of previous voyagers the expedition passed south of Australia, the Dutch 'New Holland', to discover Van Diemen's Land (Tasmania) and Staten Land (New Zealand), although the explorers gave a poor report on the former island, and failed to land in New Zealand owing to the ferocity of the Maoris. Tasman and Visscher had, however, proved that New Holland must be a comparatively small continent or group of islands, and not a vast land mass stretching across the Pacific to New Zealand or southwards towards the Pole.

❡ The Dutch were now weary of unprofitable explorations. Instead of gold and spices their New Holland had yielded little but incredibly primitive men and incredibly ugly women. As traders rather than colonisers they concentrated upon the wealth of the tropics, leaving the discovery and colonization of any temperate lands to the rising seafarers of England and France.

❡ Portugal, Spain, Holland, Britain and France were all prepared to seek God, Glory and Gold in a varied order of importance, and the time had now arrived when Britain and France realised, that, with the development of ships, navigation, and ocean routes, they must despatch official expeditions to ascertain whether or not the South Seas contained land masses which would be of value to sea power, commerce and colonization, and as sewer vents for convicts, more emphasis being laid on advancing the glory of science than on the old Spanish objective of advancing the glory of God. In France De Brosses, and in England Campbell, Callander and Dalrymple of the 'Dry Land' school, proclaimed with individual variations the existence of an immense south land with promontories or coastlines at Cape Circumcision (Bouvet Island) to the south west of South Africa; Davis Land, to the west of Chile; New Zealand, and De Quiros' Land (The New Hebrides), although these last were situated in the Pacific as far north as latitude 10° S. Already Britain, France and Spain were in fierce competition for the Falkland Islands which were regarded as the key to the South Pacific and the symbol of British determination to expand in that ocean.

❨ Immediately before the beginning of Cook's contribution, France despatched a fine explorer, Bougainville, who, sailing the Pacific by more southerly routes than his predecessors, excepting Tasman and perhaps Torres, actually forestalled Cook in sighting the Great Barrier Reef of North Eastern Australia and very narrowly avoided the shipwreck that was to overtake Cook.

❨ Similarly in Britain, at this time, 'Dry Land' propaganda, ambition, and the fear of French discoveries led the government to despatch Byron in 1764, and Wallis, with Carteret, in 1766 to search for the Southern Continent, Byron receiving additional instructions to sail to Drake's New Albion in the far North East Pacific and there to seek a North East passage to the North Atlantic. It was after the partial failure of these expeditions that Britain called on the services of James Cook, who, in his first two expeditions, solved the main problems of the supposed southern land masses, and, in his third, answered the chief unanswered questions on the Northern Pacific.

❨ A less important feature of the mystery of the southern land masses was the delineation of the eastern shores of New Holland and New Zealand, the New Zealand question looming particularly large owing to the fact that the western coastline of New Zealand might prove to be the shoreline of a continent. It was almost or wholly unperceived at this time that the Trade Winds, which made Eastern New Holland a dangerous lee shore, might also provide a well watered and fertile margin to a continent. Few geographers seemed to care whether this coastline consisted of mainland or islands, or whether it bent back westwards towards the arid regions of Dutch discovery, or bulged promisingly into the Pacific as tentatively depicted in Tasman's famous map of 1644. It was typical that the British Admiralty should order Cook to examine New Zealand and the unknown ocean to its east in the hope of finding a continent, and then, ignoring a golden opportunity for an exploration of the Southland Coasts, leave him free to voyage home by what seemed to him the most profitable route. Thus the courageous decision, which led to the discovery of Eastern Australia, and the occupation of a new continent by English-speaking peoples, although influenced to some extent by the material state of the expedition, was wholly to the glory of James Cook and his staff.

❨ The third geographical problem solved by Cook was the distribution of land and sea in the far north of the Pacific, and the existence or non-existence of a passage from the North American coast to Hudson Bay, in solving which problem he perished. Cook need not have embarked upon this adventure. He returned in glory from his long and successful second voyage only in July 1775, yet he volunteered to lead the North Pacific expedition and sailed in July 1776.

The truth was that, although the nominal excuse was the return of the Polynesian Omai to a suitable island, the real objective was the fulfilment of the task in which Byron had failed. At this time the discovery of a passage between the North Pacific and North Atlantic was becoming of increasing importance owing to the growth of the tea trade. A reward of £20,000 had been offered to any British merchant ship commander discovering a passage, and this offer was now extended to the commanders of naval vessels, provided that the passage lay north of latitude 53° N.

❡ Professor Vincent T. Harlow has pointed out that the Admiralty planned a two-pronged attack. While Cook sought a passage from the Pacific to the Atlantic Lieutenant Richard Pickersgill, who had been trained by Cook on his second expedition, was to command the brig *Lion* in an effort to penetrate from the Atlantic to the Pacific. Unfortunately Pickersgill became seriously ill while coasting along Greenland to Davis Strait, and his successor, Lieutenant Walter Young, completely disregarded his instructions and returned in 1777 with his task 'not even begun'.

❡ In the North Pacific Cook discovered the Hawaiian (Sandwich) Islands which, strangely enough, he regarded as his most important discovery long before their great strategic value was recognised. He then examined the North American coast from about Latitude 45° N.; showed that no passage to the east existed south of the Arctic, and confirmed Bering's work by passing through his Strait in a region where Cook considered that his predecessor, another martyr in the cause of exploration, had determined latitude and longitude better than could have been expected. In spite of Cook's tragic death at the hands of Hawaiian islanders on 14th February 1779, the results he achieved compare more than favourably with those of any of his predecessors in the North Pacific, and had important effects on exploration and commerce.

❡ The fourth question to be considered is the Eighteenth Century knowledge of navigation and cartography to which again Cook made a valuable contribution, that has been recently examined by Mr R. A. Skelton of the Hakluyt Society. Long before the days of Cook seamen could calculate latitude with fair accuracy, and could estimate the distance of their positions north or south of the Equator. Unfortunately the calculation of longitude, the distances east and west, was far more difficult, as was shown in the case of numerous Pacific islands which were discovered, only to be immediately lost. By Cook's time, however, watchmakers were experimenting with chronometers, instruments which would accurately record time over long periods, regardless of weather conditions, and hence enable seamen to calculate longitude, while astronomers had evolved, by the use of lunar distances, another method, which, unfortunately, involved many hours of laborious calculation, although, as Cook showed on his first voyage, the results could be extremely accurate.

☾ On the voyage of the *Endeavour* Cook carried no chronometer, but he and the Astronomer, Green, made very frequent calculations of lunar distance with the great assistance of tables recently published by the Astronomer Royal, Nevil Maskelyne. 'By these tables,' wrote Cook in 1773, 'the Calculations are rendered short beyond conception and easy to the meanest capacity.' On his second voyage Cook and the Astronomers, Wales and Bayley, continued to take frequent lunar observations, but the vessels carried three experimental and unsatisfactory chronometers made by Arnold, and a very famous and satisfactory instrument, made by Larcum Kendall to Harrison's design. So reliable was this chronometer that Harrison gained the substantial reward offered by the Board of Longitude, but not until George III had himself intervened to see that the inventor secured justice.

☾ While Cook's contribution to the solution of the long-standing and very grave problem of calculating longitude was based upon the successful work of astronomers and watchmakers his advancement of surveying and cartography gave scope for much greater individuality. Skelton writes that 'Cook's Journals repeatedly testify to his flair for predicting the trend of a coastline and for discerning and interpreting its principal features', and again his charts 'are in general notably correct in outline and accurate in their latitudes', while the errors in longitude were slight. Cook also made a great impression on his crews by his uncanny 'foreknowledge of the existence of land'. He would come up on deck and alter course when no one else had the slightest perception of any danger.

☾ Admiral Sir W. J. L. Wharton, a very high authority, paid glowing tributes to Cook's cartography both in Newfoundland and on the voyages of exploration, and pointed out that many of his charts were still the basis of those used by the Admiralty at the end of the nineteenth century, or more than a hundred years after Cook's death. Skelton summed up the position by comparing Cook's achievement with that of General Roy in the trigonometrical Survey of Britain. The standards of precision and scientific method set by the two men on land and sea dominated the early labours of the Ordnance Survey and of the Hydrographic Department.

☾ Great as were Cook's geographical achievements it was, perhaps, for his contribution to the control of sea diseases that he received in his lifetime the highest honours and greatest credit. Possibly ancient ocean navigators, such as the Polynesians or Vikings, suffered from diseases like scurvy, but, until the development of the sailing ship and long-distance ocean navigation on a substantial scale, deficiency diseases were not of great importance. Very different was the case when European nations developed the trade routes around Africa, to the Americas, and even across the North Pacific, for the casualties on these long voyages became so appalling that they played no small part in the decline of a numerically weak people, the Portuguese. Indeed as late as 1740-4, and immediately before Cook's voyages, Commodore Anson, on his circumnavigation of the world lost, principally in two outbreaks of scurvy, 626 out of 961 men on three ships. Yet the cure for scurvy had been known for many years, owing to the effective use of citrus by Sir Richard Hawkins in 1593, and Captain James Lancaster in 1605. Lancaster used lemon juice to cure any scurvy which appeared on his flagship the *Dragon* during his voyage to the East Indies, but he lost 105 out of 222 men who manned the three lesser ships that carried no lemon. In 1617 James Woodall published in his book *The Surgeon's Mate* a strong plea for the use of lemon juice to combat the disease, and it seems clear that for many years thinking seamen realised the importance of citrus and of fresh foods.

❡ In 1747 Dr James Lind, of the Royal Navy, showed by a controlled experiment that oranges and lemons were a cure for scurvy. He published papers on the health of seamen in 1754 and 1757, and was in 1758 appointed physician to the Royal Naval Hospital at Haslar where he continued to press for improved diet and hygiene on His Majesty's overcrowded ships, and for adequate supplies of fresh water. A number of naval captains followed Lind's teaching or evolved similar ideas of their own. Cook himself claimed that he made the plans for the health of his expeditions from his own long experience, and from hints given him by Sir Hugh Palliser, and by Captains Campbell, Wallis and other intelligent officers. Certainly Cook had learnt from his own sea-faring the necessity of combating scurvy, for he saw Palliser bury twenty-two men, and land 130 sick of the *Eagle's* complement of about 400 while the ship was serving near Britain, and the *Pembroke* lose 29 men in crossing the Atlantic.

❡ Cook was greatly assisted in his task by Mr Pelham, the Secretary to the Commissioners of Victualling, who had been experimenting with anti-scorbutics, and who was responsible for the remedy upon which Cook placed his chief reliance, the inspissated juice of wort or beer, a remedy that, according to Cook's biographer Arthur Kitson, had been recommended to the Admiralty by a Dr McBride.

❡ Cook also used sauerkraut (salted and fermented cabbage), portable broth, and some orange and lemon juice. Further he laid great weight on securing fresh provisions whenever possible, on keeping his ships clean, his seamen clean, dry and warmly clad, and their crowded quarters and their bedding thoroughly aired. The Journals will show the patient attention to detail and the knowledge of sea psychology which brought such extraordinary success, a success which exceeded that of his own captains owing to Cook's personality and patience.

❡ Here then, in outline, are the main aspects of the position when Cook began his great work in 1768. The scientific progress of the Eighteenth Century, and British ambition, aroused in great measure by the victories of the Seven Years' War which ended in 1763, were in a position to provide the means that could carry sea exploration far beyond its previous limits. The fact, however, that the times could produce the means, detracts nothing from the stature of the leader who by character, ability and intense personal attention to detail, could, throughout long years and many dangers and hardships, preserve his ships and crews so that they could carry exploration beyond those previous limits.

Chapter II

COOK'S EARLY LIFE AND CAREER

"Well qualified for the work performed, and for greater undertakings of the same kind."

LORD COLVILLE ON COOK, 1762

JAMES COOK WAS THIRTY-NINE YEARS OF AGE WHEN HE was called to his great task, and, like many of the sea explorers of the period, both English and French, was a product of the maritime struggle between Britain and France. The fact that he came from very humble origins makes it difficult to ascertain with accuracy some of the details of his childhood and early career, but the main facts are beyond dispute. His biographers have also been handicapped by the fact that he wrapped himself in a mantle of dignified reticence, and, as his wife probably destroyed their private correspondence, as too sacred for other eyes, it is difficult to see the husband and father behind the professional sailor and scientist.

Cook was born in a tiny, two-room clay cottage in the remote village of Marton-cum-Cleveland on 27th October 1728, and was the second of seven children. His mother, Grace Pace, was a Yorkshire woman, while his father, James Cook, who was possibly of Scottish descent, was designated as a day labourer, both at the time of his son's baptism and of his own death, although he rose to the positions of farm bailiff and builder in the years between. Little has been recorded of the childhood of the younger James, who must have been reared under conditions which may well have contributed to the remarkable stamina and self-denial which he exhibited, when necessary, throughout his explorations. In his early youth Cook, like his famous predecessor the scientific pirate Dampier, was a farm lad, first under William Walker, whose wife seems to have conducted his early schooling, and later at Ayton in Yorkshire where he received under a Mr Pullen some further education in the little school which still stands and where he is alleged to have displayed 'remarkable facility in the science of numbers'. Near the school stood a cottage which is said to have been built by Cook's father who in 1755 put his own and his wife's initials over the door. In 1933-4, an Australian, Mr Russell Grimwade, transplanted this cottage to Melbourne, erecting in its place a memorial of stone hewn from the rocks of Cape Everard near Cook's Australian landfall, Point Hicks, a name which has disappeared from the map. At Great Ayton, in the churchyard of all Saints, stands the gravestone which Cook erected to the memory of his mother Grace, who died in 1765, and to the memory of some of his brothers and sisters.

❨ At Ayton Cook's father held the position of hind or bailiff to a Mr Skottowe of Airy Holme Farm, and Cook assisted in the farm work until 1745 when his father placed him with a Mr Saunderson, a grocer in the tiny fishing port of Staithes, where the boy was to learn the trade and mystery of a grocer. Here in a little shop, on a site now beneath the waves, Cook must have lived in continuous sight and sound of the sea with ships constantly passing before his eyes. At any rate, at the end of eighteen months, he showed his preference for sea-faring, and, in July 1746, Saunderson helped him to secure an apprenticeship with John and Henry Walker, Quaker shipowners of Whitby, thus beginning a very happy association, for, even in his later and famous years, Cook conducted an important correspondence with the family.

❨ Whitby was at that time a centre for the coastal trade and shipbuilding, and for some years Cook made voyages in colliers such as the *Freelove*, working while ashore at those mathematical studies which were to prove the basis of his unique career. In the hard school of the North Sea he received a singularly appropriate training for sea exploration and cartography—a knowledge of coastal navigation and the handling of the coal ships which were to prove a mainstay of his success. So well did he serve the Walkers that, in 1755, they offered Cook, then Mate of the *Freelove*, the command of one of their vessels, an offer which was declined. The truth was that Britain was on the verge of the Seven Years' War with France and Spain, and, while Cook may have feared that he would be pressed for naval service, it is more probable that, knowing the desperate need of the navy for trained personnel, he saw before him a duty to his country and an unequalled opportunity for advancing his own career. Whatever may have been the reasons he enlisted in the only way then possible, as an ordinary seaman, and was drafted in June 1755 to the Fourth Rate *Eagle*, a ship of 60 guns. Only five weeks after his enlistment he became rated as Masters Mate, an office which again trained him for exploration as it involved a wide range of duties under the Master, who was primarily responsible for the navigation of the ship. Under Captain Palliser, who was later to become Cook's loyal patron and friend, Cook saw active service, including one very heavy engagement. He also saw the grave effects of scurvy, which Palliser himself attributed to the lack of clothing for his men. In October 1757, Cook joined the *Pembroke* as Master, and served under Admiral Saunders, whose ships and their small boats made it possible for Wolfe and his army to advance up the St. Lawrence to the famous victory at, and capture of, Quebec. In 1759 Admiral Saunders appointed Cook Master of the *Northumberland*, and by 1761 he had shown ability and service beyond the ordinary, for he received £50 for his 'indefatigable industry in making himself Master of the pilotage of the River St. Lawrence', and the Admiralty published his work. When the *Northumberland* reached England, in October 1762, Cook, who had rendered excellent service in Newfoundland and Nova Scotia, undertook family responsibilities by marrying Elizabeth Batts. It was a strange but happy alliance. Mrs Cook, who was fourteen years her husband's junior, had, in all, little more than four years of his company before she was widowed in 1779. Yet, coming as she did from well to do London trading stock, she proved herself a good wife and a woman of high character and fortitude in the face of particularly tragic family loss.

¶ In 1763 Cook was instructed to conduct surveys in the Newfoundland region, where Captain Palliser, who became Governor in 1764, secured him the command of the schooner *Grenville*. Until 1767 he was engaged in producing charts of Newfoundland and Labrador, which the high authority, Admiral Wharton, considered 'admirable' and which had not been wholly superseded at the end of the nineteenth century. Cook effected his work in spite of a very serious accident, the explosion of a powder horn which maimed a hand. In August 1766 he observed an eclipse of the sun, and, when his observations were communicated to the Royal Society, he was considered 'a good mathematician and very expert in his business'. The time had arrived when this farm lad, this obscure mate of a Whitby collier, had gained a high reputation both with the Royal Society and his employers the Admiralty. As his commanding officer, Lord Colville, wrote in references to his services while Master of the *Northumberland*, 'he was well qualified for the work performed, and for greater undertakings of the same kind'.

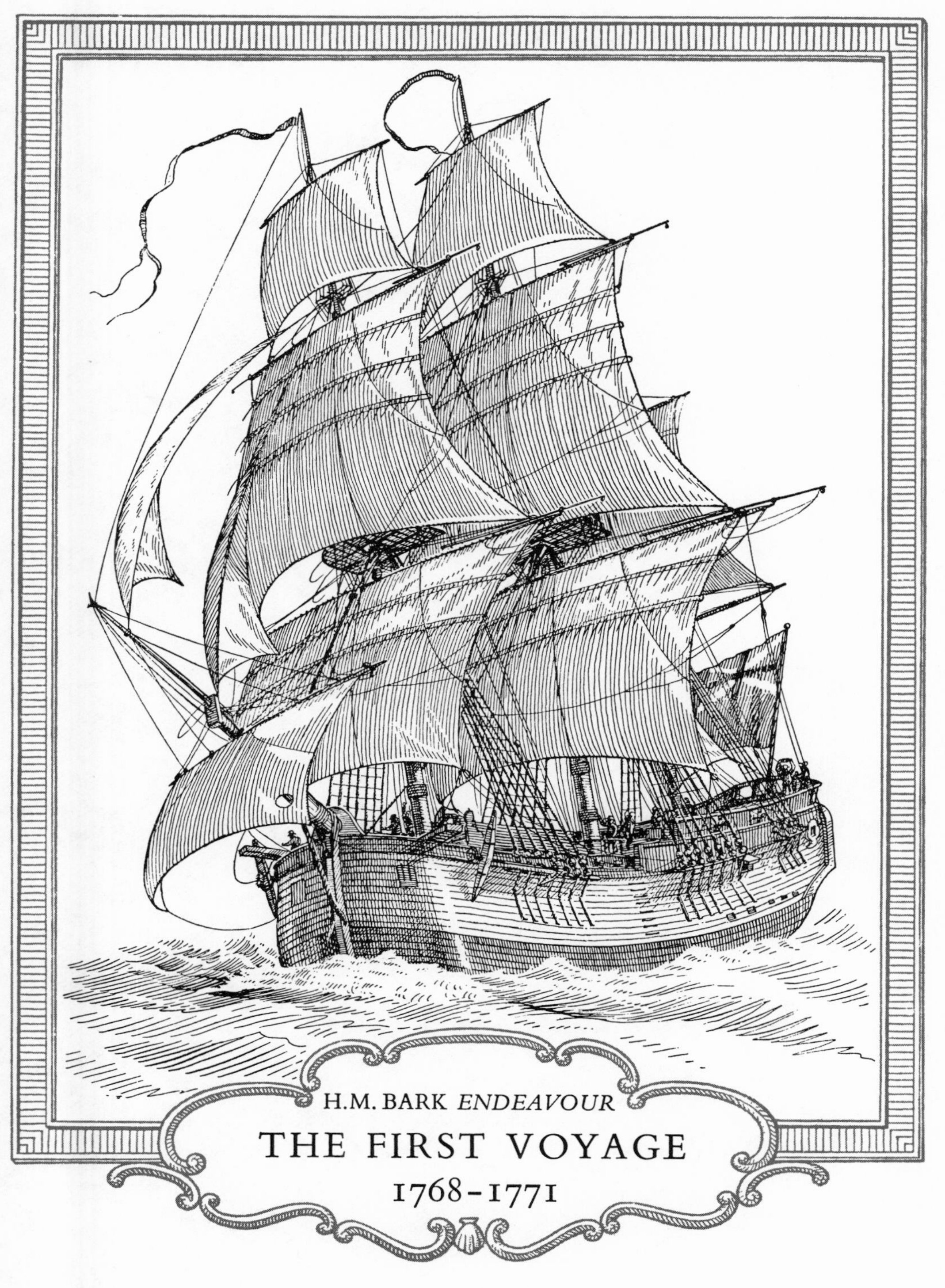
H.M. BARK *ENDEAVOUR*
THE FIRST VOYAGE
1768–1771

Chapter III

PREPARATIONS AND INSTRUCTIONS

"You are to proceed to the southward in order to make discovery of the Continent."

SECRET INSTRUCTIONS TO COOK, 1768

BY 1768 COOK HAD MADE A FAVOURABLE IMPRESSION ON both the Royal Society and the Admiralty at a moment when Britain was in urgent need of a seaman-scientist who would not only lead an expedition with greater ability than men such as Byron but who could fulfil a dual role—the open and public duty of observing the transit of Venus on 3rd June 1769, and the more important but secret task of finding a Southern Continent if one existed. The transit, predicted by an Astronomer Royal—Edmund Halley—was interesting the scientific world as a possible means of calculating the distance between the Earth and the Sun. In 1767 a Committee of the Royal Society recommended that observing stations should be established near the North Cape of Norway, in Hudson Bay, and on a Pacific Island, and the young King George III, keenly interested in science, and as wise in winning Australia as he was foolish in losing America, promised to donate £4,000 and to provide a naval vessel.

¶ At first it seemed that the leader of the expedition would be Alexander Dalrymple, who possessed both seafaring and scientific qualifications. A leader of the 'Dry Land' school of Pacific geographers, Dalrymple had discovered a copy of a memorial from a Dr Arias of Santiago, Chile, to Philip III of Spain, advocating, on behalf of the Franciscans, further exploration for religious motives and revealing the existence of Torres Strait between New Guinea and the Australian continent. Dalrymple was preparing at the moment a book and a pamphlet on Pacific discovery in which he attempted to show the existence of a Southern Continent. He had, however, in the eyes of the Admiralty, the fatal disadvantage of not being a naval officer. Moreover, he was imperious, conceited, narrow-minded and resentful, as he showed when he refused the offer of sailing in the *Endeavour* as chief scientific observer of the transit of Venus, and in his later unscrupulous and lying attacks on Cook. Very fortunately the Admiralty rejected a recommendation that Dalrymple should lead the expedition, and equally fortunately the final choice fell on Cook.

℄ In Volume I of the Hakluyt Society's edition of Cook the distinguished scholar and editor Dr J. C. Beaglehole presents evidence which indicates that Cook was appointed to command the expedition in early April 1768, but that by late March the authorities had already selected his ship. It is, however, an extraordinary coincidence if a Whitby-trained Commander and a Whitby-built collier were selected simultaneously but quite separately, and Cook's biographer Kippis may be right in his statement that, when it was decided to purchase a vessel, Palliser was entrusted with her selection, and Palliser secured advice from Cook.

℄ Whatever the causes, however, the Navy Board purchased for the Admiralty the Whitby collier *Earl of Pembroke*, then slightly less than four years old and having a burthen of 368 tons. Renamed the *Endeavour* Bark, or subsidiary vessel to distinguish her from an H.M.S. *Endeavour* already in service, the Government paid £2,800 for the vessel and £2,294 to sheath and fit her for the voyage.

℄ The *Endeavour* is one of the most famous ships in history, but, unlike Columbus' *Santa Maria*, Magellan's *Victoria*, or Drake's *Golden Hind*, we have full knowledge of her construction and dimensions. Of Scandinavian or 'cat built' design, she was an immensely strong, bluff-bowed, shallow-draft and necessarily slow vessel. Cook, as we shall see, summed up her advantages in the introduction to his Journal of the Second Voyage for which similar vessels, the *Resolution* and *Adventure*, were purchased. It is sufficient to say here that the *Endeavour* provided unusual space for stores, that her construction enabled her 'to take the ground' with less damage than most types of vessel, and that her own crew could beach her and effect repairs. The voyage was to prove the wisdom and judgment of those who made the selection.

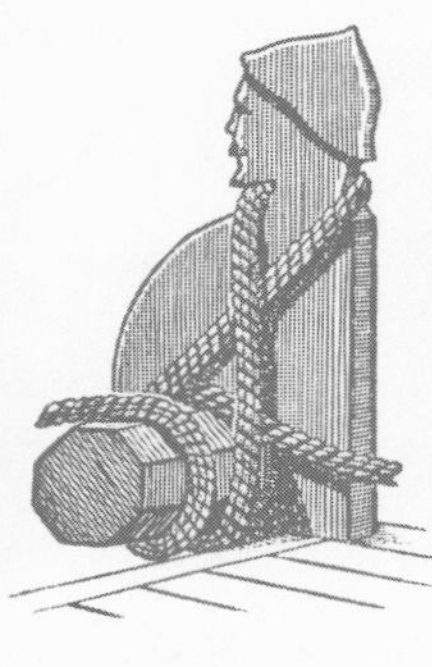

℄ In contrast to many earlier expeditions the improved type and rigging of the *Endeavour* enabled Cook to sail with a total of only 94 persons including the eleven members of a scientific party, a fact which gave the high and favourable allowance of four tons of ship capacity per person. Again in contrast to earlier official expeditions, like that of Dampier, the personnel was in general good, although Cook objected emphatically but unsuccessfully to the appointment of a cook with only one hand. Lieutenant Gore, who was also to accompany Cook on his third and last expedition, had circumnavigated the Earth under both Byron and Wallis, while five other members of Cook's crew had sailed with Wallis and hence had been present at the discovery of King George III Island, Tahiti. Dr Beaglehole notes that amongst these experienced circumnavigators was a goat which had been around the world with Wallis and 'was transferred to Cook so that South Sea coffee should still have its milk'. On the whole the crew of the *Endeavour* was very young, few being over thirty. Cook did not choose them, but five had been with him in the *Grenville* during his Newfoundland Survey, and some were to accompany him on his second, and even on his third voyage.

℄ The scientific personnel consisted of Charles Green, Assistant to the Astronomer Royal, an able scientist whom the Royal Society appointed an 'observer' with Cook, and the party led by Joseph Banks, a rich young Fellow of the Royal Society who engaged Dr Solander, a pupil of Linnaeus as Naturalist; H. Spöring, Assistant Naturalist; and A. Buchan and S. Parkinson as Artists. Both the Royal Society and Banks provided a large amount of scientific equipment, and Solander estimated that the expedition was to cost Banks some £10,000, a very large sum at that time, but relatively little in consideration of the wonderful contribution which the voyage made to Botany and other natural sciences.

℄ The *Endeavour* also carried most of the available writings on the Pacific, including extracts from Tasman's journals, Wallis' log, and, as a gift from the author to Banks, Dalrymple's unpublished pamphlet containing Arias' evidence on the existence of Torres Strait. As previously noted, Cook, with the assistance of Pelham of the Victualling Board, shipped a varied and adequate supply of anti-scorbutics for an experiment which was to have a vital effect on the future practice, health and safety of seamanship. On the advice of Wallis, who had returned to England in May 1768 after discovering Tahiti, this island, at that time known as King George III Island, was selected, with great suitability, for the observation of Venus.

COOK'S INSTRUCTIONS

℄ Cook's instructions were divided into two parts. The first and public section, which was issued by the Admiralty after consultation with the Royal Society, ordered the expedition to proceed via Cape Horn to King George's Island (Tahiti) to observe the transit of Venus in June 1769. When this work was completed, however, Cook was to open additional secret and sealed instructions which ordered him to discover whether or not the Pacific contained a great continent to the south of Tahiti and whether or not Tasman's New Zealand was part of this unknown continent. In other words, Cook was to prove or disprove the contentions of Dalrymple and the 'Dry Land' theorists, and if the theorists proved right, to prepare the way for British supremacy in the new continent.

(Cook's own Journal indicates the nature of these instructions, but they themselves lay unknown until they were discovered and published by the Navy Records Society in 1928. Their importance is so great that we give them here in full as published by the Hakluyt Society from the Naval Records and the Canberra Letter Book. Although the document was labelled "Secret" the London Gazetteer of 18th August 1768 indicated that, after observing the Transit of Venus, the expedition was 'to attempt some new discoveries in that vast unknown tract, about the latitude 40'.

Secret — By the Commissioners for executing the office of Lord High Admiral of Great Britain &c^{a}.

Additional Instructions for Lt James Cook, Appointed to Command His Majesty's Bark the Endeavour.

Whereas the making Discoverys of Countries hitherto unknown, and the Attaining a Knowledge of distant Parts which though formerly discover'd have yet been but imperfectly explored, will redound greatly to the Honour of this Nation as a Maritime Power, as well as to the Dignity of the Crown of Great Britain, and may trend greatly to the advancement of the Trade and Navigation thereof; and Whereas there is reason to imagine that a Continent or Land of great extent, may be found to the Southward of the Tract lately made by Captn Wallis in His Majesty's Ship the Dolphin (of which you will herewith receive a Copy) or of the Tract of any former Navigators in Pursuits of the like kind; You are therefore in Pursuance of His Majesty's Pleasure hereby requir'd and directed to put to Sea with the Bark you Command so soon as the Observation of the Transit of the Planet Venus shall be finished and observe the following Instructions.

You are to proceed to the southward in order to make discovery of the Continent above-mentioned until you arrive in the Latitude of 40°, unless you sooner fall in with it. But not having discover'd it or any Evident signs of it in that Run, you are to proceed in search of it to the Westward between the Latitude before mentioned and the Latitude of 35° until you discover it, or fall in with the Eastern side of the Land discover'd by Tasman and now called New Zeland.

If you discover the Continent above-mentioned either in your Run to the Southward or to the Westward as above directed, You are to employ youself diligently in exploring as great an Extent of the Coast as you can; carefully observing the true situation thereof both in Latitude and Longitude, the Variation of the Needle, bearings of Head Lands, Height, direction and Course of the Tides and Currents, Depths and Soundings of the Sea, Shoals, Rocks, &c^{a}. and also surveying and making Charts, and taking Views of such Bays, Harbours and Parts of the Coast as may be useful to Navigation.

You are also carefully to observe the Nature of the Soil, and the Products thereof; the Beasts and Fowls that inhabit or frequent it, the fishes that are to be found in the Rivers or upon the Coast and in what Plenty; and in case you find any Mines, Minerals or valuable stones you are to bring home Specimens of each, as also such Specimens of the Seeds of the Trees, Fruits and Grains as you may be able to collect, and Transmit them to our Secretary that We may cause proper Examination and Experiments to be made of them.

You are likewise to observe the Genius, Temper, Disposition and Number of the Natives, if there be any, and endeavour by all proper means to cultivate a Friendship and Alliance with them, making them presents of such Trifles as they may Value, inviting them to Traffick, and Shewing them every kind of Civility and Regard; taking Care however not to suffer yourself to be surprized by them, but to be always upon your guard against any Accident.

You are also with the Consent of the Natives to take possession of Convenient Situations in the Country in the Name of the King of Great Britain; or, if you find the Country uninhabited take Possession for His Majesty by setting up Proper Marks and Inscriptions, as first discoverers and possessors.

But if you should fail of discovering the Continent before-mention'd, you will upon falling in with New Zeland carefully observe the Latitude and Longitude in which that Land is situated, and explore as much of the Coast as the Condition of the Bark, the health of her Crew, and the State of your Provisions will admit of, having always great Attention to reserve as much of the latter as will enable you to reach some known Port where you may procure a Sufficiency to carry you to England, either round the Cape of Good Hope, or Cape Horn, as from Circumstances you may judge the Most Eligible way of returning home.

You will also observe with accuracy the Situation of such Islands as you may discover in the Course of your Voyage that have not hitherto been discover'd by any Europeans, and take possession for His Majesty and make Surveys and Draughts of such of them as may appear to be of Consequence, without Suffering yourself however to be thereby diverted from the Object which you are always to have in View, the Discovery of the Southern Continent so often Mentioned.

But for as much as in an undertaking of this nature several Emergencies may Arise not to be foreseen, and therefore not particularly to be provided for by Instruction before hand, you are in all such Cases, to proceed, as upon advice with your Officers you shall judge most advantageous to the Service on which you are employed.

You are to send by all proper Conveyances to the Secretary of the Royal Society Copys of the Observations you shall have made of the Transit of Venus; and you are at the same time to send to our Secretary, for our information, accounts of your Proceedings, and Copys of the Surveys and drawings you shall have made. And upon your Arrival in England you are immediately to repair to this Office in order to lay before us a full account of your Proceedings in the whole Course of your Voyage, taking care before you leave the Vessel to demand from your Officers and Petty Officers the Log Books and Journals they may have Kept, and to seal them up for our inspection, and enjoyning them, and the whole Crew, not to divulge where they have been until they shall have Permission so to do.

Given under our hands the 30th of July 1768.

Ed. HAWKE
Piercy BRETT
C. SPENCER

By Command of their Lordships
PH. STEPHENS

¶ The Admiralty also issued a very strong general order for all Naval Officers and Vessels to help the Expedition.

By the Commissioners for executing the office of Lord High Admiral of Great Britain &ca.

Whereas we have directed Lieut. James Cook to proceed in His Majesty's Bark the Endeavour upon a particular service, you are hereby required and directed not to demand of him a sight of the Instructions he has received from us for his proceedings on the said service, nor upon any pretence whatever to detain him, but on the contrary to give him any assistance he may stand in need of, towards enabling him to carry the said instructions into execution.

Given, etc., the 30th of July 1768.

E. HAWKE
Py. BRETT
C. SPENCER

To the Flag Officers, Captains & Commanders of His Majesty's Ships and Vessels to whom this shall be exhibited.

By Command of their Lordships
Php. Stephens

Chapter IV

TAHITI, 1769

"An Arcadia of which we are going to be Kings."

JOSEPH BANKS

COOK HOISTED HIS PENNANT AND TOOK CHARGE OF THE *Endeavour* in the Thames on 27th May 1768. He sailed from Plymouth on Friday, 26th August, and in September took in at Madeira stores, including fresh onions, and Madeira wine which kept well. The expedition reached Rio de Janeiro in November and here Cook had difficulties with an ignorant Portuguese Viceroy who refused to believe that the party had entirely scientific objectives, perhaps not without reason as Cook prepared a plan of the harbour and its fortifications. The Viceroy treated the voyagers as pirates; temporarily imprisoned some of the crew in a loathsome dungeon, and perpetrated other insults which Cook had to tolerate for fear of delay in obtaining supplies. By 11th January 1769, the *Endeavour* was off Terra del Fuego, and Cook could undertake some charting, while the scientists landed and procured plants and flowers unknown in European collections. Neither the country nor its inhabitants were, however, anything but forbidding and unpleasant.

MONDAY 16*th* January. They (the natives) are something above the Middle size of a dark copper Colour with long black hair, they paint their bodies in Streakes mostly Red and Black, their cloathing consists wholy of a Guanacoes skin or that of a Seal, in the same form as it came from the Animals back, the Women wear a peice of skin over their privey parts but the Men observe no such decency. Their Hutts are made like a behive and open on one side where they have their fire, they are made of small Sticks and cover'd with branches of trees, long grass &c[a] in such a manner that they are

January 1769 neither proff against wind, Hail, rain, or snow, a sufficient proff that these People must be a very hardy race; they live chiefly on shell fish such as Muscles which they gather from off the rocks along the seashore and this seems to be the work of the Women; their arms are Bows and Arrows neatly made, their arows are bearded some with glass and others with fine flint, several pieces of the former we saw amongst them with other European things such as Rings, Buttons, Cloth, Canvas &c[a] which I think proves that they must sometimes travel to the Northward, as we know of no ship that hath been in those parts for many years, besides they were not at all surprised at our fire arms on the contrary seem'd to know the use of them by making signs to us to fire at Seals or Birds that might come in the way. They have no boats that we saw, or any thing to go upon the water with. Their number doth not exceed 50 or 60 young and old and there are fewer Women then Men. They are extreeamly fond of any Red thing and seemed to set more Value on Beeds than any thing we could give them: in this consists their whole pride, few either men or Women are without a necklace or string of Beeds made of small Shells or bones about their necks. They would not taste any strong Liquor, neither did they seem fond of our provisions. We could not discover that they had any head or chief, or form of Government, neither have they any usefull or neccessary Utentials except it be a Bagg or Basket to gather their Muscels into: in a Word they are perhaps as miserable a set of People as are this day upon Earth. Having found a convenient place on the s side of the Bay to wood and Water at, we set about that work in the morning, and M[r] Banks with a party went into the Country to gather Plants &c[a].

THURSDAY 17*th* January. Fresh gales at South, sw, and w, with rain and Snow and of course very cold weather, notwithstanding we kept geting on board Wood and water, and finished the Survey of the Bay. M[r] Banks and his party not returning this Evening as I expected gave me great uneasiness as they were not prepared for staying out the night, however about noon they returned in no very comfortable condition and what was still worse two Blacks servants to M[r] Banks had perished in the night with cold; great part of the day they landed was spent before they got through the woods, after which they advanced so far into the Country that they were so far from being able to return that night that it was with much difficulty they got to a place of tolerable shelter where they could make a fire. These two men being intrusted with great part of the Liquor that was for the whole party had made too free with it and stupified themselves to that degree that they either could or would not travel but laid themselves down in a place where there was not the least thing to shelter them from the inclemency of the night. This was about a $\frac{1}{4}$ of a mile from where the rest took up their quarters and notwithstanding their repeted endeavours they could not get them to move one step farther, and the bad traveling made it impossible for any one to carry them, so that they were oblig'd to leave them and the next morning they were both found dead. *January* 1769

CALCULATION OF LONGITUDE

℄ Short as was the stay of the *Endeavour* in the waters of Terra del Fuego, Cook and Green made a valuable contribution to navigation, particularly by determining correct longitudes.

WEDNESDAY 25*th* Jan^{ry}. The appearance of this Cape and Hermites Islands is represented in the last View in the Chart which I have drawn of this Coast from our first making land unto Cape Horn in which is included Strait Le Maire and part of Staten land. In this Chart I have laid down no land nor figure'd out any shore but what I saw my self, and thus far the Chart may be depented upon, the Bay and inlets are left void the openings of which we only see from the Ship; it cannot be doubted but what there is Anchorage Wood and water in those bays and it must have been in some of them that the Duch Squadron Commanded by Hermite put into in the year 1624. It was the Vice Admiral Chapenham of this Squadron who first discover'd that the land of Cape Horn consisted of a number of Islands, but the Account they have given of those parts is very short and imperfect and that of Schouton and Le Maire still worse, that it is no wonder that the Charts hitherto published should be found incorrect, not only in laying down the land but in the Latitude and Longitude of the places they contain; but I can now venter to assert that the Longitude of few parts of the World are better assertain'd than that of Strait Le Maire and Cape Horn being determined by several observations of the Sun and Moon, made both by myself and Mr Green the Astronomer.

ROUNDING CAPE HORN

℄ The expedition had the good fortune to double Cape Horn in unusually calm weather.

MONDAY 13*th* February. From the foregoing observations it will appear that we are now advanced about 12° to the westward of the Strait of Magellan and $3\frac{1}{2}$° to the Northward of it, having been 33 days in doubbling Cape Horn or the land of Terra del Fuego, and arriving into the degree of Latitude and Longitude we are now in without ever being brought once under our close reefe'd Topsails since we left strait la Maire, a circumstance that perhaps never hapned before to any ship in those Seas so much dreaded for Hard gales of Wind; in so much that the doubling of Cape Horn is thought by some to be a mighty thing, and others to this day prefer the Straits of Magellan. As I have never been in those Straits I can only form my Judgement on a Carefull Comparison of the Different Ships' Journals that have passed them, and those that have sail'd round Cape Horn, particularly the DOLPHIN's two last Voyages and this of ours,

February 1769 being made at the same season of the Year, when one may reasonable expect the same Winds to prevail. The DOLPHIN in her last Voyage was three Months in getting through the Straits, not reckoning the time she lay in Port Famine; and I am firmly perswaided from the Winds we have had, that had we come by that Passage we should not have been in these Seas, besides the fatiguing of our People, the damage we must have done to our Anchors, Cables, Sails, and Rigging, none of which have suffer'd in our passage round Cape Horn.

THE SOUTHERN CONTINENT

❨ Cook now sailed north-west towards his first objectives—Tahiti and the transit of Venus—but he sailed west of the courses taken by previous navigators, and by the beginning of March was 560 leagues west of Chile, thus disposing of some of Dalrymple's miscalculations by sailing through the eastern side of the supposed southern continent.

WEDNESDAY 1*st* March. The result of the forementioned Observations gives 110° 33′ w. Longitude from Greenwich and exactly agrees with the Longitude given by the Log, from Cape Horn: this agreement of the two Longitudes after a Run of 660 Leagues is surpriseing and much more then could be expected, but as it is so, it serves to prove as well as the repeted trials we have made when the weather would permit, that we have had no Current that hath affected the Ship Since we came into these Seas, this must be a great sign that we have been near no land of any extent because near land are generally found Currents: it is well known that on the East side of the Continent in the North sea we meet with Currents above 100 Leagues from the Land, and even in the Middle of the Atlantic Ocean between Africa and America are always found Currents, and I can see no reason why currents should not be found in this Sea Supposing a Continent or lands lay not far west from us as some have immagine'd, and if such land was ever seen we cannot be far from it, as we are now 560 Leagues West of the Coast of Chili.

TAHITI, APRIL–JULY 1769

❨ In early April the *Endeavour* sighted some of the islands of the Panmotu or Low Archipelago but, although they were inhabited, Cook did not anchor but sailed west to reach Tahiti on 11th April. Already his campaign against scurvy had been outstandingly successful, partly because of his precautionary measures but partly because he possessed the vigour and psychological knowledge which ensured the adoption of those measures.

THURSDAY 13*th* April. At this time we had but a very few men upon the Sick list and these had but slite complaints, the Ships compney had in general been very healthy owing in a great measure to the Sour krout, Portable Soup and Malt; the two first were serve'd to the People, the one on Beef Days and the other on Banyan Days, Wort was made of the Malt and at the discrition of the Surgeon given to every man that had the least symptoms of Scurvy upon him, by this Means and the care and Vigilance of Mr Munkhous the Surgeon this disease was prevented from geting a footing in the Ship. The Sour Krout the Men at first would not eate untill I put in pratice a Method I never once knew to fail with seamen, and this was to have some of it dress'd every Day for the Cabbin Table, and permitted all the Officers without exception to make use of it and left it to the option of the Men either to take as much as they pleased or none at all; but this pratice was not continued above a week before I found it necessary to put every one on board to an Allowance, for such are the Tempers and disposissions of Seamen in general that whatever you give them out of the Common way, altho it be ever so much for their good yet it will not go down with them and you will hear nothing but murmurings gainest the man that first invented it; but the Moment they see their Superiors set a Value upon it, it becomes the finest stuff in the World and the inventer an honest fellow.

April 1769

(Cook anchored in Wallis' Royal Bay (Matavai) and the natives, who had felt the power of the *Dolphin's* guns, and who recognised Cook's officers that had been with Wallis, greeted them warmly. They were, however, 'prodiges expert' thieves, and some of their customs, although possibly of a religious or ceremonial nature, greatly surprised the Europeans.

THURSDAY 13*th* April. We had no sooner come to an Anchor in Royal Bay as before Mentioned than a great number of the natives in their Canoes came off to the Ship and brought with them Cocoa-nuts &ca and these they seem'd to set a great Value upon. Amongest those that came off to the Ship was an elderly Mañ whose name is *Owhaa*, him the Gentlemen that had been here before in the Dolphin knew and had often spoke of him as one that had been of service to them, this man (together with some others) I took on board, and made much of him thinking that he might on some occasion be of use to us. As our stay at this place was not likly to be very Short, I thought it very necessary that some order Should be Observed in Trafficing with the Natives: that such Merchantdize as we had on board for that purpose might continue to bear a proper value, and not leave it to every ones own particular fancy which could not fail to bring on confution and quarels between us and the Natives, and would infallible lesen the Value of such Articles as we had to Traffic with: in order to prevent this the following Rules were ordered to be observed, viz.

RULES to be observe'd by every person in or belonging to His Majestys Bark the Endevour, for the better establishing a regular and uniform Trade for Provisions &ca with the Inhabitants of Georges Island.

1st *To endeavour by every fair means to cultivate a friendship with the Natives and to treat them with all imaginable humanity.*

April 1769

2d *A proper person or persons will be appointed to trade with the Natives for all manner of Provisions, Fruit, and other productions of the earth; and no officer or Seaman, or other person belonging to the Ship, excepting such as are so appointed, shall Trade or offer to Trade for any sort of Provisions, Fruit, or other productions of the earth unless they have my leave so to do.*

3d *Every person employ'd a Shore on any duty what soever is strictly to attend to the same, and if by neglect he looseth any of his Arms or woorking tools, or suffers them to be stole, the full Value thereof will be charge'd againest his pay according to the Custom of the Navy in such cases, and he shall recive such farther punishment as the nature of the offence may deserve.*

4th *The same penalty will be inflicted on every person who is found to imbezzle, trade or offer to trade with any part of the Ships Stores of what nature soever.*

5th *No Sort of Iron, or any thing that is made of Iron, or any sort of Cloth or other usefull or necessary articles are to be given in exchange for any thing but provisions.*

J.C.

'As soon as the Ship was properly secure'd I went on shore accompanied by Mr Banks and the other gentlemen, with a party of Men under arms, we took along with us Owhaa who conducted us to the place where the Dolphin water'd, and made signs to us as well as we could understand that we might occupy that ground but it happen'd not to be fit for our purpose. No one of the Natives made the least opposission at our landing but came to us with all imaginable marks of friendship and submission.

FRIDAY 14*th* April. This morning we had a great many Canoes about the Ship, the Most of them came from the westward but brought nothing with them but a few Cocoa-nuts &ca. Two that appear'd to be Chiefs we had on board together with several others for it was a hard matter to keep them out of the Ship as they clime like Munkeys, but it was still harder to keep them from Stealing but every thing that came within their reach, in this they are prodiges expert. I made each of the two Chiefs a present of a Hatchet things that they seem'd mostly to Value. As soon as we had partly got clear of these people, I took two Boats and went to the Westward all the Gentlemen being along with me, my design was to see if there was not a more comm[o]dious Harbour and to try the disposission of the Natives having along with us the two Chiefs above mentioned: the first place we landed at was in Great Canoe Harbour (so call'd by Capt Wallis) here the Natives Flock'd about us in great Numbers and in as friendly a Manner as we could wish, only that they shew'd a great inclination to pick our pockets. We were conducted to a Chief who for distinction sake we call'd *Hercules*, after staying a Short time with him and distributing a few presents about us, we proceeded further and came to a Chief who I shall call *Lycurgus*, this Man entertain'd us with Broil'd fish Bread fruit Cocoa-nuts &ca with great hospitality,

COOK AND BANKS
GREETED AT MATAVAI BAY

and all the time took great care to tell us to take care of our pockets, as a great number of people had crowded about us. Notwithstanding the care we took D[r] Solander and D[r] Munkhouse had each of them their pockets pick'd the one of his spy glass and the other of his snuff Box, as soon as Lycurgus was made acquainted with the theift he disperse'd the people in a Moment and the method he made use of was to lay hold of the first thing that came in his way and throw it at them and happy was he or she that could get first out of his way; he seem'd very much concern'd for what had happened and by way of recompence offer'd us but every thing that was in his House, but we refuse'd to except of any thing and made signs to him that we only wanted the things again. He had already sent people out after them and it was not long before they were return'd. We found the Natives very Numerous where ever we came and from what we could judge seem'd very peaceably inclin'd.

April 1769

SATURDAY 15*th* April. This morning several of the Chiefs we had seen yesterday came on board and brought with them Hogs, Bread fruit &c[a] for these we gave them Hatchets, Linnen and such things as they Valued. Having not met with yesterday a more convenient situation for every purpose we wanted than the place where we now are, I therefore without delay resolved to pitch upon some spot upon the NE point of the Bay properly situated for observing the Transit of Venus and at the same time under the command of the Ships Guns, and there to throw up a small fort for our defence. . . . It being too late in the Day to do any thing more a party with a Petty officer was left to guard the Tent while we with a nother party took a walk into the woods and with us most of the natives. We had but just cross'd the River when M[r] Banks shott three Ducks at one shott which surprise'd them so much that the most of them fell down as tho they had been shott likewise. I was in hopes this would have had some good effect but the event did not prove it, for we had not been gone long from the Tent before the natives again began to gather about it and one of them more daring then the rest push'd one of the Centinals down, snatched the Musquet out of his hand and made a push at him and then made off and with him all the rest, emmidiatly upon this the officer order'd the party to fire and the Man who took the Musquet was shott dead before he had got far from the Tent but the Musquet was carried quite off.

FRIDAY 28*th* April. This Morning a great number of the Natives came to us in their Canoes from different parts of the Island several of whome we had not seen before, one of these was the Woman called by the Dolphin the Queen of this Island. She first went to M[r] Banks's Tent at the Fort where she was not known till the Master happening to go aShore who knew her and brought her on board with two men and several Women who seem'd to be all of her Family. I made them all some presents or other, but to Obariea, for such is this womans name, I gave several things, in return for which, as soon as I went a Shore with her,

April 1769 she gave me a Hog and several Bunches of Plantains, these she caused to be carried from her Canoe's up to the Fort in a kind of Procession she and I bringing up the rear. This Woman is about 40 years of Age and like most of the other Women very Masculine.

MONDAY *1st* May. This afternoon we set up the Observatory and took the Astronomical Quad^t^ a shore for the first time, together with some other Instruments. The Fort being no[w] finished and made as Tenable as the Time, Nature and situation of the ground, and materials we had to work upon would admit of. The North and south parts consisted of a Bank of earth 4½ feet high on the inside, and a Ditch without, 10 feet broad and 6 feet deep: on the west side faceing the Bay a Bank of earth 4 feet high and Pallisades upon that, but no ditch the works being at highwater mark: on the East side upon the Bank of the River was place'd a double row of casks: and as this was the weakest side the 2 four pounders were planted there, and the whole was defended besides these 2 guns with 6 Swivels and generally about 45 Men with small arms including the officers and gentlemen who resided aShore. I now thought my self perfectly secure from any thing these people could attempt.

TUESDAY *2nd* May. This morning about 9 oClock when Mr Green and I went to set up the Quad^t^ it was not to be found, it had never been taken out of the Packing case (which was ab^t^ 18 Inches square), sence it came from Mr Bird the Maker, and the whole was pretty heavy, so that it was a matter of astonishment to us all how it could be taken away, as a Centinal stood the whole night within 5 yards of the door of the Tent where it was put together with several other Instruments but none of them was missing but this. However it was not long before we got information that one of the natives had taken it away and carried it to the Eastward. Immidiatly a resolution was taken to detain all the large Canoes that were in the Bay, and to seize upon Tootaha and some others of the Principle people and keep them in Custody untill the Quad^t^ was produce'd, but this last we did not think proper immidiatly to put in execution as we had only Obaria in our power and the detaining of her by force would have alarm'd all the rest. In the meantime Mr Banks (who is always very alert upon all occations wherein the Natives are concern'd) and Mr Green went into the woods to enquire of Toobouratomita which way and where the Quadrant was gone; I very soon was inform'd that these Three were gone to the Eastward in quest of it and some time after I follow'd my self with a small party of Men, but before I went away I gave orders that if Tootaha came either to the Ship or the Fort he was not to be detain'd, for I found that he had no hand in takeing away the Quadrant and that there was almost a certainty of geting it again. I met Mr Banks and Mr Green about 4 Miles from the Fort returning with the Quadrant.

FRIDAY *12th* May. Clowdy weather with Showers of Rain. This Morning a Man and two young women with some others came to the Fort whome we had

not seen before: and as their manner of introduceing themselves was a little uncommon I shall insert it: Mr Banks was as usual at the gate of the Fort trading with the people, when he was told that some Strangers were coming and therefore stood to receive them, the compney had with them about a Dozn young Plantains Trees and some other small Plants, these they laid down about 20 feet from Mr Banks, the People then made a lane between him and them, when this was done the Man (who appear'd to be only a Servant to the 2 Women) brought the young Plantains Singley, together with some of the other Plants and gave them to Mr Banks, and at the delivery of each pronounce'd a Short sentence, which we understood not, after he had thus dispose'd of all his Plantain trees he took several peices of Cloth and spread them on the ground, one of the Young Women then step'd upon the Cloth and with as much Innocency as one could possibly conceve, expose'd herself intirely naked from the waist downwards, in this manner she turn'd her Self once or twice round, I am not certain which, then step'd of the Cloth and drop'd down her clothes, more Cloth was then spread upon the Former and she again perform'd the same ceremony; the Cloth was then rowled up and given to Mr Banks and the two young women went and embraced him which ended the Ceremoney.

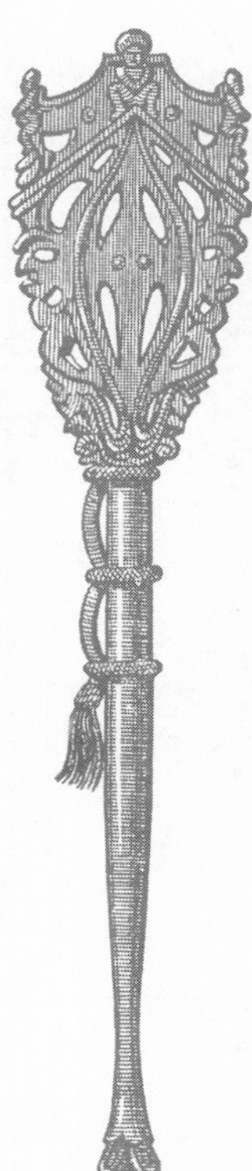

SUNDAY *14th* May. This day we perform'd divine Service in one of the Tents in the Fort where several of the Natives attended and behaved with great decency the whole time: this day closed with an odd Scene at the Gate of the Fort where a young fellow above 6 feet high lay with a little Girl about 10 or 12 years of age publickly before several of our people and a number of the Natives. What makes me mention this, is because, it appear'd to be done more from Custom than Lewdness, for there were several women present particularly Obarea and several others of the better sort and these were so far from shewing the least disaprobation that they instructed the girl how she should act her part, who young as she was, did not seem to want it.

(On 3rd June they observed the Transit of Venus in very favourable weather, although, as explained in the introduction, the results of these observations and those made elsewhere proved practically useless.

SATURDAY *3rd* June. This day prov'd as favourable to our purpose as we could wish, not a Clowd was to be seen the whole day and the Air was perfectly clear, so that we had every advantage we could desire in Observing the whole of the passage of the Planet Venus over the Suns disk: we very distinctly saw an Atmosphere or dusky shade round the body of the Planet which very much disturbed the times of the Contacts particularly the two internal ones. Dr Solander observed as well as Mr Green and my self, and we differ'd from one another in observeing the times of the Contacts much more than could be expected. Mr Greens Telescope and mine were of the same Mag[n]ifying power but that of the Dr was greater then ours. It was ne[a]rly calm the whole day and

June 1769 the Thermometer expose'd to the Sun about the middle of the Day rose to a degree of heat (119) we have not before met with.

SUNDAY *4th* June. Punished Arch[d] Wolf with two Doz[n] Lashes for theft, having broken into one of the Store rooms and stolen from thence a large quantity of spike Nails, some few of them were found upon him. This evening the gentlemen that were sent to observe the Transit of Venus returnd with success. Those that were sent to York Island were well received by the Natives; that Island appear'd to them not to be very fruitfull.

❡ During the weeks of preparation for the observations at the appropriately named 'Fort Venus' the party enjoyed the food and pleasures of this paradise of splendidly built men and beautiful coffee coloured women. Banks and others wrote enthusiastically of an 'Arcadia' inhabited by the noble savages who formed the ideal of Rousseau and other contemporary theorists. Cook with his sound judgment and sense of responsibility saw deeper, not least because he found it impossible to control sexual relations with the consequent danger of the venereal diseases which were soon to create such havoc in the Pacific islands. Beaglehole considers that Cook's crew were guiltless of introducing disease as twenty-four seamen and nine marines became infected from the islanders. The question is with what? Dr S. M. Lambert, a high authority, who examined the problem, declared against syphilis and in favour of yaws which was an endemic disease in the Pacific and produced somewhat similar symptoms to syphilis.

TUESDAY *6th* June. This Day and for some days past we have been inform'd by several of the Natives that about 10 or 15 Months ago, Two Ships touched at this Island and stay'd 10 days in a Harbour to the Eastward calle'd *Ohidea,* the Commanders name was *Toottera* so at least they call'd him and that one of the Natives call'd *Orette* Brother to the Chief of Ohidea went away with him; they likewise say that these Ship[s] brought the Venerial distemper to this Island where it is now as common as in any part of the world and which the people bear with as little concern as if they had been accustomed to it for ages past. We had not been here many days before some of our people got this disease and as no such thing happen'd to any of the Dolphins people while she was here that I ever heard off, I had reason (notwithstanding the improbability of the thing) to think that we had brought it along with us which gave me no small uneasiness and did all in my power to prevent its progress, but all I could do was to little purpose for I may safely say that I was not assisted by any one person in y[e] Ship, and was oblige'd to have the most part of the Ships Compney a Shore every day to work upon the Fort and a Strong guard every night and the Women were so very liberal with their favours, or else Nails, Shirts &c[a] were temptations that they could not withstand, that this distemper very soon spread it self over the greatest part of the Ships Compney but now I have the satisfaction to find that the Natives all agree that we did not bring it here. However this is little satisfaction to them who must suffer by it in a very great degree and may in time spread it self over all the Islands in the South Seas, to the eternal reproach of those who first brought it among them. I had taken the greatest pains to discover if any of the Ships Company had the disorder upon him for above a month before our arrival here and ordered the Surgeon to examine every man the least suspected who declar'd to me that only one man in the Ship was the least affected with it and his complaint was a carious shin bone; this man has not had connection with one woman in the Island. We have several times seen Iron tolls and other articles with these people that we suspected came not from the Dolphin and these they now say they had from these two Ships.

June 1769

☾ On the eve of the *Endeavour* sailing, the action of two marines forecast the mutiny of the *Bounty* when they decamped for the mountains with their 'wives', while a much more serious conspiracy miscarried. Cook captured his men by seizing local chiefs as hostages, a dangerous practice which ultimately led to his death in Hawaii, when he attempted to seize King Taraiopu to secure the return of a stolen cutter.

JULY 1769

'I now determin'd to get every thing off from the Shore & leave the Place as soon as Possible, the geting the several Articles on board & Scraping & Paying the Ships Sides took us up the whole of the following week without anything remarkable happening until.

SUNDAY 9*th* July. When sometime in the Middle Watch Clement Webb & Sam[l] Gibson both Marines & young Men found means to get away from the Fort (which was now no hard matter to do) & in the morning were not to be found, as it was known to every body that all hands were to go on board on the monday morning & that the ship would sail in a day or 2, there was reason to think that these 2 Men intended to stay behind, However I was willing to wait one day to see if they would return before I took any steps to find them.

MONDAY 10*th* July. The 2 Marines not returning this morning I began to enquire after them & was inform'd by some of the Natives that they were gone to the Mountains & that they had got each of them a Wife & would not return, but at the same time no one would give us any Certain intelligence where they were, upon which a resolution was taken to seize upon as many of the Chiefs as we could, this was thought to be the readiest method to induce the other natives to produce the two men. We had in our Custody Obarea, Toobouratomita, and two other Chiefs but as I know'd that Tootaha would have more weight with the Natives then all these put together, I dispatch'd Lieut[t] Hicks away in the Pinnace to the place where Tootaha was to endeavour to decoy him into the boat and bring him on board which M[r] Hicks perform'd without the least disturbance.

July 1769 TUESDAY 11*th* July. The Petty officer whom I sent in quest of the deserters told me that the Natives would give him no intellingence where they were nor those that went along with him, but on the contrary grew very troblesome and as they were returning in the evening they were suddenly Siezed upon by a number of arm'd men that had hid themselves in the woods for that purpose; this was after Tootaha had been seized upon by us so that they did this by way of retaliation in order to recover their Chief, but this method did not meet with the approbation of them all, a great many condem'd these proceedings and were for having them set at liberty, while others were for keeping them untill Tootaha was relase'd. The desputes went so far that they came from words to blowes and our people were several times very near being set at liberty but at last the party for keeping them prevail'd; but as they had still some friends no insult was offer'd them; a little while after they brought Web and Gibson the two deserters to them as prisoners likwise but at last they agree'd that Web should be sent to inform us where the others were.

'When I came to examine these two men touching the reasons that induce'd them to go away, it appear'd that an acquentence they had contracted with two Girls and to whome they had stron[g]ly attache'd themselves was the sole reason of their attempting to Stay behind.

THURSDAY 13*th* July. For some time before we left this Island several of the natives were daily offering themselves to go away with us, and as it was thought that they must be of use to us in our future discoveries, we resolved to bring away one whose name is *Tupia*, a Cheif and a Priest: This man had been with us the most part of the time we had been upon the Island which gave us an oppertunity to know some thing of him: we found him to be a very intelligent person and to know more of the Geography of the Islands situated in these seas, their produce and the religion laws and customs of the inhabitants then any one we had met with and was the likeliest person to answer our purpose; for these reasons and at the request of M[r] Banks I received him on board together with a you[n]g boy his servant.

℄ Cook's Journal contains a very long and interesting description of Tahiti, and its produce, and of the inhabitants, their manners, customs, religion, houses, arms and magnificent canoes. The following brief extracts illustrate Cook's great gifts of observation and judgment, but, as Beaglehole points out, some of Cook's anthropological observations may really be those of Banks as they drew upon each other's journals.

DESCRIPTION OF KING GEORGES ISLAND

'This Island is called by the Natives *Otaheite* and was first discover'd by Captain Wallice in His Majestys Ship Dolphin on the 19th of June 1767, and to the credit of him and his officers the Long[d] of Roy[l] Bay was settled by them to within half a degree of the truth and the whole figure of the Island not ill discribed. . . . *July 1769* The land of this Island except what is emmidiatly bordering upon the Sea Coast is of a very uneven Surface and riseth in ridges which run up into the middle of the Island, and there form mountains that are of a height sufficient to be seen at the distance of 20 Leagues. Between the foot of the ridges and the sea is a border of low land surrounding the whole Island, except in a few places where the ridges rise directly from the Sea, this low land is of various breadths but no where exceeds a mile and a half; the soil is rich and fertile being for the most part well stocked with fruit trees and small plantations and well water'd by a number of small rivulets of excellent water which come from the adjacent hills. It is upon this low land that the greatest part of the inhabitants live, not in towns or Villages but dispersed every where round the whole Island. The tops of most of the ridges and mountains are barren and as it were burnt up with the sun, yet many parts of some of them are not without their produce and many of the Vallies are fertile and inhabited.

'The produce of this Island is Bread fruit, cocoa-nuts, Bananoes, Plantains, a fruit like an apple, sweet Potatoes, yams, a fruit known by the name of Eag melloa and reckond most delicous, Sugar cane which the inhabitants eat raw, a root of the Salop kind call'd by inhabitants Pea, the root also of a plant call'd Ether and a fruit in a Pod like a Kidney bean which when roasted eats like a chestnut and is call'd Ahu, the fruit of a tree which they call Wharra something like a Pine Apple, the fruit of a tree call'd by them Nano, the roots of a Fern and the roots of a Plant call'd Theve. All these articles the Earth almost spontaniously produces or at least they are raisd with very little labour, in the article of food these people may almost be said to be exempt from the curse of our fore fathers; scarcely can it be said that they earn their bread with the sweet of their brow, benevolent nature hath not only supply'd them with necessarys but with abundance of superfluities. The Sea Coast supplies them with vast variety of most excellent fish but these they get not without some trouble and perseverance, fish seems to be one of their greatest luxuries and they eat it either raw or dress'd and seem to relish it one way as well as the other, not only fish but almost every thing that comes out of the sea is eat and esteem'd by these people. Shell fish Lobsters Crabs and even Sea Insects and what is commonly call'd Blubbers of many kinds conduce to their support. For tame Animals they have Hogs Fowls and Dogs the latter of which we learnd to eat from them and few were there of us but what allowe'd that a South Sea Dog was next to an English Lamb, one thing in their favour is that they live intirely upon Vegetables probably our Dogs would not eat half so well, little can be said in favour of their fowles but their Pork is most excellent. . . . With respect to their persons the men in general are tall, strong limb'd and well shaped, one of the tallest we saw measured Six feet 3 Inches and a half, the superior women are in every respect as large as Europeans

July 1769 but the inferior sort are in general Small owing possibbly to their early amours which they are more addicted to then their Superiors. They are of Various Colours, those of the inferior sort who are obliged to be much exposed to the sun and air are of a very dark brown, the Superiors again who spend most of their time in their Houses or under shelter are not browner than people who are born or reside long in the West Indias nay some of the women are almost as fair as Europeans. Their hair is almost universaly black thick and strong this the women wear short cropt round their ears, the men on the other hand wear it different ways, the better sort let it grow long and sometimes tying it up on the top of their heads or leting it hang loose over their Shoulders but many of the inferiors and such w[h]o in the exersice of their profession fishing &c[a] are obliged to be much upon or in the water wear it cropt short like the women. They always pluck out a part of their beards and keep that that remains neat and clean. Both sexes eradicate every hair from under their armpits and look upon it as a mark of uncleanliness in us that we do not do the same. They have all fine white teeth and for the most part short flat noses and thick lips, yet their features are agreable and their gate gracefull, and their behavour to strangers and to each other is open affable and courtious and from all I could see free from threachery, only that they are thieves to a Man and would steal but everything that came in their way and that with such dexterity as would shame the most noted pickbocket in Europe. They are a Very cleanly people both in their persons and diat always washing their hands and mouth immidiatly before and after their meals and wash or bathe themselves in fresh water three times a day, morning noon night, the only disagreable thing about them is the oyle with which they anoint their heads *Monoe* as they call it, this is made of cocoanut oyle in which some sweet earbs or flowers are infused the oyle is generaly very rancid which makes the wearer of it smell not very agreable. Another custom they have that is disagreable to Europeans which is eating lice a pretty good stock of which they generaly carry about them; however this Custom is not universal for I seldom saw it done but among children and common people and I am persuaded that had they the means they would keep themselves as free from lice as we do, but the want of Combs in a hot climate makes this hardly possible.

'There are some very few men upon this Island whose skins were whiter than any Europeans, but of a dead colour like that of the nose of [a] white horse, their Eyes, eyebrows, hair and beards were also white, their bodies were cover'd more or less with a kind of white down, their skins are spotted some parts being much whiter than others, they are short sighted with their eyes often full of rheum and always looke'd unwholesome and have neither the spirit or activity of the other natives. I did not see above three or four upon the whole Island and these were old men so that I concluded that this difference of Colour &c[a] was accidental and did not run in families for if it did they must have been more numerous. The inhabitants of this Island are troubled with a sort of Leprosie or scab all over their bodies, I have seen men women and children, but not many, who have had this distemper to that degree as not to be able to walk; this distemper I believe runs in familys because I have seen both Mother and child have it.

July 1769

'Both sexes paint their bodys *Tattow* as it is called in their language, this is done by inlaying the Colour of black under their skins in such a manner as to be indelible. Some have ill design'd figures of men birds or dogs, the women generaly have this figure Z simply on ever[y] joint of their fingures and toes, the men have it like wise and both have other defferent figures such as circles crescents &c[a] which they have on their Arms and legs. In short they are so various in the application of these figures that both the quantity and situation of them seem to depend intirely upon the humour of each individual, yet all agree in having all their buttocks cover'd with a deep black, over this most have arches drawn one over a[n]other as high as their short ribs which are near a quarter of an Inch broad; these arches seem to be their great pride as both men and women show them with great pleasure. . . . Their cloathing are either of Cloth or matting of several differen[t] sorts the dress of both men and women are much the same which is a peice of Cloth or Matting wraped two or three times round their waist and hangs down below their knees both behind and before like a peticoat, another peice or sometimes two or three, about 2 yards or 2½ yards long with a hole in the middle thro which they put their heads, this hangs over their shoulders down behind and before and is tied round their waist with a long peice of thin Cloth and being open at the sides gives free liberty to their arms. This is the Common dress of all ranks of people and there are few without such a one except the Children who go quite naked the boys untill they are Six or Seven years of Age and the girls untill 3 or 4, at these ages they begin to cover what nature teaches them to hide. . . . After their meals and in the heat of the day they often sleep middle aged people especialy, the better sort of whom seem to spend most of their time in eating and sleeping. Diversions they have but few. Shooting with the Bow and Wristling are the chief the first of which is confined almost wholy to the Chiefs; they shoot for distance only kneeling upon one knee and dropping the bow at the instant of the arrows parting from it, I have seen one of them shoot an arrow 274 yards yet he look'd upon it as no great shott. . . . The young girls when ever they can collect 8 or 10 together dance a very indecent dance which they call *Timorodee* singing most indecent songs and useing most indecent actions in the practice of which they are brought up from their earlyest Childhood, in doing this they keep time to a great nicety; this exercise is however generaly left of as soon as they arrive at years of maturity for as soon as they have form'd a connection with man they are expected to leave of dancing *Timorodee*. One amusement or Custom more I must mention tho I must confess

July 1769 I do not expect to be believed as it is founded upon a Custom so inhuman and contrary to the first principals of human nature: it is this, that more than one half of the better sort of the inhabitants have enter'd into a resolution of injoying free liberty in love without being troubled or disturbed by its concequences; these mix and cohabit together with the utmost freedom and the Children who are so unfortunate as to be thus begot are smother'd at the moment of their birth; many of these people contract intimacies and live together as Man and wife for years in the Course of which the Children that are born are destroy'd. They are so far from concealing it that they rather look upon it as a branch of freedom upon which they value themselves. They are call'd *Arreoy's* and have meetings among themselves where the men amuse themselves with wristling &c[a] and the women in dancing the indecent dance before mentioned, in the Course of which they give full liberty to their desires but I believe keep up to the appearance of decency. I never saw one of these meetings. D[r] Munkhouse saw part of one enough to make him give credit to what we had been told.

'Both sexes express the most indecent ideas in conversation without the least emotion and they delight in such conversation behond any other. Chastity indeed is but little Valued especialy among the middle people, if a wife is found guilty of a breach of it her only punishment is a beating from her husband; the men will very readily offer the young women to strangers even their own daughters and think it very strange if you refuse them but this is done meerly for the lucre of gain.

'The Houses or dwellings of these people are admirably calculated for the continual warmth of the climate, they do not build them in Towns or Villiges but seperate each from the other and always in the woods and are without walls so that the air coold by the shade of the trees has free access in whatever direction it happens to blow, no country can bost of more delightfull walks than this; the whole plains where the natives reside are cover'd with groves of Bread fruit and Cocoa nut trees without under wood and intersected in all directions by the paths which go from house to house, so that nothing can be more gratefull in a Climate where the sun hath so powerfull an influance. They are generaly built in form of an Oblong square the roofs are supported by three rows of pillors or posts and neatly cover'd with thatch made of palm leaves, a middle sized house is about 24 feet by 12 extreme height 8 or 9 and height of the eves 3½ or 4, the flowers are covered some Inches deep with hay upon which here and there lay matts for the conveniency of seting down, few houses has more than one stool which is only used by the Master of the family. In their houses are neither rooms or partitions but they all huddle and sleep to gether yet in this they generaly observe some order, the married people laying by themselves and the unmarried each sex by themselves at some small distance from each other. . . . *Their Canoes* or *Proes* are built all of them very narrow and some of the largest are

60 or 70 feet long; these co[n]sist of several peices, the bottom is round and made of large logs hollowed out to the thickness of about 3 Inches and may consist of three or four peices, the sides are of plank of nearly the same thickness and are built nearly perpendicular rounding in a little towards the gunwale, the peices in which they are built are well fited and fasten'd or sew'd together with strong platting something in the same manner as old China wooden bowls &c[a] are mended. The greatest breadth is at the after part which is generaly about 18 or 20 Inches and the fore part about ⅓ narrower, the height from the bottom to the gunwale seldom exceeds 2½ or 3 feet, they build them with high curv'd sterns which are generaly ornimented with carved work, the head or fore part curves little or nothing. The smaller Canoes are built after the same Plan some out of one, two or more trees according to their size or the use they are for. In order to prevent them from overseting when in the water all those that go single both great and small have what is call'd outriggers which are peices of wood fasten'd to the gunel and project out on one side about 6, 8 or 10 feet according to the size of the boat; at the ends is fastend in a parallel direction to the Canoe a long log of wood simply, or some have it shaped into the form of a small boat but this is not common, this lays in the water & ballanceth the boat: those that are for sailing have outriggers only on the other side abreast of the mast, these serve to fasten the shrouds to and are of use in trimming the boat when it blows fresh. The sailing Proes have some one and some two masts, the sails are off Matting and are made narrow at the head and square at the foot something like a shoulder of Mutton Sail, & generally used on Man of War Barges &c[a] I have mentioned above that the single Canoes have outriggers for those that go double that is two together, which is very common, have no need of any and it is done in this manner: two Canoes are placed in a parallel direction to each other about three or four feet asunder securing them together by small logs of wood laid aCross and lashed to each of their gunels, thus the one boat supports the other and are not in the least danger of over seting and I beleive that it is in this manner that all their large Proes are use'd, some of which will carry a great number of men by means of a platform made of bamboos or other light wood the whole length of the Proes and considerably broader, but I never saw but one fited in this manner upon the whole Island. Upon the fore part of all these large double Proes was placed an oblong platform about 10 or 12 feet in length and 6 or 8 in breadth, and supported about 4 feet above the Gunels by stout carved pillors: the use of these platforms as were told are for the Club men to stand and fight upon in time of battle, for the large Canoes from what I could learn are built mostly if not wholy for war and their method of fighting is to graple one a nother and fight it out with Clubs, spears & stones. I never saw but one of these sort of Canoes in the water the rest were all hauld a shore and seem'd to be going to decay neither were they very many of them upon the Island.

July 1769

'The Chiefs and better sort of people generaly go from one place of the Island to a nother in small double Canoes which carry a little moveable house, this not only screens them from the Sun by day but serves them to sleep in in the night and this way of traveling is extreamly commodious about such Islands as are inclosed by a reef as this is, for as these canoes draw but little water they can always keep within the reefs and by that means are never in danger. The[y] have some few other Canoes, *Pahee's* as they call them, which differ from those above discribed, but of these I saw but six upon the whole Island and was told that they were not built here, the two largest was each 76 feet long and when they had been in use had been fasten'd together, these are built sharp and narrow at both ends and broad in the middle, the bottom is likewise sharp inclining to a wedge, yet bildges out very much and rounds in again very quick just below the gunwale. They are built of several peices of thick plank and put together as the others are only these have timbers in the inside which the others have not, they have high curved sterns the head also curves a little and both are ornmented with the image of a Man carved in wood, very little inferior work of the like kind done by common ship carvers in England. When one considers the tools these people have to work with one cannot help but admire their workmanship, these are Adzes and small hatchets made of a hard stone, Chisels or gouges made of human bones, generaly the bone of the fore arm, but spike nails have pretty well supplied the place of these, with these ordinary tools that a European workman would expect to break the first stroke I have seen them work surprisingly fast; to plane or polish their work they rub upon it with a smooth stone, Coral beat small and mixt with water, this is sometimes done by scraping it with shells with which alone they perform most of their small woodwork.

'Their Proes or Canoes large and small are rowed and steer'd with paddles and notwithstanding the large ones appear to be very unwieldy they manage them very dextrusly and I beleive perform long and distant Voyages in them, otherwise they could not have the knowlidge of the Islands in these seas they seem to have. They wear for shew or or[n]ament at the Mast heads of most of their sailing canoes Pendants made of feathers. . . . I have before mentioned that this Island is divided into two districts or Kingdoms which are frequently at war with each other as happend about twelve Months ago, and each of these is again divided into smaller districts, *Whennuas* as they Call them, over each of the Kingdoms is an *Eare dehi* or head whome we call a King and in the *Whannuas* are *Eares* or Chiefs. The Kings power seems to be but very little, he may be reverenced as a father but he his neither fear'd nor respected as a Monarch and the same may be said of the other Chiefs, however they have a preeminence over the rest of the people who pay them a kind of a volantry obedience. Upon the whole these people seem to injoy liberty in its fullest extend, every man seems to be the sole judge of his own actions and to know no punishment but death and this perhaps is never inflicted but upon a publick enimy. There are three Ranks of Men and women, first the *Eares* or Chiefs, second the *Manahoona's* or midling sort and lastly the *Toutou's* which comprehends all the lower class and are by far the most numerous, these seem to live in some sort dependent on the *Eares* who together with the Manahoona's own most of not all of the lands, this is hereditary in their families and the moment the heir is born he succeeds the father both in the title and estate: at least to the name for it is most likely that the latter must have the power during his Son or Daughters minority.

July 1769

'Having given the best account I can of the manners and Customs of these people, it will be expected that I should give some account of their Religion, which is a thing I have learnt so little of that I hardly dare touch upon it, and should have pass'd it over in silance was it not my duty as well as inclination to insert in this Journal every and the least knowledge I may obtain of a people who for many centuries have been shut up from almost every other part of the world. They believe that theer is one Supreme God whome they call Tane from him sprung a number of inferior Deities *Eatuas* as they call them, these they think preside over them and intermeddle in their affairs, to these they offer oblations such as Hogs, Dogs, Fish, Fruit &c[a] and invoke them on some particular occasions as in times of real or apparrent danger, the seting out of a long Voyage sickness &c[a] but the ceremonies made use on these occasions I know not. The Mories which we at first thought were berrying places are wholy built for places of worship and for the performing of religious ceremo[n]ies in. The Viands are laid upon Altars erected 8, 10 or 12 [feet] high by stout posts and the table of the Altar on which the Viands lay is generaly made of Palm leaves, they are not always in the Mories but very often at some distance from them: their Mories as well as the tombs of the dead they seem to hold sacred and the women never enter the former whatever they may do the latter. The Viands laid near the tombs of the dead are from what I can learn not for the deceased but as an offering to the *Eatua* made upon that occasion, who if not would distroy the body and not except of the Soul for they believe of a future state of rewards and punishments, but what their ideas are of it I know not. We have seen in some few places small houses set apart on purpose for the reception of the oblations offer'd to the *Eatua* which consists in small strips of Cloth Viands &c[a]. I am of opinion that they offer to the *Eatua* a strip or small peice of every peice of cloth they make before they use it themselves and it is not unlikely but what they observe the same thing with respect to thier Victuals, but as there are but few of these houses this cannot be a common custom, it may only be observed by the priest and such families as are more regilious than others. Now I have mentioned preists, these are men who exerise that function of which number Tupia is one, they seem to be in no great repute niether can they live wholy by their profession and this leads me to think that these people are no bigots to their regelion. The priests on some occasions do the office

July 1769 of Physicions and their prescriptions consi[s]ts in performing some religious ceremony before the sick person, they likewise Crown the *Eare dehi* or King in the performing of which we are told much form and ceremony is used after which every one is at liberty to treat and play as many tricks with the new King as he pleaseth during the remainder of the day. . . . They compute time by the moon which they call *Malama* reckoning 30 days to each Moon, 2 of which they say the moon is *Matte* that is dead and this is at the time of new mo[o]n when she cannot be seen; the day is divided into smaller portions not less than two hours. Their computations is by units, tens and scores up to ten score or 200 &c^a^. In counting they generaly take hold of their fingers one by one shifting from the one hand to the other untill they come to the number they want to express but if it be a high number instead of their fingers they use peices [of] leaves &c^a^. . . . Altho this Island lies within the Tropick of Capricorn yet the heat is not troublesome nor do the winds blow constantly from the east but are subject to variations, frequently blowing a fresh gale from the SW quarter for two or three days together, but very seldome from the NW. When ever these variable winds happen they are always accompaned with a swell from the SW or WSW and the same thing happens when ever it is calm, and the Atmosphere at the same time loaded with clowds, sure indications that the winds are variable or westerly out at sea for clear weather generaly attend[s] the settle[d] trade.

'The meeting with Westerly winds within the general limets of the easterly trade is a little extraordinary, and has induced former navigators when they met with them to think that they were caused by the nearness of some large track of land but I rather think that they are owing to a nother cause; it hath been found both by the dolphin and us that the trade wind in those parts of this sea doth not extend farther to the South than 20° and without which we generaly met with a wind from the westward; now is it not reasonable to suppose that when these winds blow strong they must incroach upon and drive back the easterly winds and so cause the variable winds and SWterly Swell I have been speaking of: it is well known that the trade winds blow but faint for some distance within their limets and are therefore easily stop'd by a wind from the contrary direction. It is likewise known that these limets are subject to vary several degrees not only at different seasons of the year but at one and the same season; another reason why I think that these SW winds are not caused by the nearness of any large track of land is their being always accompaned with a large swell from the same quarter, and we find a much greater surf beating upon the shores of the SW sides of the Islands situated just within the limets of the trade winds than upon any other part of them. . . . I have before hinted that these people have an extensive knowlidge of the Islands situated in these seas, Tupia as well as several others hath given us an account of upwards of seventy, but as the account they have given of their situation is so vague and uncertain I shall refar giving a list of them untill I have learnt from Tupia the situation of each Island with a little more certainty. Four of these Islands (viz) *Huaheine*, *Ulietea*, *Otaha* and *Bolabola* we were inform'd lay only one or two days sail to the westward of Georges Island and that we might there procure there Hogs Fowls and other refreshments, articles that we had been very sparly supply'd with at this last Island and as the Ships company, what from the constant hard duty they had had at this place and the too free use of women were in a worse state of hilth then they were on our first arrival, for by this time full half of them had got the Venereal disease in which situation I thought they would be ill able to stand the cold weather we might expect to meet with to the southward at this Season of the year, and therefore I resolved to give them a little time to recover while we run down to and exploar'd the Islands before mentioned. *July 1769*

(Cook now decided to sail south-west in pursuit of his second and secret objective, the supposed continent, although he believed that no large tract of land lay near Tahiti for the reasons given below. However, as noted above, he remained for awhile in tropical waters until his men were in better health and took with him a Tahitian priest named Tupia, who probably accepted the invitation because he had been concerned in a conspiracy to kill Tootaha, the Chief of the Matavai district where the *Dolphin* and *Endeavour* anchored.

(For these reasons Cook delayed in the tropics and discovered, described and mapped the beautiful and fertile Leeward Group of the Society Islands before seeking the continent.

TUESDAY 15*th* August. The farthest Island to the southward that Tupia hath been at or knows anything of lies but two days sail from Ohetiroa and is called *Moutou* but he says that his Father once told him that their were Islands to the southward of it, but we can not find that he either knows or ever heard of a Continent or large track of land. I have no reason to doubt Tupia[s] information of these Islands, for when we left Ulietea and steer'd to the southward, he told us that if we would keep a little more to the East (which the wind would not permit us to do) we should see Mannua, but as we then steer'd we should see Ohetiroa which happend accordingly. If we meet with the Islands to the southward he speaks off it[s] well if not I shall spend no time in searching for them, being now fully resolved to Stand directly to the Southward in search of the Continent.

(By the beginning of September the *Endeavour* had reached Latitude 40° 12′ south but tempestuous weather forced Cook to change his course and sail north and west for Tasman's New Zealand.

SATURDAY 2*nd* September. *Latd in South* 39° 45′. *Longd in West* 145° 39′. Very Strong gales with heavy Squalls of Wind, hail and rain. At 4 PM being in the Lat[d] of 40° 22′ S and having not the least Visible signs of land, we wore and brought too under the fore sail and reefd the Main sail and handed it. I did intend

September 1769 to have stood to the Southward if the winds had been moderate so long as they continued westerly notwithstanding we had no prospect of meeting with land, rather then stand back to y[e] north[rd] on the same track as we came; but as the weather was so very tempestuous I laid a side this design, thought it more advisable to stand to the Northward into better weather least we should receive such damages in our sails & rigging as might hinder the further prosecutions of the Voyage.

Chapter V

NEW ZEALAND, 1769-70

"Never has a coastline been so well laid down by a first explorer."

ADMIRAL WHARTON

THE *ENDEAVOUR* HAD NOW SAILED THROUGH THE EASTERN part of the mythical Southern Continent in her voyage from Cape Horn to Tahiti, and she had shown in her southern sweep from Tahiti that the supposed northern shores of the continent were non-existent in that locality. The exploration of New Zealand would decide whether or not this land formed the western coast of the continent. Land was seen on the 7th of October, by a boy, Nicholas Young, and the S.W. point of Poverty Bay was named 'Young Nick's Head'. Cook then sailed into the Bay, which he first named 'Endeavour Bay' and later 'Poverty Bay' because 'it afforded us no one thing we wanted'. The expedition at once encountered trouble with the warlike Maoris.

SATURDAY *7th* October. *Latd in South* 38° 57′. *Longd in West* 177° 54′. Gentle breezes and settled weather. At 2 PM saw land from the mast head bearing WBN, which we stood directly for, and could but just see it at sun set.

MONDAY *9th* October. I went ashore with a party of men in the Pinnace and yawl accompaned by M[r] Banks and D[r] Solander, we land[ed] abreast of the Ship and on the east side of the river just mentioned, but seeing some of the natives on the other side of the river whome I was desirous of speaking with and finding that we could not ford the river, I order'd the yawl in to carry us over and the Pinnace to lay at the entrance. In the mean time the Indians made off; however we went as far as their hutts which lay about 2 or 3 hundred yards from the water side leaving four boys to take care of the yawl, which we had no sooner left than four men came out of the woods on the other side the river and would

October certainly have cut her off, had not the people in the pinnace discover'd them and
1769 called to her to drop down the stream which they did being closely pursued by the Indians; the Coxswain of the pinnace who had the charge of the Boats, seeing this fire'd two musquets over their heads, the first made them stop and look round them, but the 2^{d} they took no notice of upon which a third was fired and killed one of them upon the spot just as he was going to dart his spear at the boat; at this the other three stood motionless for a minute or two, seemingly quite surprised wondering no doubt what it was that had thus killed their commorade: but as soon as they recover'd themselves they made off draging the dead body a little way and then left it.

⁋ Cook and Banks were deeply grieved at an even more serious incident the following day.

TUESDAY 10*th* October. PM I rowed round the head of the Bay but could find no place to land, on account of the great surff which beat every where upon the shore; seeing two boats or Canoes coming in from Sea, I rowed to one of them in order to seize upon the people and came so near before they took notice of us that Tupia called to them to come along side and we would not hurt them, but instead of doing this they endeavoured to get away, upon which I order'd a Musquet to be fire'd over their heads thinking that this would either make them surrender or jump over board, but here I was misstaken for they immidiately took to thier arms or whatever they had in the boat and began to attack us, this obliged us to fire upon them and unfortunatly either two or three were kill'd, and one wounded, and three jumped over board, these last we took up and brought on board, where they were clothed and treated with all immaginable kindness and to the surprise of every body became at once as cheerful and as merry as if they had been with their own friends; they were all three young, the eldest not above 20 years of age and the youngest about 10 or 12.

'I am aware that most humane men who have not experienced things of this nature will cencure my conduct in fireing upon the people in this boat nor do I my self think that the reason I had for seizing upon her will att all justify me, and had I thought that they would have made the least resistance I would not have come near them, but as they did I was not to stand still and suffer either my self or those that were with me to be knocked on the head.

WEDNESDAY 11*th* October. In the PM as I intended to sail in the morning we put the three youths ashore seemingly very much againest their inclination, but whether this was owing to a desire they had to remain with us or the fear of falling into the hands of their eminies as they pretended I know not; the latter however seem'd to be ill founded for we saw them carried aCross the river in a Catamaran and walk leasurely off with the other natives.

'At 6 AM we weigh'd and stood out of the Bay which I have named *Poverty Bay* because it afforded us no one thing we wanted.

November 1769

(From Poverty Bay Cook sailed south, naming Hawke Bay after the First Lord of the Admiralty, but, as he found no good harbour and poor country, he turned north and began to circumnavigate the North Island in an anti-clockwise direction. They passed the Bay of Plenty and Mercury Bay where they observed the Transit of Mercury and where Cook was greatly impressed by the Pahs or fortified Maori villages. A long account of one of these includes the following:—

SATURDAY 11*th* November. A little with[in] the entrance of the river [the Mercury] on the East side is a high point or peninsula juting out into the River on which are the remains of one of thier Fortified towns, the Situation is such that the best Engineer in Europe could not have choose'd a better for a small number of men to defend themselves against a greater, it is strong by nature and made more so by Art. It is only accessible on the land side, and there have been cut a Ditch and a bank raised on the inside, from the top of the bank to the bottom of the ditch was about 22 feet and depth of the ditch on the land side 14 feet; its breadth was in proportion to its depth and the whole seem'd to have been done with great judgement. There had been a row of Pickets on the top of the bank and another on the outside of the ditch, these last had been set deep in the ground and sloaping with their upper ends hanging over the ditch; the whole had been burnt down, so that it is probable that this place has been taken and distroy'd by an Enimy.

(Relations with the Maoris varied. Sometimes muskets and even cannon were needed to deal with them; at other times they were most friendly—for example, on the River Thames, where the magnificent trees impressed Cook greatly.

TUESDAY 21*st* November. After land[ing] as above mentioned we had not gone a hundred yards into the Woods before we found a tree that girted 19 feet 8 Inches 6 feet above the Ground, and having a quadrant with me I found its length from the root to the first branch to be 89 feet, it was as streight as an arrow and taper'd but very little in proportion to its length, so that I judged that there was 356 solid feet of timber in this tree clear of the branches. We saw many others of the same sort several of which were taller than the one we measured and all of them very stout; there were likewise many other sorts of very stout timber-trees all of them wholy unknown to any of us. We brought away a few specimans and at 3 oClock we embarqued in order to return on board with the very first of the Ebb, but not before we had named this River the *Thames* on account of its bearing some resemblence to that river in england. In our return down the River the inhabitants of the Village where we landed in going, seeing that we return'd by a nother Channell put off in thier Canoes and met us and trafficked with us in the most friendly manner immagineable untill they had disposed of the few trifles they had.

November 1769

☾ After passing Hauraki Gulf, and the future site of Auckland, the *Endeavour* entered the Bay of Islands, where, then, as at present, the Maori population was dense.

MONDAY *27th* November. PM On the SW side of this Bay we saw several Villages situated both on Islands and on the Main land from whence came off to us several large Canoes full of people, but like those that had been along side before would not enter into a friendly traffick with us, but would cheat when ever they had an opertunity. The people in these Canoes made a very good appearence being all stout well made men, having all of them their hair which was black Comb'd up and tied upon the Crown of their heads and there stuck with white feathers, in each of the Canoes were two or three Cheifs and the habits of these were rather superior to any we had yet seen, the Cloth they were made on was of the best sort and cover'd on the out side with Dog skins put on in such a manner as to look agreeable enought to the Eye. Few of these people were tattow'd or mark'd in the face like those we have seen farther to the south, but several had their Backsides tattou'd much in the same manner as the Inhabitants of the Islands within the Tropics. In the Course of this Day, that is this afternoon and yester forenoon, we reckoned that we had not less than four or five hundred of the Natives alongside and on board the Ship, and in that time did not rainge above 6 or 8 Leagues of the Sea-Coast, a strong proff that this part of the Country must be well inhabited.

☾ In his dealings with the members of his crew and the natives Cook was scrupulously just.

THURSDAY *30th* November. PM had the winds Westerly with some very heavy showers of rain. We had no sooner come to an Anchor than between 3 and 4 hundred of the Natives Assembled in their Canoes about the Ship, some few were admited on board and to one of the Chiefs I gave a piece of Broad Cloth and distributed a few nails &c^{a} a Mongest some others of them. Many of these people had been off to the Ship when we were at sea and seem'd to be very sencible of the use of fire arms and in the little trade we had with them they behaved tollerable well, but continued not long before some of them wanted to take away the Buoy and would not desist at the fireing of several Musquets untill one of them was hurt by small shott, after which they withdrew a small distance from the Ship . . . I sent the Master with two Boats to sound the harbour, but before this I order'd Math^{w} Cox, Hen^{ry} Stevens and Man^{l} Paroyra to be punished with a doz^{n} lashes each for leaving thier duty when a shore last night and diging up Potatous out of one of the Plantations, the first of the three I remited back to confinement because he insisted that their was no harm in what he had done. All this fore noon had abundance of the Natives about the Ship and some few on board, we trafficked with them for a few trifles in which they dealt very fair and friendly.

☾ In early December came an incident which illustrated the constant dangers of navigation on an unknown coast. *December 1769*

WEDNESDAY *6th* December. PM had a gentle breeze at NNW, with which we kept turning out of the Bay but gaind little or nothing, in the evening it fell little wind and at 10 oClock it was Calm; At this time the tide or Current seting the Ship near one of the Islands, where we was very near being a shore but by the help of our boat and a light air from the southward we got clear; about an hour after when we thought our selves out of all danger the Ship struck upon a Sunken rock and went immidiatly clear without receiving any perceptible damage; just before the man in the chains had 17 fathom water and immidiatly after she struck 5 fathom, but very soon deepen'd to 20.

☾ Shortly after mid December and in very bad weather Cook passed and named North Cape and saw the Three Kings Island and Cape Maria Van Diemen which Tasman had discovered. He had now shown the probability of the Dutchman's contentions that, owing to the heavy swell from the north-west, there must be a passage from New Zealand and south-west across the Pacific. Continuing south Cook sighted and was immensely impressed by Mt. Egmont.

SATURDAY *13th* January. At 5 AM saw for a few Minutes the Top of the peaked Mountain above the Clowds, bearing NE; it is of a prodigious height and its top is cover'd with everlasting snow. It lies in the Latitude of 39° 16′ S and in the Longitude of 185° 15′ W. I have named it *Mount Egmont* in honour of the Earl of Egmont. This mountain seems to have a pretty large base and to rise with a gradual assent to the peak and what makes it more conspicuous is, its being situated near the Sea, and a flat Country in its neighbourhood which afforded a very good asspect, being cloathed with Wood and Verdure.

MONDAY *15th* January. The land seen than bearing S 63° West bore now N 59° West distant 7 or 8 Leag[s] and makes like an Island, between this land or Island and Cape Egmont is a very broad and deep Bay or Inlet the SW side of which we are now upon, and here the land is of a considerable height distinguished by hills and Vallies and the shore seems to form several Bays into one of which I intend to go with the Ship in order to Careen her (she being very foul) and to repair some few defects, recrute our stock of Wood, water &c[a] with this View we kept plying on and off al[l] night having from 80 to 63 fathoms water. At day light Stood in for an Inlet which runs in SW.

☾ The *Endeavour* now entered the great western opening of Cook Strait between the North and South Island—the strait whose existence Tasman had suspected but which he had failed to penetrate in 1642. Sailing in Cook encountered as the strait narrowed the northern fiord coast of the Southern Island, and here, he decided to stay in what was to prove his much beloved Queen Charlotte Sound, an inlet which provided timber, fresh water, and friendly natives.

January 1770 ℂ Admiral Wharton has pointed out that Cook had now effected, by an admirable mingling of 'audacity and caution', a brilliant survey of a most dangerous and stormy coastline together with 'extraordinarily accurate' observations of latitude and longitude.

ℂ In Queen Charlotte Sound the Maoris, who were comparatively few, changed in attitude from hostility and stonethrowing to lukewarm friendliness. The whites were, however, horrified to find that they were enthusiastic cannibals.

WEDNESDAY 17*th* January. Soon after we landed we met with two or three of the Natives who not long before must have been regailing themselves upon human flesh, for I got from one of them the bone of the fore arm of a Man or a Woman which was quite fresh and the flesh had been but lately pick'd off which they told us they had eat, they gave us to understand that but a few days ago they had taken Kill'd and eat a Boats crew of their enemies or strangers, for I beleive that they look upon all strangers as enemies; from what we could learn the Woman we had seen floating upon the water was in this boat and had been drownded in the fray. There was not one of us that had the least doubt but what this people were Canabals but the finding this Bone with part of the sinews fresh upon it was a stronger proof than any we had yet met with, and in order to be fully satisfied of the truth of what they had told us, we told one of them that it was not the bone of a man but that of a Dog, but he with great fervency took hold of his fore-arm and told us again that it was that bone and to convence us that they had eat the flesh he took hold of the flesh of his own arm with his teeth and made shew of eating.—AM Careen'd scrubed and pay'd the Starboard side of the Ship: While this was doing some of the natives came along side seemingly only to look at us, there was a Woman among them who had her Arms, thighs and legs cut in several places, this was done by way of Mourning for her husband who had very lately been kill'd and eat by some of their enimies as they told us and pointed towards the place where it was done which lay some where to the Eastward. Mr Banks got from one of them a bone of the fore arm much in the same state as the one before mention'd and to shew us that they had eat the flesh they bit a[nd] naw'd the bone and draw'd it thro' their mouth and this in such a manner as plainly shew'd that the flesh to them was a dainty bit.

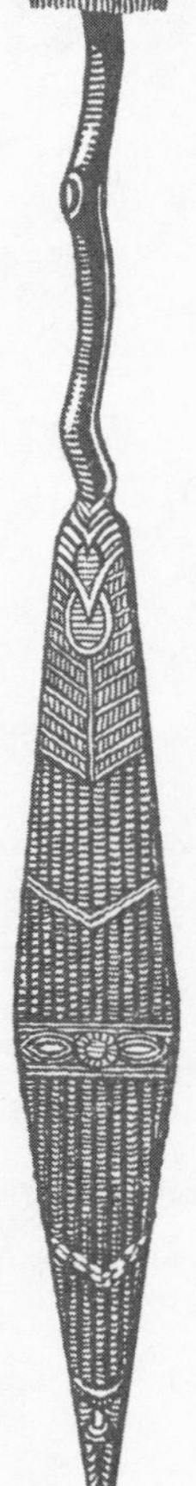

ℂ Later in the month Cook ascended the neighbouring hills and returned satisfied that he had discovered a strait running towards the east.

FRIDAY 26*th* January. In the AM I made an excursion into one of the Bays which lie on the East side of the Inlet accompanied by Mr Banks and Dr Solander, upon our landing we ascended a very high hill from which we had a full View of the passage I had before descover'd and the land on the opposite shore which appear'd to be about 4 Leagues from us, but as it was hazey near the horizon we could not see far to the SE. However, I had now seen enough of this passage to convence me that there was the greatest probabillty in the world of its runing into the Eastern Sea as the distance of that Sea from this place cannot exceed 20 Leagues even to where we were, upon this I resolve'd after puting to sea to search this passage with the Ship. *January 1770*

℄ On the 31st January, Cook took formal possession of Queen Charlotte Sound and the adjacent lands and made further enquiries from the Maoris which strengthened his belief that New Zealand consisted of islands and was not part of a continent.

WEDNESDAY 31*st* January. I next, by means of Tupia, explained to the old man and several others that we were come to set up a mark upon the Island in order to shew to any ship that might put into this place that we had been here before, they not only gave their free consent to set it up, but promise'd never to pull it down. I then gave to every one present one thing or a nother, to the old men I gave silver threepenny peices dated 1763 and spike nails with the Kings broad Arrow cut deep in them things that I thought were most likely to remain long among them.

'After I had thus prepare'd the way for seting up the post we took it up to the highest part of the Island and after fixing it fast in the ground hoisted thereon the Union flag and I dignified this Inlet with the name of *Queen Charlottes Sound* and took formal posession of it and the adjacent lands in the name and for the use of his Majesty, we then drank Her Majestys hilth in a Bottle of wine and gave the empty bottle to the old man (who had attended us up the hill) with which he was highly pleased. Whilest the post was seting up we asked the old man about the *Strait* or passage into the Eastern Sea and he very plainly told us that there was a passage and as I had some conjectors that the lands to the SW of this strait (which we are now at) was an Island and not part of a continent we questioned the old man about it who said that it consisted of two *Wannuaes*, that is two lands or Islands that might be circumnavigated in a few days, even in four.

℄ On leaving Queen Charlotte Sound the *Endeavour* sailed eastwards through Cook Strait where the currents nearly wrecked the ship.

WEDNESDAY 7*th* February. In the PM had a light breeze at NBW with which we got out of the Sound and stood over to the eastward in ord[er] to get the Strait well open before the tide of ebb made. At 7 the two small Island[s] which lies off Cape Koameroo or the SE head of Queen Charlottes Sound bore East distant 4 Miles. At this time we had it nearly calm and the tide Ebb makeing out we were carried by the rapiddity of the stream in a very short time close upon one of the Islands where we narrowly escaped being dashed againest the rocks by bringing the Ship to an Anchor in 75 fathom water with 150 fathoms of Cable out; even this would not have save'd us had not the tide, which first set SBE, by meeting with the Island changed its dire[c]tion to SE and carried us past the first point. When the Ship was brought up she was about two Cables lengths of the rocks and in the strength of the stream which set SE at least 4 or 5 Knotts or miles an hour.

February 1770

(When Cook reached the open ocean, some of his officers expressed the opinion that the coast of the North Island between Cook's Strait and Cape Turnagain might be connected with a continent lying to the east, so Cook sailed north to Cape Turnagain to settle the matter.

THURSDAY *8th* February. From this Cape we steer'd along shore SWBS untill 8 oClock when the wind died away, but an hour after a fresh breeze sprung up at SW and we put the Ship right before it. The reasons for my doing this was owing to a notion which some of the officers had just started that *Aeheinomouwe* was not an Island, founding their opinion on a suppotision that the land might extend away to the SE from between Cape Turn-again and Cape Pallisser, there being a space of about 12 or 15 Leagues which we had not seen. For my own part I had seen so far into this Sea the first time I discover'd the Strait, together with many other concurrent testimonies of its being an Island that no such supposition ever enter'd my thoughts, but being resolved to clear up every doubt that might arise on so important an object I took the oppertunity of the shifting of the wind to stand to the Eastward and accordingly steer'd NEBE all night.

FRIDAY *9th* February. We continued our Course along shore to the NE untill 11 oClock AM when the weather clearing up we saw Cape Turn-again bearing NBE$\frac{1}{4}$E distant 7 Leagues. I then called the officers upon deck and asked them if they were now satisfied that this land was an Island to which they answer'd in the affirmative.

(Cook now turned and circumnavigated the South Island of New Zealand in a clockwise direction. On four occasions foul weather drove him out of sight of land, but he completed his task in under seven weeks, although this part of the voyage lacked the frequent landings and picturesque accounts given during the four months spent in circling the North Island. By 8th March he was able to change his course to south-west for it was becoming clear that New Zealand was a group of islands and not part of a great southern continent. He could now write:

SATURDAY *10th* March. At sunset the Southermost point of land which I afterwards named *South Cape* and which lies on the Lat^{de} 47° 19′ S, Long^{d} 192° 12′ West from Greenwich bore N 38° E distant 4 Leagues and the westermost land in sight bore N 2° East, this last was a small Isl^{d} lying off the point of the Main. I began now to think that this was the southermost land and that we should be able to get round it by the west, for we have had a large hollow swell from the SW ever sence we had the last gale of wind from that quarter which makes me think that there is no land in that direction.

(Cook now worked northwards along the rugged fiord coast of the south-west with its backing of the Southern Alps, and then followed Tasman's bush-covered shoreline to Admiralty Bay and Cape Farewell, where he left New Zealand for the East Australian coast.

FRIDAY 23*rd* March. Having now nearly run down the whole of this NW Coast [of] *Tovypoenammu* it is time I should discribe the face of the Country as it hath at different times appeard to us. I have mentioned on the 11th Instant at which time we were off the Southern part of the Island, that the land seen than was Ruged and Mountainous and there is great reason to beleive that the same ridge of Mountains extends nearly the whole length of the Island. From between the Westermost land seen that day and the Eastermost seen on the 13th there is a space of about 6 or 8 Leagues of the Sea Coast unexplored but the mountains inland were Visible enough. The land near the Shore about *Cape West* is rather low and riseth with a gradual assent up to the foot of the mountains and appear'd to be mostly cover'd with Wood; from *Point five fingers* down to the Latitude of 44° 20′ there is a narrow ridge of hills rising dire[c]tly from the sea which are cloathed with wood. Close behind these hills lies the ridge of Mountains which are of a prodigious height and appear to consist of nothing but barren rocks, cover'd in many places with large patches of snow which perhaps have laid their sence the creation. No country upon earth can appear with a more ruged and barren aspect than this doth from the sea for as far inland as the eye can reach nothing is to be seen but the sumits of these Rocky mountains which seem to lay so near one another as not to admit any Vallies between them. From the Latitude of 44° 20′ to the Latitude 42° 8′ these mountains lay farther inland. The Country between them and the Sea consists of woody hills and Vallies of various extent both for height and depth and hath much the appearence of fertility, many of the Vallies are large low and flat and appeard to be wholy cover'd with Wood but it is very probable that great part of the land is taken up in Lak[e]s Ponds &ca as is very common in such like places. From the last mentioned Latitude to *Cape Farewell*, (afterwards so call'd) the Land is not distinguished by anything remarkable, it riseth into hills directly from the sea and is cover'd with wood. While we were upon this part of the coast the weather was foggy in so much that we could see but a very little way in land, however we sometimes saw the summits of the Mountains above the fogg and clowds which plainly shew'd that the inland parts were high and Mountainous and gave me great reason to think that thier is a continued chain of Mountains from the one end of the Island to the other.

March 1770

¶ Cook had now fulfilled his instructions and could sail back to England by any route which he thought fit. He wished to return by Cape Horn in order to prove or disprove the existence of a continent to the south of his outward route, but the *Endeavour* was in no state for such a voyage in high latitudes. The Cape of Good Hope route offered similar disadvantages and no prospects for exploration, so he decided to refit in the East Indies, sailing thither by the unknown East Coast of New Holland and the lands which Quiros had discovered. His officers agreed with this brilliant and momentous decision.

March 1770 SATURDAY 31*st* March. Upon my return to the Ship in the evening I found the water &c[a] all on board and the Ship ready for sea and being now resolved to quit this country altogether and to bend my thoughts towards returning home by such a rout as might conduce most to the advantage of the service I am upon, I consulted with the officers upon the most eligible way of puting this in execution. To return by the way of *Cape Horn* was what I most wish'd because by this rout we should have been able to prove the existence or non existence of a Southern Continent which yet remains doubtfull; but in order to ascertain this we must have kept in a high latitude in the very depth of winter but the condition of the ship in every respect was not thought sufficient for such an undertaking. For the same reason the thoughts of proceeding directly to the Cape of Good Hope was laid a side especialy as no discovery of any moment could be hoped for in that rout. It was therefore resolved to return by way of the East Indies by the following rout: upon leaving this coast to steer to the westward untill we fall in with the East Coast of New Holland and than to follow the deriction of that Coast to the northward or what other direction it may take untill we arrive at its northern extremity, and if this should be found impractical than to endeavour to fall in with the lands or Islands discover'd by Quiros.

NEW ZEALAND AND THE MAORIS

(Under the heading of 31st March, the day before he left New Zealand, Cook gave a most interesting account of the islands and their picturesque cannibal inhabitants. The following extracts also show that he was not merely an explorer, but an empire builder who looked towards the possibilities of future British settlement.

SATURDAY 31*st* March. Before I quit this land altogether I shall give a short and general discription of the Country, its inhabitants their manners, Customs &c[a] in which it is necessary to observe that many things are founded only on Conjector for we were too short a time in any one place to learn much of their interior policy and therefore could only draw conclutions from what we saw at different times.

'Part of the East Coast of this Country was first discover'd by *Abel Tasman* in 1642 and by him calld *New Zeland*, he however never landed upon it probably he was discouraged from it by the natives killing 3 or 4 of his people at the first and only place he anchor'd at. This country, which before now was thought to be a part of the imaginary southern continent, co[n]sists of Two large Islands divided from each other by a strait or passage of 4 or 5 Leagues broad. They are Situated between the Latitudes of 34° and 48° s and between the Longitude of 181° and 194° West from the Meridion of Greenw[h]. The situation of few parts of the world are better determined than these Islands are being settled by some hundreds of Observations of the Sun and Moon and one of the transit of Mercury made by M[r] Green who was sent out by the Roy[l] Society to observe the Transit of Venus. *March 1770*

'The Northermost of these Islands, as I have before Observed is call'd by the Natives *Aehei no mouwe* and the Southermost *Tovy Poenammu*, the former name we were well assurd comprehended the whole of the Northern Island, but we were not so well satisfied with the latter whether it comprehended the whole of the Southern Island or only a part of it. This last according to the accounts of the Natives of Queen Charlottes Sound ought to consist of two Il[ds] one of which at least we were to have saild round in a few days, but this was not verify[ed] by our own observations. I am inclinable to think that they know'd no more of this land than what came within the limets of their sight. The Chart which I have drawn will best point out the figure and extent of these Islands, the situation of the Bays and harbours they contain and the lesser Islands lay about them. . . . Mention is likewise made in the Chart of the appearence or Aspect of the face of the Country. With respect to *Tovy poenammu* it is for the most part of a very Mountainous and to all appearences a barren Country. The people in Queen Charlottes Sound, those that came off to us from under the Snowey Mountain and the fire we saw to the sw of Cape Saunders were all the inhabitants or signs of inhabitants we saw upon the whole Island. But most part of the Sea Coast of *Aeheinomouwe* except the sw side is well inhabited and altho it is a hilly mountainous Country yet the very hills and mountains are many of them cover'd with wood, and the Soil of the planes and Vallies appeared to be rich and fertile and such as we had an oppertunity to examine we found to be so in a high degree and not very much incumbered with woods; it was the opinion of every body on board that all sorts of European grain fruits Plants &c[a] would thrive here. In short was this Country settled by an Industrus people they would very soon be supply'd not only with the necessarys but many of the luxuries of life. The Sea Bays and Rivers abound with a great varity of excellent fish the most of them unknown in England, besides Lobsters which were allow'd by every body to be the best they ever had eat, Oy[s]ters and many other sorts of shell fish all excellent in their kind. Sea and water fowles of all sorts are however in no great plenty, those known in Europe are Ducks, Shags, Gannets & Gulls all of which were eat by us and found exceeding good, indeed hardly any thing came amiss to us that could be eat by man. Land fowl are likewise in no great plenty and all of them except quals are I beleive unknown in Europe, these are exactly like those we have in England. The country is certainly destitute of all sorts of beasts either wild or tame except Dogs and Ratts, the former are tame and live with the people who breed and bring them up for no other purpose than to eat and ratts are so scarce that not only I but many others in the ship never saw one. Altho we have seen some few Seals and once a Sea Lyon upon this coast yet I beleive

March 1770 that they are not only very scarce but seldom or ever come a shore, for if they did the natives would certainly find out some method of Killing them the Skins of which they no doubt would preserve for Clothing as well as the skins of Dogs and birds the only skins we ever saw among them. But they must sometimes get whales because many of their Patoo patoos are made of the bones of some such like fish and an orament they wear at their breasts (on which they set great Value) which we suppose'd to be made of the tooth of a whale and yet we know of no method or instrument they have to kill these animals.

'In the woods are plenty of excellent timber fit for all purposes excepting Ships Mast[s] and perhaps upon a close examination some might be found not improper for that purpose. There grows spontaneously every where a kind of very broad pladed grass like flags of the nature of hemp of which might be made the very best of Cordage Canvas &c[a]. There are of two sorts the one finer than the other, of these the natives make cloth, rope, lines, netts &c[a]. Iron ore is undoubtedly to be found here particularly about Mercury bay where we found great quantities of Iron sand, however we met with no ore of any sort neither did we ever see any sort of Metal with the natives. . . . Should it ever become an object of settleing this Country the best place for the first fixing of a Colony would be either in the River Thames or the Bay of Islands, for at either of these places they would have the advantage of a good harbour and by means of the former an easy communication would be had and settlements might be extended into the inland parts of the Country, for at a very little trouble and expence small Vessels might be built in the River proper for the Navigating thereof. . . . So far as I have been able to judge of the genius of these people it doth not appear to me to be attall difficult for Strangers to form a settleme[n]t in this Country. They seem to be too much divided among themselves to unite in opposing, by which means and kind and gentle usuage the Colonists would be able to form strong parties among them.

'The Natives of this Country are a strong raw boned well made Active people rather above than under the common size especialy the men, they are all of a very dark brown Colour with black hair, thin black beards and white teeth and such as do not disfigure their faces by tattowing &c[a] have in general very good features. The men generaly wear their hair long coombd up and tied upon the crown of their heads, some of the women wear it long and loose upon their Shoulders, old women especialy, others again wear it crop'd short: their coombs are some made of bone and others of wood, they sometimes wear them as an ornament stuck upright in thier hair. They seem to injoy a good state of hilth and many of them live to a good old age. Many of the old and some of the middle aged men have thier faces mark'd or tattow'd with black and some few we have seen who have had their buttocks thighs and other parts of their bodies mark'd but this is less common.

'One day a[t] Tolago I saw a strong proff that the women never appear naked at least before strangers. Some of us happen'd to land upon a small Island where several of them were naked in the water gathering Lobsters and Shell fish. As soon as they saw us some of them hid themselves among the rocks and the rest remain'd in the Sea untill they had made themselves aprons of the Sea weed and even than when they came out to us they shew'd manifest signs of Shame and those who had no method of hiding their nakedness would by no means appear before us. The women have all very soft Voices and may by that alone be known from the men. The makeing of Cloth and all other Domestick work is I beleive wholy done by them and the more labourous work such as build[g] Boats, Houses, Tilling the ground, fishing &c[a] by the Men. Both men and women wear oraments at their ears and about their necks. These are made of Stone, bone, Shells &c[a] and are variously shaped, and some I have seen wear human teeth and finger nails and I think we were told that they did belong to thier deceas'd friends. The men when they are dress'd generaly wear two or three long white feathers stuck upright in their hair and at Queen Charlottes sound many both men and women wore round Caps made of black feathers. . . . When ever we were Viseted by any number of them that had never heard or seen any thing of us before they generaly came off in the largest Canoes they had, some of which will carry 60, 80 or 100 people, they always brought their best close along with them which they put on as soon as they came near the Ship. In each Canoe were generaly an Old man, in some two or three, these use'd always to dire[c]t the others, were better Clothed and generaly carried a halbard or battle ax in their hands or some such like thing that distinguished them from the others. As soon as they came within about a stones throw of the Ship they would there lay and call out *Haromai hareuta a patoo age*, that is come here, come a shore with us and we will kill you with our patoo patoo's, and at the same time would shake them at us, at times they would dance the war dance, and other times they would trade with and talk to us and answer such questons as were put to them with all the Calmness emaginable and then again begin the war dance, shaking their paddles patoo patoo's &c[a] and make strange contorsions at the same time, and as soon as they had worked themselves up to a proper pitch they would begin to attack us with stones and darts and oblige us whether we would or no to fire upon them. Musquetary they never regarded unless they felt the effect but great guns they did because these threw stones farther than they could comprehend. After they found that our Arms were so much Superior to theirs and that we took no advantage of that superiority and a little time given them to reflect upon it they ever after were our very good friends and we never had an Instance of their attempting to surprize or cut off any of our people when they were ashore, oppertunities for so doing they must have had at one time or a nother.

March 1770

March 1770 'It is hard to account for what we have every w[h]ere been told of their eating their enimies kill'd in battle which they most certainly do, circumstance enough we have seen to convince of the truth of this. Tupia who holds this custom in great aversion hath very often argued with them against it but they always as strenuously supported it and never would own that it was wrong. It is reasonable to suppose that men with whome this Custom is found seldom or never give quarter to those they overcome in battle and if so they must fight desperatly to the very last. A strong proff of this supposision we had from the people of Queen Charlottes Sound who told us but a few days before we arrived that they had kill'd and eat a whole boats crew; surely a single boats crew or at least a part of them when they found themselves beset and over powerd by number would have surrender'd themselves prisioners was such a thing practised among them. The heads of these unfortunate people they preserved as trophies; four or five of them they brought off to shew to us, one of which M[r] Banks bought or rather forced them to sell for they parted with it with the utmost reluctancy and afterwards would not so much as let us see one more for anything we could offer them. . . . The People shew great ingenuity and good workmanship in the building and framing their Boats or Canoes; the[y] are long and narrow and shaped very much like a New England Whale boat. Their large Canoes are I beleive built wholy for war and will carry from 40 to 80 or 100 men with their arms &c[a]. I shall give the demensions of one which I measured that lay a shore at *Tolaga*. Length 68½ feet, breadth 5 feet and depth 3½ feet. The bottom sharp inclining to a wedge and was made of three pieces hollow'd out to about 2 inches or an inch and a half thick and well fasten'd together with strong plating; each side consisted of one plank only which was 63 feet long and 10 to 12 Inches broad and about an inch and a quarter thick and these were well fited and lash'd to the bottom part; there were a number of Thwarts laid across and lashed to each gunel as a strengthening to the boat. The head orament projected 5 or 6 feet without the body of the Boat and was 4½ feet high; the stern orament was 14 feet high, about 2 feet broad and about an 1½ Inch thick, it was fix'd upon the Stern of the Canoe like the Stern post of a Ship upon her keel. The oraments of both head and stern and the two side boards were of carved work and in my opinion neither ill designed nor executed. All their Canoes are built after this plan and few are less than 20 feet long—some of the small ones we have seen with out-riggers but this is not common. . . . The tools with which they work in building their Canoes houses &c[a] are adzes or axes some made of a hard black stone, and others of green Talk; they have chisels made of the same but these are more commonly made of human bones. In working small work and carving I believe they use mostly peices of Jasper breaking small peices from a large lump they have for that purpose. As soon as the small peice is blunted they throw it a way and take another. To till or turn up the ground they have wooden

spades (if I may so call them) made like stout pickets with a peice of wood tyed aCross near the lower end to put the foot upon to force them into the ground. There green talk axes that are whole and good they set much value upon and never wold part with them for any thing we could offer. I offer'd one day for one, one of the best axes I had in the Ship besides a number of other things but nothing would induce the owner to part with it: from this I infer'd that good ones were scarce among them. . . . We were never able to learn with any degree of certainty in what manner they bury their dead, we were generaly told that they put them in the ground, if so it must be in some secrete or by place for we never saw the least signs of a burying place in the whole Country. Their Custom of Mourning for a friend or a relation is by cuting and scarifying their bodies particularly their Arms and breasts in such a Manner that the scars remain indelible and I beleive have some signification such as to shew how near related the deceas'd was to them.

March 1770

'With respect to Religion I beleive these People trouble themselves very little about it. They however beleive that their is one Supream God whome they call Tane and likewise a number of other inferior Deities, but whether or no they Worship or Pray to either one or the other we know not with any degree of certainty. It is reasonable to suppose that they do and I beleive it, yet I never saw the least action or thing a mong them that tended to prove it.

'They have the same notions of the Creation of the World Mankind &c[a] as the People of the South Sea Islands have, indeed many of there Notions and Customs are the very same, but nothing is so great a proff of they all having had one Source as their Language which differs but in a very few words the one from the other . . . There are some small difference in the Language spoke by the *Aehei-no mouweans* and those of *Tovy poe nammu* but this difference seem'd to me to be only in the pronunciation and is no more than what we find between one part of England and another: what is here inserted as a specemen is that spoke by the People of *Ae hei no mouwe*. What is meant by the South Sea Islands are those Islands we our selves touch'd at, but I gave it that title because we have a[l]ways been told that the same Language is Universally spoke by all the Islanders and this is a sufficient proff that both they and the New Zelanders have had one Origin or Source but where this is, even time perhaps may never discover. It certainly is neither to the Southward nor Eastward for I cannot preswaid my self that ever they came from America.

❨ Although in his rapid survey Cook made the mistake of thinking that Bank's Peninsula was an island and Stewart Island a peninsula, he could now complete a very fine map. He had given the islands 'a sure and defined outline'. It is only just to say that Cook had 'found New Zealand a line on the map and left it an Archipelago'. In this region at least he had dispelled the myth of the Southern Continent which he dismissed as follows.

March 1770 SATURDAY 31*st* March. As to a Southern Continent I do not beleive any such thing exists unless in a high Latitude, but as the Contrary oppinion hath for many years prevaild and may yet prevail it is necessary I should say some thing in support of mine more than what will be dire[c]tly point out by the track of this Ship in those seas; for from that alone it will evidently appear that there is a large space of Sea extending quite to the Tropick in which we were not or any other before us that we can aver for certain. In our rout to the northward after doubling Cape Horn when in the Latitude of 40° we were in the Longitude of 110°, and in our return to the Southward after leaving Ulietea when in the same Latitude we were in the Longitude of 145°; the difference in this Latitude is 35°. In the Latitude of 30° the difference of the two tracks is 21° and that difference continues as low as 20° but a view of the Chart will best illusterate this. Here is now room enough for the North Cape of the Southern Continent to extend to the Northward even to a pretty low Latitude. But what foundation have we for such a Supposision, none that I know of but this that it must be either here or no where.

'Geographers have indeed laid down part of *Quiros's* discoveries in this Longitude and have told us that he had their signs of a Continent a part of which they have actually laid down in their Maps but by what authority I know not. *Quiros* in the Latitude of 25° or 26° s discover'd Two Islands which I Suppose may lay between the Longitudes of 130° and 140° West. *Dalrymple* lays them down in 146° w and says that Quiros saw to the Southward very large hanging clowds and a very thick horizon, with other known signs of a Continent: other accounts of the Voyage says not a word about this but supposing it to be true, hanging Clowds and a thick horizon are certainly no known Signs of a Continent, I have had ma[n]y proofs to the contrary in the Course of this Voyage, neither do I beleive that Quiros himself looked upon such things as known signs of land, for if he had he certainly would have stood to the Southward in order to have satisfied himself before he had gone to the northward for no man seems to have had discoveries more at heart than he had; besides this was the ultimate object of his Voyage. If Quiros was in the Latitude of 26° and Longitude 146° west than I am certain that no part of the Southern continent can no where extend so far to the Northward as the above mentioned Latitude. But the Voyage which seems to thrust it farthest back in the Longitude I am speaking of viz. betwixt 130° and 150° West, is that of *Admiral Roggeween* a Dutch man made in 1722, who after leaving *Juan Fernandes* went in search of *Davis's Island*, but not finding it he ran 12° More to the West and in the Latitude of 28½° discover'd *Easter Island*. Dalrymple and some others have laid it down in 27° s & 106° 30′ West and supposes it to be the same as *Davis's Isle* which I think cannot be from the circumstance of the Voyage. On the other hand *M. Pingre* in his Treatise concerning the Transit of Venus gives an extract of Roggeween's Voyage and a

Map of the *South Seas*, where in he place[s] *Easter Island* in the Latitude of 28½° S and in the Longitude of 123° West. His reasons for so doing may be seen at large in the said treatise, he like wise lays down *Roggeween's* rout thro' these Seas very different from any other author I have seen, for after leaving *Easter Island* he makes him to steer SW to the height of 34° South and afterwards WNW. If *Roggeween* realy took this rout than it is not probable that there is any main land to the Northward of 35° South. However Mr Dalrymple and some Geographers have laid down *Roggeween's* track very different from *M. Pingre*. From *Easter Isle* they have laid down his track to the NW and afterwards very little different from that of *Le Maire*, and this I think is not probable that a Man who at his own request was sent to discover the Southern Continent should take the same rout thro' these Seas as others had done before who had the same thing in View, by so doing he most be morally certain of not finding what he was in search of and of course must fail as they had done. Be this as it may it is a point that cannot be clear'd up from the published accounts of the Voyage which so far from takeing proper Notice of their Longitude have not even mentioned the Latitude of several of the Islands they discover'd so that I find it impossible to lay down *Roggeween's* rout with the least degree of accuracy.

March 1770

'But to return to our own Voyage which must be allow'd to have set a side the most if not all the arguments and proofs that have been advance'd by different Authors to prove that there must be a Southern Continent, I mean to the northward of 40° S for what may lay to the Southward of that Latitude I know not. Certain it is that we saw no visible signs of land, according to my opinion, neither in our rout to the Northward, Southward or Westward untill a few days before we made the east Coast of *New-Zeland*. It is true we have often seen large flocks of Birds but they were generaly such as are always seen at a very great distance from land, we likewise saw frequintly peices of Sea or rock weed, but how is one to know how far this may drive to Sea. I am told and that from undoubted Authority that there is yearly thrown up upon the Coast of Ireland a sort of Beans call'd Ox Eys which are known to grow no where but in the West Indias and yet these two places are not less than [11 or 1200] Leagues asunder; was such things found floating upon the water in the South Seas one would hardly be perswaided that one was even out of sight of land so apt are we to catch at every thing that may in the least point out to us the favourat object we are in persute of and yet experience shews that we may be as far from it as ever.

'Thus I have given my Opinion freely and without prejudicy not with any view to discourage any future attempts being made towards discovering the *Southern Continent*, on the Contrary, as this Voyage will evidently make it appear that there is left but a small space to the Northward of 40° where the grand Object can lay, I think it would be a great pitty that this thing which at times has been

March 1770 the object of many ages and Nations should not now be wholy clear'd up, which might very easily be done in one Voyage without either much trouble or danger or fear of misscarrying as the Navigator would know where to go to look for it; but if after all no Continent was to be found than he might turn his thoughts towards the discovery of those multitude of Islands which we are told lay within the Tropical Regions to the South of the line, and this we have from very good Authority as I have before hinted. This he will always have in his Power, for unless he be directed to search for the Southern lands in a high Latitude he will not, as we were, be obliged to go farther to the westward in the Latitude of 40° than 140° or 145° West and therefore will always have it in his power to go to Georges Island where he will be sure of meeting with refreshments to rec[r]ute his people before he sets out upon the discovery of the Islands. But, should it be thought proper to send a ship out upon this service while *Tupia* lieves and he to come out in her, in that case she would have a prodigious advantage over every ship that had been upon discoveries in those seas before; for by means of Tupia, supposeing he did not accompany you himself, you would always get people to direct you from Island to Island and would be sure of meeting with a friendly reseption and refreshments at every Island you came to; this would inable the Navigator to make his discoveries the more perfect and compleat, at least it would give him time so to do for he would not be obliged to hurry through those seas from an apprehinsion of wanting provisions.

Chapter VI

EASTERN AUSTRALIA, 1770

"Coasted the shore to the Northward through the most dangerous Navigation that perhaps ever ship was in."

COOK

COOK PROBABLY SAILED FOR AUSTRALIA WITH TWO GREAT geographical problems in his mind. First, how far did New Holland, the lands skirted by Tasman, Van Nuyts and others, stretch towards New Zealand? Second, were these lands one great continent of which Van Diemen's Land, New Guinea and de Quiros' Espiritu Santo were all parts, or were they only island groups? To answer these questions, which had puzzled Europe for over a century, Cook sailed in the *Endeavour* on 1st April 1770, to discover the east coast of Australia.

THE EAST AUSTRALIAN COAST

¶ Cook's Journal shows that he intended to pick up Tasman's work where the Dutch navigator left Van Diemen's Land. On 16th April he took soundings all night in case he was approaching land in Latitude 39° 40′, which means that the *Endeavour* was nearing the completely unknown region of Bass Strait. At this moment a heavy gale from the south drove the explorer north and

April 1770 unfortunately prevented him from settling whether or not Van Diemen's Land was joined to New Holland, a matter on which he was clearly in doubt, for he wrote as follows:—

THURSDAY 19*th* April. In the PM had fresh gales at SSW and Clowdy Squaly weather with a large Southerly Sea. At 6 took in the Topsails and at 1 AM brought too and sounded but had no ground with 130 fathoms of line. At 5 Set the Topsails Close reef'd and at 6 saw land extending from NE to West at the distance of 5 or 6 Leagues having 80 fathom water a fine sandy bottom. We continued Standing to the westward with the wind at SSW untill 8 oClock at which time we got topg^{t} yards aCross, made all sail and bore away along shore NE for the Eastermost land we had in sight, being at this time in the Latitude of 37° 58′ S and Long^{d} of 210° 39′ West. The Southermost Point of land we had in sight which bore from us W¼S I judged to lay in the Latitude of 38° 0′ S and in the Longitude of 211° 07′ W from the Meridion of Greenwich. I have Named it *Point Hicks*, because Leuit^{t} Hicks was the first who discover'd this land.

'To the Southward of this point we could see no land and yet it was very clear in that quarter and by our Longitude compared with that of Tasmans the body of Vandiemens land ought to have bore due south from us and from the soon falling of the Sea after the wind abated I had reason to think it did, but as we did not see it and finding this coast to trend NE and SW or rather more to the westward makes me doubtfull whether they are one land or no: however every one who compares this Journal with that of Tasmans will be as good a judge [as] I am, but it is necessary to observe that I do not take the situation of Vandiemens from the prented Charts but from the extract of Tasmens *Journal* published by *Dirk Rembrantse*.

⁅ According to Professor G. A. Wood, Point Hicks was unfortunately renamed Cape Everard in 1843 by Stokes.

⁅ From Point Hicks Cook sailed north from 20th April to 29th April, as he considered Bateman's Bay and Jervis Bay insufficiently sheltered as anchorages. On 29th April, however, he anchored in Botany Bay where a week's stay led to the choice of this spot as the tentative site of the first British settlement. Strangely enough this was partly due to the fact that Cook, usually the most careful and accurate observer, overestimated the potentialities of the harbour and surrounding soils.

⁅ Also on Sunday, 6th May, he wrote that the Bay was 'Capacious, safe and commodious', whereas Governor Phillip found in 1783 that the harbour was exposed to easterly winds, while disgruntled colonists hunted in vain for the 'fine Meadow', with the result that Botany Bay was abandoned for Sydney. Professor G. A. Wood in his *Discovery of Australia*, points out the very curious fact that Banks, whose advice was primarily responsible for the despatch of the convicts, was much less impressed by Botany Bay than was Cook.

(Cook's accounts of the Australian aboriginals were less enthusiastic and more accurate than his accounts of the surrounding country.

(In 1779, in giving his evidence to a committee of the House of Commons on the choice of a site for a British colony in the Pacific, Banks strengthened what was already an unduly optimistic statement by giving his opinion that the natives were 'few and cowardly'. One suspects that this was a main reason for the choice of Botany Bay rather than New Zealand, for, much as the British Government wished to rid itself of its convicts, it must have feared the danger of disposing of them as the pièce de résistance in Maori feasts.

(Cook at first named the harbour Stingray Bay owing to the capture of a number of huge fish. When, however, Banks and Solander secured the wealth of plants which was to revolutionize botanical science, he changed his original Journal first to 'Botanist' and later to 'Botany Bay'.

SATURDAY 28*th* April. At day light in the morning we discoverd a Bay which appeard to be tollerably well shelterd from all winds into which I resoloved to go with the Ship and with this view sent the Master in the Pinnace to sound the entrance while we kept turning up with the Ship haveing the wind right out. At Noon the entran[c]e bore NNW distance 1 Mile.

SUNDAY 29*th* April. Saw as we came in on both points of the bay Several of the natives and a few hutts, Men, women and children on the south shore abreast of the Ship, to which place I went in the boats in hopes of speaking with them accompaned by M[r] Banks D[r] Solander and Tupia; as we approached the shore they all made off except two Men who seemd resolved to oppose our landing. As soon as I saw this I orderd the boats to lay upon their oars in order to speake to them but this was to little purpose for neither us nor Tupia could understand one word they said. We then threw them some nails beeds &c[a] a shore which they took up and seem'd not ill pleased in so much that I thout that they beckon'd to us to come a shore; but in this we were mistaken, for as soon as we put the boat in they again came to oppose us upon which I fired a musket between the two which had no other effect than to make them retire back where bundles of thier darts lay, and one of them took up a stone and threw at us which caused my fireing a second Musquet load with small shott, and altho some of the shott struck the man yet it had no other effect than to make him lay hold of a Shield or target to defend himself. Emmidiatly after this we landed which we had no sooner done than they throw'd two darts at us, this obliged me to fire a third shott soon after which they both made off, but not in such haste but what we might have taken one, but M[r] Banks being of opinion that the darts were poisoned, made me cautious how I advanced into the woods. We found here a few Small hutts made of the bark of trees in one of which were four or five small children with whome we left some strings of beeds &c[a]. A quantity of darts lay about the hutts these we took away with us.

April 1770 Three Canoes lay upon the bea[c]h the worst I think I ever saw, they were about 12 or 14 feet long made of one peice of the bark of a tree drawn or tied up at each end and the middle kept open by means of peices of sticks by way of Thwarts.

[MAY 1770]

TUESDAY 1*st* May. Last night Torby Sutherland seaman departed this life and in the AM his body was buried a shore at the watering place which occasioned my calling the south point of this Bay after his name. This morning a party of us went ashore to some hutts not far from the watering place where some of the natives are daly seen, here we left several articles such as Cloth, Looking glasses, Combs, Beeds Nails &c[a]. After this we made an excursion into the country which we found deversified with woods, Lawns and Marshes; the woods are free from under wood of every kind and the trees are at such a distance from one a nother that the whole Country or at least great part of it might be cultivated without being oblig'd to cut down a single tree; we found the soil every where except in the Marshes to be a light white sand and produceth a quant[it]y of good grass which grows in little tufts about as big as one can hold in ones hand and pretty close to one another, in this manner the surface of the ground is coated in the woods between the trees. D[r] Solander had a bad sight of a small Animal some thing like a rabbit and we found the dung of an Animal which must feed upon grass and which we judged could not be less than a deer, we also saw the track of a dog or some such like Animal.

FRIDAY 4*th* May. In the AM as the wind would not permit us to sail I sent out some parties into the Country to try to form some Connections with the natives. One of the Midshipmen met with a very old man and woman and two small Children; they were close to the water side where several more were in their canoes gathering shell fish and he being alone was afraid to make any stay with the two old people least he should be discoverd by those in the Canoes. He gave them a bird he had shott which they would not touch neither did they speak one word but seem'd to be much frighten'd, they were quite naked even the woman had nothing to cover her nuditie. D[r] Munkhouse and a nother man being in the woods not far from the watering place discoverd Six more of the natives who at first seemd to wait his coming but as he was going up to them had a dart thrown at him out of a tree which narrowly escaped him, as soon as the fellow had thrown the dart he desended the tree and made off and with him all the rest and these were all that were met with in the Course of this day.

SUNDAY 6*th* May. In the evening the yawl return'd from fishing having caught two Sting rays weighing near 600 pounds. The great quantity of New Plants &c[a] M[r] Banks & D[r] Solander collected in this place occasioned my giveing it the name of *Botany Bay*. It is situated in the Latitude of 34° 0′ S, Longitude 208° 37′ West; it is Capacious safe and commodious. . . . We anchord near

LANDING AT BOTANY BAY
APRIL 1770

the south shore about a Mile within the entrance for the conveniency of sailing with a Southerly wind and the geting of fresh water but I afterwards found a very fine stream of fresh water on the north shore in the first sandy cove within the Island before which a Ship might lay almost land lock'd and wood for fual may be got every where: altho wood is here in great plenty yet there is very little variety, the largest trees are as large or larger than our oaks in England and grows a good deal like them and yeilds a redish gum, the wood itself is heavy hard and black like Lignum Vitae; another sort that grows tall and strait some thing like Pines, the wood of this is hard and Ponderous and something of the nature of American live oaks, these two are all the timber trees I met with. There are a few sorts of Shrubs and several Palm trees, and Mangroves about the head of the harbour. The Country is woody low and flat as far inland as we could see and I believe that the soil is in general sandy, in the wood are a variety of very boutifull birds such as Cocatoo's, Lorryquets, Parrots &c[a] and Crows exactly like those we have in England.

May 1770

'The natives do not appear to be numberous neither do they seem to live in large bodies but dispers'd in small parties along by the water side; those I saw were about as tall as Europeans, of a very dark brown colour but not black nor had they wooly frizled hair, but black and lank much like ours. No sort of cloathing or ornaments were ever seen by any of us upon any one of them or in or about any of their hutts, from which I conclude that they never wear any. Some we saw that had their faces and bodies painted with a sort of white paint or Pigment. Altho I have said that shell fish is their chief support yet they catch other sorts of fish some of which we found roasting on the fire the first time we landed, some of these they strike with gigs and others they catch with hook and line; we have seen them strike fish with gigs & hooks and lines were found in their hutts. Sting rays I believe they do not eat because I never saw the least remains of one near any of their hutts or fire places. However we could know but very little of their customs as we never were able to form any connections with them, they had not so much as touch'd the things we had left in their hutts on purpose for them to take away. During our stay in this Harbour I caused the English Colours to be display'd ashore every day and an inscription to be cut out upon one of the trees near the watering place seting forth the Ships name, date &c[a]. Having seen every thing this place afforded we at day light in the Morning weigh'd with a light breeze at NW and put to sea.

SHIPWRECK

(After leaving Botany Bay on 7th May 1770, Cook steered northwards along the East Australian coast encountering no serious trouble for some five weeks excepting the fact that unknown persons assaulted his clerk, Orton, the chief suspects being Midshipmen Magra and Saunders. Magra, or Matra, later

May 1770 played an interesting part in proposing to the British Government the colonization of Eastern Australia by American 'loyalists' with their slaves.

❨ Returning to the *Endeavour*, we find that Cook named the entrance of Sydney Harbour, Port Jackson, in honour of a Secretary of the Admiralty, but did not steer close enough to discover the magnificent harbour itself. He also missed the discovery of the splendid colonising site of Newcastle at the mouth of the Hunter River, and, although he named Moreton Bay, he missed the Brisbane River. He then landed at Bustard Bay, crossed the Tropic of Capricorn, and entered without knowing his danger, the perilous waters between the Great Barrier Reef and the Queensland coast. On the night of 11th June, when standing very slowly northwards in bright moonlight and deep water according to the lead, the *Endeavour* struck and remained fast on a coral reef, where she lay miles from shore and in desperate peril for 23 hours during which time Cook, and all on board, showed the utmost coolness and bravery.

WEDNESDAY 23*rd* May. Last Night some time in the Middle watch a very extraordinary affair happend to M[r] Orton my Clerk, he having been drinking in the Evening, some Malicious person or persons in the Ship took the advantage of his being drunk and cut off all the cloaths from off his back, not being satisfied with this they some time after went into his Cabbin and cut off a part of both his Ears as he lay asleep in his bed. The person whome he suspected to have done this was M[r] Magra one of the Midshipmen, but this did not appear to me upon inquirey. However as I know'd Magra had once or twice before this in their drunken frolicks cut of his Cloaths and had been heard to say (as I was told) that if it was not for the Law he would Murder him, these things consider'd induce'd me to think that Magra was not altogether innocent.

MONDAY 11*th* June. Wind at ESE with which we steer'd along shore NBW at the distance of 3 or 4 Leagues off having from 14 to 10 & 12 fm [with] saw two small Islands in the offing which lay in the latitude of 16° 0′ S and about 6 or 7 Leagues from the Main. At 6 oClock the northermost land in sight bore NBW½W and two low woody Islands which some took to be rocks above water bore N½W. At this time we shortend sail and hauld off shore ENE and NEBE close upon a wind. My intention was to stretch off all night as well to avoid the dangers we saw ahead as to see if any Islands lay in the offing, especialy as we now begin to draw the Latitude of those discover'd by Quiros which some Geographers, for what reason I know not have thought proper to tack to this land, having the advantage of a fine breeze of wind and a clear moonlight night. In standing off from 6 untill near 9 oClock we deepen'd our water from 14 to 21 fathom when all at once we fell into 12, 10 and 8 fathom. At this time I had every body at their stations to put about and come too an anchor but in this I was not so fortunate for meeting again with deep water I thought there could be no danger in stand[g] on. Before 10 oClock we has 20 and 21 fathom and continued in that depth untill a few Minutes before a 11 when we had 17 and before the Man at the lead could heave another cast the Ship Struck and stuck fast. Emmidiatly upon this we took in all our sails hoisted out the boats and sounded round the Ship, and found that we had got upon the SE edge of a reef of Coral rocks having in some places round the Ship 3 and 4 fathom water and in other places not quite as many feet, and about a Ships length from us on our starboard side (the ship laying with her head to the NE) were 8, 10 and 12 fathom. As soon as the long boat was out we struck yards and Topm[ts] and carried out the stream Anchor upon the starboard bow, got the Costing anchor and cable into the boat and were going to carry it out the same way; but upon my sounding the second time round the Ship I found the most water a stern, and therefore had this anchor carried out upon the Starboard quarter and hove upon it a very great strean which was to no purpose the Ship being quite fast, upon which we went to work to lighten her as fast as possible which seem'd to be the only means we had left to get her off as we went a Shore about the top of high-water. We not only started water but throw'd over board our guns Iron and stone ballast Casks, Hoops staves oyle Jars, decay'd stores &c[a], many of these last articles lay in the way at coming at heavyer. All this time the Ship made little or no water. At a 11 oClock in the AM being high-water as we thought we try'd to heave her off without success, she not being a float by a foot or more notwithstanding by this time we had thrown over board 40 or 50 Tun weight; as this was not found sufficient we continued to Lighten her by every method we could think off. As the Tide fell the Ship began to make water as much as two Pumps could free. At Noon she lay with 3 or 4 Strakes heel to Starboard. Latitude Observed 15° 45′ South.

June 1770

TUESDAY 12*th* June. Fortunatly we had little wind fine weather and a smooth Sea all these 24 hours which in the PM gave us an oppertunity to carry out the two bower Anchors, the one on the Starboard quarter and the other right a stern. Got blocks and tackles upon the Cables brought the falls in abaft and hove taught. By this time it was 5 oClock in the pm, the tide we observed now begun to rise and the leak increased upon us which obliged us to set the 3rd Pump to work as we should have done the 4th also, but could not make it work. At 9 oClock the Ship righted and the leak gaind upon the Pumps considerably. This was an alarming and I may say terrible Circumstance and threatend immidiate destruction to us as soon as the Ship was afloat. However I resolved to resk all and heave her off in case it was practical and accordingly turnd as many hands to the Capstan & windlass as could be spared from the Pumps and about 20′ past 10 oClock the Ship floated and we hove her off into deep water having at this time 3 feet 9 Inches water in the hold. This done I sent the Long boat to take up the stream anchor—got the anchor but lost the Cable among the rocks, after this turn'd all hands to the Pumps the leak increasing upon us.

June 1770 A Mistake soon after happened which for the first time caused fear to operate upon every man in the Ship. The man which attend[ed] the well took y[e] depth of water above the ceiling, he being relieved by another who did not know in what manner the former had sounded, took the depth of water from the out side plank, the difference being 16 or 18 Inches and made it appear that the leak had gain'd this upon the pumps in a short time, this mistake was no sooner clear'd up than [it] acted upon every man like a charm; they redoubled their Vigour in so much that before 8 oClock in the Morning they gain'd considerably upon the leak. We now hove up the best bower but found it impossible to save the small bower so cut it away at a whole Cable. Got up the fore topmast and fore yard, warped the Ship to the SE and at a 11 got under Sail and Stood in for the land with a light breeze at ESE, some hands employ'd sowing ockam wool &c[a] into a lower Studding sail to fother the Ship, others emplo'd at the Pumps which still gain'd upon the leak. . . . The Ledge of rocks or Shoal we have been upon lies in the Lat[de] of 15° 45′ and about 6 or 7 Leagues from the Main land. . . . At Noon we were about 3 Leagues from the land and in the latitude of 15° 37′ South, the northermost part of the Main in sight bore N 3° west and the above Islands extending from S 30° E to South 40° E, in this situation had 12 fathoms water and sever[l] Sand Banks without us. The leak now decreaseth but for fear it should break out again we got the Sail ready fill'd for fothering. The manner this is done is thus, we Mix ockam & wool together (but ockam alone would do) and chop it up small and than stick it loosly by handfulls all over the sail and throw over it sheeps dung or other filth. Horse dung for this purpose is the best. The sail thus prepared is hauld under the Ships bottom by ropes and if the place of the leak is uncertain it must be hauld from one part of her bottom to a nother untill the place is found where it takes effect; while the sail is under the Ship the Ockam &c[a] is washed off and part of it carried along with the water into the leak and in part stops up the hole. M[r] Munkhouse one of my Midshipmen was once in a Merchant ship which sprung a leak and made 48 inches water per hour but by this means was brought home from Virginia to London with only her proper crew, to him I gave the deriction of this who exicuted it very much to my satisfaction.

⁅ Cook then took the vessel into Cook Harbour, Endeavour River, near the present Cooktown, where a careful examination showed how nearly she had foundered.

FRIDAY *22nd* June. Winds at SE fair weather. At 4 In the PM having got out most of the Coals, cast loose the moorings and warped the Ship a little higher up the harbour to a place I had pitched upon to lay a Shore for stoping the leak, her draught of Water forward 7 feet 9 Inches and abaft 13 feet 6 Inches. At 8 being high water hauld her bow close a shore but kept her stern a float because I was afraid of neeping her, and yet it was necessary to lay the whole of her as near the ground as possible. At 2 oClock in the AM the tide left her which gave us an oppertunity to examine the leak which we found to be at her floor heads a little before the Starboard fore chains. Here the rocks had made their way thro' four Planks quite to and even into the timbers and wound'd three more. The manner these planks were damaged or cut out as I may say is hardly credable, scarce a splinter was to be seen but the whole was cut away as if it had been done by the hands of Man with a blunt edge tool. Fortunatly for us the timbers in this place were very close, other ways it would have been impossible to have saved the ship and even as it was it appear'd very extraordinary that she made no more water than what she did. A large piece of Coral rock was sticking in one hole and several pieces of the fothering, small stones, sand &c[a] had made its way in and lodged between the timbers which had stoped the water from forceing its way in in great quantities.

June 1770

❨ It may be noted in the above account that a large piece of coral was blocking one of the holes in the *Endeavour.* The casual as well as the causal creates history and but for this piece of coral there might have been no British colonisation of Australia.

❨ The *Endeavour* remained in Cook's River until 4th August, the stay being marked by the exciting discovery and shooting of Kangaroos, and by the arrival of natives who wanted only turtle meat and created trouble when it was refused, as they no doubt thought that they owned both the country and the turtles.

SATURDAY 14*th* July. Gentle breezes at SE and Hazey weather. In the PM compleated our water got on board all the Bread and part of the Boatswains stores; in the evening sent the turtlers out again. In the AM employd geting on board stone ballast and airing the Spare sails. M[r] Gore being out in the Country shott one of the Animals before spoke of, it was a small one of the sort weighing only 28 pound clear of the entrails. The head neck and shoulders of this Animal was very small in proportion to the other parts; the tail was nearly as long as the body, thick next the rump and tapering towards the end; the fore legs were 8 Inch long and the hind 22, its progression is by hoping or jumping 7 or 8 feet at each hop upon its hind legs only, for in this it makes no use of the fore, which seem to be only design'd for scratching in the ground &c[a]. The skin is cover'd with a short hairy fur of a dark Mouse or Grey Colour. Excepting the head and ears which I thought was something like a Hare's, it bears no sort of resemblance to any European Animal I ever saw; it is said to bear much resemblance to the Gerbua excepting in size, the Gerbua being no larger than a common rat.

THURSDAY 19*th* July. Gentle breezes at SE and fair weather. Employ'd geting every thing in readiness for sea. In the AM we were viseted by 10 or 11 of the natives, the most of them came from the other side of the River where we saw six or seven more the most of them women and like the men quite naked; those that came on board were very desirous of having some of our turtle and took

July 1770 the liberty to haul two to the gang way to put over the side, being disapointed in this they grew a little troublesome and were for throwing every thing over board they could lay their hands upon; as we had no victuals dress'd at this time I offer'd them some bread to eat, which they rejected with scorn as I believe they would have done any thing else excepting turtle. Soon after this they all went a shore, M[r] Banks my self and five or six or our people being a shore at the same time; emmidiatly upon their landing one of them took a handfull of dry grass and lighted it at a fire we had a shore, and before we well know'd what he was going about he made a large circuit round about us and set fire to the grass in his way and in an Instant the whole place was in flames, luckily at this time we had hardly any thing ashore besides the forge and a sow with a Litter of young pigs one of which was scorched to death in the fire. As soon as they had done this they all went to a place where some of our people were washing and where all our nets and a good deal of linnen were laid out to dry, here with the greatest obstinacy they again set fire to the grass which I and some others who were present could not prevent, untill I was obliged to fire a musquet load[ed] with small shott at one of the ri[n]g leaders which sent them off.

⁅ Throughout his stay Cook took the greatest precautions against scurvy. To quote his own words of the supplies secured at Endeavour River.

SATURDAY 4*th* August. The refreshments we got here were chiefly Turtle, but as we had to go five leagues out to Sea for them and had much blowing weather we were not over stock'd with this article, however what with these and the fish we caught in the Sain we had not much reason to complain considering the Country we were in. Whatever refreshment we got that would bear a division I caused to be equally divided amongest the whole compney generally by weight, the meanest person in the Ship had an equal share with my self or any one on board, and this method every commander of a Ship on such a Voyage as this ought ever to observe. We found in several places on the sandy beaches and sand Hills near the sea Purslain and beans which growes on a creeping kind of a Vine, the first we found very good when boild and the latter not to be despised and were at first very servicable to the sick, but the best greens we found here was the Tarra or Cocco tops call'd in the West Indias Indian Kale, which grow in most Boggy places, these eat as well or better than spinnage; the roots for want of being transplanted and properly cultivated were not good yet we could have dispenced with them could we have got them in any tolerable plenty, but having a good way to go for them it took up too much time and too many hands to gather both root and branch: the few Cabbage Palms we found here were in general small and yeilded so little Cabbage that they were not worth the looking after and this was the case with most of the fruits &c[a] we found in the woods. Besides the Animal which I have before mentioned called by the natives *Kangooroo* or *Kanguru* here are Wolves, Possums, an Animal like a ratt,

August 1770

and snakes both of the Venomous and other sorts. Tame Animals here are none except Dogs and of these we never saw but one who frequently came about our tents to pick up bones &c[a]. The Kangura are in the greatest number for we seldom went into the Country without seeing some.

⁅ Cook sailed with a ship that was making water 'at not quite an inch an hour, with worn out sails, and with all pumps' in a state of decay. Barring his passage north were banks and shoals that gave him 'no small uneasiness'. By Tuesday 7th August, they were again in deadly peril and Cook wrote:

TUESDAY *7th* August. After having well View'd our situation from the mast head I saw that we were surrounded on every side with Shoals and no such thing as a passage to Sea but through the winding channels between them, dangerous to the highest degree in so much that I was quite at a loss which way to steer when the weather would permit us to get under sail; for to beat back to the SE the way we came as the Master would have had me done would be an endless peice of work, as the winds blow now constantly strong from that quarter without hardly any intermission—on the other hand if we do not find a passage to the north[d] we shall have to come [back] at last.

⁅ After eight perilous days in this nightmare of navigation, Cook decided to stand out to the open ocean.

MONDAY *13th* August. After well considering both what I had seen my self and the report of the Master, who was of opinion that the Passage to Leeward would prove danger[ou]s; this I was pretty well convince'd of my self that by keeping in with the main land we should be in continual danger besides the risk we should run of being locke'd in within the Main reef at last and have to return back to seek a passage out, an accident of this kind or any other that might happen to the Ship would infallibly loose our passage to the East Indias this season and might prove the ruin of the Voyage, as we have now little more than 3 Months provisions on board and that short allowance in many Arti[c]les. These reasons had the [same] weight with all the officers, I therefore resolved to weigh in the morning and endeavour to quet the coast altogether untill we could approach it with less danger: With this View we got under sail at day light and stood out NE for the NW end of Lizard Island, leaving Eagle Island to windward of us and some other Islands & Shoals to le[e]ward having the Pinnace a head sounding, in this channell we had from 9 to 14 fathom. At Noon the NW end of Lizard Island bore ESE distant one mile, Lat[de] observed 14° 38′ S, depth of water 14 fathom.—We now took the Pinnace in tow knowing that there was no danger till we got out to the Reefs without the Island.

TUESDAY *14th* August. Winds at SE a steady fresh gale. By 2 oClock we just fetched to windward of one of the Channels in the outer Reef I had seen from the Island, we now tacked and made a short trip to the SW while the Master in the Pinnace examind the channell, he soon made the Signal for the Ship to

August 1770 follow which we accordingly did and in a short time got safe out, we had no sooner got without the breakers than we had no ground with 150 fathom of line and found a well growen Sea rowling in from the SE, certain signs that nither land nor shoals were in our neighbourhood in that direction, which made us quite easy at being free'd from fears of Shoals &c[a]—after having been intangled among them more or less ever sence the 26th of May, in which time we have saild 360 Leagues without ever having a Man out of the cheans heaving the Lead when the Ship was under way, a circumstance that I dare say never happen'd to any ship before and yet here it was absolutely necessary. It was with great regret I was obliged to quit this coast unexplored to its No[r]thern extremity which I think we were not far off, for I firmly believe that it doth not join to *New Guinea*, however this I hope yet to clear up being resolved to get in with the land again as soon as I can do it with safety and the reasons I have before assigned will I presume be thought sufficient for my haveing left it at this time.

⸿ In the last two sentences Cook refers to one of the most important geographical problems which he hoped to solve on the east coast of New Holland—the question of whether or not New Holland was joined to New Guinea. Banks, as we have seen, had on board the *Endeavour* a copy of Dalrymple's booklet with a map marking Torres' route between Australia and New Guinea in 1606, and although Cook had so far proved all Dalrymple's speculations on a southern continent to be wild and ill-founded, the great explorer was broad-minded enough to admit that his rival's views might, on this point, prove correct. He had already decided that New Holland was not joined to Quiros' Espiritu Santo, which now lay some 1200 miles to his east, as he wrote—

'I had forgot to mention in its proper place that not only on these Islands but in sever[l] places on the Sea beach in and about Endeavour River we found Bamboos, Cocoa-nutts, the Seeds of Plants, and Pummick Stones which were not the produce of this Country from all the discoveries we have been able to make in it. It is reasonable to suppose that they are the produce of some Country lying to the Eastward and brought here by the Easterly Trade winds. The Islands discover'd by Quiros call'd by him Astralia del Espiritu Santo lays in this parallel but how far to the East is hard to say, most charts place them as far to the west as this Country, but we are morally certain that he never was upon any part of this coast. The published account of the Voyage which we must depend upon untill we have better Authority places his discoveries about 22° to the East of the Coast of New Holland.

⸿ Although the *Endeavour* was free for the moment from the perilous reefs, the ocean swell increased the leaks to beyond the capacity of a single pump, while she soon sighted the reefs again to her leeward, which exposed her to the dangers that Bougainville, in the same locality, had only just escaped.

THURSDAY *16th* August. By one oClock in the PM or before we saw high land from y[e] Masthead bearing WSW and at 2 oClock saw more land to the NW of the former makeing in hills like Islands but we judged it to be the continuation of the Main land. An hour after this we saw breakers between us and the land extending to the Southward farther than we could see, but we thought we saw them terminate to the northward abreast of us, this however proved only an opening for soon after we saw the Reef or breakers extend away to the northward as far as we could see, upon this we hauld close upon a wind which was now at ESE. We had hardly trimed our sails before the wind came to EBN which was right upon the Reef and of Course made our clearing of it doubtfull, the northermost of it that we could see at sun set bore from us NBE distant about 2 or 3 Leagues. However this being the best tack to clear it we kept standing to the northward with all the Sail we could set untill 12 oClock at night when fearing to Stand too far up this tack we tacked and stood to the Southward having run 6 Leagues North and NBE sence Sun set. We had not stood above 2 Miles SSE before it fell quite Calm, we both sounded now and several times in the night but had no ground with 140 fathoms of line. A little after 4 oClock the roaring of the Surf was plainly heard and at day break the vast foaming breakers were too plainly to be seen not a Mile from us towards which we found the Ship was carried by the waves surprisingly fast. We had at this time not an air of wind and the depth of water was unfathomable so that there was not a possibility of Anchoring, in this distressed situation we had nothing but Providence and the small Assistance our boats could give us to trust to; the Pinnace was under a repair and could not immidiately be hoisted out, the Yawl was put into the water and the Long-boat hoisted out and both sent ahead to tow which together with the help of our sweeps abaft got the Ships head round to the northward which seem'd to be the only way to keep her off the reef or at least to delay time, before this was effected it was 6 oClock and we were not above 80 or 100 Yards from the breakers, the same Sea that washed the sides of the Ship rose in a breaker prodigiously high the very next time it did rise so that between us and distruction was only a dismal Vally the breadth of one wave and even now no ground could be felt with 120 fathoms. The Pinnace by this time was patched up and hoisted out and sent ahead to tow; still we had hardly any hopes of saving the Ship and full as little our lives as we were full 10 Leagues from the nearest land and the boats not sufficient to carry the whole of us, yet in this truly terrible situation not one man ceased to do his utmost and that with as much calmness as if no danger had been near. All the dangers we had escaped were little in comparison of being thrown upon this Reef where the Ship must be dashed to peices in a Moment. A Reef such as is here spoke of is scarcely known in Europe, it is a wall of Coral Rock rising all most perpendicular out of the unfathomable Ocean, always overflown at high-water generally 7 or 8 feet and dry in places

August 1770 at low-water; the large waves of the vast Ocean meeting with so sudden a resistance make a most terrible surf breaking mountains high especially as in our case when the general trade wind blowes directly upon it. At this critical juncture when all our endeavours seem'd too little a small air of wind sprung up, but so small that at any other time in a Calm we should not have observed it, with this and the assistance of our boats we could observe the Ship to move off from the Reef in a slanting direction, but in less than 10 Minutes we had as flat a Calm as ever when our fears were again renewed for as yet we were not above 200 Yards from the breakers. Soon after our friendly breeze Viseted us again and lasted about as long as before. A small opening was now seen in the Reef about a quarter of a Mile from us which I sent one of the Mates to examine, its breadth was not more than the length of the Ship but within was smooth water, into this place it was resolve'd to push her if possible haveing no other probable Views to save her, for we were still in the very jaws of distruction and it was a doubt whether or no we could reach this opening, however we soon got off it when to our surprise we found the Tide of Ebb gushing out like a Mill stream so that it was impossible to get in; we however took all the advantage possible of it and it carried us out about a ¼ of a Mile from the breakers, but it was too narrow for us to keep in long; how ever what with the help of Ebb and our boats we by noon had got an offing of one and half or two Miles, yet we could hardly flater our selves with hopes of geting clear even if a breeze should spring up as we were by this time imbayed by the Reef, and the Ship in spite of our endeavours driving before the Sea into the bight, the Ebb had been in our favour and we had reason to suppose that the flood which was now making would be againest us, the only hopes we had was another opening we saw about a Mile to the Westward of us which I sent Lieut[en]ant Hick[s] in the Small boat to examine. Latitude Observed 12° 37′ S, the Main land in sight distant about 10 Leagues.

FRIDAY 17*th* August. While Mr Hicks was examining the opening we strugled hard with the flood some times gaining a little and at other times looseing. At 2 oClock Mr Hicks returnd with a favourable account of the opening, it was immidiately resolved to try to secure the Ship in it, narrow and dangerous as it was it seem'd to be the only means we had of saving her as well as our selves. A light breeze soon after sprung up at ENE which with the help of our boats and a flood tide we soon enter'd the opening and was hurried through in a short time by a rappid tide like a Mill race which kept us from driving againest either side, tho the c[h]annell was not more than a quarter of a Mile broad, we had however two boats a head to direct us through, our depth of water in the Channell was from 30 to 7 fathom very erregular soundings and foul ground untill we had got quite within the Reef where we anchor'd in 19 fathom a Corally & Shelly bottom happy once more to incounter those shoals which but

two days ago our utmost wishes were crowned by geting clear of, such are the Vicissitudes attending this kind of service and must always attend an unknown Navigation: Was it not for the pleasure which naturly results to a Man from being the first discoverer, even was it nothing more than sands and Shoals, this service would be insuportable especialy in far distant parts, like this, short of Provisions and almost every other necessary. The world will hardly admit of an excuse for a man leaving a Coast unexplored he has once discover'd, if dangers are his excuse he is than charged with *Timorousness* and want of Perseverance and at once pronounced the unfitest man in the world to be employ'd as a discoverer; if on the other hand he boldly incounters all the dangers and obstacles he meets and is unfortunate enough not to succeed he is than charged with *Temerity* and want of conduct. The former of these aspersins cannot with Justice be laid to my charge and if I am fortunate enough to surmount all the dangers we may meet the latter will never be brought in question. I must own I have ingaged more among the Islands and shoals upon this coast than may be thought with prudence I ought to have done with a single Ship and every other thing considered, but if I had not we should not have been able to give any better account of the one half of it than if we had never seen it, that is we should not have been able to say whether it consisted of main land or Islands and as to its produce, we must have been totally ignorant of as being inseparable with the other.

'I now came to a fix'd resolution to keep the Main land on board in our rout to the norward let the concequence be what it will, indeed now it was not adviseable to go without the reef, for by it we might be carried so far from the Coast as not to be able to determine whether or no New Guinea joins to or makes a part of this land. This doubtfull point I had from my first coming upon the Coast determined if possible to clear up.

☾ Even Cook must have been gravely shaken to voice so strongly the terrible dangers and hardships.

☾ Once more within the Great Barrier Reef, Cook again crept northwards and on Tuesday, 21st August, discovered the north-easterly point of Australia, Cape York, with the adjoining islands that fringe the Eastern entrance of Torres Strait.

TUESDAY 21*st* August. The Point of the Main which forms one side of the Passage before mentioned and which is the Northern Promontary of this country I have Named *York Cape* in honour of His late Royal Highness the Duke of York. It lies in the Longitude of 218° 24′ w, the North point in ye Lat^de^ of 10° 37′ s & the E^t^ point in 10° 41′ s. The land over and to the Southward of this last point is rather low and very flat as far in land as the eye could r[e]ach and looks barren to the Southward of the Cape.

☾ Sailing westwards around the Cape, Cook discovered and passed through Endeavour Strait between Prince of Wales Island and the mainland, and, feeling that he would now enter the region of Dutch discovery, he landed on Possession

August 1770 Island, and on 22nd August 1770, took possession of Eastern Australia for the British Crown.

WEDNESDAY *22nd* August. At 4 oClock we anchor'd about a Mile and a half or 2 Miles within the entrance in 6½ fathom clear ground, distant from the Islands on each side of us one mile, the Main land extending away to the SW, the farthest point of which that we could see bore from us S 48° West and the South-wester-most point of the Islands on the NW side of the Passage bore S 76° West. Between these two points we could see no land so that we were in great hopes that we had at last found a Passage into the Indian Seas, but in order to be better informd I landed with a party of Men accompan'd by Mr Banks and Dr Solander upon the Island which lies at the SE point of the Passage. Before and after we Anchor'd we saw a number of People upon this Island arm'd in the same manner as all the others we have seen, except one man who had a bow and a bundle of Arrows, the first we have seen on this coast. From the appearence of these People we expected that they would have opposed our landing but as we approachd the Shore they all made off and left us in peaceable posession of as much of the Island as served our purpose. After landing I went upon the highest hill which however was of no great height, yet not less than twice or thrice the height of the Ships Mast heads, but I could see from it no land between SW and WSW so that I did not doubt but what there was a passage. I could see plainly that the Lands laying to the NW of this passage were composed of a number of Island[s] of various extent both for height and circuit, rainged one behind another as far to the Northward and Westward as I could see, which could not be less than 12 or 14 Leagues. Having satisfied my self of the great Probabillity of a Passage, thro' which I intend going with the Ship, and therefore may land no more upon this Eastern coast of *New Holland*, and on the Western side I can make no new discovery the honour of which belongs to the Dutch Navigators; but the Eastern Coast from the Latitude of 38° South down to this place I am confident was never seen or viseted by any European before us, and Notwithstand[ing] I had in the Name of His Majesty taken posession of several places upon this coast, I now once more hoisted English Coulers and in the Name of His Majesty King George the Third took posession of the whole Eastern Coast from the above Latitude down to this place by the name of *New South Wales*, together with all the Bays, Harbours Rivers and Islands situate upon the said coast, after which we fired three Volleys of small Arms which were Answerd by the like number from the Ship.

℄ By 23rd August the swell from the south-west and other factors convinced Cook that he had proved that New Holland and New Guinea were separated by water, and that open sea lay to the westward. He could thus write:

THURSDAY *23rd* August. Being now near the Island and having but little wind Mr Banks and I landed upon it and found it to be mostly a barren Rock frequented by birds such as Boobies, a few of which we Shott and occasioned my giving it the Name of *Booby Island.* I made but a very short stay at this Island before I returnd to the Ship. In the mean time the wind had got to SW and altho it blowed but very faint yet it was accompaned with a swell from the same quarter; this together with other concuring circumstances left me no room to doubt but we were got to the Westward of *Carpentaria* or the Northern extremety of *New-Holland* and had now an open Sea to the westward, which gave me no small satisfaction not only because the dangers and fatigues of the Voyage was drawing near to an end, but by being able to prove that New-Holland and New-Guinea are two Seperate Lands or Islands, which untill this day hath been a doubtfull point with Geographers.

August 1770

❨ Before leaving North-East Australia Cook wrote an account of this land that he called 'New Wales' in his original Journal, and in the 'Corner' or 'Mitchell' copy which he despatched from Batavia, but later named 'New South Wales'. He saw with great shrewdness the potentialities offered for the introduction of exotic animals and food plants, and it was not until many years later that anthropologists realised as clearly as Cook that the aboriginals possessed many good qualities and were well adjusted to the environment.

THURSDAY *23rd* August. In the Course of this Journal I have at different times made mention of the appearence or Aspect of the face of the Country, the nature of the Soil, its produce &c[a]. By the first it will appear that to the Southward of 33° or 34° the Land in general is low and level with very few Hills or Mountains, further to the northward it may in some places be called a Hilly, but hardly any where can be call'd a Mountainous Country, for the Hills and Mountains put together take up but a small part of the Surface in comparison to what the Planes and Vallies do which intersect or divide these Hills and Mountains: It is indefferently well watered, even in the dry Seasons, with small Brooks and springs, but no great Rivers, unless it be in the wet Season when the low lands and Vallies near the Sea I do suppose are mostly laid under water; the small brooks may then become large Rivers but this can only happen with the Tropick. It was only in *Thirsty Sound* where we could find no fresh Water, excepting one small pool or two which Gore saw in the woods, which no doubt was owing to the Country being there very much intersected with Salt creeks and Mangrove land.

'The low Land by the Sea and even as far in land as we were, is for the most part friable, loose, sandy Soil; yet indefferently fertile and cloathed with woods, long grass, shrubs, Plants &c[a]. The Mountains or Hills are Chequered with woods and Lawns. Some of the Hills are wholy covered with flourishing Trees; others but thinly, and the few that are on them are small and the spots of Lawns or Savannahs are Rocky and barren, especially to the northward where the country did not afford or produce near the Vegetation that it does to the southward, nor were the Trees in the woods half so tall and stout.

August 1770 'The Woods do not produce any great variety of Trees, there are only 2 or 3 sorts that can be call'd Timber; the largest is the Gum Tree which growes all over the Country, the Wood of this Tree is too hard and ponderous for most common uses. The Tree which resembles our Pines, I saw no where in perfection but in Botany Bay, this wood as I have before observed is some thing of the same nature as America Live Oak; in short most of the large Trees in this Country are of a hard and ponderous nature and could not be applied to many purposes. Here are several sorts of the Palm kind, Mangro[v]es and several other sorts of small Trees and shrubs quite unknown to me besides a very great Variety of Plants hetherto unknown, but these things are wholy out of my way to describe, nor will this be of any loss sence not only Plants but everything that can be of use to the Learn'd World will be very accuratly described by Mr Banks and Dr Solander. The Land naturly produces hardly any thing fit for man to eat and the Natives know nothing of Cultivation. There are indeed found growing wild in the woods a few sorts of fruits (the most of them unknown to us) which when ripe do not eat a miss, one sort especially which we call'd Apples, being about the size of a Crab-Apple, it is black and pulpy when ripe and tastes like a Damson, it hath a large hard stone or kernel and grows on Trees or Shrubs.

'In the Northern parts of the Country as about *Endeavour River*, and probably in many other places, the Boggy or watery Lands produce Taara or Cocos which when properly cultivated are very good roots, without which they are hardly eatable, the tops however make very good greens.

'Land Animals are scarce, as so far as we know confined to a very few species; all that we saw I have before mentioned, the sort that is in the greatest plenty is the Kangooroo, or Kanguru so call'd by the Natives; we saw a good many of them about Endeavour River, but kill'd only Three which we found very good eating. Here are like wise Batts, Lizards, Snakes, Scorpions, Centumpees &c^a^ but not in any plenty. Tame Animals they have none but Dogs, and of these we saw but one and therefore must be very scarce, probably they eat them faster than they breed them, we should not have seen this one had he not made us frequent Visets while we lay in Endeavour River.

'The Land Fowles are Bustards, Eagles, Hawks, Crows such as we have in England, Cockatoes of two sorts, white and brown, very beautifull Birds of the Parrot kind such as Lorryquets &c^a^, Pidgeons, Doves, Quales, and several sorts of smaller birds. The Sea and Water Fowls are Herons, Boobies, Nodies, Guls, Curlews, Ducks, Pelicans &c^a^ and when Mr Banks and Mr Gore were in the Country at the head of Endeavour River they saw and heard in the night great numbers of Geese. The sea is indifferently well stock'd with Fish of various sorts, such as Sharks, Dog-fish, Rock-fish, Mullets, Breames, Cavallies, Mackarel, old wives, Leather-Jackets, Five-fingers, Sting-Rays, Whip-rays &c^a^—all excellent in their kind. The Shell-fish are Oysters of 3 or 4 sorts, viz Rock oysters and Mangrove Oysters which are small, Pearl Oysters, and Mud Oysters, these last are the best and largest; Cockles and Clams of Several sorts, many of these that are found upon the Reefs are of a Prodigious size; Craw-fish, Crabs, Musles, and a variety of other sorts. Here are also among and upon the Shoals & reefs great numbers of the finest Gree[n] Turtle in the world and in the Rivers and salt Creeks are some Aligators. *August 1770*

'The Natives of this Country are of a middle Stature straight bodied and slender-limbd, their skins the Colour of Wood soot or of a dark Chocolate, their hair mostly black, some lank and others curled, they all wear it crop'd short, their Beards which are generaly black they like wise crop short or singe off. Their features are far from being disagreeable and their Voices are soft and tunable. They go quite naked both Men and women without any manner of Cloathing whatever, even the Women do not so much as Cover their privities. Altho none of us were ever very near any of their women, one gentleman excepted, yet we are all as well satisfied of this as if we had lived among them. Notwithstanding we had several interviews with the Men while we lay in Endeavour River, yet whether through Jealousy or disrigard they never brought any of their women along with them to the Ship, but always left them on the opposite side of the River where we had frequent oppertunities [of] Viewing them through our glasses. They wear as Oraments Necklaces made of shells, Bracelets or hoops about their arms, made mostly of hair twisted and made like a cord hoop, these they wear teight about the uper parts of their Arms, and some have girdles made in the same manner. The men wear a bone about 3 or 4 Inches long and a fingers thick, run through the Bridge of the nose, which the Seamen call'd a sprit sail yard; they like wise have holes in their ears for Earrings but we never saw them wear any, neither are all the other oraments wore in common for we have seen as many without as with them. Some of those we saw on Posession Island wore Breast Plates which we suppose'd were made of Mother of Pearl shells. Many of them paint their bodies and faces with a sort of White paist or Pigment, this they apply different ways each according to his fancy. Their Offensive weaphons are Darts, some are only pointed at one end others are barb'd, some with wood others with the Stings of Rays and some with Sharks teeth &c[a], these last are stuck fast on with gum. They throw the dart with only one hand, in the doing of which they make use of a peice of wood about 3 feet long made thin like the blade of a Cutlass, with a little hook at one end to take hold of the end of the Dart, and at the other end is fix'd a thin peice of bone about 3 or 4 Inches long; the use of this is, I beleive, to keep the dart steady and to make it quit the hand in a proper direction; by the help of these throwing sticks, as we call them, they will hit a Mark at the distance of 40 or 50 Yards, with almost, if not as much certainty as we can do with a Musquet, and much more so than with a ball. These throwing sticks we at first took for wooden swords,

August 1770 and perhaps on some occasions they may use them as such, that is when all their darts are expended, be this as it may they never travel without both them and their darts, not altogether for fear of enimies but for killing of Game &c[a] as I shall shew hereafter. Their defensive weapons are Shields made of wood but these we never saw use'd but once in Botany Bay. I do not look upon them to be a warlike People, on the Contrary I think them a timorous and inoffensive race, no ways inclinable to cruelty, as appear'd from their behavour to one of our people in Endeavour River which I have before mentioned. Neither are they very numerous, they live in small parties along by the Sea Coast, the banks of Lakes, Rivers creeks &c[a]. They seem to have no fix'd habitation but move about from place to place like wild Beasts in search of food, and I beleive depend wholy upon the success of the present day for their subsistance. They have wooden fish gigs with 2, 3 or 4 prongs each very ingeniously made with which they strike fish; we have also seen them strike both fish and birds with their darts. With these they like wise kill other Animals; they have also wooden Harpoons for striking Turtle, but of these I beleive they got but few, except at the Season they come a shore to lay. In short these people live wholy by fishing and hunting, but mostly by the former, for we never saw one Inch of Cultivated land in the whole Country; they know however the use of Taara and sometimes eat them. We do not know that they eat any thing raw but roast or broil all they eat on slow small fires.

'Their Houses are mean small hovels not much bigger than an oven, made of peices of Sticks, Bark, Grass &c[a], and even these are seldom used but in the wet seasons for in the dry times we know that they as often sleep in the open air as any where else. We have seen many of their Sleeping places where there has been only some branches, or peices of bark ris about a foot from the ground on the windward side. Their Canoes are as mean as can be conceived, especially to the southward where all we saw were made of one peice of the bark of Trees, about 12 or 14 feet long, drawn or tied together at one end as I have before made mention. These Canoes will not carry above 2 people, in general their is never more than one in them, but bad as they are they do very well for the purpose they apply them to, better then if they were larger, for as they draw but little water they go in them upon the Mud banks and pick up shell fish &c[a] without going out of the Canoe. The few Canoes we saw to the northward were made of a log of wood hollow'd out, about 14 feet long and very narrow with out-riggers, these will carry 4 people. During our whole stay in Endevour River we saw but one Canoe and had great reason to think that the few people that resided about this place had no more; this one served them to cross the River and to go a fishing in &c[a]. They Attend the Shoals and flatts one where or a nother every Day at Low-water to gather Shell fish or what ever they can find to eat, and have each a little bag to put what they get in: this bag is made of net work.

They have not the least knowlidge of Iron or any other Metal that we know of; their working tools must be made of stone, bone and shells, those made of the former are very bad if I may judge from one of their Adzes I have seen.

August 1770

'Bad and mean as their Canoes are they at certain Seasons of the Year, so far as we know, go in them to the most Distant Islands which lay upon the Coast, for we never landed upon one but what we saw signs of people having been there before. We were supprised to find Houses &c[a] upon Lizard Island which lies 5 Leagues from the nearest part of the Main, a distance we before thought that they could not have gone in their Canoes.

'The Coast of this Country, at least so much of it as lays to the Northward of 25° of Latitude, abounds with a great Number of fine Bays and Harbours, which are shelter'd from all Winds. But, the Country it self so far as we know doth not produce any one thing that can become an Article in trade to invite Europeans to fix a settlement upon it. However this Eastern side is not that barren and Miserable Country that *Dampier* and others have discribed the western side to be. We are to Consider that we see this Country in the pure state of Nature, the Industry of Man has had nothing to do with any part of it and yet we find all such things as nature hath bestow'd upon it in a flourishing state. In this Extensive Country it can never be doubted but what most sorts of Grain, Fruits, Roots &c[a] of every kind would flourish here were they once brought hither, planted and cultivated by the hand of Industry, and here are Provender for more Cattle at all seasons of the year than ever can be brought into this Country.

'When one considers the Proximity of this Country with New-Guiney, New-Britain and several other Islands which produce Cocoa-Nutts and many other fruits proper for the Support of Man, it seems strange that they should not long ago have been transplanted here; by its not being done it should seem that the Natives of this Country have no Commerce with their neighbours the New-Guinians, it is very probable that they are a different people and speake a different Language. . . . From what I have said of the Natives of New-Holland they may appear to some to be the most wretched people upon Earth, but in reality they are far more happier than we Europeans; being wholy unacquainted not only with the superfluous but the necessary Conveniences so much sought after in Europe, they are happy in not knowing the use of them. They live in a Tranquility which is not disturb'd by the Inequality of Condition: The Earth and sea of their own accord furnishes them with all things necessary for life, they covet not Magnificent Houses, Houshold-stuff &c[a], they live in a warm and fine Climate and enjoy a very wholsome Air, so that they have very little need of Clothing and this they seem to be fully sencible of, for many to whome we gave Cloth &c[a] to, left it carlessly upon the Sea beach and in the woods as a thing they had no manner of use for. In short they seem'd to set no Value upon any thing we gave them.

Chapter VII
THE VOYAGE CONCLUDED

"No discoverer ever measured his claim with more moderation."

J. C. BEAGLEHOLE

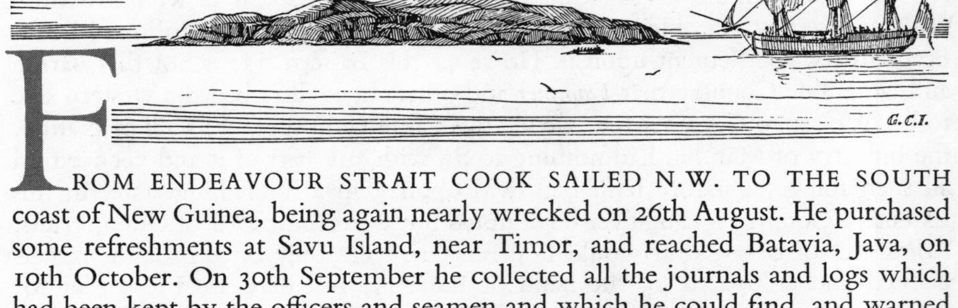

FROM ENDEAVOUR STRAIT COOK SAILED N.W. TO THE SOUTH coast of New Guinea, being again nearly wrecked on 26th August. He purchased some refreshments at Savu Island, near Timor, and reached Batavia, Java, on 10th October. On 30th September he collected all the journals and logs which had been kept by the officers and seamen and which he could find, and warned the crew not to say where they had been. On 24th October he despatched the 'Mitchell' or 'Corner' copy of his own journal to London, but the Canberra copy records events until the voyage terminated.

¶ In Batavia the Dutch gave Cook generous assistance, as was necessary, for the damage to the *Endeavour* was even worse than Cook and the carpenters had suspected.

FRIDAY *9th* November. In the PM Hove the Larboard side of the Ship Keel out and found her bottom to be in a far worse condition than we expected, the False Keel was gone to within 20 feet of the stern post, the Main Keel wounded in ma[n]y places very considerably, a great quantity of Sheathing [off], several planks much damaged especially under the Main channell near the Keel, where two planks and a half near 6 feet in length were within ⅛ of a Inch of being cut through, and here the worms had made their way quite into the Timbers, so that it was a Matter of Surprise to every one who saw her bottom how we had kept her above water; and yet in this condition we had sailed some hundreds of Leagues in as dangerous a Navigation as is in any part of the world, happy in being ignorant of the continual danger we were in. In the Evening righted the Ship, Having only time to patch up some of the worst places to prevent the water geting in in large quantitys for the present. In the Morning hove her down again and most of the Carpenters and Caulkers in the yard (which are not a few) were set to work upon her bottom, and at the same time a number of slaves were employ'd bailing the water out of the hold. Our people altho they attend were seldom called upon, indeed by this time we were so weake[n]d by sickness that we could not muster above 20 Men and officers that were able to do duty, so little should we have been able to have hove her down and repair'd her our selves as I at one time thought us capable of.

November 1770

₵ The repairs kept Cook in Batavia until 27th December and during his stay dysentery and malaria killed a number of the crew and left others desperately ill. Even Banks and Solander became very sick but bought a Malay woman apiece and took them to a country house 'hoping that the tenderness of the sex would prevail even here, which indeed we found it to do'. Cook had written in his Journal on Monday, 15th October, 'I forgot to mention, that upon our arrival here I had not one man upon the sick list; Lieut. Hicks, Mr Green and Tupia were the only people that had any complaints occasioned by a long continuance at sea'. Yet, in spite of the wonderful results of his anti-scorbutic and other health precautions, he was forced to write on the eve of his departure:

WEDNESDAY *26th* December. In the PM My self Mr Banks and all the Gentlemen came on board and at 6 in the AM we weigh'd and came to sail with a light breeze at SW. The Elgin Indiaman saluted with three Cheers and 13 Guns and soon after the Garrison with 14 both of which we returnd. Soon after this the Sea breeze set in at NBW which obliged us to anchor just without the Ships in the Road. The Number sick on board at this time amounts to 40 or upwards and the rest of the Ships company are in a Weakly condition, having been ev[er]y one sick except the Sail maker an old Man about 70 or 80 Years of age, and what was still more extraordinary in this man his being generally more or less drunk every day. But notwithstanding this general sickness we lost but Seven Men in the whole: the Surgeon three Seamen, Mr Greens Servant and Tupia and his servant, both of which fell a sacrifice to this unwholsom climate before they had reached the Object of their wishes. Tupia['s] death indeed cannot be said to be owing wholy to the unwholsom air of Batavia, the long want of a Vegetable diat which he had all his life before been use'd to had brought upon him all the disorders attending a sea life. He was a Shrewd Sensible, Ingenious Man, but proud and obstinate which often made his situation on board both disagreable to himself and those about him, and tended much to promote the deceases which put a period to his life. . . . Batavia is certainly a place that Europeans need not covet to go to, but if necessity obliges them they will do well to make their stay as short a[s] possible otherwise they will soon feel the effects of the unwholsome air of Batavia which I firmly beleive is the death of more Europeans than any other place upon the Globe of the same extent, such at least is my opinion of it which is founded on facts. We came in here with as

December 1770 healthy a ships company as need [go] to Sea and after a stay of not quite 3 Months lift it in the condition of an Hospital Ship besides the loss of 7 Men and yet all the Dutch Captains I had an oppertunity to convers with said that we had been very lucky and wondered that we had not lost half our people in that time.

⁅ The *Endeavour* was indeed 'an Hospital Ship', and on the way to England via the Cape of Good Hope she lost 23 more of her people, the great majority before the immediate 'happy Effect' of the S.E. Trade Wind. Amongst these were Charles Green, the Astronomer; Sydney Parkinson, Bank's Natural History Painter; Midshipman Monkhouse, who had fothered the *Endeavour*, and John Satterly, the much esteemed carpenter.

THURSDAY 31*st* January. In the Course of this 24 hours we have had 4 Men died of the Flux—A Melancholy proff of the Calamitous Situation we are at present in, having hardly men enough to tend the Sails and look after the Sick, many of the latter are so ill that we have not the least hopes of their recovery.

⁅ As mentioned above, however, matters improved in the Trades, and, after taking in refreshments at Cape Town, the *Endeavour* anchored in the Downs on Saturday 13th July 1771, the voyage having lasted very nearly three years.

⁅ The results of this historic voyage can best be summarised by quoting Cook's own letter to Philip Stephens, Secretary of the Admiralty, written on 23rd October 1770.

'Sir,—

'Please to acquaint my Lords Commissioners of the Admiralty that I left Rio de Janeiro the 8th of December 1768, and on the 16th January following arrived in Success Bay in Straits La Maire, where we recruited our Wood and Water; on the 21st of the same month we quitted Straits La Maire, and arrived at Georges Island on the 13th of April. In our Passage to this Island I made a far more Westerly Track than any Ship had ever done before; yet it was attended with no discovery until we arrived within the Tropick, where we discovered several Islands. We met with as Friendly a reception by the Natives of Georges Island as I could wish, and I took care to secure ourselves in such a manner as to put it out of the power of the whole Island to drive us off. Some days preceeding the 3rd of June I sent Lieut[t] Hicks to the Eastern part of this Island, and Lieut[t] Gore to York Island, with others of the officers (M[r] Green having furnished them with Instruments), to observe the Transit of Venus, that we may have the better Chance of succeeding should the day prove unfavourable; but in this We were so fortunate that the observations were everywhere attended with every favourable Circumstance. It was the 13th of July before I was ready to quitt this Island, after which I spent near a month in exploring some other Islands which lay to the Westward, before we steer'd to the Southward. On the 14th of August we discovered a small Island laying in the Latitude of 22° 27′ S., Long. 150° 47′ W. After quitting this Island I steered to the S., inclining a little to the East, until we arrived in the Lat. 40° 12′ S., without seeing the least signs of Land. After this I steer'd to the Westward, between the Latitude of 30° and 40° until the 6th of October, on which day we discovered the East Coast of New Zeland, which I found to consist of 2 large Islands, extending from 34° to 48° of South Latitude, both of which I circumnavigated. On the 1st of April, 1770, I quitted New Zeland, and steer'd to the Westward, until I fell in with the East Coast of New Holland, in the Latitude of 30°S. I coasted the shore of this Country to the N., putting in at such places as I saw Convenient, until we arrived in the Latitude of 15° 45′ S., where, on the night of the 10th of June, we struck upon a Reef of Rocks, where we lay 23 Hours, and received some very considerable damage. This proved a fatal stroke to the remainder of the Voyage, as we were obliged to take shelter in the first Port we met with, where we were detain'd repairing the damage we had sustain'd until the 4th of August, and after all put to Sea with a leaky Ship, and afterwards coasted the Shore to the Northward through the most dangerous Navigation that perhaps ever ship was in, until the 22nd of same month, when, being in the Latitude of 10° 30′ S., we found a Passage into the Indian Sea between the Northern extremity of New Holland and New Guinea. After getting through the Passage I stood for the Coast of New Guinea, which we made on the 29th; but as we found it absolutely necessary to heave the Ship down to Stop her leaks before we proceeded home, I made no stay here, but quitted this Coast on the 30th of September, and made the best of my way to Batavia, where we Arrived on the 10th instant, and soon after obtained leave of the Governor and Council to be hove down at Onrust, where we have but just got alongside of the Wharft in order to take out our Stores, &c[a].

'I send herewith a copy of my Journal, containing the Proceedings of the whole Voyage, together with such Charts as I have had time to Copy, which I judge will be sufficient for the present to illustrate said Journal. In this Journal I have with undisguised truth and without gloss inserted the whole Transactions of the Voyage, and made such remarks and have given such discriptions of things as I thought was necessary in the best manner I was Capable off. Altho' the discoverys made in this Voyage are not great, yet I flatter myself they are such as may Merit the Attention of their Lordships; and altho' I have failed in discovering the so much talked of Southern Continent (which perhaps do not exist), and which I myself had much at heart, yet I am confident that no part of the failure of such discovery can be laid to my charge. Had we been so fortunate not to have run a shore much more would have been done in the latter part of the Voyage than what was; but as it is, I presume this Voyage will be found as compleat as any before made to the So. Seas on the same account. The plans I have drawn of the places I have been at were made with all the Care and accuracy that time and Circumstance would admit of. Thus far I am certain that the

Latitude and Longitude of few parts of the World are better settled than these. In this I was very much assisted by Mr Green, who let slip no one opportunity for making of Observations for settling the Longitude during the whole Course of the Voyage; and the many Valuable discoveries made by Mr Banks and Dr Solander in Natural History, and other things useful to the learned World, cannot fail of contributing very much to the Success of the Voyage. In justice to the Officers and the whole Crew, I must say they have gone through the fatigues and dangers of the whole Voyage with that cheerfulness and Allertness that will always do Honour to British Seamen, and I have the satisfaction to say that I have not lost one Man by sickness during the whole Voyage. Had we been so fortunate not to have run a shore much more would have been done in the latter part of the Voyage that what was, but, as it is I presume this Voyage will be found as Compleat as any before made to the South Seas, on the same account. I hope that the repairs wanting to the Ship will not be so great as to detain us any length of time. You may be assured that I shall make no unnecessary delay either here or at any other place, but shall make the best of my way home. I have the Honour to be with the greatest respect,

Sir,

Your most Obedient Humble Servant,

(Signed) JAMES COOK'.

THE RESULTS OF THE EXPEDITION 1771

¶ In his modest way Cook stated 'the discoveries made in this voyage are not great'. Actually, like several other results of the expedition, they were of outstanding importance. It is true that the primary objective of the voyage, as openly published, was not achieved, for, although the Tahitian observations of the Transit of Venus were conducted in favourable weather and with success, an unforeseen optical distortion vitiated all the readings in the Pacific, at North Cape and in Hudson Bay, and no calculation of the distance between the Earth and Sun could be obtained from them. Against this scientific failure could, however, be put the fact that in the sphere of Natural History Banks and Solander made 'many valuable discoveries', and returned 'laden with the greatest treasure of natural history that ever was brought into any country at one time by two persons'. Of no less importance was the fact that Cook could claim that through his anti-scorbutic precautions he had 'not lost one man by sickness during the whole voyage'. Deaths, many deaths, he had had through dysentery and fever contracted in Batavia, and, although these deaths clouded the medical achievements of his first expedition, he had at last shown the world how ships could keep the sea for long periods without the devastating ravages of diseases such as scurvy.

⁋ Far from the discoveries of the voyage being 'not great', they made a momentous contribution to world history. By sailing south-west and south of the tracks of previous voyagers Cook had shown it unlikely that any great continent existed in the South Pacific. Nevertheless he proved, and depicted on splendid charts, that New Zealand consisted of two large, fertile and alluring islands which obviously offered enticing prospects for colonization. Most important of all, however, he showed that, although the Dutch land of New Holland was separated from Quiros' Espiritu Santo and from New Guinea by Torres' long forgotten Strait, it was a country of continental dimensions; with a vast eastern coastline which appeared continuous from Point Hicks to Cape York. Moreover, his journals showed that these trade wind coasts had no resemblance to the sterile or desert regions which had seemed to the Dutch so repellant. By brilliantly fulfilling his secret instructions in regard to New Zealand, and by even more brilliantly discovering and exploring eastern Australia when permitted to find his own way home, Cook paved the way for English-speaking peoples to occupy the South-West Pacific.

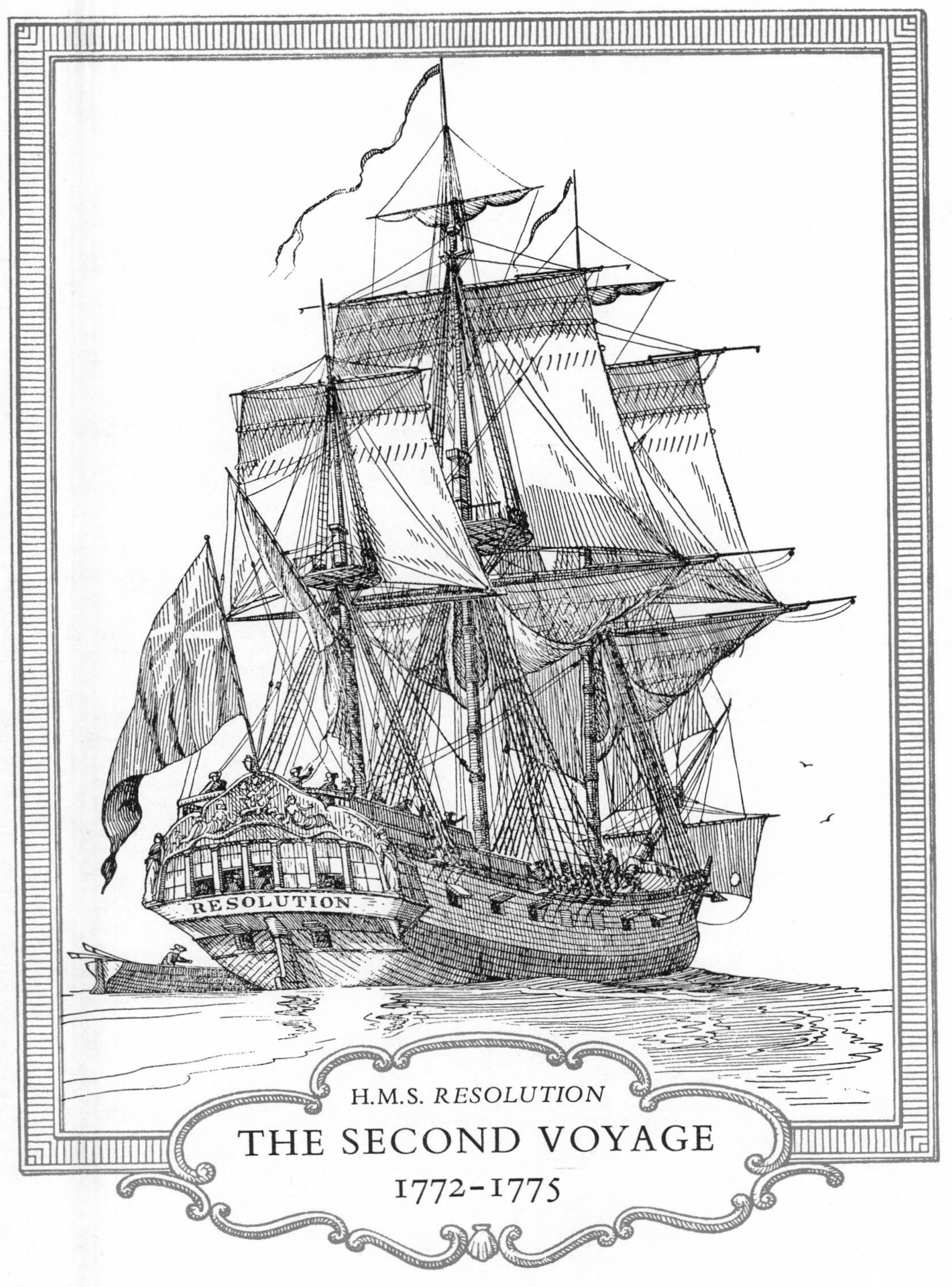
RESOLUTION
H.M.S. *RESOLUTION*
THE SECOND VOYAGE
1772–1775

Chapter VIII

SEEKING THE SOUTHERN CONTINENT

"Prosecuting your discoveries . . . as near the Pole as possible until I had circumnavigated the globe."

COOK'S INSTRUCTIONS FOR THE SECOND VOYAGE, 1772

ON THE POSITIVE SIDE COOK'S FIRST EXPEDITION HAD discovered the long and fertile eastern coast of the Australian continent and had shown that Tasman's New Zealand was a group of promising islands nearly as large as the British Isles. On the negative side, however, Cook's achievement had been less definite. He had proved that no great continent existed in the region of the alleged Davis Land off the coast of Chile, nor as far south as 40° 22′, in approximately the longitude of Tahiti. These facts were of great significance, but they still left unknown immense areas that might contain important land masses.

❡ Moreover international rivalry had not lessened on this subject. During Cook's first expedition Britain had, in 1770, almost gone to war with France and Spain over the Falkland Islands which as noted previously were then regarded as commanding a vital gateway to the Pacific. In 1769-70 a Frenchman, Jean François de Surville, sailed from Pondicherry through the East Indies and Solomons, to New Zealand, where he just missed sighting Cook. He then crossed to Callao on the South American coast where he was drowned, so that his enterprise failed to reward his employers, a private Syndicate which sought a Pacific continent. In 1772, a second Frenchman, Marion du Fresne, sailed from the Cape of Good Hope as far south as Latitude 46° 45′, discovered the small Prince Edward Islands which he thought were part of a continent, and, in May 1772, was murdered and eaten by the Maoris in the Bay of Islands. In 1771 a third Frenchman, Kerguelen-Trémarec, gained the support of his government, in a continent hunt which resulted in his visits to the desolate Kerguelen Land in 1772 and 1773.

⁅ English and French voyages made the Spanish nervous, and Don Manuel de Amat, Viceroy of Peru, despatched, in 1770, two ships that naturally failed to find a continent in the Davis Land region, but made a report on Easter Island, which, however, seemed less promising for settlement than Tahiti, whither Spain sent three expeditions in 1772-5. Some missionary efforts by unusually timorous Franciscans proved a complete failure and Spain made no further attempts to establish settlements in Tahiti, which, as Beaglehole has shown, the Spaniards thought would have no effect on Peru, and would be of no use to other nations 'because of its distance from their several bases'.

⁅ On the academic side the voyage of the *Endeavour* had failed to shake Alexander Dalrymple's belief in his vast southern continent. Although partially defeated in the western, or Australasian side of the Pacific, Dalrymple now claimed that his continent must be further east. When Hawkesworth published the official but unsatisfactory account of the voyage of the *Endeavour*, after Cook had left on his second expedition, Dalrymple attacked Cook most viciously, particularly on the totally false charge that he must have known of the mysterious Dieppe maps, brought to light by Banks, because these maps, apparently Portuguese in origin, marked a 'coste des herbaiges' near Cook's Botany Bay, and a 'coste dangereuse' in the region where the *Endeavour* struck the Barrier Reef.

⁅ Scholars differ strongly on the question of these maps. Professor Sir Ernest Scott believed that at least one Portuguese ship must have skirted the coast of Western Australia to delineate the general shape with such accuracy. Professor G. A. Wood, however, considered them brilliant guesses following those of Ptolemy and Mercator. A more recent authority, T. D. Mutch, has pointed out that the author of the Dieppe map of 1555 wrote on it that the alleged South land was drawn only from imagination because it had not yet been discovered. Whatever may have been the origin of these strange documents they presented no excuse whatever for the jealous, inaccurate, and imaginative Dalrymple's making unjust and baseless attacks on a great explorer who drew his place names from contemporary and well recorded events.

⁅ The international rivalry and academic theory which made further explorations advisable were reinforced by the great public interest aroused by the voyage of the *Endeavour*. Although Cook had followed Admiralty instructions and had collected at Batavia the private journals of his personnel, much information became public. A small anonymous journal, possibly by James Magra, was rushed out with a preface dated 28th September 1771, or only about two months after the *Endeavour* returned, while Cook himself wrote to John Walker of Whitby in 1770 and 1771 letters which described the voyage in part. Unfortunately, Lord Sandwich, at the Admiralty, and others, including Cook himself, considered that Cook's own journal with its nautical terminology and details; its abbreviations, and its chaotic spelling and punctuation, was unfit for publication, although we now realise that Cook's knowledge and vision, together with his seaman's outlook and turn of phrase, make his own journals the best account of his exploits. In view of contemporary opinion, however, the Cook and Banks papers were handed over to a Dr Hawkesworth, together with what was then a very large remuneration. Hawkesworth appears to have given more weight in his volume to the journals of the 'gentleman Joseph Banks Esquire' than to those of the unlettered sailor who commanded the expedition, and he not only weakened the primary accounts with his flamboyant style but added his own brief but sometimes inaccurate comments. Hawkesworth's volumes did not appear until 1773. Copies met Cook at St. Helena when he was returning home in 1775, and immediately involved him in trouble with the principal people of the island who were offended by Hawkesworth's account of Cook's previous visit. Hawkesworth himself did not survive to enjoy his financial gains for any length of time. Attacked by critics for follies such as the inclusion of his heterodox religious sentiments in Cook's work, he died in November 1773, possibly by his own hand. It was not until 1893, one hundred and twenty years later, that Admiral Wharton published a satisfactory edition of Cook's journal using the 'Mitchell' or 'Corner' copy, and the world has had to wait until 1955 for the production of Cook's holograph by the Hakluyt Society.

¶ Cook himself advocated a second voyage to solve the mystery of the Southern continent. There was no question as to the choice of leader, for My Lords Commissioners of the Admiralty extremely well approved the whole of his proceedings on the first voyage, and enough of the story had leaked out to make him embarrassingly famous with the public. The King himself was interested. He received Cook in August 1771, accepted a copy of his journal, and had him promoted Commander, a recognition too long overlooked. By September 1771 Cook could tell Walker that he was probably leading another expedition, this time of two ships. Towards the end of the year the Admiralty purchased, for reasons of safety, two Whitby colliers like the *Endeavour*, and, after renaming them the *Drake* and *Raleigh*, changed their names to *Resolution* and *Adventure* lest the Spaniards should resent the remembrance of two famous Elizabethan seadogs.

¶ Beaglehole has brilliantly portrayed the growth in wisdom and stature that Cook had achieved as a result of his explorations and their success. Prior to

1768 he had commanded only small crews, engaged largely on coastal surveys, and when he took command of the *Endeavour* he was a man of relatively slight education and of somewhat limited experience.

⁋ Now, however, good fortune gave him some years of close contact with Banks, Solander and other men of vision and ability and he possessed the genius to acquire scientific and other knowledge with the facility with which he had grasped mathematics. As Beaglehole says he led out his first expedition as 'a good sailor, a first rate marine surveyor and an able mathematician, and returned a great commander, a great discoverer, and a man with a greatly heightened sense of the scope of human thought'.

⁋ Banks also advocated a second voyage which he was so anxious to accompany that he spent the then large sum of £5,000 on equipment. Unfortunately the events which follow seem to indicate that the great scientific successes of the First Voyage rather turned his youthful head, as was not unlikely in view of the fact that various progress reports of the voyage mentioned only the 'scientific gentlemen' and completely ignored the unfortunate Cook. Whatever the cause, however, Banks, with the influence of Lord Sandwich, overlooked the fact that the major objective of the voyage was exploration, and attempted to rebuild the little *Resolution* as a species of floating laboratory and conservatorium for a growing retinue of scientific and musical experts. Cook handled a most difficult situation by a superb exhibition of silence and tact but, when a Trinity House pilot showed that this Banksian fantasy was dangerously unseaworthy even in the waters of the Thames estuary, Sir Hugh Palliser, Comptroller of the Navy, restored the *Resolution* to her former dimensions of 462 tons which was rather larger than the *Endeavour*. Banks was furious, and it is now known that he not only tried to persuade Sandwich to substitute a larger vessel, a frigate or an East Indiaman, although a vessel of this type could never have braved successfully the dangers surmounted by the *Endeavour* amongst the Barrier reefs, but even suggested that the Admiralty should put another commander in Cook's place. When the Navy Board stood firm Banks withdrew and took his scientific party to Iceland. Fortunately, although Banks never forgave Palliser, there was no serious breach between him and Cook.

⁋ Perhaps the most unfortunate result of the withdrawal of the scientists was the fact that the Admiralty appointed as naturalist John Reinhold Forster, a naturalised Prussian, querulous and unpleasant, who was accompanied by his son as Assistant. A parliamentary remuneration of £4,000 was colossal in comparison with the salary paid to Cook. Banks' artist, Zoffany, was replaced by William Hodges, who, although prone to clothe the Polynesians in classical garb, was a capable artist.

⁋ Very important was the fact that the party included two astronomers, Wales and Bayly, to whom was entrusted a most important object of the expedition, the further improvement of the means of recording longitude. Although Cook and Green had obtained some extremely satisfactory results on the *Endeavour* by lunar observations, accuracy was difficult to secure in bad weather and on heaving decks. Obviously the greatest hope lay in the chronometer, provided that clockmakers could produce a watch that could maintain the time at the prime meridian under any and all conditions of temperature and humidity. Cook was now to carry four chronometers, three made by Arnold and one by Larcum Kendall on the principles of John Harrison who had constructed four watches over a period of fifty years, and had won part of the £20,000 prize which the British Parliament had offered in 1714.

❨ The crews of the *Resolution* and *Adventure* were picked men, including a number who had sailed in the *Endeavour*. The *Adventure* was commanded by Lieutenant Tobias Furneaux, who had circumnavigated the globe with Wallis. Lieutenant Cooper of the *Resolution* was a fine officer while Clerke, Pickersgill and Edgecumbe had been promoted on the recommendation of Cook himself. The commander secured all the anti-scorbutic precautions of the previous voyage whose brilliant results had been clouded by the fact that the *Endeavour* had lost so many of her crew from land diseases. On this voyage there was to be no Batavia to cloak Cook's brilliant results.

❨ Dr Beaglehole has pointed out that Cook's high reputation in the experienced eyes of the Admiralty enabled him to plan and submit to the Board the instructions for the Second Voyage, which he conceived brilliantly. He proposed to use the westerly winds of the high southern latitudes to circumnavigate the Antarctic during two summers, sailing eastwards from Africa as Tasman had done and using the beloved base of Queen Charlotte Sound, New Zealand, as the point of refreshment between the winters. Moreover, as 'South lands of great extent' could still be found in the longitude of about 140° west he planned during the winter months to sweep northwards in the Pacific using Tahiti as a second base. The Mitchell Library, Sydney, now contains the memorandum and map of the proposed route which Cook submitted to Lord Sandwich, First Lord of the Admiralty, on 6th February 1772. The memorandum runs as follows:—

UPON due consideration of the discoveries that have been made in the Southern Ocean, and the tracks of the Ships which have made these discoveries; it appears that no Southern lands of great extent can extend to the Northward of 40° Latitude, except about the Meridian of 140° West, every other part of the Southern Ocean have at different times been explored to the northward of the above parallel. Therefore to make new discoveries the Navigator must Traverse or Circumnavigate the Globe in a higher parallel than has hitherto been done, and this will be best accomplished by an Easterly Course on account of the prevailing westerly winds in all high Latitudes. The principle thing to be attended to is the proper Seasons of Year, for Winter is

November 1771 by no means favourable for discoveries in these Latitudes; for which reason it is humbly proposed that the Ships may not leave the Cape of Good Hope before the latter end of September or begining of October, when having the whole summer before them may safely Steer to the Southward and make their way for New Zealand, between the parallels of 45° and 60° or in as high a Latitude as the weather and other circumstances will admit. If no land is discovered in this rout the Ships will be obliged to touch at New Zealand to recrute their water.

'From New Zealand the same rout must be continued to Cape Horn, but before this can be accomplished they will be overtaken by Winter, and must seek Shelter in the more Hospitable Latitudes, for which purpose Otahieta will probably be found to be the most convenient, at, and in its Neighbourhood the Winter Months may be spent, after which they must steer to the Southward and continue their rout for Cape Horn in the Neighbourhood of which they may again recrute their water, and afterwords proceed for the Cape of Good Hope.

'The Yellow line on the Map shews the track I would propose the Ships to make, Supposeing no land to intervene, for if land is discovered the track will be altered according to the directing of the land, but the general rout must be pursued otherwise some part of the Southern Ocean will remain unexplored.

⁋ We shall see that Cook resolutely and successfully followed this plan except that the circumnavigation of the Antarctic occupied the three winters of 1772–3, 1773–4, and 1774–5, while the two intervening summers of 1773 and 1774 enabled Cook to conduct two highly important sweeps of the South Pacific.

⁋ The printed addition of Cook's Journals of the Second Voyage was edited by Canon Douglas who, unlike Hawkesworth, gained Cook's approval. It is interesting to note, however, that, whereas the Douglas edition opens with an historical résumé of South Sea exploration, Cook's holograph found in the British Museum begins with a detailed account of the actions of Joseph Banks, who, as Cook says, would have caused the expedition 'to be laid aside' but for the loyalty and perseverance of Lord Sandwich and Hugh Palliser. As this text follows Cook's original journals as closely as possible this chapter opens with Cook's candid views on Banks which were omitted from the Douglas edition of the Journal.

NOVR. 28. 1771 TO JANRY. 2nd. 1773

NOVEMBER 28*th*. I received a Commission to command His Majestys sloop Drake at this time in the Dock at Deptford, Burdthen 462 Tons to be man'd with 110 Men including officers & to carry twelve guns: at the same time Captain Tobias Furneaux was appointed to the command of the Raleigh at Woolwich Burdthen 336 Tons 80 Men & ten guns. These two sloops were both built at Whitby by Mr Fisburn the same as built the Endeavour Bark, the

November 1771

former about fourteen and the latter eighteen months ago, and had just been purchased into the Navy from Cap[p]. William Hammond of Hull in order to be sent on discoveries to the South Sea under my directions. The Admiralty gave orders that they sould be fitted in the best manner possible, the Earl of Sandwich at this time first Lord intrested himself very much in the Equipment and he was well seconded by M[r] Palliser and S[r] J[no] Williams the one Comptroller and the other Surveyor of the Navy, the Victualling Board was also very attentive in procuring the very best of every kind of Provisions in short every department seemed to vie with each other in equiping these two Sloops: every standing Rule and order in the Navy was dispenced with, every alteration, every necessary and usefull article was granted as soon as ask'd for.

'Two days after I received my Commission I hoisted the Pendant and took charge of the Sloop accordingly and began to enter Seamen. The Vestal Frigate at this time in ordnary, was appoint to receive them untill the sloop came out of Dock.

'The Admiralty changed the sloops Names to Resolution and Adventure and the officers were order'd to take out new Comisions & Warrants accordingly.

'M[r] Banks and D[r] Solander who accompanied me in my last Voyage intended to embark with me in this in order to prosecute their discoveries in Natural History and Botany and other usefull knowlidge. For this purpose M[r] Banks intend to take with him several Draughtsmen &c[a]. The Board of Longitude also came to a Resolution to send out an Astronomer in each sloop to make Astronomical Observations and also to make tryal of M[r] Arnolds Watches and M[r] Kendals Timepiece which were intended to be sent out with them. The Parliament voted Four thousand pounds towards carrying on Discoveries to the South Pole, this sum was intinded for D[r] Lynd of Edinburgh as an incouragement for him to embark with us, but what the discoveries were, the Parliament meant he was to make, and for which they made so liberal a Vote, I know not. M[r] Zoffani the famous portrait painter was one of those who had engaged to accompany M[r] Banks. All these gentlemen except one Astronomer were to embark in the Resolution and to have large and seperate apartments: three of these gentlemen were not thought of when the sloop was purchased (viz.) the Astronomer, D[r] Lynd and M[r] Zoffani. The addition of these three persons intirely altered the plan of accommodations and it was found difficult to find room for the whole and at the same time to leave room for her officers and crew and stowage for the necessary stores and provisions, for this end the Navy Board was prevailed upon, tho contrary to the opinion of some of the members particularly the Comptroller, to alter their former plan which was to leave her in her original state and to raise her upper Works about a foot, to lay a spar deck upon her from the quarter deck to the forecastle (she having at this time a low waist) and to build a round house or couch for my accommodations so

November 1771

that the great Cabbin might be appropriated to the use of Mr Banks alone. Things being thus resolved upon they were carried into execution with all possible dispatch and were about finished by the 6th Febry following on which day we hauld out of the dry into the Wet Dock, and began to taken in Ballast, stores and to Rigg the masts &ca having by this time compleated our complement of men. . . . Mr Banks gave an entertainment on board to the Earl of Sandwich, the French Embassador Cont de Guines and several other persons of distinction. The[y] were complimented at their coming on board and going a shore with all the honours due to their high ranks. The Earl of Sandwich was so attentive to the equipment of these two sloops that he had honour'd us with his presence on board several times before in order to be an eye witness of their state and condition, a laudable tho rare thing in a first Lord of the Admiralty.

'In the night of the 7th Mr Sandford one of the Midshipmen fell out of the Launch, at this time lying along side of the Sheer hulk at Woolwich, and was unfortunatly drown'd, he was a young man of good parts and much esteem'd by the officers; some officious persons the next day inform'd Sr George Saville that James Strong one of the Seamen threw him overboard in consequence of which he was taken into custody, but upon examination this charge could not be proved and he thereupon was released, he however found means to escape from the officer who was sent to take him on board and we saw him no more.

'Captain Furneaux having received orders to proceed to Plymouth she sail'd accordingly, at the same time the Resolution had orders to proceed to the Downs under the direction of the first Lieutenent, I having obtain'd leave to be absent untill she arrived at that place, accordingly on the 10th in the morning they got under sail with a light breeze at North where it did not continue long before it came to the Eastward and obliged her to work down the River in which she made so little progress that it was the 14th before she reached the Nore, in this short passage she was found so crank that it was thought unsafe to proceed any further with her. This being represented to me with all its circumstances by Mr Cooper the first Lieutenant I laid the same before the Admiralty and seeing that it was absolutely necessary that something should be done to remove the evil complain'd of I proposed to cut down her poop, shorten her masts and to change her guns from six to four pounders; the Navy Board who was immediately consulted upon the matter, propos'd not only to cut down her poop, but to take of her spar deck, lower her waist and to reduce her as near to her original sate as could conveniently be done. Orders were now sent down for her to put into Sheerness where she anchored on the 18th and the officers of that yard received orders to cut her down agreeable to a Plan sent them by the Navy Board and which was confirmable to their proposals. While these matters were under consideration of the Admiralty and Navy Board others of a contrary nature were in aggitation by Mr Banks and his friends. As this gentleman seem'd not to approve of the Ship at the first he now used all his influence to have her condem'd as totally unfit for the service she was going upon and to have a 40 gun ship or an East Indiaman fitted out in her room, either of which would have been highly improper for making discoveries in remot parts. I shall not mention the arguments made use of by Mr Banks and his friends as many of them were highly absurd and advanced by people who were not judges of the subject one or two sea officers excepted who upon this occasion I believe sacrificed their judment in support of their friendship, or some other moutive. Be this as it may the clamour was so great that it was thought it would be brought before the house of commons. The Admiralty and Navy Board, however persevered in their resolution of clearing her of all her superfluous works and remain'd firm in their opinion that after this was done she would answer in every respect better then any ship the[y] could get. I was accordingly ordered to join her immidiately, to inspect into and forward these works and to point out such others as might tend to remove the evil complain'd of a piece of service I went the more readily about as having not the least doubt with my self but that I must succeed indeed I had it much at heart as she was the ship of my choice and as I then thought and still think the properest ship for the service she is intended for of any I ever saw. On the 20th I set out for Sheerness and arrived thier the same evening and found everything in great forwardness, the Poop and Spar deck was already taken away and Mr Huntt the Builder only waited to consult me about some little alteration he proposed to make in the waist from the Navy Boards Plan which the Board afterwards approved of. The next day I proposed to the Navy Board by letter to shorten her lower Masts two feet which they approved of and it was done accordingly. On Sunday 24th Mr Banks and Dr Solender came down to take a view of the Sloop as she was now altered and return'd to town again the same even^g^ and soon after Mr Banks declared his resolution not to go the Voyage, aledging that the Sleop was neither roomy nor convenient enough for his purpose, nor noways proper for the Voyage, these were the principal reasons Mr Banks assign'd for giving up a Voyage the preparing for which had cost him about five Thousand pounds, he probably had others which he did not care to declare, at least whoever saw the Sloop and the apartments that were alloted to him and his people could not help but think so. Be this as it may, not only Mr Banks and his whole suite but Dr Lind gave up the Voyage and their Baggage &c^a^ were got out of the Sloop and sent to London, after which no more complaints were heard for want of room &c^a^.

'On the 30th Mr Palliser Comptroller of the Navy paid us a Visit in order to inspect into the several alterations that had been and were still to make, for this gentleman had taken upon him in spite of all that had been alledged against her to make her compleatly fit not only for the sea but for the service she was intended for, indeed if his advice had not been over ruled at first a great deal of

November 1771 annoying trouble and expence would have been saved not only to the Crown but to Mr Banks and every other person concerned. . . .

¶ The departure of the expedition with exploration as its main objective, in spite of the misbehaviour of the influential Banks, was clearly a personal triumph for Cook, who had gained the loyal support, and indeed the deep admiration, of King George III, Lord Sandwich and Palliser. The strong pressure, which the last two could, and did, exert, is shown by their visits to the ships; the unique wage concessions to the crews, and the bountiful supply of scientific instruments and anti-scorbutics. By June 1772 Cook could write:

'Every thing being now nearly upon the point of finishing and having some business to settle in London I set out for that place in the Even[g] and upon my arrival learnt that M[r] John Reinhold Forster and his Son M[r] George Forster were to imbark with me, gentlemen skill'd in Natural history and Botany but more especially the former, who from the first was desireous of going the Voyage and therefore no sooner heard that M[r] Banks had given it up than he applyed to go. The Earl of Sandwich favoured his proposals which were approved of by His Majesty and a very handsome stipend allowed him and his son, their Baggage and other necessarys being sent on board and I having finished by Business in Town I on Sunday morn the 21st tooke leave of my Family and set out, in company with M[r] Wales the Astronomer for Sheerness where we arrived that evening and the next day sailed out of the Harbour. . . . The evening before we met between the Start and Plymouth Lord Sandwich in the Augusta Yacht, the Glory Frigate & Hazard Sloop. His Lordship was upon his return from visiting Plym[h] yard and where he had waited some days longer than he had occasion for my arrival, as soon as we joind this little squadron we saluted his Lordship with 17 guns, and soon after he and M[r] Palliser came on board. Their intintion for making us this Visit was to be informed personaly from me of the true state and quallities of the Sloop and which I was now well able to give them and so much in her favour that I had not one fault to alledge against her. So far from being crank I found her remarkably stiff and to work and sail better than could be expected from a ship of her burdthensome construction and at the same time deeply laden. Being able to give this information with so much Candor as could not be confuted they no doubt received great satisfaction therefrom. It is owing to the perseverance of these two persons that the expedition is in so much forwardness, had they given way to the general Clamour and not steadily adhered to their own better judgement the Voyage in all probability would have been laid aside. After a stay of something more than an hour they took their leave and we gave his Lordship three cheers at parting. . . . At Plymouth I received my Instruction the heads of which I had seen before I left London, indeed I was consulted at the time they were drawn up and nothing was inserted that I did not fully comprehend and approve of.

'The manner in which they (the ships) are victualed will best appear from the following account of Provisions which are now on board exclusive of what the officers have provided for themselves. *June* 1772

Quallity	Resolution	Adventure
Biscuit	59531 pounds	39990 } Pounds
Flour	17437 Do.	12767 } Pounds
Salt Beef	7637 four pd. pieces	4300 } pieces
Do. Pork	14214 two pd. pieces	8820 } pieces
Beer	19 Ton	30 Punch[n]
Wine	642 gallons	400 } Gallons
Spirit	1397 Do.	300 } Gallons
Pease	358 Bushels	216 Bushels
Wheat	188 Do.	820 } Gallons
Oatmeal	300 gallons	460 } Gallons
Butter	1963 } Pounds	1000 } Pounds
Cheese	797 } Pounds	1200 } Pounds
Sugar	1959 } Pounds	1441 } Pounds
Oyle olive	210 Galln[s]	237 } Gallons
Vinegar	259 Do	320 } Gallons
Suet	1900 } Pounds	1267 } Pounds
Raisins	3102 } Pounds	2776 } Pounds
Salt	101 Bush[l]	51 } Bushels
*Malt	80 Bushels	60 } Bushels
		T. Cwt. Q. lb.
*Sour Krout	19337 } Pounds	5 5 0 4
*Salted Cabbage	4773 } Pounds	1 16 1 0
*Portable Broth	3000 } Pounds	2000 } Pounds
*Saloup	70 } Pounds	47 } Pounds
*Mustard	400 } Pounds	300 } Pounds
*Mermalde of Carrots	30 gallons	22 gallons
Water	45 Tons	40 Tons
Experl Beef	1384 pounds	298 pieces 4 lb. each
Inspisated Juce of Beer	19 half Barrels	12 half Barrels

* The articles marked thus (*) are antiscorbuticks and are to be issued occasionally

June 1772 Besides the Provisions &c[a] mentioned above we have casks on board the two Sloops for the reception of about 4000 gallons of Madeira Wine which we intend to take in at that Island, so that upon the whole including what the officers and gentlemen had provided for themselves, we have full two years Provisions on board at whole allowance of most articles and of some much more and this exclusive of the antiscorbuticks before mentioned. We were also provided with M[r] Irvings apparatus for distillation by which we can at any time get a small supply of fresh Water from the Sea, in case we should be short of that article .... The Board of Longitude were not wanting on their part in providing the Astronomers with the very best of Instruments both for makeing Celestial and Nautical Observations but as the principal object these gentlemen are sent out upon is to ascertain the going of M[r] Kendall's Watch and three of M[r] Arnolds, they employed themselves during our stay at Plymouth in makeing the necessary Observations on Drakes Island—& at 7 o'Clock in ye even.g on the Friday before we departed the Watches were put in motion in the presence of myself Captain Furneaux, the first Lieutenant of each of the Sloops, the two Astronomers and M[r] Arnold and afterward put on board: M[r] Kendals and one of M[r] Arnolds on board the Resolution and the other two of M[r] Arnolds on board the Adventure: the Commander, First Lieutenant and Astronomer on board each of the Sloops had each of them Keys of the Boxes which containd the Watches and were allways to be present at the winding them up and comparing the one with the other.

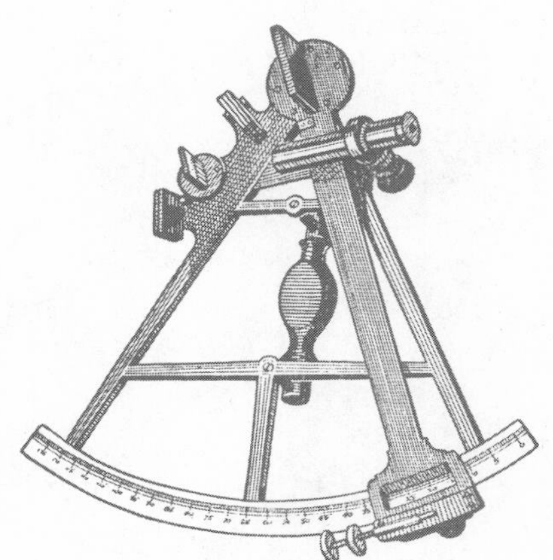

Chapter IX

THE ANTARCTIC, 1772-3

"No ship had ever before penetrated so far South, nor suffered such dangers from pack ice and floating islands."

J. C. BEAGLEHOLE ON COOK

COOK SAILED FROM PLYMOUTH ON 13TH JULY 1772; STOPPED for supplies at Madeira and Porto Praya and reached Cape Town without important incident on 30th October 1772. Several entries in the Journal indicate the stringent precautions which he enforced in order to preserve health.

SATURDAY 8*th* August. *Therm.* 78. *Latd. in North* 27° 7′. *Longd in West pr. Reck.g & Obsern* 19° 33′; *Pr. Kendalls Watch* 20° 3¼. Hazey weather with gentle gales. Made 3 Puncheons of Beer of the Inspissated juce, the proportion being about ten of Water to one of Juce; I have mentioned in the account of Provisions that we had 19 half Barrels of Inspissated Juce of Beer or Malt whereas only four were of Beer, the rest of Wort that was hopped before inspissated. Mr Pelham Secretary to the Commissioners of the Victualing having some years ago considered (and I think made tryal) that if the Juce of Malt, either made into Beer or Wort, was Inspissated by evaporation it would keep good a considerable length of time and by mixing it with Water a supply of Beer might at any time be had, several experiments were made last winter by Mr Pelham himself which so far promised success that the Commisrs caused the quantity before mentioned to be prepared and put on board the Sloops for tryal. . . . In the am Cleaned and smoaked the Sloop betwixt Decks.

THURSDAY 20*th* August. *Latd in North* 9° 17′. *Longd in Wt. pr. Reck.g & Obn.* 18° 55′. Gentle breezes and Dark gloomy hot weather and fair untill 4 o'Clock

August 1772 in the am when we had squals attended with showers of rain. At Noon it rain'd excessive hard. In the pm we had the misfortune to loose Henry Smock one of the Carpenters Mates, he was at work over the side fitting one of the Scuttles from whence we supposed he fell into the Sea for he was not seen untill the moment he sunk under the Stern when all assistance was too late.

THURSDAY 27*th* August. Spoke with the Adventure and Captain Furneaux inform'd us that one of his young Gentlemen was dead. At this time we have not one Sick on board.

FRIDAY 28*th* August. *Therm.* 77. *Latd in North* 3° 44′. *Longd in Wt. pr. Reck.g & Obsern* 11° 29′; *Kendalls Watch* 10° 21¼′. Got by the Still 14 gallons of Fresh Water from one Copper the time the Pease was boiling (viz) from half past 7 o'Clock in the Morning till Noon. Saw two Men of War Birds—and some Tropick Birds.

WEDNESDAY 9*th* September. Gentle gales and pleasent weather. In the PM after it was known that we were South of the Line or Equator, the ancient custom of Ducking, &c[a] was observed and in the evening the People were made not a little merry with the liquor given them by the Gentle[n]. on this occasion.

MONDAY 14*th* September. Capt[n]. Furneaux dine with me to day, a nother of his Midshipmen is dead. His crew are however healthy. At this time I have not one Sick on board.

SATURDAY 30*th* October. *Therm.* 61. *Winds NNW. Latd in South* 33° 53′. Fresh gales with rain in the night. At 2 p.m. Saw the land of the Cape of Good Hope, the Table Mountain which is over the Cape Town bore ESE Distant 12 or 13 Leagues. . . . At this time we have not one man on the Sick list. The People in general have injoy'd a good state of health ever since we left England. . . . During this stay the Crews of both Sloops were served every Day with new baked Bread fresh Beef or Mutton and as much greens as they could eat, they had also leave to go on shore 10 or 12 at a time to refresh themselves.

'Mess[rs]. Wales and Baily the two Astronomers were on Shore all the time makeing the necessary astronomical observations in order to ascertain the going of the Watches and other purposes. M[r] Kendalls Watch thus far has been found to answer beyond all expection but this cannot be said of Mr Arnolds. . . . However one of M[r] Arnolds on board the Adventure kept time in such a manner as not to be complained on. M[r] Forster met with a Swedish Gentleman here, one M[r] Sparman, who understood something of Botany and Natural History and who was willing to embarque with us, M[r] Forster thinking that he would be of great assistance to him in the Course of the Voyage strongly importuned me to take him on board which I accordingly did.

⁅ After taking in provisions at the Cape and hearing news of French expeditions which had been exploring to the south, Cook set sail towards the south-west at the end of November to search for Cape Circumcision, which was thought to be part of a continent, but which was really a small and barren island that the French explorer Bouvet had found. *November 1772*

TUESDAY *24th* November. *Latd in South* 35° 25′. *Longd in East of Greenwch* 17° 44′. Moderate gales and Clowdy Weather with a large swell from Southward. In the PM served to each Man a Fearnought Jacket and a pair of Trowers which were allowed by the Admiralty. Many Albatross about the Ship, some of which we caught with Hook and line and were not thought dispiseable food even at a time when all hands were served fresh Mutton.

SATURDAY *12th* December. *Latd in South* 52° 56′. *Longd in E. Greenwhich Reck.g* 20° 50′. Fresh gales and Hazy Foggy weather with sleet and snow. In the PM stood to the SW with the Wind at West & WNW which in the night veer'd to North at which time the Therm[r] was one degree below the Freezing point, kept on a wind all night under an easy sail and in the Morn made all the Sail we could and Steer'd SW with the Wind at NW. Pass'd Six Islands of Ice this 24 hours, some of which were near two Miles in circuit and about 200 feet high, on the Weather side of them the Sea broke very high, some Gentlemen on Deck saw some Penguins.

MONDAY *14th* December. *Therm. In the Night* 29. *Latd in South* 54° 55′. *Longd in E. Greenwhich Reck.g* 22° 13′, *Watch* 22° 1′. At half past six we were stopped by an immence field of Ice to which we could see no end. Over it, to the SWBS we thought we saw high land, but can by no means assert it. We now bore away SSE, SE & SEBS as the Ice trended, keeping close by the edge of it, where we saw many Penguins and Whales and many of the Ice Birds, small grey Birds and Pintadoes. At 8 o'Clock brot to under a Point of the Ice and sent on board for Captain Furneaux, fixed on Rendizvouze in case of seperation agreed on some other matters for the better keeping Company and after breakfast he return'd to his Sloop and we made sail along the Ice, but before we hoisted the boat in we took up several pieces which yeilded fresh Water, at Noon had a good observation both for determining the Latitude and Longitude by the Watch.

WEDNESDAY *16th* December. *Latd in South* 55° 8′. *Longd in Greenwich pr. Reck.g* 22° 45′. Very thick Foggy weather with Snow, so that we could do nothing but make short boards first one way and then a nother. Thermometer generally at the freezing point and some times below it, Rigging and Sails hung with Icikles. Many Whales playing about the Ship.

FRIDAY *18th* December. *Therm.* 31. *Latd in South* 54° 57′. *Longd in Greenwh pr. Reckg.* 24° 6′. The gale freshened and brought with it snow and sleet which freezed on our Rigging and Sails as it fell, the Wind however veer'd more & more to the NE which inabled us to clear the Field Ice, though at the same time it carried us a mong the Islands which we had enough to do to keep clear of. Of two evils I thought this the least. Dangerous as it is sailing a mongest the

December 1772 floating Rocks in a thick Fog and unknown Sea, yet it is preferable to being intangled with Field Ice under the same circumstances. The danger to be apprehended from this Ice is the geting fast in it where beside the damage a Ship might receive might be detaind some time. I have heard of a Greenland Ship lying nine Weeks fast in this kind of Ice and at present we have no more appearance of them than they can have in Greenland. On the Contrary Fahrenheits Thermometer keeps generally below the freezing point and yet it may be said to be the middle of summer. We have now sail'd 30 Leagues a long the firm Ice, which has extended nearly East and West, the Several Bays formed by it excepted, every one of which we have looked into without finding one open g to the South. I think it reasonable to suppose that this Ice either joins to or that there is land behind it and the appearance we had of land the day we fell in with it serves to increase the probability, we however could see nothing like land either last night or this Morn altho' the Weather was clearer than it has been for many days past. I now intend, after geting a few miles farther to the North, to run 30 or 40 Leagues to the East before I haul again to the South, for here nothing can be done.

SUNDAY 20*th* December. *Thermr.* 34. *Lat. in South* 54° 0′. *Longde in East pr. Reck.g* 28° 14′. In the PM had thick hazy Weather untill 6 o'Clock when it cleared up and continued so till 6 am when the gale freshend at NNE and brought with it hazey weather Sleet and Snow the Thermometer from 31° to 34. Ice Islands as usual of various extend both for height and circuit. Set all the Taylors to work to lengthen the Sleves of the Seamens Jackets and to make Caps to shelter them from the Severity of the Weather, having ordered a quantity of Red Baize to be converted to that purpose. Also began to make Wort from the Malt and give to such People as had symptoms of the Scurvy; one of them indeed is highly Scorbutick altho he has been taking of the Rob, for some time past without finding himself benifited therefrom, on the other hand the Adventure has had two men in a manner cured by it who came, even, from the Cape highly Scorbutick. Such a nother large brown bird or Albatross as we saw near the feild Ice I saw near the Ship last night: the Common sort of Albatross seem not to like an Icy sea for we have only seen one now and then sence we came a mong the Islands.

FRIDAY 25*th* December. *Thermr.* 31 *to* 35½. *Lat. in South* 57° 50′. *Longd. in East of Greenwich pr. Reck.g* 29° 32′. *Longd. from C.G.H.* 11° 9′. Gentle gales fair & Clowdy. Thermr. from 31 to 35. At 2 pm being near an Island of Ice which was about 100 feet high and four cables in circuit I sent the Master in the Jolly Boat to see if any Fresh Water run from it, he soon returned with an account that thier was not one Drop or the least appearance of thaw. From 8 to 12 am Sailed thro' several Floats or fields of loose Ice extending in length SE and NW as far as we could see and about 1/4 of a Mile in breadth, at the same time we had several Islands of the same composition in sight. At Noon seeing that the People were inclinable to celebrate Christmas Day in their own way, I brought the Sloops under a very snug sail least I should be surprised with a gale wind with a drunken crew, this caution was however unnecessary for the Wind continued to blow in a gentle gale and the Weather such that had it not been for the length of the Day one might have supposed themselves keeping Christmas in the Latitude of 58° North for the air was exceeding sharp and cold. *December 1772*

SATURDAY *26th* December. *Thermr.* 35 *to* 31. *Lat. in South* 58° 31′. *Longde. East of Greenwich Reck.g* 27° 37′. Fresh gales fair & Clowdy till towards Noon when it cleared up and we had a very good Observation; in the Course of this Days sail we passed thro Several Fields of Broken loose Ice all of which lay in the direction of NW to SE. The Ice was so close in one that it would hardly admitt of a Passage thro, the pieces of this Ice was from 4 to 6 or 8 Inches thick, broke into various sized pieces and heaped 3 or 4 one upon the other, it appeared to have been constituted from clear water which occasioned some on board to think that it came from some River. The Ice in some other of the loose feilds appeared like Corral Rocks, honey combed and as it were rotten and exhibited such a variety of figuers that there it not a animal on Earth that was not in some degree represented by it. We supposed these loose feilds to have broken from the large feild we had lately left and which I now determined to get behind, if possible, to satisfy myself whether it joined to any land or no. To Day we saw some of the White Albatross with black tiped Wings, some of the Smow birds or White Peterls, Blue Peterls &c[a] and a nother kind of a Peterls, which are a good deal like the Pintadoes, these as well as the White we have seen no where but a mong the Ice and but few at a time.

¶ At the beginning of January Cook reached the Longitude of Cape Circumcision, and, as he could not find Bouvet Island, thought that Bouvet must have been misled by the sight of ‘mountains of Ice’.

JANRY. 3rd. 1773 TO MAY 11th.

SUNDAY *3rd* January. *Lat. in South* 59° 18′. *Longde. in East of Greenwich pr. Reck.g* 11° 9′. We were now about 1½° or 2° of Longitude to the West of the Meridian of Cape Circumcision and at the going down of the sun 4° 45′ of Latitude to the Southward of it, the Weather was so clear, that Land even of a Moderate height might have been seen 15 Leagues, so that there could be no land betwixt us and the Latitude of 48°. In short, I am of opinion that what M[r] Bouvet took for Land and named Cape Circumcision was nothing but Mountains of Ice surrounded by field Ice. We ourselves were undoubtedly deceived by the Ice Hills the Day we first fell in with the field Ice and many were of the opinion that the Ice we run along join’d to land to the Southward, indeed this was a very probably supposition, the probability is however now very much

January 1773 lessened if not intirely set aside for the Distance betwixt the Northern edge of that Ice and our Track to the West, South of it, hath no where exceeded 100 Leagues and in some places not Sixty, from this it is plain that if there is land it can have no great extent North and South, but I am so fully of opinion that there is none that I shall not go in search of it, being now determined to make the best of my way to the East in the Latitude of 60° or upwards, and am only sorry that in searching after those imaginary Lands, I have spent so much time, which will become the more valuable as the Season advanceth. It is a general received opinion that Ice is formed near land, if so then there must be land in the Neighbourhood of this Ice, that is either to the Southward or Westward. I think it most probable that it lies to the West and the Ice is brought from it by the prevailing Westerly Winds and Sea. I however have no inclination to go any farther West in search of it, having a greater desire to proceed to the East in Search of the land said to have been lately discovered by the French in the Latitude of 48½° South and in about the Longitude of 57° or 58° East.

MONDAY 4*th* January. *Lat. in South* 58° 55′. *Long. in East of Greenwich per Reck.g* 14° 43′. First and middle parts strong gales attended with a thick Fogg Sleet and Snow, all the Rigging covered with Ice and the air excessive cold, the Crew however stand it tolerable well, each being cloathed with a fearnought jacket, a pair of Trowsers of the same and a large cap made of Canvas and Baize, these together with an additional glass of Brandy every Morning enables them to bear the Cold without Flinshing.

SUNDAY 10*th* January. *Lat. in South* 61° 58′. *Longd. in East pr. Reckg. Corrected* 36° 7′ *Watch* 35° 48′. Gentle gales, first part fair and Clowdy, remainder hazy with showers of snow. In the PM hoisted in the Boats after having taken up all the loose Ice with which our Decks were full; having got on board this seasonable supply of fresh Water, I did not hesitate one moment whether or no I should steer farther to the South but directed my course South East by South and as we had once broke the Ice I did not doubt of geting a supply of Water whenever I stood in need.

THURSDAY 14*th* January. *Lat. in South* 63° 57′. *Longde in East of Greenwich Reck.g* 39° 38½′ *Watch* 38° 35½′. Very gentle breezes of Wind with tolerable Clear and Serene Weather. We have now had five tolerable good Days succeeding one another, which have been usefull to us more ways than one; having on board plenty of Fresh Water or Ice which is the same thing, the People have had an opportunity to Wash and Dry their Linnen &c[a] a thing that was not a little wanting. . . . We are sure of finding a Ships place at sea to a Degree and a half and generally to less than a half a Degree. Such are the improvements Navigation has received from the Astronomers of this Age by the Valuable Table they have communicated to the Publick under the direction of the Board of Longitude contained in the Astronomical Ephemeris and the Tables for correcting the Apparent Distance of the Moon and a Star from the effects of Refraction and Parallax, by these Tables the Calculations are rendred short beyond conception and easy to the meanest capacity and can never be enought recommended to the Attention of all Sea officers, who now have no cause left for not making themselves acquainted with this useful and necessary part of their Duty. Much Credit is also due to the Mathematical Instrument makers for the improvements and accuracy with which they make their Instruments for without good Instruments the Tables would loose part of their use.

January 1773

☾ On 17th January they crossed the Antarctic Circle, being, as Cook said, 'the first and only Ship that ever crossed that line'. The crews of both sloops were in good health in spite of the hardship and cold, while the ice was at least providing the adequate supplies of fresh water that were so essential to Cook's use of anti-scorbutics.

SUNDAY *17th* January. *Thermr.* 34. *Lat. in South* 66° 36½′. *Longde. in E. Greenwich* 39° 35′. In the AM had hazy weather with Snow Showers and saw but one Island of Ice in the Course of these 24 hours so that we begin to think that we have got into a clear Sea. At about a 1/4 past 11 o'Clock we crossed the Antarctic Circle for at Noon we were by observation four Miles and a half South of it and are undoubtedly the first and only Ship that ever cross'd that line. We now saw several Flocks of the Brown and White Pintadoes which we have named Antarctic Petrels because they seem to be natives of that Region; the White Petrels also appear in greater numbers than of late and some few Dark Grey Albatrosses, our constant companions, the Blue Petrels have not forsaken us but the Common Pintadoes have quite disappeared as well as many other sorts which are Commin in lower Latitudes.

MONDAY *18th* January. The Ice was so thinck and close that we could proceed no further but were fain to Tack and stand from it. From the mast head I could see no thing to the Southward but Ice, in the whole extent from East to WSW without the least appearance of any partition, this immense Feild was composed of different kinds of Ice, such as high Hills or Islands, smaller pieces packed close together and what Greenland men properly call field Ice, a piece of this kind of such extend that I could see no end to it, lay to the SE of us, it was 16 or 18 feet high at least and appeared of a pretty equal height. I did not think it was consistant with the safty of the Sloops or any ways prudent for me to persevere in going farther to the South as the summer was already half spent and it would have taken up some time to have got round this Ice, even supposing this to have been practicable, which however is doubtfull. The Winds Continued at East and EBS and increased to a strong gale attended with a large Sea, hazy weather Sleet and Snow and obliged us to close reef our Topsails.

TUESDAY *2nd* February. *Lat. in South* 48° 36′. *Longde. in East* 59° 35′ *Watch* 59° 33′. Hazey Clowdy weather and a fresh gale at NW with which we stood

February 1773 NEBN till 4 o'Clock in the PM when being in the Latitude of 48° 30′ S. and nearly in the Meridian of the Isle of Mauritius where we were to expect to find the Land said lately to have been discovered by the French, but seeing nothing of it we bore away East and made the Signal to the Adventure to keep on our Starboard beam at 4 miles distance. In this manner we proceeded till half past Six o'Clock when the Adventure made the Signal to speak with me, we accordingly shortn[d] sail, bro[t] to to wait for her to come up, when Captain Furneaux informed us that they just had seen a large Float of Sea or Rock Weed and several Birds (Divers) about it. This was certainly a great sign of the vicinity of land but wheather it laid to the East or West was not possible for us to know.

SATURDAY *6th* February. *Thermr.* 43¾. *Lat. in South* 48° 6′. *Longd. in East Reck.g* 58° 22′ *Watch* 58° 32′. In the pm had a fresh gale and fair weather, at 6 o'Clock the Variation was 30° 26′ W. We continued our Course to the North and NE till 4 o'Clock am, by which time the Wind had veered to North, we Tacked and stood West with a fresh gale attended with rain. At 10 o'Clock the Wind veered back again to WNW I now gave over all thoughts of beating any longer against it and bore away East a little Southerly all sails set. Indeed I had no sort of incouragement to proceed farther to the West as we have continually a long heavy Swell from that quarter which made it very improbable that any large land lay to the West.

SUNDAY *7th* February. At 4 o'Clock made the Signal for the Adventure to keep at the Distance of 4 miles on our Starboard beam. Having fair and clear weather, I had all the peoples Bedding &c[a] upon deck to air a thing that was absolutely necessary.

⁅ Cook now sailed eastwards and in February was in the Southern Indian Ocean but passed about midway between Kerguelen and the Crozet Islands which the French had seen. On 9th February the *Resolution* lost sight of the *Adventure* in foggy weather. Contact was not re-established, and the two vessels followed different tracks to New Zealand.

TUESDAY *9th* February. The Thick Foggy Weather continuing and being apprehensive that the Adventure was still on the other Tack, we at 2 pm, after being run 2 Leagues to the West, made the Signal and Tacked to which we heard no Answer, we now continued to afire a gun every half hour. . . . We still continued to fire half our guns and the Fogg dissipated at times so to admit us to see two or three Miles or more round us, we however could neither hear nor see any thing of her. Being now well assured that a Separation had taken place I had nothing to do but to repair to the place where we last saw her, Captain Furneaux being directed to do the same and there to cruze three days.

WEDNESDAY *10th* February. Having now spent two Days out of the three assigned to look for each other, I thought it would be to little purpose to wait any longer and still less to attempt to beat back to the appointed station well-knowing that the Adventure must have been drove to leeward equally with ourselves. I therefore made sail to the SE with a very fresh gale at WBN accompanied with a high Sea, many dark grey Albatrosses, Blue Petrels and Sheerwaters about the Ship but only two or three divers were seen and not one Penguin.

February 1773

SATURDAY 13*th* February. The meeting with so many of these Birds gave us still some hopes of meeting with land and various were the oppinions among the officers of its situation. Some said we should find it to East others to the North, but it was remarkable that not one gave it as his opinion that any was be found to the South which served to convince me that they had no inclination to proceed any farther that way. I however was resolved to get as far to the South as I conveniently could without loosing too much easting altho I must confess I had little hopes of meeting with land, for the high Swell or Sea which we have had for some time from the West came now gradually round to SSE so that it was not probable that any land was near between these two points and it is less probable that land of any extent can lie to the North as we are not above 160 Leagues South of Tasmans track and this space I expect Captain Furneaux will explore, who I expect is to the North of me.

WEDNESDAY 24*th* February. *Lat. in South* 61° 21′. *Longd. in East Reckg.* 95° 15′. At noon we were about 6 or 7 miles East of the place where we last saw the Adventure and could see 3 or 4 Leagues round us, by this time the wind had increased so as to oblege us to take in our Topsails & the Sea began to rise from the same quarter, we still continued to see Penguins & divers which made us conjecter that land was not far off.

'Under these circumstances and surrounded on every side with huge pieces of Ice equally as dangerous as so many rocks, it was natural for us to wish for daylight which when it came was so far from lessening the danger that it served to increase our apprehensions thereof by exhibiting to our view those mountains of ice which in the night would have been passed unseen. These obstacles together with dark nights and the advanced season of the year, discouraged me from carrying into execution a resolution I had taken of crossing the Antarctick Circle once more. According at 4 o'Clock in the AM we Tacked and Stood to the North under our two Courses and double reefed Topsails, stormy Weather still continuing which together with a great Sea from the East, made great distruction among the Islands of Ice. This was so far from being any advantage to us that it served only to increase the number of pieces we had to avoide, for the pieces which break from the large Islands are more dangerous than the Islands themselves, the latter are generally seen at sufficient distance to give time to steer clear of them, whereas the others cannot be seen in the night or thick weather till they are under the Bows: great as these dangers are they are now become so very familiar to us that the apprehensions they cause are never

February 1773 of long duration and are in some measure compencated by the very curious and romantick views many of these Islands exhibit and which are greatly heightned by the foaming and dashing of the waves against them and into the several holes and caverns which are formed in the most of them, in short the whole exhibits a View which can only be discribed by the pencil of an able painter and at once fills the mind with admiration and horror, the first is occasioned by the beautifullness of the Picture and the latter by the danger attending it, for was a ship to fall aboard one of these large pieces of ice she would be dashed to pieces in a moment.

SUNDAY 28*th* February. *Thermr.* 36½. *Lat. in South* 59° 58′. *Longd. in East Reck.g* 104° 44′. In the pm the gale abated and the Wind veered to SSW and SWBS. Hazey weather with sleet continued till 8 o'Clock in the am when it became fair and tolerable clear, at day light in the morn got Topg^{n} yards across and set all the sail we could, having a fine fresh gale and but few Islands of Ice to impede us, the late gale having probably distroyed great numbers of them. A large hollow sea hath continued to accompany the Wind that is from the East round by the South to SW, so that no land can be hoped for betwixt these two extreme points. We have a breeding sow on board which yesterday morning Farrowed nine Pigs every one of which were killed by the cold before 4 o'Clock in the afternoon notwithstanding all the care we could take of them, from the same cause People on board have their feet and hands chilblain'd, from the circumstances a judgement may be formed of the summer weather we injoy here.

TUESDAY 16*th* March. *Thermr.* 32 *to* 35½. *Lat. in South* 58° 52′. *Longd. in East Reck.g* 143° 27′. The same Weather continued till the evening when it cleared up and became fair and the Wind veered back to SE, we nevertheless had a long hollow swell from WSW such as assured us we had left no land behind us in that direction.

❡ Cook now continued eastwards in high latitudes to the south of Australia, and, although he wished to settle the question of whether or not Van Diemen's Land (Tasmania) was an island, decided that he must at once refresh his crew in Southern New Zealand where he sought Dusky Bay, partly for immediate refreshment and partly to see if it would provide an adequate harbour in this region. This fortunately proved to be the case as an abundance of wild fowl, seals and fish, together with spruce beer fortified the general health.

WEDNESDAY 17*th* March. *Thermr.* 33 *to* 35½. *Lat. in South* 58° 40′. *Longd. in East Reck.g* 147° 43′. We continued to steer to the East inclining a little to the South till 5 o'Clock in the am at which time we were in the Latitude of 50° 7′ S Long^{g} 146° 53′ E. We then bore. away NE and at Noon steer'd North inclining to the East with a resolution of making the best of my way to *New Holland* or *New Zealand*, my sole motive for wishing to make the former is to inform myself whether or no Van Diemens Land makes a part of that continent. If the reader of this Journal desires to know my reasons for taking the resolution just mentioned I desire he will only consider that after crusing four months in these high Latitudes it must be natural for me to wish to injoy some short repose in a harbour where I can procure some refreshments for my people of which they begin to stand in need of, to this point too great attention could not be paid as the Voyage is but in its infancy. *March 1773*

FRIDAY *26th* March. Intending to put into *Dusky Bay* or any other Port I could find on the Southern part of *New Zealand*, we steered in for the land under all the Sail I could set . . . and entred Dusky Bay about Noon in the mouth of which we found 44 fathom water, a Sandy Bottom, the West cape bearing SSE and the North point of the Bay North, here we found a vast swell roll in from the SW, tho Water Shoalden'd to 40 f^m^, after which we had no ground with 60, we were however too far advanced to return and therefore pushed on not doubting but what we should find anchorage, for in this Bay we were all strangers, in my last Voyage I did no more than discover it.

SATURDAY *27th* March. After runing about two Leagues up the Bay without find^g^ Anchorage and having pass'd come of the Islands which lie in it, I brought to, hoisted out two Boats and sent one of them with an officer round a point on the Larboard hand and upon her making the Signal for anchorage we followed with the Ship and came to an Anchor in 50 f^m^ water so near the shore as to reach it with a hawser after having been 117 Days at Sea in which time we have Sailed [3660] Leagues without once having sight of land. I cannot however help thinking but that there is some near the Meridian of the Mauritius and about the Latitude of 49° or 50° which I have been unfortunate enough not to find, at least the many Penguins and Divers we saw there seemed to indicate as much, but I shall refer making my remarks on this subject till I join the Adventure which cannot be far off if not already in *Queen Charlottes Sound* provided she has met with nothing to retard her. It may be asked why I did not proceed directly for that place as being the Rendesvouze. The Discovery of a good Port in the Southern part of this Country and to find out its produce were objects more intresting, it is quite immaterial whether the Adventure joins us now or a Month or two hence. Mention has already been made of sweet wort being given to the Scorbutick People; the Marmalade of Carrots alone was also given to one man and we found that both had the desired effect in so much that we have only one man on board that can be called ill of this disease and two or three more on the Sick list of slight complaints.

'My first care after the Ship was moored was to send a Boat & People afishing, in the mean time some of the gentle^m^ went in a Boat to a rock a small distance from the ship on which were many Seals, one of which they killed which afforded us a fresh Meal.

March 1773 SUNDAY 28*th* March. In the PM hauled the Sloop into a small creek and moored her head and Stern to the Trees and so near the Shore as to reach it with a Brow or stage which nature had in a manner prepared for us by a large tree which growed in a horizontal direction over the Water so long that the top of it reached our gunwale. Wood for fuel was here so convenient that our Yards were locked in the branches of the trees, about one hundred yards from our stern was a fine stream of fresh Water and every place abounded with excellent fish and the shores and Woods we found not distitute of wild fowl, so that we expected to injoy with ease what in our situation might be call'd the luxuries of life. The few sheep and goats we had left were not likely to fair quite so well here being neither pasture nor grass to eat but what is course and harsh, nevertheless we were supprised to find that they would not eat it as they had not tasted either grass or hay for these many Weeks past, nor did they seem over fond of the leaves of more tender plants and shrubs, upon examination we found their teeth loose and that many of them had every symptom of an inveterate Sea Scurvy; out of four Ewes and Two Rams I brought from the Cape with an intent to put ashore in this Country or any other I might have found, I have only been able to preserve one of each and even they are in so bad a state that it is doubtfull if they may recover.

THURSDAY 1*st* April. Little Wind and tolerable fair. Began to cut down Wood for fuel, got our empty casks ashore to fill with Water and to repair such as were in want of repair, set up the Forge to repair our Iron Work and put the Sail-makers to Work upon the Sails all of which were absolutely necessary occupations. Also began to Brew Beer with the leaves and branches of a tree which resembles the Americo black Spruce Inspissated Juce of Wort and Melasses; now I have mentioned the Inspissated Juce of Wort it may not be a miss to inform the reader that I have made several trials of it since we left the Cape of Good Hope and find it to answer in a cold climate beyond all expectation.

SUNDAY 11*th* April. Rain continued all the PM but the Morning was clear and Serene which afforded an opportunity for us to dry our linnen a thing very much wanting not having had fair weather enough for that purpose since we put into this Bay. Mr Forster and his party profited by the day in Botanizing. About 10 o'Clock the family of the Natives paid us a visit, seeing that they approached the Ship with great caution I met them in my Boat which I quited and went into their Canoe, nevertheless I could not prevail upon them to put along side the Ship and was at last obliged to leave them to follow their own inclinations; at length they put ashore in a little creek hard by us and afterwards came and sat down on the shore abreast of the Ship near enough to speak to us. I caused the Bagpipes and fife to be played and the Drum to be beat, this last they admired most, nothing however would induce them to come on board but they entered with great familiarity into conversation with such of the

IN PICKERSGILL HARBOUR
NEW ZEALAND

officers & Seamen as went to them and paid a much greater regard to some more than others and these we had reason to believe they took to be Women, to one man in particular the Girl showed an extraordinary fondness untill she discovered his sex and then she would not suffer him to come near her, whether it was because that she before realy took him for a Woman or that the Man had taken some liberties with her which she thus resented I know not. *April 1773*

☾ Cook was delighted with Dusky Bay, a safe harbour in an area which provided refreshment, and whose inhabitants were a small group of not unfriendly Maoris. After a fortnight spent on refitting he sailed northwards to Queen Charlotte Sound, where, as he expected, the *Adventure* was anchored.

TUESDAY 11*th* May. As there is no Port in New Zealand I have been in that affords the necessary refreshments in such plenty as Dusky Bay, and altho' in (it) lies far remote from the trading part of the World, nevertheless a short account of the adjacent Country and a discription of the Bay may not only be acceptable to the curious reader but may be of use to some future Navigators for we can by no means tell what use future ages may make of the discoveries made in the present. The north entrance of this Bay is situated on the North side of *Cape West* in the Latitude of 45°. South, it is formed by the Cape to the South and Point five fingers to the North, this point is remarkable by several peaked rocks lying off it, the land of this point is still more remarkable by the little Similarity it bears to the lands adjacent being a narrow Peninsula lying north and South of a moderate height and covered with Wood. To sail into this Bay is by no means difficult as I know of no danger but what shows it self. The worst that attends it is the depth of Water which is too great to admit of Anchorage except in the Coves or Harbours and near the Shores and even in many places this last is not to be done, the Anchoring places are however numerous enough and equally safe and commodious. . . . The Inhabitants of this Bay are of the same race as those in the other parts of this Country, speak the same language and observe nearly the same customs; these indeed whether from custom or a more generous disposition make you presents before they receive any, in this they come nearer to the Otaheitians than the rest of their Country men. What could induce three or four families to seperate themselves so far from the Society of the rest of their fellow creatures is not easy to guess, by our meeting with Inhabitants in this place makes it probable that there are Inhabitants in most of the Bays and harbours in the Southern parts of this Island, the many vestigias we saw of People in different parts of this Bay indicates that they live a wandering life never remaining long in one spott, and if one can judge from appearences & circumstances few as they are they live not in perfect amity one family with another for if they do why do not they form themselves into some society a thing not only natural to Man but is even observed by the brute creation.

May 1773 'If the Inhabitants of Dusky Bay feel at any time the effects of cold they never can that of hunger, as every corner of the Bay abounds with fish, the Coal fish (as we call it) is here in vast plenty, is larger and better flavoured than I have any where tasted, nor are there any want of Craw and other shell fish, Seals are also here in Plenty, they chiefly inhabit the Rocks & small Isles which lie near the Sea, the flesh of many of them we found excellent eating, not a bit inferior to the finest Beef Stakes and the Harslets of them all are little inferior to a Hogs. The Wild fowl are Ducks, Shaggs, Cormorrants, Oyster Catchers or Sea pies, Water or wood Hens, which are something like our English Kails, these inhabit the Skirts of the Woods and feed upon the Sea beach they are very like a Common Hen and eat very well in a Pye or Fricasee, they are so scarce in other parts of New Zealand that I never saw one but at this place. Albatroses, Gannets, Gulls, Penguins and other aquatick birds, the Land fowl are Hawks, Parrots, Pigeons and such other birds as are common to this country. The flax plant is as common here as in any other part of New Zealand and the natives apply it to the same use, in generally the produce of the land is much the same with this difference that there is not so great a variety. Mention hath already be made of our having seen a quadruped, it is to be wished we could have given some better account of it as it is more than probable that it is of a new species: we are however now certain that this Country is not so clear of these sort of animals as was once thought. The most mischievous animal here is the small black sandfly which are exceeding numerous and are so troublesome that they exceed everything of the kind I ever met with, wherever they light they cause a swelling and such an intolerable itching that it is not possible to refrain from scratching and at last ends in ulcers like the small Pox. The almost continual rain may be reckoned a nother ilconveniency attending this Bay but perhaps this may only happen at some seasons of the year, yet the situation of the Country, vast height and nearness of the Mountains seem to subject it to much rain at all times. Notwithstanding our people were continually exposed to the rain yet they felt no ill effects from it, on the contrary such as were sick or ailing when we arrived recovered strength daily and the whole crew became strong and vigorous.

'I have already made mention of our brewing Beer which we at first made with a decoction of the leaves of the spruce tree mixed with Inspissated juce of Wort and Mellasses but finding that the decoction of Spruce alone made the Beer to astringent we mixed with it an equal quantity of the Tea plant which partly distroyed the Astringency of the other and made the Beer exceeding Palatable and esteemed by every one on board.

Chapter X
SEARCHING THE PACIFIC, 1773

"In the evening we all returned aboard everyone highly dilighted . . . the friendly behaver of the Natives who seem'd to [vie] with each other in doing what they thought would give us pleasure."

COOK ON THE FRIENDLY ISLANDS, 1773

AS EXPECTED COOK FOUND THE 'ADVENTURE' AT THE rendezvous, Queen Charlotte Sound, where she had been waiting for some six weeks while Cook had been risking the dangers of the Antarctic with a single ship. Both as an explorer and a commander Furneaux cuts a somewhat sorry figure beside Cook. Having visited Tasmania after the vessels were separated Furneaux now gave Cook information which led the latter to conclude, somewhat unwisely, that Tasmania was part of the Australian continent. Even more serious was the fact that Furneaux's slackness in enforcing Cook's unpopular precautions against scurvy exposed the crew of the *Adventure* to ill health and rendered them a drag on the expedition. Cook did his best to meet the situation by going ashore, discovering anti-scorbutic plants and ordering their use on both vessels, although he added what for him was an unusually sarcastic comment that his orders were at any rate enforced in his own sloop.

MAY 12*th*. Having quited Dusky Bay as has been already mentioned I directed my Course along shore for Queen Charlottes Sound having a gentle breeze at SE and South with fair weather.

TUESDAY 18*th* May. At Daylight in the Morn we were the length of Point Jackson at the entrance of Queen Charlottes Sound and soon after we discovered the Adventure in Ship Cove by the Signals she made, what little wind we had was out of the Sound so that we had to work in, in the doing of which we discovered a rock which we did not see in my last voyage. . . . A little while

May 1773 before we anchored Captain Furneaux came on board and informed me that he arrived here on the 7th of Apr[l] having first touched at Van Diemens Land.

WEDNESDAY 19*th* May. I have some were in this Journal mentioned a desire I had of Visiting Vandiemens land in order to inform my self whether or no it made a part of New Holland, but sence Captain Furneaux hath in a great degree cleared up this point I have given up all thoughts of going thither, but that I might not Idle away the whole Winter in Port I proposed to Captain Furneaux to spend that time in exploring the unknown parts of the Sea to the East and North, acquainting him at the same time with the rout I intended to take and the time I meant to spend in this cruse. To this proposition he readily agreed; and in concequence thereof I desired him to get his Sloop ready for sea as soon as possible for at this time she was striped. Knowing that sellery and Scurvey grass and other vegetables were to be found in this Sound and that when boiled with Wheat or Pease and Portable Soups a very nourishing and wholesom Diet which is extremely beneficial both in curing and preventing the Scurvey, I went my self at day light in the Morn in search of some and returned by breakfast with a board load and having satisfied my self that enough was to be [had] I gave orders that it should be boild with Wheat or Oatmeal and Portable Soup for the Crew of both Sloops every morning for breakfast and also with Pease every day for dinner and I took care that this order was punctually complied with at least in my sloop. . . . Now I have had the perusal of Captain Furneaux's Journal it is necessary to mention before I proceed with our transactions in this place, such general remarks as hath occur'd to me and not before taken notice of. My reason for quiting the high Latitudes in the latter end of January and Steering to the North was to search for the land said to have been lately descovered by the French; what Am I now to think of that land? I cannot suppose as some doth that the whole is a fiction, no, if I had had no such information the several Signs of land we met with in the neighbourhood would have induced me to believe that there is land, the small divers which we saw there, which Captain Furneaux calls Dip Chicks, we have no where else met with but on the Coast of New Zealand, these therefore must be looked upon as signs of the Vicinity of land without paying any regard to Penguins and Seals which are everywhere to be found, it is nevertheless certain that it can only be an Island and one of very small extent unless it lies to the West of the Longitude of 57°. there indeed is room for a pretty large land as will more fully appear by the Chart. If the French have really made the descovery they will no doubt make it Publick and then this point will be cleared up, it was not my business to spend much time in search of an Island I was not sure existed, the discovery of a Southern Continent is the object I have in view, besides at that time it was just as probable that I should meet with it to the East or South as any other way; I shall now drop this subject and follow Captain Furneaux to Van Diemens

Land in which rout he seems to have met with nothing remarkable. . . . *May* When they hauld up for New Zealand they were in the Latitude of 39° 20′ at 1773 that time they saw land from the mast head bearing NNW distant by estimation 12 Leagues and is distant from Point Hicks, the most Southern part of my discovery, 17 or 18 Leagues and about the same distance or some thing more from the northern point of Furneaux's Islands; it is therefore highly probable that the whole is one continued land and that Van Diemens Land is a part of New Holland, the Similarity of the Countrys Soil Produce Inhabitants &c[a] all serve to increase the probability. The direction of the Coast from the Southermost of Marias Islands down to the Northermost land is nearly North and lies under the Meridian of 148° 06′ East. Captain Furneaux had no intercourse with the Natives, nor did he I believe see any, but he saw many of their fires and some of their hutts, the same Custom of burning the Country prevails here as in *New South Wales*, upon the whole, by what I can learn, the account I have given of the Southern parts of this last Country in my former Voyage will convey a very good Idea of Van Diemens land, which I have now done with and shall return to our transactions in Queen Charlottes Sound.

❨ At Queen Charlotte Sound relations with the Maoris continued, on the whole, to be friendly, and efforts were made to introduce useful animals and plants.

THURSDAY *20th* May. This morning I put ashore at the Watering place near the Adventure's Tent, a Ewe and a Ram (the only two remaining of those I brought from the Cape of Good Hope) untill I found a proper place to put them a shore for good for my intention was to leave them in this Country, at the same time I visited the different Gardens Captain Furneaux and his officers had planted with garden seeds roots &c[a] all of which were in flourishing condition and if improved or taken care of by the natives might prove of great use to them.

FRIDAY *21st* May. My self with a party of men employed digging up ground on Long Island, which we planted with several sorts of garden seeds and return'd on board in the evening with a quantity of selery and scurvy grass. Some hands a Shore cuting Wood & filling Water.

SATURDAY *22nd* May. Some hands employed Wooding and Watering, Lieu[t] Pickersgill with the Cutter collecting Selery and Scurvy grass, M[r] Forster and his party Botanizing, and my self accomp[d] by Captain Furneaux out in the Pinnace a Shooting.

SUNDAY *23rd* May. Last Night the Ewe and Ram I had with so much care and trouble brought to this place, died, we did suppose that they were poisoned by eating of some poisonous plant, thus all my fine hopes of stocking this Country with a breed of Sheep were blasted in a moment. Towards noon we were visited for the first time by some of the Natives, & they stayed and dined with us and it was not a little they devoured, they were dismiss'd in the evening Loaded with presents.

June 1773 TUESDAY *1st* June. This morning I went over to the East side of the Sound accompanied by Captain Furnequx and Mr Forster, then I put a Shore two Goats male and female, the latter was old but had two fine Kids, some time before we arrived in *Dusky Bay*, which were both kill'd by the cold as I have already mentioned, the male was some thing more than twelve months old: Captain Furneaux hath put a Shore in Canibals Cove a Boar and a Breeding Sow so that we have reason to hope that in process of time this Country will be stocked with Goats and Hoggs; there is no great danger that the Natives will destroy them as they are exceedingly afraid of both, besides as they have not the least knowledge of them being left, they will grow so Wild before they are discovered as not to suffer any one to come near them.

WEDNESDAY *2nd* June. The Goats will undoubtedly take to the Mountains and the Hoggs to the Woods where there is plenty of food for both.

THURSDAY *3rd* June. Yesterday morning a Man brought his Son a boy about 10 years of age and presented him to me and as the report was then currant I thought he wanted to sell him, but at last I found out that he wanted me to give him a Shirt which I accordingly did the Boy was so fond of his new dress that he went all over the Ship presenting himself to every boddy that came in his way, this liberty of the Boy offended old Will the Ram Goat who up with his head and knock'd the boy backwards on the Deck, Will would have repeated his blow had not some of the people got to the boys assistance, this misfortune however seem'd to him irrepairable, the Shirt was dirted and he was afraid to appear in the Cabbin before his father untill brought in Mr Forster, when he told a very lamentable story against Goure the great Dog, for so they call all the quadrupeds we have aboard, nor could he be pacified untill his Shirt was wash'd and dry'd. . . . A trade soon Commenced between our people and these, it was not possible to hinder the former from giving the clothes from of their backs for the merest trifles, things that were neither usefull nor curious, such was the prevailing passion for curiosities, and caused me to dismiss these strangers sooner than I would have done. When they departed they went over to Moutara where, by the help of our Glasses we discover'd four or five more Canoes and a number of people on the Shore, this induced me to go over in my boat accompanied by Mr Forster and one of the Officers, we were well received by the Chief and the whole trib[l]e which consisted of between 90 & 100 people Men Women and Children, having with them Six Canoes and all their utensils which made it probable that they were come to reside in this Sound, but this is only conjector for it is very common for them when they even go but a little way to carry their whole property with them, every place being equally alike to them if it affords the necessary subsistance so that it can hardly be said that they are ever from home, thus we may easily account for the migration of those few small families we found in *Dusky Bay*. Living thus dispersed in small parties knowing no head but the chief of the family or tribe whose authority may be very little, subjects them to many inconveniences a well regulated society united under one head or any other form of government are not subject to, these form Laws and regulations for their general security, are not alarm'd at the appearance of every stranger and if attack'd or invaded by a publick enimy have strong holds to retire to where they can with advantage defend themselves, their proper[i]ty & their Country, this seems to be the state of most of the Inhabitants of *Eahei nomauwe*, whereas those of *Tavai pocnammoo*, by living a wandering life in small parties are distitute of most of the advantages which subjects them to perpetual alarms, and we generally find them upon their guard travelling and working as it were with their Arms in their hands even the Women are not exempted from carrying Arms as appear'd at the first interview I had with the family in Dusky Bay when each of the two Women were Arm'd with a Spear not less than 18 feet in length.

June 1773

(As noted above, when the *Resolution* arrived Furneaux was preparing to spend the winter in Queen Charlotte Sound, a course by no means palatable to his energetic Commander, who decided to seek a continent eastwards of New Zealand in Latitudes 41 to 46 South. For this purpose he was able to use the westerly winds and sail south of the course followed in 1769 when he had used the easterly winds further north to sail from Tahiti to New Zealand.

'Both Sloops being now ready to put to Sea I gave Captain Furneaux an account in writing of the rout I intended to take which was to proceed immidiately to the East between the Latitude of 41° and 46° untill I arrived in the Longitude of 140° or 135° East and then, providing no land was discovered, to proceed to *Otaheite*, from thence to return back to this place by the Shortest rout, and after taking in wood and Water to proceed to the South and explore all the unknown parts of the Sea bet^{n} the Meridian of New Zealand and Cape Horn and therefore in case of seperation before we reach'd Otaheite I appointed that Island for the place of Rendezvouz where he was to wait untill the 20th of Augt. Not being join'd by me before that time he was then to make the best of his way back to Queen Charlottes Sound and there remain untill the 20th of Novr after which he was to put to Sea & carry into execution their Lordships Instructions. It may be thought by some an extraordinary step in me to proceed on discoveries as far South as 46° in the very depth of Winter for it must be own'd that this is a Season by no means favourable for discoveries. It nevertheless appear'd to me necessary that something must be done in it, in order to lessen the work I am upon least I should not be able to finish the discovery of the Southern part of the South Pacifick Ocean the insuing Summer, besides if I should discover any land in my rout to the East I shall be ready to begin with the Summer to explore it, seting aside all the considerations, I have little to fear, having two good Ships well provided and healthy crews.

June 1773 'During our short stay in this Sound I have observed that this Second Visit of ours hath not mended the morals of the Natives of either Sex, the Women of this Country I always looked upon to be more chaste than the generality of Indian Women, whatever favours a few of them might have granted to the Crew of the Endeavour it was generally done in a private manner and without the men seeming to intrest themselves in it, but now we find the men are the chief promoters of this vice, and for a spikenail or any other thing they value will oblige[d] their Wives and Daughters to prostitute themselves whether they will or no and that not with the privacy decency seems to require, such are the concequences of a commerce with Europeans and what is still more to our Shame civilized Christians, we debauch their morals already too prone to vice and we interduce among them wants and perhaps diseases which they never before knew and which serve only to disturb that happy tranquillity they and their fore Fathers had injoyed. If any one denies the truth of this assertion let him tell me what the Natives of the whole extent of America have gained by the commerce they have had with Europeans.

TUESDAY *8th* June. To day when we attended the Winding up of the Watches the fusee of Mr Arnolds would not turn round and after several unsuccessful tryals we were obliged to let it go down, this is the second of this gentlemans Watches that hath faild, one of these on board the Adventure stop'd at the Cape of Good Hope and hath not gone sence.

TUESDAY *22nd* June. *Therm.r* 48 *to* 50. *Lat. in South* 44° 41′. *Long. in West Reck.g* 162° 39′ *Watch* 162° 47′. Gentle breezes and pleasent weather. A very great Swell from the South such as makes it probable that no land can be near in that direction at least not on this side of 50° Latitude.

☾ By mid July Cook had sailed eastwards to and beyond Longitude 130 west keeping, despite the winter, in Latitudes for the most part south of Latitude 40. On 17th July he turned northwards towards Pitcairn Island, which had been discovered by Captain Carteret in 1767, and which lay about half way between New Zealand and South America. In spite of winter weather he had now proved that no continent lay approximately north of Latitude 40° south in this area.

SATURDAY *17th* July. *Lat. in South* 39° 44′. *Long. in West Reck.g* 133° 32′. First part Strong gales and fair weather, the latter Squally showers of rain. At 4 pm close reef'd the Top-sails and handled the Mizen Top-sail. In the Morning loosed them out again but was obliged to reef again before Noon at which time we had run down the whole of the Longitude I at first intended and being nearly midway betwixt my trip to the north in 1769 and return to the South the same year as will appear by the Chart, I steer'd N1/2E having the Advantage of a strong gale at SSW, with a view of exploring that part of the Sea between the two tracks just mentioned down as low as the Latitude of 27° S in which space no one has been that I know of. A Great Swell from SW.

July 1773

℄ The importance of seeking refreshment in warmer seas was increased by a severe outbreak of scurvy on the *Adventure* when the cook died and twenty men became sick, whereas the *Resolution* had at the time only one case of scurvy, and a few men whose symptoms were suspicious. Cook crossed to the *Adventure* and gave Furneaux written proposals as to the use of anti-scorbutics, but, in the circumstances, he passed some fifteen leagues west of Pitcairn and by various other islands, without halting, until, on 15th August, his old love Tahiti lay in sight. Her greeting was, however, far from loving, as a dead calm surrendered the sloops to currents which very nearly wrecked them on the island reefs.

THURSDAY *29th* July. *Lat. in South* 27° 30′. *Long. in West Reck.g* 136° 14′. Gentle breezes with some Showers in the night. Stood to the Westward till 4 AM when we Tacked to the NE being then in Latitude 27° 49′. Being a fine day I hoisted a boat out and sent aboard the Adventure to inquire into the state of her crew when I learnt that her cook was dead and about Twenty more were attacked with the Scurvy and Flux; at this time we had only three men on the Sick list and only one of them of the Scurvy, several more however began to shew some symptoms of it and were accordingly put upon the Wort, Marmalade of Carrots, Rot of Lemons and Oranges. I appointed one of my people Cook of the Adventure and wrote to Captain Furneaux proposing such methods as I thought would tend to stop the spreading of the disease among his people. The methods I proposed were to Brew Beer of the Inspissated juce of Wort, Essence of Spruce and Tea plant (all of which he had aboard) for all hands, if he could spare Water, if not, for the Sick, to inlarge their allowance of Sour Krout, to boil Cabbage in their Pease, to serve Wine in lieu of Spirit and lastly to shorten their allowance of Salt Meat. Swell from WSW.

MONDAY *2nd* August. *Therm.r* 68. *Lat. in South* 23° 14′. *Longde. in West Reck.g* 134° 6′. First part fresh gales and Clowdy remainder gentle breeze and clear weather. Being in the Latitude of *Pitcairn* Island discovered by Captain Carteret in 1767 we looked out for it but could see no thing excepting two Tropick Birds, we undoubtedly left this Island to the East of us. Having now crossed or got to the north of Captain Carteret's Track, no discovery of importance can be made, some few Islands is all that can be expected while I remain within the Tropical Seas. As I have now in this and my former Voyage crossed this Ocean from 40° South and upwards it will hardly be denied but what I must have formed some judgement concerning the great object of my researches, viz. the Southern Continent. Circumstances seem to point out to us that there is none, but this is too important a point to be left to conjector, facts must determine it and these can only be had by viseting the remaining unexplored parts of this Sea which will be the work of the remaining part of this voyage. I shall now collect into one View such general remarks as hath occured to me since we left New Zealand. After leaving the Coast we dayly saw Rock Weed floating

August *1773* in the Sea for the space of 18° of Longitude. In my passage to New Zealand in 1769 we saw the same sort of Weed and in greater quantities between the Latitudes of 37° and 39° for the space of 12° or 14° of Longitude before we discovered the land, this Weed is undoubtedly the produce of New Zealand because the nearer we are to this Coast the greater is the quantity of weed we see, what we see at the greatest distance in (is) always in small pieces and generally covered with Barnacles and rotten; it was necessary to mention this otherwise conjectors might arise that some other large land lay in this neighbourhood. I say large land because it cannot be a small extent of Sea Coast than (that) can produce such a quantity as to spread over such a large space of Sea. After leaving the land we continued for some days to have a large hollow [swell] from the SE untill we arrived in the Latitu[de] of 46° Longed. 177° W where we had large billows from the North and NE and which continued for the space of 5° of Longitude more to the East altho the wind generally blue from a contrary direction, this was a Strong indication that there was no land between us and my Track to the West in 1769. In short the wind never blew a fresh gale but what it brought before it a long hollow swell which never ceased with the wind which first put it in motion, which plainly showed that we were never in the neighbourhood of any large land and this opinion I hold to this hour for this day at Noon we had a large western swell higher than usual which convinced me that there was no land between us and my former Track to the South from which we were distant 230 Leagues.

WEDNESDAY 11*th* August. *Lat. in South* 17° 18′. *Long. in West Reck.g* 142° 3′ *Watch* 142° 29′. Gentle gales and fair weather. At 6 o'Clock in the morning land was seen to the Southward, we soon discovered it to be an Island about 2 Leagues in extent NW to SE. low and cloathed with wood above which the Cocoa-nutts shew'd their lofty heads. I believe it to be one of the Isles discovered by M[r] de Bougainville (Latitude 17° 24′ Longitude 141° 39′ West). The Scorbutic state of the Adventure's Crew made it necessary for me to make the best of my way to Otaheite where I was sure of finding refreshments for them, concequently I did not wait to examine this Island which appear'd too small to supply our wants.

SATURDAY 14*th* August. At 5 o'Clock in the pm saw land extending from WSW to SW dis[r] 3 or 4 Leagues. I judged it to be Chain Island discovered in my last Voyage. Fearing to fall in with some of these low Islands in night and being desirous of avoiding the delay which lying too occasions I hoisted out the Cutter, equiped her properly and sent her a head to carry a light with proper signals to direct the Sloops in case she met with danger, in this manner we proceeded all night without meeting with any thing, at 6 in the morning I called her on board and hoisted her in as it did not appear that she would be wanted again for this purpose, as we had now a large swell from the South a sure indication that we were clear of the low Islands.

SUNDAY 15*th* August. *Lat. in South* 17° 45′. *Long. in West Reck.g.* 148° 16′ *Watch* 148° 34′. Gentle breezes and pleasant weather. At 5 am saw Osnaburg Island bearing SBW1/2W. At 9 o'Clock I sent for Captain Furneaux on board to acquaint him that I intended to put into Oaiti-piha Bay in the SE end of Otaheite in order to get what refreshment we could from that part of the Island before we went down to Matavai Bay. At Noon Osnaburg Island bore ESE distent 5 or 6 Leagues. Swell from the Southward still continues. *August 1773*

'At 6 PM saw the Island of Otaheite extending from WBS to WNW distant about 8 Leagues. We stood on till midnight then brought too till 4 o'Clock when we made sail in for the land. I had given directions in what posision the land was to be kept but by some mistake it was not properly attended to for when I got up at break of day I found we were steering a wrong course and were not more than half a league from the reef which guards the South end of the Island. I immidiately gave orders to haul off to the Northward and had the breeze of wind which we now had continued we should have gone clear of every thing but the wind soon died away and at last flatened to a Calm. We then hoisted out our Boats but even with their assistance the Sloops could not be kept from nearing the reef, but the current seem'd to be in our favour, we were in hopes of geting round the point of the reef into the Bay. At this time many of the natives were on board the Sloops and about them in their canoes, bring off with them some fruit and fish which they exchanged for Nails, Beads, &c[a].

TUESDAY 17*th* August. About 2 o'Clock in the PM we came before an opening in the reef by which I hoped to enter with the Sloops as our situation became more and more dangerous, but when I examined the natives about it they told me that the Water was not deep and this I found upon examination, it however caused such an indraught of the Tide as was very near proving fatal to both the Sloops, the Resolution especially, for as soon as the Sloops came into this indraught they were carried by it toward the reef at a great rate; the moment I preceived this I order'd one of the Warping Machines which we had in readiness to be carried out with about 3 or 4 hundred fathoms of rope to it, this proved of no service to us, it even would not bring her head to Sea. We then let go an anchor as soon as we could find bottom but by such time as the Ship was brought up she was in less then 3 fathom water and Struck at every fall of the Sea which broke with great violence against the reef close under our stern and threatened us every moment with shipwreck, the Adventure anchored close to us on our starboard bow and happily did not touch. We presently carried out a Kedge Anchor and a hawser and the Coasting Anchor with an 8 inch Hawser bent to it, by heaving upon these and cuting away the Bower Anchor we saved the Ship; by the time this was done the current or Tide had ceased to act in the same direction and then I order'd all the Boats to try to tow off the Resolution, as soon as I saw it was practical we hove up the two small anchors. At that moment

August 1773 a very light air came of from the land which with the assistance of the Boats by 7 o'Clock gave us an offing of about 2 Miles and I sent all the Boats to the assistance of the Adventure, but before they reached her she had got under sail with the land wind, leaving behind her three anchors, her coasting Cable and two Hawsers which were never recovered: thus the Sloops were got once more into safety after a narrow escape of being Wrecked on the very Island we but a few days ago so ardently wished to be at. We spent the night making short board and in the morning stood in for Oaiti-piha Bay where we anchored about Noon in 12 fathom water about 2 Cables length from the shore and moor'd with our stream anchors, both Sloops being by this time surrounded by a great number of the natives in their Canoes, the[y] brought with them Cocoa-nutts, Plantans, Bananoes, Apples, Yams and other roots which they exchanged for Nails and Beeds. To Several who call'd themselves *arree's* (Chiefs) I made presents of Shirts, Axes and various other articles and in return they promised to bring me Hogs and Fowls, a promise they neither did nor never intended to perform.

TUESDAY *24th* August. In the Morning I put to Sea with a light land breeze which soon after we got out came to the Westward and blew in Squals attended with heavy showers of rain. I left Lieutenant Pickersgill with the Cutter in the Bay to purchase Hogs as several had been promised to day. Many Canoes followed us out to Sea with Cocoa-nutts and other fruits and did not leave us till they had disposed of their cargoes. The fruits we got here contributed greatly towards the recovery of the Adventures Sick many of whom were so weak when we put in as not to be able to get on deck without assistance were now so far recovered as to be able to Walk about of themselves, they were put ashore under the care of the Surgeons mate every morning and taken aboard in the evening. When we put in here the Resolution had only one Scorbutic person on board and a Marine that had been long ill and who died the 2nd day after our arrival of a complication of disorders without the least touch of the Scurvy.

THURSDAY *26th* August. At 4 o'Clock in the PM we anchored in Matavai Bay after which I sent our Boats to assist the Adventure who got in about two hours after. At the time we anchored many of the natives came of to us, several of whom I knew and almost all of them me, a great crowd were got together on the Shore.

❨ Cook spent only seventeen days in Tahitian anchorages finishing at Fort Venus. The Tahitians, particularly some of his 'old friends', were kind and hospitable, but the islanders had suffered from internecine warfare, while the visit of Spanish vessels seems to have introduced or increased exotic disease.

WEDNESDAY *1st* September. The Sick being all pretty well recovered, our Water Casks repaired and fill'd and the necessary repairs of the Sloops compleated I determined to put to sea without Loss of time, accordingly I ordered everything to be got off from the Shore and the Sloops to be unmoor'd. . . . We will now leave the Sloops proceeding for the Island of Huaheine and take a short view of Otaheite. Soon after our arrival we were informed that a Ship about the sieze of the Resolution Commanded by one Opeppe had put into OWhaiurua Harbour near the Sound end of the Island, various were the accounts the natives gave us concerning this Ship, from what I could learn she stayed here about three Weeks, that she had been gone near three when we arrived . . . probably this was one of the two French Ships that were fited out at the Mauritius and touched at the Cape of Good Hope in March 1772 in their way to this Sea having Aotourou on board the man Mr Bougainville took from this Island and who died while the Ships lay at the Cape as was reported, be this as it may we are sure that he is not return'd and now seems to be quite forgot by his Countrymen as well as Tupia who came away much later.

'This fine Island which in the years 1767 and 8 swarmed as it were with Hogs and Fowls is now so scarce of these Animals that hard[l]y any thing will induce the owners to part with them, the few that are now remaining seem in a great measure to be at the disposal of the King, for while we lay in Oaiti-piha Bay in the Kingdom of Tearrabou and at any time saw a Hog they never fail'd to say it belonged to Oheatooa, the same while we lay in Matavai in the Kingdom of *Opoureonu* they there all belonged to [Otoo]. During the Seventeen days we were at the Island we got but 25 Hogs and one Fowl, half the Hogs were had from the two Kings and I believe most part of the other half were sold us by their permission. We were however abundantly supplyed with all the fruits the Island produceth, except Bread fruit of which we got but little this not being the Proper season for it. I every day had a trading party on Shore by which means we got sufficient for present consumption and to take to Sea. The scarcity of Hogs and Fowls may be owing to two causes, first to the number which have been consumed and carried off by the Shiping which have touched here of late years and secondly by their frequent wars which not only distroy great numbers but does not allow time to breed others. Two distructive Wars hath happen'd between the two Kindoms sence the year 1767, at present they are at Peace but doth not seem to entertain much friendship for each other. I never could learn the cause of the late War or how [who] got the better in the conflict in the Battle which I think put an end to the dispute, many were kill'd on both sides. . . . The Veneral disease which was so common in this Isle in the year 1769 is now far less so, they say they can cure it and it fully appears so for altho most of our people made pritty free use of their Women and these of the common sort, very few of them were affected by this disease in both Sloops and this in such a gentle manner as was easy to remove. They complain of a disease communicated to them by Opeppe's Ship (as they say) they told us that it affected the head, Throat and Stomach and at last kills them, they dread it much and

September 1773 constantly enquiring if we had it, they call it by the name of the communicator Apo na Peppe. I am however of opinion that it was some epidemical disease that broke out among them at the time the Ship was there without her contributing in the least towards it. Some of our people pretend to have seen some who have had the Pox in a high degree.

☾ Cook left Tahiti, on 2nd September 1773, and sailed westwards to other Society Islands where the inhabitants knew him and welcomed him warmly, although the usual thieving incidents occurred, and two natives assaulted a naturalist, Mr Sparman, possibly because he unknowingly violated some tabu.

THURSDAY *2nd* September. After leaving the Bay of Matavai as before mentioned I directed my course for the Island of *Huaheine* and at 6 o'Clock the following evening we were wit^h^ two or three Leagues of its northern point where we spent the night laying too and making short boards, and on Friday morning at day light made sail round the point for the Harbour Owharre where we anchored at 9 o'Clock in 24 fathom water, as the wind blew out of the Harbour I choose to turn in by the Southern Channell, the Resolution turn'd in very well, but the Adventure missing stays got a shore on the reef on the north side of the Channell.

FRIDAY *3rd* September. I had the Resolutions Launch in the Water ready in case of an axcedent of this kind, and sent her immidiately to the Adventure by this timely assistance she was got off without receiving any damage. As soon as the Sloops were in safety I landed and was received by the natives with the utmost cordiality.

SUNDAY *5th* September. Early in the morning Oree made me a visit accompanied by some of his friends, he brought me a present of a Hog and some fruit for which I made him a suitable return, this good old Chief never faild to send me every day for my Table the best of ready dress'd fruit and roots and in great plenty. Lieu^t^ Pickersgill was again detached to the South end of the Island with both Cutter and Launch, he returned the same day with Twenty-eight Hogs and about four times as many more were got ashore and along side the Sloops.

MONDAY *6th* September. In the morning I sent the tradeing party a shore as usual and after breakfast went my self when I found that one of the natives had been a little troublesome, this fellow being pointed out to me compleatly equiped in the War habit with a club in each hand, as he seem'd to be intent on Mischief I took from him the two clubs and broke them and with some difficulty forced him to retire from the place, they told me that he was an Aru which made me the more suspicious of him and occasioned me to send for a guard which before I had thought unnecessary. About this time Mr Sparman being out alone botanizing was set upon by two men who striped him of everything he had but his Trowsers, they struck him several times with his own hanger but

September 1773

happily did him no harm, as soon as they had accomplished their end they made off after which a man came to him, gave him a piece of cloth to cover himself and conducted him to me. I went immidiately to Oree to complain of this outrage takeing with me the man who came back with Mr Sparman to confirm the complaint, as soon as the Chief heard it he wept a lowd as did several others and after the first transports of his grief was over expostulated with the people shewing them how well I had treated them both in this and my former voyage or some thing to this purpose, he then promised to do all in his power to recover what was taken from Mr Sparman. . . . We immidiately imbarqued in the Boat in order to go aboard without so much as asking the Chief to accompany us, he however insisted on going with us in spite of the opposition he met with from those about him, his Sister followed his example contrary to the tears and intreaties of her Daughter a young woman about 16 or 18 years of age. The Chief sit at table with us and made a hearty meal, his Sister sit behind us as it is not the custom for the Women to eat with the men. After dinner I made them both presents and in the Evening carried them a shore to the place w[h]ere I first took him in where some hundreds waited to receive him many of whom imbraced him with tears of joy in their eyes, all was now harmony and Peace. . . . Oree and I were profess'd friends in all the forms customary among them and he had no idea that this could be broke by the act of any other person, indeed this seem'd to be the great Argument he made use on to his people when they opposed his going into my boat, his words were to this effect: Oree (for so I was always called) and I am friends, I have done nothing to forfeit his friendship, why should I not go with him. We however may never meet with another chief who will act in the same manner on any similiar occasion.

TUESDAY *7th* September. Early in the morn we began to unmoor, while this was doing I went to take my leave of the chief accompanied by Captain Furneaux and Mr Forster. I took with me such things for a present as I knew were most useful and valuable to him. I also left with him the Inscription plate he had before in keeping and another small copper plate on which was engraved these words: Anchor'd here His Britannic Majesty's Ships Resolution and Adventure September 1773, together with some Midals all put up in a Small Bag, the chief promised to take great care of the whole and to produce them to the first Ship that should come to the Isle. He next gave me a Hog and after trading for six or eight more and loading the boat with fruit we took leave at which the good old Chief embraced me with Tears in his eyes. At this interview nothing was said about the remainder of Mr Sparmans Clothes. I judged they were not brought in and for that reason did not mention them least I should give the chief pain about a thing I did not give him time to recover. When I came aboard I found the Sloops crowded round with Canoes full of Hogs, Fowls and Fruit as at our first arrival.

September 1773 ℭ On 18th September 1773 Cook left the Society Islands in order to check native reports that to the westward lay islands which Cook believed must include Amsterdam Island, discovered by Tasman in 1643. The result was the rediscovery of the very delightful Friendly Islands with their fertile soil and charming inhabitants of whom Cook gave a long and interesting account.

SEPTR. 18TH 1773 TO FEBRY. 6TH 1774

SATURDAY 18*th* September. *Lat. in St.* 17° 17′ *W. Longd. Greenwich pr. Reck.g.* 153° 10′. Having left Ulietea as before related, I directed my Course to the West inclining to the South as well to avoid the tracks of former Navigators as to get into the Latitude of Amsterdam Island discovered by Tasman in 1643, my intention being to run as far west as that Island and even to touch there if I found it convenient before I proceeded to the South. In the PM we saw the Island of Maurua, one of the Society Isles bearing NBW distant 10 Leagues.

FRIDAY 24*th* September. At 2 o'Clock pass'd the Land above mentioned at the distance of one League which proved to be three small Islands connected together by a reef of rocks in which they were incircled and which might be about 18 miles in circuit. They are low and cloathed with wood among which the Cocoa-nutt trees were the most conspicious, we saw no people or signs of inhabitants. I named them Sandwich in honour of my noble Patron the Earl of Sandwich. Latitude 19° 18′ S. Longitude 158° 54′ West. Having no time to loose to attempted(ed) a landing altho' this seemed Practical on the NW side, we reassumed our Course to the West. In the night had a few hours Calm which was succeeded by a fresh trade wind at SE attended with some showers of rain.

SATURDAY 2*nd* October. *Winds Easterly*. Fresh gales and fair Weather. At 2 pm Saw the Island of Middleburg bearing WSW. At 6 o'Clock we were about 12 miles from the East side the extream bearing from SWBW to NW and another land bearing NNW. at this time we hauled to the Southward in order to get round the South end of the Island. At 8 o'Clock we discovered a small Island lying WSW from the South end of Middleburg, not knowing but these two Islands might be connected to each other by a reef the extent of which we might be ignorant of and in order to guard against the worst, we haul'd the wind and spent the night making short boards under an easy sail. . . . Soon after we had come to an Anchor, I went a Shore with Captain Furneaux and some of the officers and gentlemen, having in the Boat with us Tioonee who conducted us to the proper landing place where we were welcomed a shore by acclamations from an immence crowd of Men and Women not one of which had so much as a stick in their hands, they crowded so thick round the boats with Cloth, Matting, &c[a] to exchange for Nails that it was some time before we could get room to land, at last the Chief cleared the way and conducted us up to his house which was situated hard by in a most delightfull spot, the floor was laid with

Matting on which we were seated, the Islanders who accompanied us seated themselves in a circle round the out sides. I ordered the Bag-pipes to be pla(y)ed and in return the Chief ordered three young women to Sing a Song which they did with a very good grace. When they had done I gave each of them a necklace, this set most of the Women in the Circle a Singing, their songs were musical and harmonious, noways harsh or disagreeable. . . . Captain Furneaux and I were conducted to the Chiefs house where we had fruit brought us to eat, afterwards he accompanied us into the Country through several Plantations Planted with fruit trees, roots, &c[a] in great tast and ellegancy and inclose by neat fences made of reeds. In the lanes and about their house were runing about Hogs and large fowls which were the only domistick Animals we saw and these they did not seem desireous to part with, nor did they during this day offer to exchange any fruit or roots worth mentioning, this determined me to leave the Island in the morning and go down to that of Amsterdam where Tasman in 1643 found refreshments in plenty. In the evening we all returned aboard every one highly dilighted with his little excursion and the friendly behaver of the Natives who seem'd to [vie] with each other in doing what they thought would give us pleasure.

SUNDAY *3rd* October. As soon as I was aboard we bore away for the Island of Amsterdam all sails set, we ran a long the South Side of the Isle half a mile from shore and had an opportunity with the assistance of our glasses to view the face of the Country every acre of which was laid out in Plantations, we could see the natives in different parts runing a long the shore, some having little white flags in their hands which we took for signs of Peace and answered them by hoisting a S[t] Georges Ensign. . . .

MONDAY *4th* October. After breakfast I went a shore with Captain Furneaux, M[r] Forster and several of the officers, a chief or man of some note to whom I had made several presents was in the Boat with us, his name was Hātago by which name he desired I might be called and he by mine (Otootee) we were lucky in having anchored before a narrow creek in the rocks which just admitted our Boats within the breakers where they laid secure and at high water we could land dry on the shore; into this place Hatago conducted us, there on the shore an immense crowd of men Women and children who welcomed us in the same manner as those of Middleburg and were like them all un arm'd. All the officers and gentlemen set out into the Country as soon as we land, excepting Captain Furneaux who stayed with me on the shore, we two Hatago seated on the grass and ordered the People to set down in a circle round us which they did, never once attempting to push themselves upon us as the Otahieteans and the people of the neighbouring Isles generally do. After distributing some trifles among them we signified our desire to see the Country, this was no sooner done than the chief shewed us the way, conducting us along a lane which led us to an open

October 1773 green on the one side of which was a house of Worship built on a Mount which had been raised by the hand of Man about 16 or 18 feet above the common level. . . . After we had [d]one examining this place of worship which in their Language is called *Afiā-tou-ca*, we desired to return, but instead of conducting us directly to the Water side they struck into a road leading into the Country, this road which was a very publick one, was about [15] feet broad and as even as a B[owling] green, there was a fence of reeds on each side and here and there doors which opened into the adjoining Plantations several other Roads from different parts joined this, some equally as broad and others narrower, the most part of them shaded from the Scorching Sun by fruit trees, I thought I was transported into one of the most fertile plains in Europe, here was not an inch of waste ground, the roads occupied no more space than was absolutely necessary and each fence did not take up above 4 Inches and even this was not wholy lost for in many of the fences were planted fruit trees and the Cloth plant, these served as a support to them, it was every were the same, change of place altered not the scene. Nature, assisted by a little art, no were appears in a more florishing state than at this Isle. In these delightfull Walks we met numbers of people some were travering down to the Ships with their burdthens of fruit, others returning back empty, they all gave us the road and either sit down or stood up with their backs against the fences till we had passed. . . . As soon as dinner was over we all went a shore again were we found the old Chief who presented me with a Hog and he and some others took a Walk with us into the Isle, our rout was by the first mentioned Afiā-tou-ca before which we again seated our selves, but had no praying on the contrary here the good natured old Chief interduced to me a woman and gave me to understand that I might retire with her, she was next offered to Captain Furneaux but met with a refusal from both, tho she was neither old nor ugly, our stay here was but short. The Chief probably thinking that we might want water on board the Sloops conducted us to a Plantation hard by and there shewed us a pool of fresh Water without our making the least enquiry after such a thing. I believe it to be the same as Tasman calls the Washing place for the King and his nobles.

WEDNESDAY *6th* October. My friend Otago visited me this morning as usual, brought with him a Hog and assisted me in purchasing several others, after this I wint a shore, visited the old Chief where I stayed till noon and then returned aboard to dinner with my friend who never quited me.

THURSDAY *7th* October. Otago was very desirous for me to return again to the isle and to bring with me Cloth, Axes, Nails &c[a] telling me that I should have Hogs, Fowls, Fruit and roots in a bundance, he particularly desired me to bring him such a sute of Cloths as I had then on and which was my uniform. This good natured Islander was very serviceable to be (me) on many occasions, during our short stay he constantly came aboard every Morning soon after it was light

October 1773

and never quited me during the remainder of the day, he was always ready either a board or a shore to do me all the service that lay in his power, his fidelity was rewarded a small expense and I found my account in having such a friend. . . . At 10 o'Clock we got under sail but as our decks were very much lumbered with fruit &c^a we kept plying with our Topsails under the land till they were cleared. The Supplies we got at this Island were about 150 Pigs, double that number of fowls, Bananas and Cocoa-nutts as many as we could dispence with and a few yams and, had we stayed longer we might no dought have got a great deal more, this in some degree shews the fertillity of the isle which together with the neighbouring isle of Middleburg I shall now give a more particular account of. These Islands were first discovered by Captain Tasman in Janr^y 1643 who named them Amsterdam and Middleburg, but the former is called by the Natives *Ton-ga-tabu* and the latter *Ea-ōō-we*. . . . The Island of Tango-tabu and the skirts of Ea-oo-we are as I have before observed wholy laid out in Plantations in which are some of the richest Productions of Nature, in these plantations are the greatest part of the Houses of the Inhabitants built with no other order than conveniency requires, paths leading from one to a nother and publick lanes which (which) open a free communication to every part of the Island.

'The Chief Productions of these isles are Cocoa-nutts, Bread fruit, Plantains or Bananas, Shaddocks, Lemons, a fruit like an Apple called by them Fezhega and in Otaheite Aheiya, Sugar Cane, Yams and several other Roots and fruits which are common in the other Isles. In general Mr Forster has found the same sort of Plants here as are at Otaheite besides several others which are not to be found there and I probably may have added to their Stock of Vegetables by leaving at both the isles an assortment of Garden Seeds, Pulse &c^a. Bread fruit as at all the other isles was now out of Season, Shaddocks and Lemons the same, of the former we got but a few at Ea-ōō-we and as to the latter we found only the tree nor was this the Season for roots. We saw no other Domistick Animals among them but Hogs and Fowls, the former are of the same sort as at the other isles, but the latter are far superior being as large as any we have in Europe and full as well tasted. We believe that they have no Dogs as they were exceeding desirous of those we had on board, their desire was satisfied so far as a Dog and a Bitch would do it, the one was from New Zealand and the other from Huaheino or Ulietea. The name of a Dog in their Language is [Korree] the same as at New Zealand, this shows that they are no strangers to the name what ever they may be to the Animal. . . . Nothing shews their ingenuity so much as the manner in which their Canoes are built and constructed, they are long and narrow with out-riggers and built of several pieces which are curiously sew'd together with platting made of the outside fibers of Cocoa-nutt. The sewing is all in the inside, they work a sort of kant on the insides edges of the pieces to be

October 1773 joined together in which they make holes through which they pass the platting so that no part of it is to be seen on the outside and the Seams are so closely fitted to each other as hardly to admit in any Water altho' they are neither caulked nor payd. The Common Canoes are about [twenty to thirty] feet in length and [twenty inches] in breadth, the body nearly round, the Stern terminates in a point and the head something like a wedge which has its edges rounded: neither the one nor the other is raised above the common level of the Gunwale, over each is a kind of deck about 1/4 part the length of the Canoe, the middle of these decks in some are decorated with a row of white shells stuck of little pegs which are worked out of the same piece as composeth the deck; the middle is open where there are thwarts secured to each gun [whale] which serve as seats to the rowers and a security to the Canoe, they are rowed by Paddles the blades of which are short and broadest in the middle, some are fitted with a mast and sail, we however saw but one of these small Canoes thus equiped, the generality of those that are intended for sailing are a great deal larger, but constructed in the very same manner with the addition of a rising in the middle round the open part of the Canoe in the form of a long trunck or trough which is open longitudinally at the uper and under sides, it is composed of boards closely fitted together and well secured to the body of the Canoe. Two such Canoes they fasten together alongside each other (leaving a space of about [six] feet between them) by means of Strong beams secured to the upper parts of the rising above mentioned. The ends of these beams project but very little without the off sides of the Canoes, over them is laid a boarded platform the ends of which project considerably over the beams, at the one end it preserves its breadth and is supported by stations fitted to the body of the Canoe and the other end the projecting part is no broader than the space between the Canoes and is supported by longitudinal spars fasten'd to the beams. I have already observed that the risings are open at the uper part, nor are the(y) covered by the platform concequently remain as hatchways leading into the Canoes from off the platform and as all parts which compose these two bodies are made as tight as the nature of the work will admit, they may be immerged in Water to the very platform without being in danger of filling nor is it possible under any circumstances whatever for them to sink so long as the(y) hold together. Thus they are not only made Vessels of burdthen but fit for distant Navigation, they are rigged with one mast which steps upon the Platform and can easily be raised or taken down a long one not being necessary as they are sailed with a Lateene sail, or a triangular sail extended by a long yard which is a little bent or crooked, the sail is made of Matting, some of the rope necessary for rigging of these vessels is 4 or 5 Inches thick and made exactly like ours. They fix a little hut or shed (for it is open on one side) on the Platform in which they keep their provisions &c[a]. It also serves to screen them from the Sun and shelter them from the Weather;

they carry likewise a Firehearth which is a square trough of Wood about 8 Inches deep fill'd with Stones, for the conveniency of making a fire to dress their Victuals. I think these Vessels are navigated either end foremost and that in changing tacks they only shift the Sail, but of this I am not certain as having seen none under sail, or with the Mast and sail on end but what were at some distance off. . . . They make the same kind of Cloth as at Otaheite and of the same Materials, they have not such a variety nor do they make it so fine, but as it is all died with a thick gummy glossy Colour it is perhaps more durable, these Colours are black, Brow(n), Purple, yellow and Red, I am unacquainted with the material with which they are made, a kind of Red and Yellow pigment we have seen. They also make various sorts of Matts of a very fine texture which serve them both for Cloathing and beding. Their Dress is a piece of Cloth or Matting wrapped round their Middle reaching from the breast down below the knee, they seldom wear anything over their Shoulders or upon their heads. The dress of the Men and Women are the same. With respect to their persons and colour I neither think them ugly nor handsome, there are none so fair, so tall or so well made as some of the natives of Otaheite and the neighbouring isles: on the other hand they are not so dark, so little or ill shaped as some we see at these isles, nor is there that disproportion between the men and Women. . . . As we had yet some Venereal complaints on board I took all possible means to prevent its being communicated to the Natives by not suffering a Man to go on shore on whom there was the least suspicion nor did I permit that any women should be allowed to come on board the Sloops. I cannot tell if the women are so free of their favours as at Otaheite, I think not and yet I beleive incontinency to be no great crime among them, with the unmarried especially.

October 1773

'Their Common method of Saluting or embracing one a nother is by join[in]g or touching Noses the same as in New Zealand and their Signs of Peace seems to be the displaying a white flag or flags, at least such were displayed on the Shore in several places as we rainged along the Coast and before the place where we Anchored, but those people who came first off to us in their Canoes brought with them some [of the pepper plant] Root of which they made their drink which they sent aboard before they came in themselves. One would not wish for a better sign of friendship than this; can we make a friend more welcome than by seting before him the best liquor in our posession or that can be got? In this manner did those friendly people receive us; I never Visited the old Chief but he ordered some of the root just mentioned to be brought me and would also set some of his people to chew it and prepare the liquor, notwithstanding I seldom tasted any, he even carried his hospitality farther by procuring me a Woman as I have before related.

'Every thing you give them they apply to their heads by way of thanks, this Custom they are taught from their infancy, when I have given things to little

October 1773 children the Mother has lifted up the Child's hands to its head just as we in England teach a child to pay a compliment by kissing its hand. They also made use of this Custom in the exchanges between us, whatever we gave them for their goods was applied to the head, just the same as if we had given it for nothing, sometimes they would take our goods and examine them and if not liked return them back, but when ever they applied them to the head the bargin was infallibly struck. . . . I am likewise of opinion that all the lands on the Islands, especially on Tonga-tabu, is private property and that there are among them, as at Otaheite Servants or Slaves who can have no share in it, indeed it would be absurd to suppose everything to be in Common in a Country so well cultivated as this. Intrest is the great Spring which animates the hand of industry, few would toil themselves in cultivating and planting the land if he did not expect to injoy the fruits of his labour, if everything was in common the Industerous man would be upon a worse footing than the Idle Sluggard. M. Bougainville is vastly misstaken where he says, page 252, that the people of Otaheite gathers fruit from the first tree they meet with or takes some in any house into which they enter &c[a]. I question if there is a fruit tree on that whole island that is not the property of some individual in it, Oediddu tells me that he who takes fruit &c[a] in the Manner just mentioned is punishable with death, be these things as they will, no one seems to want the Common necessaries of life, joy and Contentment is painted in every face and their whole behaviour to us was mild and benevolent, were they less addicted to thieving we should not, perhaps, be able to charge them with any other vice, they are however far less addicted to this vice than the people of Otaheite, indeed when I consider their whole conduct towards us and the manner in which the few arts they have among them are executed I must also allow them to be in a higher state of civilization. . . . We know so little of their Religion that I hardly dare mention it, the building called *Afiā-tou-ca* before spoke of is undoubtedly set apart for this purpose. M[r] Forster and one or two of the officers think that they understood for certain that their dead was enterred in them, this is even probable enough as we saw no other place so likely; I however could by no means satisfy my self on this point, but one thing I am certain of which is, that they are places to which they direct their prayers for this I have both seen and heard in the manner already related but to whome or on what account the prayer is made I know not it was from thence I concluded that there are priests or men among them who exercise the sacret function: the old chief which I have had occasion more than once to mention was constantly attended by one of the Reverand fathers, he seemed to be the head of the church.

Chapter XI
THE ANTARCTIC, 1773-4

> *"That there may be a Continent or large tract of land near the Pole, I will not deny, on the contrary I am of opinion there is, and it is probable that we have seen part of it."*
>
> COOK IN THE ANTARCTIC, 1774-5

OFF THE COAST OF THE NORTH ISLAND OF NEW ZEALAND the expedition experienced very stormy weather, and, during the night of 30th October 1773 the *Adventure* lost contact, and although Cook realised that stormy winds from the west had driven her eastwards he had no apprehension, but that she would soon beat up to the rendezvous, Queen Charlotte Sound.

SATURDAY 30*th* October. The breeze continued between the SW and South till 5 o'Clock in the PM when it fell calm, we being about 3 Leagues short of Cape Palliser. At 7 o'Clock a breeze sprung us (up) at NNE which was as favourable as we could wish, it proved however of short duration for about 9 the wind shifted into its old quarter NW and increased to a fresh gale with which we stretched to the SW under Courses and single-reefed top-sails. At Middnight the Adventure was two or three Miles a stern soon after she disapeared nor was she to be seen at day-light we supposed she had tacked and stood to the NE by which means we had lost sight of her. we however continued to stand to the westward with the wind at NNW and which increased in such a manner as at last to bring us under our two Courses, after spliting a new Main top-sail. At Noon Cape Campbell bore NBW distant 7 or 8 Leagues.

SUNDAY 31*st* October. At 8 o'Clock in the pm the gale became somewhat more moderate and veered more to the north so that we fetched in with the shore under the Snowey mountains about four or five leagues to windward

October 1773 of the Lookerson, where there was all the appearance of a large bay, had the Adventure been now with me I should have given up all thoughts of going to Queen Charlottes Sound to Wood and Water and sought for these articles farther South as the wind was now favourable for rainging a long the coast but as we were now seperated I was under a necessity (of) going to the Sound as being the place of rendezvous.

⸿ Cook was completely mystified by the non-appearance of the *Adventure*. His officers agreed that she could not be stranded in New Zealand, and Cook himself concluded that Furneaux had become weary of beating against the westerly winds and had sailed for the Cape of Good Hope. As the season for Antarctic exploration was already advanced Cook decided to wait no longer, but, having buried information for Furneaux, sailed south.

⸿ On the eve of their departure the Maoris gave the party a practical proof of their cannibalism by eating Maori flesh on the *Resolution's* deck, and when the belated *Adventure* arrived a few days after Cook sailed the Maoris gave Furneaux another practical demonstration by killing and partly eating the crew of one of the *Adventure's* boats, an outrage which the generous minded Cook refused to avenge on his third voyage.

⸿ Furneaux did not rejoin Cook. He sailed to Cape Horn in high latitudes and then from Cape Horn to the Cape of Good Hope, proving on the way that, in the region of the supposed Cape Circumcision (Bouvet Island) no large land mass could exist. Reaching England in July 1774, or a year before Cook he became the first commander to circumnavigate the earth from west to east.

MONDAY 15*th* November. Fair weather winds northerly a gentle breeze. In the Morning I went in the Pinnace over to the East Bay, accompanied by some of the officers and gentlemen, as soon as we landed we went upon one of the hills in order to take a view of the Straits, to see if we could discover any thing of the Adventure, we had a fatiguing walk to little purpose for when we got to the top of the hill we found the Eastern horizon so foggy that we could not see above two or three miles. M[r] Forster who was one of the party profited by this excursion in collecting some new plants; as to the Adventure I dispair of seeing her any more but am totally at a loss to conceive what is become of her till now. I thought she might have put into some port in the Strait when the wind came at NW the day we Anchor'd in Ship Cove and there stayed to compleat her wood and Water, this conjector was reasonable enough at first, but the elapsation of twelve day has now made it scarce probable.

TUESDAY 23*rd* November. Calm or light airs from the Northward so that we could not get to Sea as I intended, some of the officers went on shore to amuse themselves among the Natives where they saw the head and bowels of a youth who had lately been killed, the heart was stuck upon a forked stick and fixed to the head of their largest Canoe, the gentlemen brought the head on board

November 1773

with them, I was on shore at this time but soon after returned on board when I was informed of the above circumstances, and found the quarter deck crowded with the Natives. I now saw the mangled head or rather the remains of it for the under jaw, lips &c[a] were wanting, the scul was broke on the left side just above the temple, the face had all the appearance of a youth about fourteen or fifteen, a peice of the flesh had been broiled and eat by one of the Natives in the presince of most of the officers. The sight of the head and the relation of the circumstances just mentioned struck me with horor and filled my mind with indignation against these Canibals, but when I considered that any resentment I could shew would avail but little and being desireous of being an eye wittness to a fact which many people had their doubts about I concealed my indignation and ordered apiece of the flesh to be broiled and brought on the quarter deck where one of these Canibals eat it with a seeming good relish before the whole ships Company had such effect on some of them as to cause them to vomit. . . . That the New Zealanders are Canibals can now no longer be doubted, the account I gave of it in my former voyage was partly founded on circumstances and was, as I afterwrds found, discredited by many people. I have often been asked, after relating all the circumstances, if I had actually seen them eat human flesh my self, such a question was sufficient to convince me that they either disbelieved all I had said or formed a very different opinion from it, few consider what a savage man is in his original state and even after he is in some degree civilized; the New Zealanders are certainly in a state of civilization, their behaviour to us has been Manly and Mild, shewing allways a readiness to oblige us; they have some arts among them which they execute with great judgement and unwearied patience; they are far less addicted to thieving than the other Islanders and are I believe strictly honist among them-selves. This custom of eating their enimies slain in battle (for I firmly believe they eat the flesh of no others) has undoubtedly been handed down to them from the earliest times and we know that it is not an easy matter to break a nation of its ancient customs let them be even so inhuman and savage, especially if that nation is void of all religious principles as I believe the new zealanders in general are and like them without any settled form of government; as they become more united they will of concequence have fewer enemies and become more civilized and then and not till then this custom may be forgot, at present they seem to have but little idea of treating other men as they themselves would wish to be treated but treat them as they think they should be treated under the same circumstances. If I remember right one of the arguments they made use on against Tupia who frequently expostulated with them against this custom, was that there could be no harm in killing and eating the man who would do the same by you if it was in his power, for said they 'can there be any harm in eating our Enimies whom we have killed in battle, would not those very enimies have done the same to us?'

November 1773 THURSDAY 25*th* November. At 4 o'Clock in the Morning we weiged with a light breeze out of the Cove which carried us no farther than betwen Motuara and Long-island where we were obliged to anchor, presently after a breeze sprung up at North with which we weighed and turned out of the Sound by 12 o'Clock. During our stay in this place we were well supplyed with fish which we purchased of the Natives at a very easy rate and besides the vegetables our own gardens produced we found every were plenty of Scurvy grass and sellery which I caused to be dressed every day for all hands, by this means they have been mostly on a fresh diet for these three months past and at this time we had neither a sick or scorbutic person on board. . . . The morning before we sailed I wrote a memorandum seting forth the time we arrived last here, the day we sailed, the rout I intended to take & such other information as I thought necessary for Captain Furneaux and buried it in a bottle under the root of a tree in the garden in the bottom of the Cove in such a manner that it must be found by any European who may but into the Cove. I however have not the least reason to think that it will ever fall into the hands of the person I intended it for, for it is hardly possible that Captain Furneaux can be in any part of New Zealand and I not have heard of him in all this time, nevertheless I was determined not to leave the country without looking for him where I thought it was most likely for him to be found, and accordingly as soon as we were clear of the Sound I hauled over for Cape Teerawhitte and ran along the shore from point to point to Cape Palliser firing guns every half hour without seeing or hearing the least signs of what we were in search after. . . . All the officers being unanimous of opinion that the Adventure could neither be stranded on the Coast or be in any of the Ports in this Country determined me to spend no more time in search of her, but to proceed dire(c)tly to the Southward. I am under apprehensions for the safety of the Adventure nor can I even guess which way she is gone, the manner she was seperated from me and coming to the Rendez-vouze has left me no grounds to form any conjectors upon, I can only suppose that Captain Furneaux was tired with beating against the NW winds and had taken a resolution to make the best of his way to the Cape of Good hope, be this as it may I have no expectation of joining him any more.

(Sailing with a crew in excellent health Cook spent from early December 1773 to early February 1774 in high latitudes, sailing eastwards until he was in the longitude of Mexico City. He twice crossed the Antarctic Circle and on 30th January reached latitude 71° 10′ south, where, in longitude 106° 54′ west, he encountered the immense barrier of ice which, in that area, lies off the Antarctic continent. J. A. Williamson says that no other explorer 'reached this latitude for half a century, and no one has reached it in that area since Cook'. The references to the sighting of whales are important, as possibly bearing on the development of the whaling industry in southern waters.

WEDNESDAY 15*th* December. *Therm.r. Noon* 31. *Lat. in South* 65° 52′. *Longde. in West Reck.g.* 159° 20′. The Ice begins to increase fast, from Noon till 8 o'Clock in the evening we saw but two islands, but from 8 to 4 am we passed fifteen, besides a quantity of loose Ice which we sailed through, this last increased so fast upon us that at 6 o'Clock we were obliged to alter the Course more to the East, haveing to the South an extensive feild of loose ice; there were several partitions in the feild and clear water behind it, but as the wind blew strong the Weather foggy the going in among this Ice might have been attended with bad concequences, especially as the wind would not permit us to return. We therefore hauled to the NE on which Course we had stretched but a little way before we found our selves quite imbayed by the ice and were obliged to Tack and stretch back to the SW having the loose field ice to the South and many large island to the North. After standing two hours on this tack the wind very luckily veered to the westward with which we tacked and stretched to the Northward and soon got clear of all the loose ice but had many huge islands to incounter, which were so numerous that we had to luff for one and bear up for a nother, one of these mases was very near proving fatal to us, we had not weather it more than once or twice our length, had we not succeeded this circumstance could never have been related. According to the old proverb a miss is as good as a mile, but our situation requires more misses than we can expect, this together with the improbability of meeting with land to the South and the impossibility of exploreing it for the ice if we did find any, determined me to haul to the north.

December 1773

TUESDAY 21*st* December. *Therm.r. Noon* 33. *Lat. in South* 66° 50′. *Longde. in West Reck.g.* 66° 50′. In the pm the wind increased to a strong gale attended with a thick fogg Sleet and rain which constitutes the very worst of weather, our rigging was so loaded with ice that we had enough to do to get our Top-sails down to double reef. At 7 o'Clock we came the second time under the Polar Circle and stood to the SE till 6 o'Clock in the am when being in La^{t} 67° 5′ South Longitude 143° 49′ West, the fogg being exceeding thick we came close aboard a large Island of ice and being at the same time a good deal imbarrass'd with loose ice we with some difficulty wore and stood to the NW untill Noon when the fogg being some what disipated we resumed our Course again to the SE. The ice island we fell in with in the morning, for there were more than one, were very high and rugged terminating in many Peaks, whereas all those we have seen before were quite flat at top and not so high. A great Sea from the North. Grey Albatroses and a few Antarctick Petrels.

FRIDAY 24*th* December. *Therm.r. Noon* 32. *Lat. in South* 67° 19′. *Longde. in West Reck.g.* 138° 15′. At 4 o'Clock in the PM as we were standing to the SE, fell in with such a vast quantity of field or loose ice as covered the whole Sea from South to East and was so thick and close as to obstruct our passsage, the wind at this time being pretty moderate, brought to in the edge of this field,

December 1773 hoisted out two boats and sent them to take some up, and in the mean time we slung several large pieces along side and hoisted them in with our tackles; by such time as the Boats had made two trips it was Eight o'Clock when we hoisted them in and made sail to the westward under double reef'd Top-sails and Courses, with the wind northerly a strong gale attended with a thick fog sleet and Snow which froze to the Rigging as it fell and decorated the whole with icicles. Our ropes were like wires, Sails like board or plates of Metal and the Shivers froze fast in the blocks so that it required our utmost effort to get a Top-sail down and up; the cold so intense as hardly to be endured the whole Sea in a manner covered with ice, a hard gale and a thick fog: under all these unfavourable circumstances it was natural for me to think of returning more to the North, seeing there was no probability of finding land here nor a possibility of yet farther to the South and to have proceeded to the East in this Latitude would not have been prudent as well on account of the ice as the vast space of Sea we must Leave lying to the north unexplored, a space of 24° of Latitude in which a large track of land might lie, this point could only be determined by making a stretch to the North.

SUNDAY 26*th* December. *Therm.r.* 37. *Lat. in South* 65° 15′. *Longdc. in West Reck.g.* 134° 22′. At 2 o'Clock in the pm it fell calm, we had before preceived this would happen and got the ship into as clear a birth as we could where she drifted along with the ice islands and by taking the advantage of every light air of wind was kept from falling foul of any one; we were fortunate in two things, continual day light and clear weather, had it been foggy nothing less than a miracle could have kept us clear of them, for in the morning the whole sea was in a manner wholy covered with ice, 200 islands and upwards, none less than the Ships hull and some more than a mile in circuit were seen in the compass of five miles, the extent of our sight, and smaller peices innumerable. At 4 in the AM a light breeze sprung up at WSW and enabled us to Steer north the most probable way to extricate our selves from these dangers.

TUESDAY 4*th* January. *Therm.r. Noon* 460. *Lat. in* 54° 55′. *Longd. in West Greenwich Reck.g.* 139° 4′. As the wind seems now fixed in the western board, we shall be under a necessity of leaving unexplored to the west a space of Sea containing 40° of Longitude and 20° or 21° of Latitude, had the wind been favourable I intended to have run 15° or 20° of longitude to the west in the Latitude we are now in and back again to the East in the Latitude of 50° or near it, this rout would have so intersected the space above mentioned as to have hardly left room for the bare supposision of any large land lying there. Indeed as it is we have no reason to suppose that there is any for we have had now for these several days past a great swell from west and NW, a great sign we have not been covered by any land between these two points. In the AM saw some Pie bald porpuses.

THURSDAY *6th* January. *Lat. in* 52° 0′. *Longde. in W. Greenwh. Reck.g.* 135° 32′ *Watch* 135° 38′. At Noon loosed all the reefs out and bore away NE with a fresh gale at WSW fair weather, the distance between us now and our rout to Otaheite being little more than two hundred leagues in which space it is not probable there can be any land, and it is less probable there can be any to the west from the vast high billows we now have from that quarter. *January 1774*

SATURDAY *8th* January. *Lat. in South* 49° 7′. *Longde. W. Greenwh. Reck.g.* 131° 2′ *Watch* 131° 8′. Fresh gales with now and then showers of rain. In the PM found the variation to be 6° 2′ E and in the AM 6° 26′ East. At 9 o'Clock had again several Observations of the Sun and Moon the results were confirmable to yesterday and determined our Longde beyond a doubt. Indeed our error can never be great so long as we have so good a guide as Mr Kendalls watch. At Noon altered the Course to ENE Easterly.

TUESDAY *11th* January. Little wind continued most part of the PM. In the night it began to freshen, blew in Squalls attended with rain, afterwards the weather became clear and the wind settled. At Noon being little more than two hundred Leagues from my track to Otaheite in 1769 in which space it was not probable any thing was to be found, we therefore hauled up SE with a fresh gale at SWBW.

THURSDAY *13th* January. At Noon had a great northerly swell a sign we had left no land behind us in that direction.

THURSDAY *20th* January. *Therm.r.* 40. *Lat. in South* 62° 34′. *Longde. in West Reck.g.* 116° 24′. First part fresh gales and hazey with rain, remainder little wind and Mostly fair. At 7 PM saw a large piece of Weed. In the AM two ice islands one of which was very high terminating in a peak or like the Cupala of St Pauls Church we judged it to be 200 feet high. A great Westerly swell still continues a probable certainty there is no land between us and the Meridian of 133½° which we were under when last in this Latitude.

WEDNESDAY *26th* January. *Therm.r. Noon* 40. *Lat. in South* 66° 36′. *Longd. in W. Greenwh. Reck.g.* 109° 31′. At this time saw Nine Ice islands, the most of them small, several Whales and a few blue Petrels. At 8 o'Clock we came the third time within the Antarctick Polar Circle. Soon after saw an appearance of land to the East and SE, hauld up for it and presently after it disappeared in the haze. Sounded but found no ground with a line of 130 fathom. A few Whales & Petrels seen.

THURSDAY *27th* January. Continued to stretch to the SE till 8 o'Clock am by which time we were assured our supposed land was vanished into clouds and therefore resumed our Course to the South.

SATURDAY *29th* January. *Therm.r.* 36½. *Lat. in South* 70° 00′ *Obn. Longd. in W. Greenwh. Reck.g.* 107° 27′ *Watch* 107° 36′. A little after 4 a.m. we perceived the Clowds to the South near the horizon to be of an unusual Snow white brightness which denounced our approach to field ice, soon after it was seen from the

January 1774 mast-head and at 8 o'Clock we were close to the edge of it which extended East and West in a streight line far beyond our sight as appear'd by the brightness of the horizon, in the situation we were now in just the Southern half of the horizon was enlightned by the Reflected rays of the Ice to a considerable height. The Clowds near the horizon were of a perfect Snow whiteness and were difficult to be distinguished from the Ice hills whose lofty summits reached the Clowds. The outer or Northern edge of this immence Icefield was compose of loose or broken ice so close packed together that nothing could enter it, about a Mile in began the firm ice, in one compact solid boddy and seemed to increased in height as you traced it to the South; In this field we counted Ninety Seven Ice Hills or Mountains, many of them vastly large. Such Ice Mountains as these are never seen in Greenland, so that we cannot draw a comparison between the Greenland Ice and this now before us: Was it not for the Greenland Ships fishing yearly among such Ice (the ice hills excepted) I should not have hisitated one moment in declaring it as my opinion that the Ice we now see extended in a solid body quite to the Pole and that it is here, i.e. to the South of this parallel, where the many Ice Islands we find floating about in the Sea are first form'd, and afterwards broke off by gales of wind and other causes, be this as it may, we must allow that these numberless and large Ice Hills must add such weight to the Ice fields, to which they are fixed, as must make a wide difference between the Navigating this Icy Sea and that of Greenland: I will not say however it was impossible.

SUNDAY 30*th* January. [No date given] *Lat. in South* 70° 48′. *Longd. in W. Reck.g.* 106° 34′. Anywhere to get in among this Ice, but I will assert that the bare attempting of it would be a very dangerous enterprise and what I believe no man in my situation would have thought of. I whose ambition leads me not only farther than any other man has been before me, but as far as I think it possible for man to go, was not sorry at meeting with this interruption, as it in some measure relieved us from the dangers and hardships, inseparable with the Navigation of the Southern Polar regions. Sence therefore we could not proceed one Inch farther South, no other reason need be assigned for our Tacking and stretching back to the North, being at that time in the Latitude of 71° 10′ South, Longitude 106° 54′ West.

¶ Cook now concluded that no continent could exist in the high latitudes he was exploring, at any rate not to the west of Cape Horn. His ship and crew had experienced severe trials, but both were still in excellent condition, while there were ample provisions remaining for the expedition to spend the approaching southern winter in a second, and even more ambitious sweep of the Pacific than that undertaken in 1773. Cook therefore decided to sail northwards from his February position in the antarctic to the land reported by Juan Fernandes in latitude 38° south; to Easter Island, and then westwards through the tropics by a new route to Quiros' 'Tierra Austral del Espiritu Santo' (the New Hebrides), off the North East Australian coast. *February 1774*

(Then, in the coming southern summer of 1774-5, he would round Cape Horn, and complete his search for the Southern Continent, and incidentally his eastwards navigation of the globe, by returning to the Cape of Good Hope by the high latitudes of the South Atlantic.

SUNDAY *6th* February. In the AM we got the wind from the South, loosed all the reefs out, got top-g[t] yards and set the Sails and steered North-Easterly, with a resolution to proceed directly to the North as there was no probability of finding Land in these high Latitudes, at least not on this side Cape Horn and I thought it equally as improbable any should be found on the other side, but supposing the Land laid down in M[r] Dalrymple's Chart to exist or that of Bouvet, before we could reach either the one or the other the Season would be too far spent to explore it this Summer, and obliged us either to have wintered upon it, or retired to Falkland Isles or the Cape of Good Hope, which ever had been done, Six or Seven Months must have been spent without being able in that time to make any discovery whatever, but if we had met with no land or other impediment we might have reached the last of these places by April at farthest when the expedition would have been finished so far as it related to the finding a Southern Continent, mentioned by all Authors who have written on this subject whose assertions and conjectures are now intirely refuted as all there enquiries were confined to this Southern Pacific Ocean in which altho' there lies no continent there is however room for very large Islands, and many of those formerly discover'd within the Southern Tropick are very imperfectly explored and there situations as imperfectly known. All these things considered, and more especially as I had a good Ship, a hea[l]thy crew and no want of Stores or Provisions I thought I cou'd not do better than to spend the insuing Winter within the Tropicks: I must own I have little expectation of makeing any valuable discovery, nevertheless it must be allowed that the Sciences will receive some improvement therefrom especially Navigation and Geography. I had several times communicated my thoughts on this subject to Captain Furneaux, at first he seem'd not to approve of it, but was inclinable to get to the Cape of Good Hope, afterwards he seem'd to come into my opinion; I however could not well give any Instructions about it, as at that time it depended on so many circumstances and therefore cannot even guess how Captain Furneaux will act, be this as it will, my intintion is now to go in search of the Land said to be discovered by Juan Fernandes in the Latitude of 38° S, not finding any such Land, to look for Easter Island, the situation of which is so variously laid down that I have little hopes of finding. I next intind to get within the Tropicks and proceed to the west on a rout differing from former Navigators, touching at, and settling the Situation of such Isles as we may meet with, and if I have time,

February 1774 to proceed in this manner as far west as Quiros's Land or what M. de Bougainville calls the Great Cyclades. Quiros describes this Land, which he calls Tierra Austral del Espiritu Santo, as being very large. M. de Bougainville neither confirms nor refutes this account. I think it a point well worth clearing up, from these isles my design is to get to the South and proceed back to the East between the Latitudes of 50 and 60°, designing if Possible to be the Length of Cape Horn in November next, when we shall have the best part of the Summer before us to explore the Southern part of the Atlantick Ocean. This I must own is a great undertakeing and perhaps more than I shall be able to perform as various impediments may (*left unfinished*)

Chapter XII
SEARCHING THE PACIFIC, 1774

"By twice visiting the tropical sea I had not only settled the situation of some old discoveries but made these many new ones and left . . . very little more to be done."

COOK, 1775

COOK'S JOURNAL OF THE EXPEDITION OF 1772-5 DEALS WITH the second sweep of the Pacific in such detail and at such great length that attention can be directed only to a few outstanding discoveries or events, amongst these are the description of the mysterious Easter Island; the appearance of the Canoe Armada in the Society Islands; the re-examination of Quiros' New Hebrides; and the discovery of the large and important island of New Caledonia. Outstanding in Cook's straightforward narrative are the constant risk of shipwreck during island navigation; the superb courage of the leader, who again and again landed amidst hordes of armed natives to demonstrate his unique gifts as a peacemaker, and the almost invariable quarrels over theft, which, on the third voyage, produced the final disaster.

(Outstanding, too, in these difficult weeks were Cook's unceasing efforts to save the lives of the natives, and his endeavours, in general successful, to discipline subordinates, who were sometimes 'gun happy' and sometimes fearful.

SATURDAY 19*th* February. We are now nearly upon the track of the Dolphin, Captain Wallis having cross'd that of the Endeavour two days ago, my intention was to have kept more to the West, but the winds prevailing in that quarter has unavoidably forced me on the Tracks of these two Ships.

TUESDAY 22*nd* February. Being now in the Latitude in which most Geographers place the discovery of Juan Fernandes, M[r] Dalrymple places the Eastern side fo

February 1774 this Land under the meridian of 90° and Mr Pengre in 111°, and in a note quotes the Authority from whence he has it, by which indeed it appears, they are two different discoveries or else the same land discovered at two different Periods. I think it can'ot lie to the East of the Situation Mr Dalrymple has given it and if it lies in that situation it can have no great extent East and west for if it has we ought either to see it or some signs of it. Mr Pengres situation falls under the like observation for the Endeavour cross'd these Latitudes in the Meridian of 112°; and Captain Wallis in about 98 or 100 without seeing the least signs of land; it is therefore plain that it can be no more than a small Island but I think it as probable that the whole is a fiction and that no such discoveries were ever made. See what is said on this Subject in Mr Dalrymple's Co^l^ of Voyage to the SS.

WEDNESDAY *23rd* February. At 2 pm the wind veer'd to SE blew a gentle gale attended with small rain, we now steer'd WSW in order to make a nother search for the land, being at this time in the Latitude of 36° 39′, Longd^e^ 97° 10′ W circumstances gave us no hopes of finding what we were in search after, having continually a large swell from SW and West.

SATURDAY *5th* March. Saw some Tropick and Egg birds, had a prodigeous swell from SW so that no large land can possible be in that quarter but from the many birds we see, which generally frequent the shores of land, we are in hopes of meeting with Davis or Easter Island.

MONDAY *7th* March. Gentle breezes and pleasent weather. AM a large piece of Spung floated past the Ship. Variation 4° 47′ E. In the a.m. caught four Albacores about 25 or 30 pound each, which were very acceptable, they were about the Ship in vast numbers, but unfortunately we have no one on board who know the art of catching them. The SW swell as high as ever(y). Saw a Tropic and Man of War bird.

TUESDAY *8th* March. Gentle gales and fine pleasent weather. In the AM saw many Birds, such as Tropick, Men of War and Egg Birds of two sorts, grey and White, many sheer-waters or Petrels of two or three sorts, one sort small and almost all black, another sort much larger with dark grey backs and white bellies. Swell not much and from the East.

WEDNESDAY *9th* March. Weather and winds as yesterday. Judgeing our selves by observation to be nearly in the Latitude of Davis's land or Easter Island we steer'd nearly due west meeting with the same sort of Birds as yesterday.

℄ The expedition missed 'Juan Fernandes' but on 11th March, 1774 sighted the small but interesting Easter Island with its mysterious images. Although Cook wrote a fairly long description of the island he hurried away owing to the difficulty of obtaining fresh water and provisions.

℄ The inhabitants of the island were clearly of Polynesian type.

FRIDAY *11th* March. Gentle breeze and pleasant weather. At Midd[n]ight brought to till day-light then made sail and soon after saw the Land from the

March 1774

Mast head bearing West. At Noon it was seen from the deck extending from W3/4N to WBS. Distant about 12 Leagues.

SUNDAY 13*th* March. In stretching in for the land we discovered people and those Monements or Idols mentioned by the authors of Roggewiens Voyage which left us no room to doubt but it was Easter Island.

TUESDAY 15*th* March. PM Got on board a few Casks of Water and Traded with the Natives for some of the produce of the island which appeared in no great plenty and the Water so bad as not to be worth carrying on board, and the Ship not in safety determined me to shorten my stay here. Accordingly I sent Lieutenants Pickersgill and Edgcumb with a party of Men, accompanied by Mr Forster and several more of the gentlemen, to examine the Country. I was not sufficiently recovered from a fit of illness to make one of the party. At the Ship employed geting on Board Water and trading with the Natives.

THURSDAY 17*th* March. This is undoubtedly the same Island as was seen by Roggewein in Apl 1722 altho' the description given of it by the author of that Voyage does by no means correspond with it now, it may also be the same as was seen by Captain Davis in 1686, but this is not altogether so certain. In short if this is not the land and if it is not then his discovery cannot lie far from the continent of America for this Latitude seems to have been very well explored between the Meridian of 80 and 110, Captain Carteret carries it much farther, but his Track seems to be a little too far to the South. Had I found fresh Water on this isle I intended to have determined this point by looking for the low sandy isle mentioned by Wafer, but as I did not, and had a long run to make before I was assured of geting any and being at the same time in want of refreshments, I declined it, as a small delay might have been attended with bad consequence. No Nation will ever contend for the honour of the discovery of Easter Island as there is hardly an Island in this sea which affords less refreshments, and conveniences for Shiping than it does. Nature has hardly provided it with any thing fit for man to eat or drink, and as the Natives are but few and may be supposed to plant no more than sufficient for themselves, they cannot have much to spare to new comers. The produce is Potatoes, Yams, Taro or the Edoy root, Plantains and Sugar Cane, all excellent in its kind, the Potatoes are the best of the sort I ever tasted; they have also Gourds and the same sort of Cloth Plant as at the other isles but not much, Cocks and Hens like ours which are small and but few of them and these are the only domestick Animals we saw a mong them, nor did we see any quadrupedes, but ratts which I believe they eat as I saw a man with some in his hand which he seem'd unwilling to part with. Land Birds we saw hardly any and Sea Birds but a few, these were Men of War Birds, Noddies, Egg Birds, &ca. The Sea seems as barren of fish for we could not catch any altho we try'd in several places with hook and line and it was very little we saw a mong the Natives.

March 1774 Such is the produce of *Easter* Island which is situated in the Latitude of 27° 6′ South and the Longitude of 109° 51′ 40″ w. it is about 10 Leagues in circuit an hath hilly Rocky surface, the hills are of such a height as to be seen 15 or 16 Leagues. . . . The Inhabitants of this isle from what we have been able to see of them do not exceed six or seven hundred souls and a bove two thirds of these are Men, they either have but a few Women among them or else many were not suffer'd to make their appearence, the latter seems most Probable. They are certainly of the same race of People as the New Zealanders and the other islanders, the affinity of the Language, Colour and some of their customs all tend to prove it, I think they bearing more affinity to the Inhabitants of Amsterdam and New Zealand, than those of the more northern isles which makes it probable that there lies a chain of isles in about this Parallel or under, some of which have at different times been seen. . . . They have enormous holes in their Ears, but what their Chief Ear ornaments are I cannot saw. I have seen some with a ring fixed in the hole of the ear, but not hanging to it, also some with rings made of some elastick substance roled up like the Spring of a Watch, the design of this must be to extend or increase the hole.

'Their Arms are wooden Patta pattows and Clubs very much like those of New Zealand and spears about 6 or 8 feet long which are pointed at one end with pieces of black flit.

'Their Houses are low long and narrow and have much the appearance of a large boat turned bottom up whose keel is curved or bent, the largest I saw was 60 feet in length, 8 or 9 high in the middle and 3 or 4 at each end, its breadth was nearly the same; the door was in the middle of one Side, built like a Porch so low and narrow as just to admit a man to creep in upon all fours. The framing is made of small twigs and the covering of the tops of Sugar Cane and Plantains leaves and extends from the foundation to the roof so that they have no light but what the small door admits. These people dress their victuals in the same mann^{r} as at the other Isles.

'Of their Religion, Government &c^{a} we can say nothing with certainty. The Stupendous stone statues errected in different places along the Coast are certainly no representation of any Diety or places of worship; but most probable Burial Places for certain Tribes or Families. I my self saw a human Skeleton lying in the foundation of one just covered with Stones, what I call the foundation is an oblong square about 20 or 30 feet by 10 or 12 built of and faced with hewn stones of a vast size, errected in so masterly a manner as sufficiently shews the ingenuity of the age in which they were built. . . . Some pieces of Carving were found a mongest these people which were neither ill disigned nor executed. They have no other tools than what are made of Stone, Bone, Shells &c^{a}. They set but little value on Iron and yet they knew the use of it, perhaps they obtained their knowledge of this Metal from the Spaniards who Visited this Isle in 1769 some Vistiges of which still remained amongest them, such as pieces of Cloth &c[a]. *March 1774*

℄ From Easter Island Cook sailed north of the Tuamotus and rediscovered the Marquesas Islands which Mendaña had found in 1595. Here, as so often happened, a native theft led to a native death.

THURSDAY *7th* April. At 4 o'Clock in the PM after runing 4 Leagues West sence Noon, Land was seen bearing WBS distant about 9 Leagues, two hours after saw a nother land bearing SWBS and appeared more extensive than the first, hauld up for this land and kept under an easy Sail all night having Squally unsittled weather with rain. At 6 am the Land first seen bore NW the other SW/2W and a third West, I directed my Course for the Channell between these two last lands, under all the Sail we could set, having unsittled Squally Showery weather. Soon after we discovered a fourth land still more to the westward and were now well assured that these were the Marquesas discovered by Mendana in 1595. At Noon we were in the Channell which divides S[t] Pedro and La dominica.

FRIDAY *8th* April. I was going in a Boat to look for the most convenient place to more her in; observing so many of the Natives on board, I said to the officers, you must look well after these people or they certainly will carry off some thing or other, these words were no sooner out of my mouth and had hardly got into my Boat, when I was told they had stolen one of the Iron Stanchions from the opposite gang-way, I told the officers to fire over the Canoe till I could get round in the Boat, unluckily for the thief they took better aim that I ever intend and killed him the third Shott, two others that were in the same Canoe jumped overboard but got in again just as I got to the Canoe, the one was a Man and seem'd to laugh at what had happen'd, the other was a youth about 14 or 15 years of age, he looked at the dead man with a serious and dejected countinance and we had afterwards reason to believe that he was son to the disceas'd. This accident made all the Canoes retire from us with precipitation. I followed them into the Bay and prevaild upon the people in one Canoe to come along side the Boat and receive some Nails and other things I gave them.

MONDAY *11th* April. When I saw that this place was not likely to supply us with sufficient refreshments, not very convenient for geting off wood and Water nor for giving the Ship the necessary repairs I resolved forth with to leave it and seack for some place that would supply our wants better, for it must be supposed that after having been 19 Weeks at Sea (for I cannot call the two or 3 days spent at Easter Island any thing else) living all the time upon a Salt Diet, but what we must want some refrishments altho I must own and that with pleasure that on our arrival here, it could hardly be said that we had one Sick Man on board and not above two or three who had the least complaint, this was undoubtedly owing to the many antiscorbutic articles we had on board

April 1774 and the great care and Attention of the Surgeon who took special care to apply them in time.

TUESDAY 12*th* April. These Isles as I have before observed were first discovered by Mendana and by him called Marquesas, he likewise gave names to the different isles. The Nautical discription of them in M[r] Dalrymple Collection of Voyages is diffecient in nothing but Situation and this was the chief point I wanted to settle and my reason for touching at them as it will in a great measure fix the Situation of all Mendana's other discoveries. . . . The Inhabitants of these Isles are without exceptions as fine a race of people as any in this Sea or perhaps any whatever; the Men are Tattowed or curiously Marked from head to foot which makes them look dark but the Women (who are but little Tattow'd) youths and young children are as fair as some Europeans, they cloath them Selves with the Same sort of Cloth and Matting as the Otaheiteans; they wear as Ornaments a kind of Fillit curiously ornamented with Tortice and Mother of Pearl Shills, Feathers &c[a]. Round their Necks an ornament of this form, it is made with Wood on which are stuck with gum a great number of small red Pease, they also wear bunches of human hair round their legs and arms &c[a].

'The Men in general are tall that is about Six feet high, but we saw none so lusty as at Otaheite and the neighbouring isles, nevertheless they are of the same race of People, their language customs &c[a] all tend to prove it.

'They dwell in the Vallies and on the sides of the hills near their plantations, their Houses are built after the same manner as at Otaheite, but are much meaner and only covered with the leaves of the bread tree. They have also dwellings or Strong holds on the Summits of the highest Mountains, these we saw by the help of our Glasses for I did not permit any of our people to go to them for fear of being attack'd by the Natives whose deposission we were not sufficiently acquainted with.

'The Bay or Port of *Madre de Dios* so named by Mendana is situated near the middle of the West side. S[t] Christina under the highest land on the island in Latitude 9° 55′ 30″ S Longitude 139° 8′ 40″ E and N 1° 5″ W from the West end of La Dominica. . . . Here is the little Waterfall mentioned by Quiros . . .

(From the Marquesas Cook sailed westwards to Tahiti, which, after visiting Coral Island, named by Byron, he sighted on 21st April and anchored in Matavai Bay on the 22nd.

WEDNESDAY 13*th* April. Gentle breezes with rain. At 3 o'Clock in the PM the Harbour of Madre de Fios bore ENE1/2E distant 5 Leagues and the body of the Island Magdalena SE about 9 Leagues, this was the only View we had of this last island. From hence I directed my Course SSW1/2W for Otaheite and likewise with a view of falling in with Some of those isles discovered by former Navigators whose Situations are not well determined.

THURSDAY *21st* April. First part fresh gales with rain, remainder fair and Clowdy. At 10 AM Saw the high land of Otaheite and at Noon Point Venus bore west-northerly distant 13 Leagues. *April 1774*

FRIDAY *22nd* April. Moderate breezes and Clowdy. At 7 Shortned Sail and spent the night plying of find on. AM Squally with heavy Showers of rain. At 8 Anchored in *Matavai* Bay in 7 fathom Water.

☾ The expedition spent from 22nd April until 4th June, 1774 in the Society and Friendly Islands, renewing friendships, punishing, when possible, assaults and thefts, and collecting yams, and yaws or social diseases. A new and welcome addition to the old story came with the appearance of a huge armada of canoes, obviously training for an inter-island assault which the natives refused to undertake until the *Resolution* left, much to the chagrin of Cook who was most anxious to observe native methods of sea fighting.

TUESDAY *26th* April. In the Morning I set out for Oparre accompanyed by the two M[r] Forsters and some of the officers to pay Otou a formal Viset by appointment, as we approached Oparre we observed and number of large Canoes in Motion, but we were surprised when we got there to see upwards of three hundred of them all rainged in good order for some distance along the Shore all Compleatly equip'd and Man'd, and a vast Crown of Men on the Shore; So unexpected an Armament collected together in our Neighbour-hood in the space of one night gave rise to various conjectures. . . . When we had got into our boat we took our time to view this fleet, the Vessels of War consisted of 160 large double Canoes, very well equip'd, Man'd and Arm'd, altho' I am not sure that they had on board either their full compliment of Fighting men or rowers, I rather think not. The Chief and all those on the Fighting Stages were drist in their War habits, that is in a vast quantity of Cloth, Turbands, breast Plates and Helmmets, some of the latter are of such a length as to greatly incumber the wearer, indeed their whole dress seem'd ill caculated for the day of Battle and seems to be design'd more for Shew than use, be this as it may they certainly added grandure to the Prospect, as they were complesant enough to Shew themselves to the best advantage, their Vessels were decorated with Flags, Streamers &c[a] so that the whole made a grand and Noble appearence such as was never seen before in this Sea, their implements of war were Clups, pikes and Stones. These Canoes were rainged close along side each other with their heads a Shore and Sterns to the Sea, the Admirals vesel was, as near as I could guess, in the center. Besides these Vesels of War there were 170 Sail of Smaller double Canoes all with a little house upon them and rigg'd with Masts and sails which the others had not; These Canoes must be design'd for Transport or Victulars or both and to receive the wounded Men &c[a] in the War Canoes were no sort of Provisions whatever. In these 303 Canoes I judged there were no less than 7760 Men a number which appears incredable, especially as we were

April 1774 told that they all belonged to the districts of Attahourou and Ahopatea; in this computation I allow to each War Canoe one with a nother 40 Men, rowers and fighting Men, and to each of the Small Canoes eight, but most of the gentlemen who saw this fleet thinks the number of Men to the War Canoes were more than I have reckoned. . . . We had not long left Oparre before the whole fleet was in Motion and proceeded back to the westward from whence they came. When we got on board the Ship we were told that this fleet was a part of the Armament intended to go against Eimeo whose Chief had revolted from Otou his Lawfull Sovereign. I was also inform'd that Otou was not nor had been at Matavai and therefore after dinner I went again to Oparre where I found him, I now learn that his fears and the reason of his not seeing us in the Morning was occasioned by some of his people stealing (owing to the neglect of the washerman) a quantity of my Clothes and was fearfull least I should demand restitution, when I assured him I should not disturb the peace of the isle on any such occasion he was satisfied.

SATURDAY 30*th* April. I had an oppertunity this Mor[ng] at Matavai to see the people in Ten War Canoes go through their exercize in Padling, they were at the same time properly equip'd for war, the chiefs in their war habits &c[a]. I was present at their lan[dg] and observed that the moment the Canoe touched the Shore all the padlers jump'd out and with the assistance of a few people on the shore draged her on the Strand when without stoping the Canoe those on the Stage and in the Stern got out, all those on the Stage except one Walked off with their Arms &c[a] but the one which remained walked between the two heads of the Canoe till She was in her proper place where she was left, every one carrying off his Padle, Arms &c[a] so that in Five minutes time you could not tell that any thing of this kind had been going forward.

SATURDAY 14*th* May. We had no sooner dispatched our friends than we saw a Number of War Canoes coming round the point of Oparre, being desirous to have a nearer view of them I hastened down to Oparre (accompanied by some of the officers &c[a]) which we reached before the Canoes were all landed and had an oportunity to see in what manner they approached the Shore which was in divisions consisting of three or four or more lashed close a long side each other, such a division one would think must be very unwieldy, yet it was a pleasure to see how well they were conducted, they Paddled in for the Shore with all their might conducted in so judicious a manner that they closed the line a Shore to an inch, we landed with the last and took a view of them as they lay in along the Shore. This fleet consisted of Forty sail, were equiped in the same manner as those we had seen before and belonged to the little district of Tettaha and were come to Oparre to be reviewed before *Otou* as those we had seen before had done, there were tending on this Fleet one or more Small double Canoes which they call'd Marai having on their fore part a kind of double bed place laid over with green leaves each just sufficient to contain one Man, these they told us was to lay their Slain upon, their Chiefs I suppose they meant, otherways their Slain must be very few. . . . I went with Otou to one of his large double Canoes which was building and nearly ready to launch. She was by far the largest I had seen at any of the isles, he beged me a grapling and a grapling rope for her to which I added an English Jack and Pendant, the use of which he had been before fully informed in. I desired that these two Joint Canoes, i.e. what is understood as a double Canoe might be Call'd Brit-tania (the name they have adopted for our Country) to which he very readily consented and she was Christened accordingly. . . . As soon as the Boat was hoisted in again we directed our Course for Huaheine in order to pay a Visit to our freinds there, but it will be necessary first to give some account of the present s(t)ate of Otaheite especially as it differs very much from what it was Eight Months ago. *May 1774*

'I have already mentioned the improvements we found in the Plains of Oparre and Matavai: the same was observed in every other part into which we came, it seem'd to us allmost incredable that so many large Canoes and Houses could be built in so short a space of time as Eight Months, the tools which they got from the English and the other Nations who have touched here have no doubt greatly accelerated the work and according to the old Proverb many hands make light work, for I shall soon make it appear there are no want of these; the Number of Hoggs too was a nother thing which struck our attention, but this is more easy accounted for, they might and certainly had a good many when we were here before but not chusing to part with any had conve'd them out of our Sight, be this as it will we now got as many as we could consume during our Stay, but some to take to Sea with us. . . . I must confess I would willingly have stayed five days longer had I been sure the expedition would then take place, but it rather seem'd that they wanted us to be gone first. . . . Thus we were deprived of seeing the whole of this grand Fleet and perhaps too of being Spectators of a Sea Fight, a Sight, I am well convinced, well worth the seeing. I took some pains to inform my Self in what manner they joined Battle and fought at Sea, but knowing but little of their Language and they none of ours, the account I got must be very imperfect. It however gave me a tolerable Idea of it, which I shall endeavour to convey to the reader. I have before said that all their Vessels of War have a raised platform or Stage at the very fore part of them which will contain Eight or Ten Men, these are the Tataotai's or fighting Men. In forming the line of battle they draw up a breast of each other with their heads to the Enimy and as I understood in divisions as when they land, for the more readier closing the line when the action begins: the enemies fleet being drawn up in like manner, they rush with all their might upon each other, the Attack is first begun with Stones, but as soon as they Close they take

May 1774 to their other weapons for the stages of the one fleet will be as it were joined to those of the other.

SUNDAY 15*th* May. I have already mentioned that after leaving Otaheite we directed our Course for Huahine and at one o'Clock in the after noon of this day Anchor'd in the North entrance of OWharre Harbour, hoisted out the boats and Warp'd into a proper birth and there Moor'd the Ship. While this was doing several of the Natives came on board amongest whom was Oree the Chief, he brought with him a Hog and some other Articles which he presented to me with the usual cerimony.

MONDAY 23*rd* May. Winds Easterly as it has been every sence we have been here. The Ship being un moor'd and every thing in readiness to Sail, at 8 a.m. weighed and put to Sea, the good old Chief was the last of the Natives who went out to the Ship, when he took leave I told him we should see each other no more at which he wept saying then let your Sons come we will treat them well. Oree is a good Man to the utmost sence of the word, but many of the people are far from being of that disposision and seem to take advantage of his old age. The gentle treatment they have ever met with from me and the careless and imprudent manner many of our people have rambled about in their country from a Vain opinion that fire Arms rendred them invincible hath incouraged some of these people to commit Acts of Violence no man at Otaheite ever dar'd attempt.

MONDAY 23*rd* May. As soon as we were clear of Huaheine we made Sail and steer'd over for the South end of Ulietea, one of the Natives of the first isle took a Passage with us as some others had done from Otaheite.

FRIDAY 27*th* May. In the Morning Oreo, his Wife, Son and Daughters and several more of his friends came aboard and brought with them a supply of refreshments. After dinner we went on Shore and were entertained with a Play which ended with a representation of a Woman in Labour, who at last brought forth a thumping Boy near six feet high who ran about the stage draging what was to represent the [after birth] after him. I had an opportunity to see this acted afterwards and observed that as soon as they got hold of the fellow who represented the Child they fatned his nose or pressed it to his face which may be a Custom among them and be the reason why they have all in general flat, or what we call pug noses.

SATURDAY 4*th* June. I made all the others presents sutable to their rank and the service they had done me after which they took a very affectionate leave, Oreo's last request was for me to return and when he found I would not make him the Promise he asked the name of my *Marai* (burial place) a strange quistion to ask a Seaman, however I hesitated not one moment to tell him Stepney the Parish in which I lived when in London. I was made to repeated it several times over till they could well pronounce it, then Stepney Marai no Tootu was echoed through a hundred mouths at once. I afterwards found that the same question

THE *RESOLUTION*
ARRIVES AT TAHITI, APRIL 1774

was put to M[r] F. by a Person a Shore but he gave a different and indeed more proper answer by saying no man who used the Sea could tell were he would be buried. It is the Custom here as well as in most other Nations for all the great families to have burial places of their own were their bones are enterr'd, these go with the estate to the next heir, as for instance at Otaheite wen Toutaha held the sceptre the Marai at Oparre was Marai no Toutaha, but now they say Marai no Otoo. What greater proof could we have of these people esteeming and loving us as friends whom they wished to remember, they had been repeatedly told we should see them no more, they then wanted to know the name of the place were our bodies were to return to dust. . . . When I first came to these isles I had some thoughts of Visiting the famous Island of Bola bola, but having now got all the necessary repairs of the Ship done and got a plentifull Supply of all manner of refreshments I thought it would be answering no end going there and therefore laid it a side and directed my Course to the West and took our final leave of these happy isles and the Good People in them.

June 1774

(The expedition now sailed westwards from the Society and Friendly Islands in order to examine Quiros' Australia del Espiritu Santo (the New Hebrides) which had just been rediscovered and reported on by Bougainville.

(They saw Wallis's Howe Island; had a brush with the inhabitants of an island which Cook named 'Savage Island', but secured some provisions in the Society Islands in spite of the usual thefts.

SUNDAY *5th* June. Gentle breezes and fine Weather, I have before taken notice of after leaving Ulietea I directed my Course to the West, this was with a View of carrying into execution the resolution I had taken of Visiting Quiros's discoveries.

MONDAY *27th* June. Early in the Morn the Master and I went a Shore to look for fresh water, we were received with great Courtesy by the Natives and conducted to a Pond of Brackish Water the same I suppose as Tasman Water at. . . .

TUESDAY *28th* June. I was no sooner return'd from the Pond the first time I landed that this Woman and a Man presented to me a young woman and gave me to understand she was at my Service. Miss, who probably had received her instructions, I found wanted by way of Handsel a Shirt or a Nail, neither the one nor the other I had to give without giving her the Shirt on my back which I was not in a humour to do. I soon made them sencible of my Poverty and thought by that means to have come off with flying Colours but I was mistaken, for I was made to understand that I might retire with her on credit, this not suting me neither the old Lady began first to argue with me and when that fail'd she abused me, I understood very little of what she said, but her actions were expressive enough and shew'd that her words were to this effect: Sneering in my face and saying 'what sort of a man are you thus to refuse the embraces

June 1774 of so fine a young Woman', for the girl certainly did not [lack] beauty which I could however withstand, but the abuse of the old Woman I could not and therefore hastned into the Boat, they then would needs have me take the girl on board with me, but this could not be done as I had come to a Resolution not to suffer a Woman to come on board the Ship on any pretence whatever and had given strict orders to the officers to that purpose for reasons which I shall mention in a nother place.

THURSDAY 30*th* June. The Wind being contrary and but little of it the after noon and night was spent in plying with the precaution necessary to such navigation. In the Morning Stretched out for the high Islands having the Advantage of a gentle breeze at WSW. Day no sooner dawned than we saw Canoes coming from all parts, their Traffick was much the same as yesterday or rather better for out of one Canoe I got two Pigs which were Scarce Articles with them.

FRIDAY 1*st* July. Gentle breezes and Clowdy Weather. At 4 o'Clock in the PM we reached the two high Islands the Southernmost and the one on which the Vulcano is or is supposed to be is called by the Natives Amattafoa and the other which is round high and Peaked Oghao. . . . While we were in the Passage between the two Isles we had little wind which gave time for a large Sailing Canoe which had been chasing us all day to get up with us as well as several others with Padles which had been thrown a Stern when the breeze was fresh, several of these people came on board the Ship, these as also the others along side continued to exchange articles as usual. I had now an opertunity to verify a fact which before I was in doubt about which was whether or no their great sailing Vessels put about in changeing Tacks or only shifted the sail and so proceeded with either end foremost, the one now by us worked in this Manner, the Sail is Latteen, extended to a Latteen yard above and the foot to a Boom, the yard is slung nearly in the Middle or upon equipoise, so that when they want to change Tacks have only to ease of the sheet and bring the heel or Tack end of the yard to the other end of the Boat and the Sheet in like manner. . . . The out riggers to these Canoes necessary to support the Mast and yard are of a size sufficient to heave down a Vessel of two or three hundred Tons and were secured with equal Strength and the ropes used for shrouds, guies &c[a] are 4 inches at least, indeed the Sail yard and Boom are altogether of such an enormous weight that strength is required to Support them. . . . The Inhabitants, Productions, &c[a] of Rotterdam or Annamocka and the neighbouring isles are much the Same as at Amsterdam. Hoggs and Fowles indeed are scarce, of the former we got but Six and not very many of the latter, yams and Shaddocks were what we got the most of, other fruits being scarcer and not in such great perfection. Not half the isle is laid out in inclosed Plantations as at Amsterdam but the other parts are not less fertile or less cultivated, here is however far more waste land on this isle in proportion to its Size then upon Amsterdam and the People seem much poorer, I mean in respect to Cloth, Matting, Ornaments &c[a] which constitute a great part of the Riches of these people. The people of this isle seem to be more affected with the Leprous or some other Scrofulous disease than any I have yet seen, it breaks out in the face more than in any other parts of the Body. I have seen several who had quite lost their Noses by it. . . .

SUNDAY 17*th* July. Continued to Steer to the West till 3 o'Clock in the PM when we saw land bearing SW . . . I made no doubt but this was the Australia Del Espiritu Santo of Quiros or what M[r] D. Bougainville calls the Great Cyclades and the coast we were now upon the East side of Aurora Island whose Longitude by the Observations we have lately had is 17° E.

☾ In the New Hebrides the expedition encountered a fresh type of Pacific islander, a negroid, who in spite of his, or her unattractive appearance was less addicted to theft than the Polynesian farther to the east. Nevertheless the inhabitants of some of the islands were so fierce that the use of firearms was necessary.

FRIDAY 22*nd* July. About 9 o'Clock we landed in the face of about 4 or 500 Men who were assembled on the Shore, arm'd with Bows and Arrows, Clubs and Spears, but they made not the least opposission, on the contrary one Man gave his Arms to a nother and Met us in the water with a green branch in his hand, which exchanged for the one I held in my hand, took me by the other hand and led me up to the crowd to whom I distributed Medals, Pieces of Cloth &c[a]. . . . They set no sort of Value upon Nails nor did they seem much to esteem any thing we had, they would now and then give an arrow for a Piece of Cloth but constantly refused to part with their bows, they were unwilling we should go into the Country and very desireous for us to go on board, we understood not a word they said, they a quite different to all we have yet seen and Speak a different language, they are almost black or rather a dark Chocolate Colour, Slenderly made, not tall, have Monkey faces and Woolly hair. About Noon after sending what wood we had cut on board we all embarqued and went of after which they all retired some one way and some a nother.

SATURDAY 23*rd* July. Some time last night the Natives had taken away the Buoy from the Kedge Anchor we lay moor'd by, which I now saw a fellow bringing along the Strand to the landing place. I therefore took a boat and went for it accompained by some of the Gentlemen, the moment we landed the Buoy was put into our boat by a man who walked of again without Speaking one word; it ought to be observed that this was the only thing they even so much as attempted to take from us by any means whatever and that they seem'd to Observe Strict honisty in all their dealings. Having landed near some of their houses and Plantations which were just within the Skirts of the Woods, I prevailed on one man to let me see them, they Suffered M[r] F. to go with me but were unwilling any more should follow. Their houses are low and covered

July 1774 with thick Palm thatch, their form is oblong and some are boarded at the ends where the entrance is by a Square Port hole which at this time was Shut up, they did not chouse we should enter any of them and we attempted nothing against their inclinations; here were about half a Dozen houses, some small Plantations which were fenced round with reeds. . . . We next proceed to the Point of the harbour where we could see the three distant Isles already mentioned the names of which we now obtained as well as the land on which we were which they call *Mallecollo*, a name which we find mentioned by Quiros or at least one so like it that there is not room for a Doubt but that they both mean the same land.

'At 7 o'Clock AM weighed and with some variable light Airs of Wind and the assistance of our Boat towing got out of the Harbour the South point of which at Noon WSW distant two or three Miles, Lat Obd 16° 24′ 30″. We now got a gentle breeze at ESE which we stretched off NE with a view of geting to windward in order to explore the Isles which layd there. . . . The people of this country are in general the most Ugly and ill-proportioned of any I ever saw, to what hath been already said of them I have only to add that they have thick lips flat noses and [monkey countenances].

'Their Beards as well as most of their Woolly heads are of a Colour between brown and black, the former is much brighter than the latter and is rather more of hair than wool, short and curly. The Men go naked, it can hardly be said they cover their Natural parts, the Testicles are quite exposed, but they wrap a piece of cloth or leafe round the yard which they tye up to the belly to a Cord or bandage which they wear round the waist just under the Short Ribbs and over the belly and so tight that it was a wonder to us how they could endure it. They have curious bracelets which they wear on the Arm just above the Elbow, these are work'd with thread or Cord and studed with Shells and are four or five inches broad, they never would part with one, they also wear round the wrist Hoggs Tusks and rings made of large Shells; the bridge of the nose is pierced in which they wear an ornament of this form, it is made of a stone which is not unlike alabaster they likewise wear small ear Rings made of Tortise shell. We saw but few Women and they were full as disagreeable as the Men, their head face and Shoulders were painted with a Red Colour, they wear a piece of Cloth wraped round the Middle and Some thing over their Shoulders in which they carry their Children.

'Their Arms are Bows and Arrows, Clubs and Spears made of hard or Iron wood, the Arrows are rude and some are arm'd with a long sharp point made of the Iron wood, others are Armed with a very sharp point of bone and covered with a green gummy substance which we took to be poison and the Natives conform'd our Su[spicion] by making signs to us not to touch the point. I have seen some Arm'd with two or three of these points with little prikles on the edges to prevent the Arrows being drawn out of the wound.

SUNDAY 24*th* July. The Night before we came out of Port two Red fish about the Size of large Bream and not unlike them were caught with hook and line of which Most of the Officers and Some of the Petty officers dined the next day. In the Evening every one who had eat of these fish were seiz'd with Violent pains in the head and Limbs, so as to be unable to stand, together with a kind of Scorching heat all over the Skin, there remained no doubt but that it was occasioned by the fish being of a Poisonous nature and communicated its bad effects to every one who had the ill luck to eat of it even to the Dogs and Hogs, one of the latter died in about Sixteen hours after and a young dog soon after shared the same fate. These must be the same sort of fish as Quiros mentions under the name of *Pargon* which Poisoned the Crews of his Ships so that it was some time before they recovered. We had reason to be thankfull in not having caught more of them for if we had should have been in the Same Situation. *July 1774*

THURSDAY 4*th* August. At 6 o'Clock in the PM we got in under the NW side of the head where we Anchored in 17 fathom Water half a Mile from the Shore, the bottom black sand.

'At Day-break I went with two boats to view the coast and to look from a proper landing place wood and Water. Several people appeared on the Shore and by signs invited us to go to them, I with some difficulty on account of the rocks which every where lined the Coast, put a Shore at one place where a few men came to us to whom I gave pieces of cloth, medals &c[a] for this treatment they offered to haul the boat over some breakers to a Sandy beach, I thought this a friendly offer, but afterwards had reason to think otherwise. When they saw I was determin'd to proceed to some other place, they ran along the Shore keeping always abreast of the boats and at last directed us to a place, a Sandy beach, where I could step out of the boat without weting a foot. I landed in the face of a great Multitude with nothing but a green brance in my hand I had got from of of them, I was received very courteously and upon their pressing near the boat, retired upon my makeing Signs to keep off, one Man who seem'd to a Chief a Mongest them at once comprehending what I meant, made them form a kind of Semicircle round the bow of the boat and beat any one who broke through this order. . . . I was charmed with their behaviour, the only thing which could give the least Suspicion was the most of them being Arm'd with Clubs, Darts, stones and bows and Arrows. The Chief made a sign to me to haul the Boat up upon the Shore but I gave him to understand that I must first go on board and then I would return and do as he disired and so step'd into the boat and order her to be put of, but they were not for parting with us to soon and now attempted by force to accomplish what they could not obtain by more gentler means, the gang-board having been put out for me to come in some seized hold of it while others snatched hold of the Oars, upon my pointing a musquet at them they in some measure desisted, but return'd again in an instant seemingly

August *1774* ditermined to hauld the boat up upon Shore, at the head of this party was the Chief, and the others who had not room to come at the boat stood ready with their darts and bows and arrows in hand to support them: our own safety became now the only consideration and yet I was very loath to fire upon such a Multitude and resolved to make the chief a lone fall a Victim to his own treachery, but my Musquet at this critical Moment refused to perform its part and made it absolutely necessary for me to give orders to fire as they now began to Shoot their Arrows and throw darts and Stones at us, the first discharge threw them into confusion but a nother discharge was hardly sufficient to drive them of the beach and after all they continued to throw Stones from behind the trees and bushes and one would peep out now and then and throw a dart, four laid to all appearence dead on the shore, but two of them afterwards cript into the bushes, happy for many of these poor people not half our Musquets would go of otherwise many more must have fallen. . . . These Islanders are a different race of people to those on Mallecollo and seem'd to speake a quite different language; they are of the Middle Size, have a good Shape and tolerable features, they are of a dark Chocolate Colour and paint their faces with a sort of black or Red Pigment, their hair is very curly and crisp and some what Woolly: I saw some few Women which I thought ugly, they wore a kind of Petticoat made of Palm leaves or some plant like to them. The Men like those of Mallecollo have no other covering than the Case to the Penis which they tie up to a belt or string which they wear round the waist.

WEDNESDAY 10*th* August. Yesterday Mr Forster obtained from these people the Name of the Island (Tanna) and to day I got from them the names of those in the neighbourhood. They gave us to understand in such a manner which admitted of no doubt that they eat human flesh, they began the subject themselves by asking us if we did: they like wise gave us to understand that Circumcision was practised amongest them.

THURSDAY 11*th* August. Wind at South with some heavy showers of rain in the night. In the p.m. two or three boy's got behind some thickets and threw 2 or 3 stones at our people who were cuting wood, for which they were fired at by the petty officers present. I was much displeased at such an abuse of our fire Arms and took measures to prevent it for the future. During the night and all the nest day the Volcano made a terrible noise throwing up prodigeous Columns of Smoak and fire at every irruption, at one time great stones were seen high in the air.

SUNDAY 14*th* August. We found these people Civil and good Natured when not prompted by jealousy to a contrary conduct, a conduct one cannot blame them for when one considers the light in which they must look upon us in, its impossible for them to know our real design, we enter their Ports without their daring to make opposition, we attempt to land in a peaceable manner if this succeeds its well, if not we land nevertheless and mentain the footing we thus got by the Superiority of our fire arms, in what other light can they than at first look upon us as invaders of their Country; time and some acquaintance with us can only convince them of their mistake. *August 1774*

FRIDAY 19*th* August. Winds northerly a gentle gale. In the Tiller was finished and Shiped, so that we only waited for a fair Wind to put to sea. In the AM as the wind would not admit of our geting to sea I sent the guard on with Mr Wales as usual and at the same time a party to cut up and bring off the remainder of the tree we had Cut a spare tiller of. A good many of the Natives were, as usual, assembled near the landing place and unfortunately one of them was Shott by one of our Centinals, I who was present and on the spot saw not the least cause for the committing of such an Outrage and was astonished beyond Measure at the inhumanity of the act, the rascal who perpetrated this crime pretended that one of the Natives laid his arrow across his bow and held it in the Attitude of Shooting so that he apprehended himself in danger, but this was no more than what was done hourly and I believe with not other View than to let us see they were Armed as well as us: what made this affair the more unfortunate it not appearing to be the man who bent the Bow but a nother who was near him.

TUESDAY 23*rd* August. Wind at ESE a fresh gale and fair weather. At 4 PM we began to draw near the Island we were steering for which at this time extended from N 42° E to NW. As we were not like to have any intercourse with the Inhabtants of this fine isle by which we might obtain its true name, I called it Sandwich Island in honour of My Noble Patron the Earl of Sandwich.

❨ On 25th August Cook found himself at the entrance of the Bay of St. Philip and St. James where Quiros had tried to found his New Jerusalem in 1606. While it must be admitted that Cook's motives, as an explorer, were less noble than those of Quiros with his Franciscan friars and Knights of the Holy Ghost, the British, in spite of some unhappy incidents, were far less cruel and oppressive to the natives than were Quiros' Spanish followers.

THURSDAY 25*th* August. After doubling the Cape we found the Coast trend away to the South and to form a very large and deep bay of which the land above mentioned was its western boundaries. Every thing conspired to make us believe this was the Bay of St Philip and St James discovered by Quiros in 1606. To determine this point it was necessary to search it to the very bottom for at this time we could see no end to it, for this purpose hauled the wind on the Larboard tack, having a gentle breeze at South which at Noon began to veer towards East and being well over to the Western shore taked and stood to NE Latitude 14° 55′ 30″, Longd^e^ 16° ″ East, the Mouth of the Bay extending from N 64° W′ to S 86° East.

SATURDAY 27*th* August. At 1 PM the Calm was succeeded by a gentle breeze at NBW with which we stood up the bay till 3 when being but about two Miles from

August 1774 the shore, I sent away M[r] Cooper and the Master to sound and reconnoitre the Coast and in the Meantime we stood off and on with the Ship, this gave time for three sailing Canoes who had been following us some time to come up with us; there were 5 or 6 Men in each; they came near enough to take hold of such things as were thrown them fastned to a rope but would not come along side. They were the same sort of people as we saw last night and had some resemblance to those of Mallicollo but seemed to be stouter and better shaped and so far as we could judge spoke a different language which made us believe they were of a nother Nation: probably the same as Annamoka and the neighbouring isles, as one of them, on some occasion, mentioned the Numerals as far as five or Six in that language, some other circumstance increased the Probabillity such as giving us the Names of such parts of the Country as we pointed to, but we could not obtain from them the Name of the Island. Some had hair short a crisp which looked like wool, others had it tyed up on the crown of the head and Ornamented with feathers like the New Zealanders, their other Ornaments were Bracelets and Necklaces and one wore some thing like a white shell on his forehead. Some were painted with a kind of black Pigment. It did not appear to me that they had any other weapons with them than darts and fishgigs intended only for stricking of fish. The Canoes which were by no means a Master piece of workman Ship, were fitted with outriggers. The Sail was triangular, extended between two sticks one of which was the Mast and the other the Yard or boom, at least so they appeared to us who only saw them under Sail at some distance off. . . . It was not unanimously concluded that this was the bay of S[t] Philip and S[t] James, as the Port of VARA CRUZ was not to be found, for my own part I had no doubt about it, I found general points to agree very well with Quiros's description, and as to what he calls the Port of Vara Cruz is undoubtedly the Anchorage at the head of the bay which in some places may extend farther off than where our boats sounded: it was but natural for them to give a name to a place, independant of so large a bay, where they laid so long at Anchor. Port is a vague term, like many others used in geography, as is very often applied to a much less sheltred place than the head of this bay. The officers observed that there is seldom any surf on the beach, as grass and other plants grew close to high-water mark which is a sure sign of Pacifick anchorage; the judged that the tides rose about 4 feet and that boats might enter the River at high-water, so that it is very probbly it is one of those mentioned by Quiros and appearance inclined us to believe we saw the other.

¶ The expedition now made the important and entirely new discovery of the large island of New Caledonia, but, with the southern summer and the Antarctic season approaching, Cook could spare only ten days and was unable to examine more than half the coast.

September 1774

MONDAY 5*th* September. Continued to Stand to the South with a light breeze at East till 6 PM when we were three leagues from the land the extremes of which bore from SEBS to WBN. Some openings appeared in the coast to the West so that we could not tell if it was continued; the extremes to the SE seem'd to terminate in an elevated point (at least we could see no land beyond it) which I named Cape [Colnett] after one of my Midshipmen who first saw this land.

'We had hardly Anchored before we were surrounded by a Vast number of People, the most of them without Arms: at first they were alittle Shy, but it was not long before we prevail'd on the people in one Canoe to come near enough to receive some presents we lowered down to them by a line to which they tyed in return two fish which stunk intollerable as did those they gave us in the Morning, these mutual exchanges soon brought on a kind of confidence so that two ventured aboard and presently after the Ship was full of them and we had the Company of several at dinner in the Cabbin. Our dinner was Pease Soup, Salt Beef and Pork which they had no curiosity to taste but the eat some Yam which they call Oobee, which is not unlike Oofee the name they are called by at all the isles we have been at except Mallicollo. Nevertheless we found these people spoke a language quite new to us and like all these we have lately seen had no other covering than a little cap to the Penis which was suffered to hang down. They were curious to look into every corner of the Ship which they viewed with some attention; they had not the least knowlidge of Goats, Hogs, Dogs or Catts, they had not so much as a name for one of them; they seem'd fond of Iron, large spike Nails especially, and pieces of red cloth or indeed any other colour, but red was their favourite.

WEDNESDAY 7*th* September. Some time after a party of us went to take a View of the Country having two of the Natives to be our guides who conducted us up the hills by a tollerable good path way, meeting in our rout several people most of whom followed us so that at last our train was numerous, some indeed wanted us to turn back but we paid no regard to their Signs and they seem'd not uneasy when we proceeded. At length we reached the Summit of one of the hills from whence we saw the Sea between some Advanced hills at a considerable distance on the opposite side of the Island. Between those advanced hills and the ridge we were upon is a large Vally through which ran a Serpentine river which added no little beauty to the prospect. The plains along the Coast on the side we lay appeared from the hills to great advantage, the winding streams which ran through them which had their direction from Nature, the lesser streams conveyed by art through the different plantations, the little Stragling Villages, the Variety in the Woods, the Shoals on the Coast so variegated the Scene that the whole might afford a Picture for romance.

THURSDAY 8*th* September. In the PM we made a little excursion along the Coast to the Westward, but met with nothing remarkable, the Natives every

September 1774 where behaving with all the civility imaginable. A Fish was procured for the Natives by my Clerk and given to me after my return a board, it was of a new genius, something like a sun fish, without the least suspicion of its being of a poisonous quality we had ordered it for supper, but luckily for us the opperation of describeing and drawing took up so much time till it was too late so that only the Liver and Roe was dressed of which the two Mr Forsters and myself did but just taste. About 3 or 4 o'Clock in the Morning we were siezed with an extraordinary weakness in all our limbs attended with a numness or Sensation like to that caused by exposing ones hands or feet to a fire after having been pinched much by forst, I had almost lost the Sence of feeling nor could I distinguish between light and heavy bodies, a quart pot full of Water and a feather was the same in my hand. We each of us took a Vomet and after that a Sweat which gave great relief. (In) one of the Pigs which had eat the entrails was found dead, the Dogs got the start of the Servants of what went from our table so that they escaped, it soon made the dogs sick and they t[h]rew it all up again and were not much effected by it. In the Morning when the Natives came on board and saw the fish hanging up, they immidiately gave us to understand it was by no means to be eat expressing the utmost abhorrance of it and yet no one was observed to do this when it was to be sold or even after it was bought.

MONDAY 12*th* September. Mention hath been made of my puting a Dog and a Bitch a shore, I also wanted to lay a foundation for stocking the Country with Hogs having kept some alive for such purposes. As Teabooma the Chief had not been seen sence the day he got the Dogs, I took a young Boar and a Sow with me in the Boat and went up the Mangrove creek to look for my friend [Teabooma] but when we came there we were told he lived at some distance off but they would send for him, but whether they did or no I cannot say, in short he did not come and as the tide would not permit us to stay much longer, I resolved to give them to any man I could find of some note, our guide we had to the hills happened to be here. I made him understand I wanted to leave the two pigs a Shore, which I had now ordered out of the boat, several people present made signs to me to take them away one of which was a grave elderly man, him I made understand that it was my intention they should remain there, at which he shook his head and repeated his signs to take them away; but when they saw I did not do it they seemed to consult what was to be done and at last our guide told me to carry them to the *Alekee* (Chief) accordingly I ordered them to be taken up by my people, for none of the others would come near them; our guide conducted us to a house wherein were seated in a circle eight or ten middle aged men to whom I and my Pigs were interduced and with great courtesy I was desired to sit down, when I began to expatiate on the merits of the two Pigs, shewing them the distinction of their sex, telling them how many young ones the female would have at a time, in short I multiplyed them to some hundreds in a trice, my only view was to enhance the value of the present that they might take the more care of them and I had reason to think I in some measure succeeded. . . . Here was a pretty large scatering Village and a good deal of Cultivated land, regularly laid out in plantations, mostly planted with Tarro or Eddy roots, some yams, Sug^{r} Cane & Plantans: the Tarro Plantations were prettily Watered by little rills, continually supplyed from the main Channel where the Water was conducted by art from a River at the foot of the mountains. They have two methods in Planting and raising these roots, some are planted in square or oblong Plantations which lay perfectly horizontal and sunk below the common level of the adjacent lands, so that they can let in as much water upon them as is necessary. I have generally seen them wholy covered 2 or 3 inches deep, but I do not know if this is always necessary; others are planted in ridges about 4 feet Broad and 2½ in height, in the middle or top of the ridge is a narrow gutter along which is conveyed a small stream of Water which Waters the roots planted on each side, the plantations are so judiciously laid out that the same stream will Water several.

September 1774

THURSDAY 15*th* September. PM a gentle breeze at ESE with which we steered NWBW, NWBN and NNE along the out side of the reef, following its direction. . . . At Sun-rise made sail and steer'd NWBW at this time saw neither land nor breakers. Two hours after saw the latter extending NW farther than the eye could reach, but no land was to be seen, so that we had all the reason in the world to believe that we had seen its termination to the NW. We were already carried far out of sight of land and there was no knowing how much farther we might be carrid before we found the ends of the shoals, the exploreing of them must, and was now attended with great risk, a gale of wind or a Calm, both of which we had often enough experienced, might have been attended with fatal consequences. . . .

(On leaving New Caledonia Cook encountered very grave dangers near the reef-encircled Isle of Pines, but he refused to leave the locality until he had satisfied himself that the fine timber was suitable for shipping purposes. He then was fortunate to discover the small but useful Norfolk Island with its splendid pines, after which he sailed south to reach Queen Charlotte Sound, New Zealand, on 18th October.

TUESDAY 27*th* September. In the PM the wind veered to SSE and increased to a fresh gale. Continued to stretch to East and NE till 2 AM when we tacked and stood SW with a very fresh gale at SE we had some hopes of weathering the isle, but we fell a few miles short of our expectation, for at 10 o'Clock we had to tack, being about one mile from the East shore of the isle, the Hill bearing west, the extremes from NWBN to SW and some low isles lying off the SE point SBN, these seem'd to be connected to the large isle by breakers. Had no soundings with 80 fathoms of line. The Skirts of this isle is wholy covered with the trees so often mention on which account it obtained the name of *Isle of Pines*.

September 1774 THURSDAY *29th* September. After a short trip to the NNE we stood again to the south in order to have a nearer and better view of the shoals at Sun-set, we gained nothing by this but the Melancholy prospect of a sea strewed with Shoals: Anchoring in a strong gale with a Chain of breakers to leeward was the last resource, it was thought safer to spend the night makeing short boards over that space we had in some measure made our selves acquainted with in the day. Proper persons we stationed to look out and each man held the rope in his hand he was to manage, to this we perhaps owe our safety, for as we were stranding to the Northward the People on the Forecastle and lee gang way saw breakers under the lee-bow which we escaped by the expeditious manner the Ship was tack'd. Thus we spent the night under the terrible apprehensions of every moment falling on some of the many dangers which surrounded us. Day-light shewed that our fears were not ilfounded and that we had spent the night in the most eminent danger hav[g] had shoals and breakers continually under our lee at a very little distance from us. We found by the bearings and situations of the lands a round us that we had gained nothing to windward during the night. I was now almost tired of a Coast I could no longer explore but at the risk of loosing the ship and ruining the whole Voyage, but I was determined not to leave it till I was satisfied what sort of trees those were which had been the subject of our speculation.

FRIDAY *30th* September. After dinner I landed again with two boats accompaned by several of the officers and gentlemen takeing with me the Carpenter and some of his crew to cut down such trees as we wanted. . . . The hull of a Canoe laid wrecked in the sand, it was precisely of the same sort as we had seen at Ballade, we are now no longer at a loss to know of what trees they make their Canoes, they can be no other than the Pines. On this little isle were some which measured twenty inches diameter and between Sixty and Seventy feet in length and would have done very well for a Fore-mast for the Resolution if one had been wanting. Sence trees of this size are to be found on so small a spot is it not reasonable to expect to find some vastly larger on the Main and on the larger isles, if appearances have not deceived us we can assert it. If I except New Zealand I know of no Island in the South Pacifick Ocean where a Ship could supply herself with a Mast or a Yard, was she ever so much distress'd for want of one; nay you cannot even get a Studing-sail boom of Wood att all fit for the purpose much less a lower mast or yard; thus far the discovery may be both usefull and valuable.

SATURDAY *1st* October. When I considered that summer was at hand, the Sea which was yet to explore to the South which could only be done in summer, the state and condition of the Ship already in want of some necessary stores and the vast distance we were from any European Port where we could get supplies in case we should be detained by any accident in this Sea nother year, I did not think it adviseable to loose time evening in attempting to regain the Coast, and thus I was constrained as it were by necessity to leave it sooner than otherwise I should have done. I called the land we had lately discovered New Caledonia If we except New Zealand it is perhaps the largest Island in the whole South Pacifick Ocean. *October 1774*

TUESDAY 11*th* October. Gentle gales at SE and ESE. After dinner hoisted out two boats in which my self, some of the officers and gentlemen went to take a view of the Island and its produce, we found no difficulty in landing behind some rocks which lined part of the coast and defended it from the Surf. We found the Island uninhabited and near a kin to New Zealand, the Flax plant, many other Plants and Trees common to that country was found here but the chief produce of the isle is Spruce Pines which grow here in vast a bundance and to a vast size, from two or three feet diameter and upwards, it is of a different sort to those in New Caledonia and also to those in New Zealand and for Masts, Yards &c[a] superior to both. We cut down one of the Smallest trees we could find and Cut a length of the uper end to make a Topg[t] Mast or Yard. My Carpenter tells me that the wood is exactly of the same nature as the Quebeck Pines. Here then is a nother Isle where Masts for the largest Ships may be had. Here are the same sort of Pigions, Parrots and Parrokeets as in New Zealand, Rails and some small birds. The Sea fowl are White Boobies, guls, Tern &c[a] which breed undisturbed on the Rocks and in the Clifts. The Coast is not distitute of Fish, our people caught some which were excellent, while in the boats a long side the rocks. I took posission of this Isle as I had done of all the others we had discovered, and named it *Norfolk Isle* in honour of that noble family. . . . Being clear of the isle we stretched to the South with a fresh breeze at ESE. My design was to touch at Queen Charlottes Sound in New Zealand, there to refresh my people and put the Ship in a condition to Cross this great Ocean in a high Latitude once more.

Chapter XIII

THE ANTARCTIC AND HOME, 1774–5

"The intention of the voyage has in every respect been fully answered, the Southern Hemisphere sufficiently explored and the final end put to the searching after a Southern Continent."

COOK, 1775

THE *RESOLUTION* RETURNED TO QUEEN CHARLOTTE SOUND on 18th October 1774, and found signs that the *Adventure* had reached that place. Maori reports were confused but it seemed that some white crew might have met with disaster. Although Furneaux had taken the bottle with Cook's message and plans, he seems to have left nothing to inform Cook that, after losing a boat's crew of about a dozen men in an unpremeditated clash with the Maoris he was returning to England via Cape Horn and the Cape of Good Hope.

TUESDAY 18*th* October. Very strong gales at Westerly and Cloudy. Steered SSE for Queen Charlotte's Sound. . . . At 11 Anchored before Ship Cove the strong fluries from the land not permiting us to get in.

WEDNESDAY 19*th* October. We now found that some Ship had been here sence we last left it not only by the bottle being gone as mentioned above, but by several trees having been Cut down with Saws and Axes which were standing when we sailed. This Ship could be no other than the Adventure Captain Furneaux.

MONDAY 24*th* October. Pleasent weather. AM went on with the various works in hand. Two Canoes were seen coming down the Sound but retired behind a point on the west side upon discovering us as was supposed. After breakfast I went in a boat to look for them accompanid by the Botanists. As we proceeded a long shore we shott sever[l] birds, the report of our guns gave notice of our approach and the Natives discovered themselves by hollaing to us but when we came before their habitations only two men appeared on a rising ground, the rest had taken to the Woods and hills, but the moment we landed they knew us again, joy took place of fear, they hurried out of the woods embraced us over and over and skiped about like Mad men. *October 1774*

FRIDAY 28*th* October. Sence the Natives have been with us a report has risen said to have come first from them that a ship has lately been lost, some where in the Strait, and all the crew killed by them, when I examined them on this head they not only denied it but seem'd wholy ignorant of the matter.

❨ After a brief stay for refitting and refreshment Cook sailed on Friday 11th November 1774 with the object of crossing from New Zealand to Cape Horn in Latitudes 54°-55° south, which would show that no continent lay in that part of the South Pacific.

FRIDAY 11*th* November. After a few hours calm a breeze sprung up at North with which we steered SBE all sails Set, with a view of geting into the Latitude of 54° or 55°. My intention was to cross this vast Ocean nearly in these Parallels, and so as to pass over those parts which were left unexplored last summer.

❨ The concluding sections of the Journal contain important references to the contribution made to navigation, particularly by Mr Wales and by the Kendall-Harrison chronometer.

THURSDAY 17*th* November. Morning fresh gale and hazy weather. Saw a Seal and several pieces of weed. At noon Latitude in 51° 12′, Longitude 173° 17′ West. Mr Wales having from time to time communicated to me the observations he had made in this Sound for determining the Longitude the mean results of which gives 174° 25′ 07½″ East for the bottom of Ship Cove where the observations were made the Latitude of which is 41° 5′ 56½″ South.

'In my Chart constructed in my former Voyage this place is laid down in 184° 54′ 30″ W equal to 175° 5′ 30″ East, the error of the Chart is therefore 0° 40′ and nearly equal to what was found at Duskey Bay, by which it appears that the whole of TAVAI-POE-NAMMOO, is laid down 40′ too far East in the said Chart, as well as in the Journal of the Voyage, but the error in EAHEI-NO-MAUWE is not more than half a degree or 30′ because the distance between Queen Charlottes Sound and Cape Palliser has been found to be greater by 10′ of Longitude than it is laid down in the Chart. I mention these errors not from a supposition that they will much affect either Navigation or Geography but because I have no doubt of their existance, for from this multitude of observations which Mr Wales took the situation of few parts of the word are better ascertained than that of Queen Charlotte's Sound. Indeed I might with equal truth say the same of all the other places where we have made any stay at. For Mr Wales whose abilities is equal to his assiduity lost no one observation that could possibly be obtained. Even the situation of such islands as we past without touching at are by means of Mr Kendalls Watch determined with almost equal accuracy.

November 1774 ℂ When on 27th November the *Resolution* reached Latitude 55° 6′ south and Longitude 138° 56′ west Cook decided that no important land lay awaiting discovery in that part of the Pacific and sailed direct to the Straits of Magellan.

SATURDAY *26th* and SUNDAY *27th* November. Had a steady fresh gale at NNW with which steered East and at Noon on the latter we were in the Latitude of 55° 6′. Longitude 138° 56′ west. I now gave up all hopes of finding any more land in this Ocean and came to a Resolution to steer directly for the West entrance of the Straits of Magelhanes, with a view of coasting the out, or South side of Terra del Fuego round Cape Horn to Strait La Maire. As the world has but a very imperfect knowledge of this Coast, I thought the Coasting it would be of more advantage to both Navigation and Geography than anything I could expect to find in a higher latitude. In the afternoon of this day the Wind blew in squalls and occasioned the Main Topg[t] mast to be carried away.

ℂ The *Resolution* sighted the South American coast on 17th December 1774. Cook felt that his work in the South Pacific had been completed and expressed his relief with some candour.

SATURDAY *17th* December. The land now before us can be no other than the west Coast of Terra del Fuego and near the West entrance to the Straits of Magelhanes. As this was the first run that had been made directly a Cross this ocean in a high Sothern Latitude [Cook did not know at this time that the *Adventure* had preceded him] I have been a little particular in noteing every circumstance that appeared attall Intresting and after all I must observe that I never was makeing a passage anywhere of such length or even much shorter where so few intresting circumstance occrued. . . . I have now done with the SOUTHERN PACIFIC OCEAN. I hope those who honoured me and flatter myself that no one will think that I have left it unexplored or that more could have been done in one voyage towards obtaining that end than has been done in this.

THURSDAY *29th* December. At 3 o'Clock in the Morning made sail and steered SEBS with a fresh breeze at WSW the Weather somewhat hazy. At this time the West entrance to Nassau bay extended from NBE to NE1/2E and the South side of Hermites isles EBS. At 4 Cape Horn, for which we now steered, bore EBS, it is known at a distance by a high round hill, over it a point to the WNW shews a surface not unlike this but their situations alone will allways distinguish the one from the other. At half past 7 we passed this famous Cape and entered the *Southern Atlantick Ocean*.

ℂ Cook spent some weeks in exploring and charting the bleak and desolate shoreline in the vicinity of Cape Horn, and wrote wise advice to mariners to sail well south of the Cape and so give its dangerous currents a wide berth. He recorded many interesting facts of natural history, and his accounts of the colonies of sea animals and seabirds, which follow, will be appreciated particularly by those who have visited such colonies themselves.

December 1774

SATURDAY 31*st* December. After dinner hoisted out three boats and landed with a large party of men, some to kill seals, others to catch or kill birds fish or what came in our way. To find of the former it mattered not where we landed for the whole shore was covered with them and by the noise they made one would have thought that the island was stocked with cows and calves. On landing we found they were a different Animal to Seals, we called them Lions on account of the great resemblance the Male has to a land Lion. Here were also the same sort of Seals which we found in New Zealand generally known by the name of Sea Bears, at least so we called them. They were all so tame, or rather so stupid as to suffer us to come so near as to knock them down with a stick but the large ones we shot as it was rather dangerous to go near them. We also found on the island abundance of Penguins and Shaggs, the latter had young ones almost fledged and just to our taste; here were geese and Ducks but not many; Birds of prey and a few small birds. In the evening we returned on board with our boats well Laden with one thing or a nother.

TUESDAY 3*rd* January. The Animals which Inhabit this little spot are Sea Lyons, Sea Bears, a variety of aquatick and some land birds. The Sea Lion is pretty well described by Pernety, but these have not such forefeet or fins as the one he has given a plate of, but such fins as the one he calls a Sea Wolf, nor did we see any so large as he speaks of, the largest were not more than 12 or 14 feet in length and perhaps 8 or 10 in circumference. They are not of that sort described under the same name by Lord Anson, but for aught I know these are more like a lion of the Wood, the long hair with which the back of the head, the neck and shoulders are covered gives them greatly the air and appeerences of one. The other part of the body is covered with a short hair little longer than that of a cow or a horse and the whole is a dark brown. The female is not half so big as the male, it is covered with a short hair of an ash or light dun colour. They live as it were in herds, upon the rocks and near the Sea Shore. As this was the time for ingendering as well as bringing forth their young, we have seen a male with 20 or 30 females about him and was always very attentive to keep them all to himself by beating off every other male who attempted to come into his flock; others again have a less number and some no more than one or two, and here and there we have seen one lying growling in a retired place by himself and would neither suffer males nor females to come near him, we judged these were old and superannuated. The Sea bears are not by far so large as the Lions but rather larger than a Common Seal; they have none of that long hair which distinguishes the lion, something like an otters and the general colour is a kind of Iron grey. This is the sort which the French call Sea Wolfs and the English Seals; they are however different from the Seals we have in Europe and in North America. The Lions may too, without any great impropriety, be called over grown Seals for they are all of the same Species. It was not attall dangerous to go

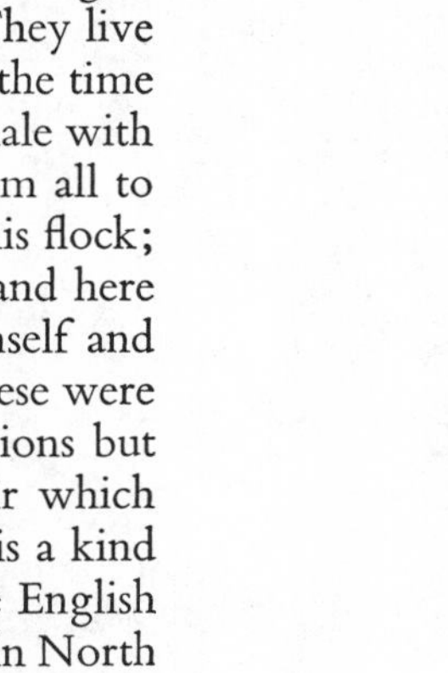

January 1775 among them, they either fled or laid still, the only danger was in going between them and the Sea for if they took fright at any thing they would come down in such numbers that if you could not get out of their way you would be run over. Sometimes when we came suddenly upon them or waked them out of their sleep (for they are slugish sleeping ahimals) they would raise up their heads, snort and snarl and look as fearce as if they meant to devour one in a moment, but by retorting it upon them I observed that they allways run away. so that they were down right bullies. The Penguin is an amphibious bird so well known to most people that I shall only observe that they are here in prodigious numbers and we could knock down as many as we pleased with a stick. I cannot say they are good eating, I have indeed made several good meals of them but it was for want of beter victuals. They either do not breed here, or else this was not the Season, for we saw neither egs nor young ones. Shags breed here in vast numbers and we took on board not a few, as they are very good eating. . . . It is wonderfull to see how the different Animals which inhabit this little spot are reconciled to each other, they seem to have entered into a league not to disturb each others tranquillity. The Sea lions occupy most of the Sea Coast, the Sea bears take up their aboad in the isle; the Shags take post on the highest clifts, the Penguins fix their quarters where there is the most easiest communication to and from the sea and the other birds chuse more retired places. We have seen all these animals mix together like domesticated Cattle and Poultry in a farm yard without the one attempting to disturb or molest the other. Nay I have often seen the Eagles and Vultures siting on the hillocks among the Shags, without the latter either young or old being disturbed by it. It may be asked how these birds of prey live, I suppose on the carcases of Seals and birds which die by various causes and probably not a few where they are so numerous. This very imperfect account is written more with a view to assist my own memory than to give information to others. I am neither a botanist nor a Naturalist and have not words to describe the productions of Nature either in the one Science or the other.

☾ In early January 1775, Cook sailed south east from South America in order to explore the far south of the Atlantic, the last remaining region in which the 'Dry Land theorists' might still try and locate a vast southern continent.

☾ The *Resolution* passed through this desolate region with fruitless results, excepting that she rediscovered the island which Cook named South Georgia, and discovered the islands which he called Sandwich Land as ice prevented a thorough examination. This, however, seemed unnecessary, as the region was icebound, desolate and worthless.

WEDNESDAY 4*th* January. Having left the land the preceeding evening . . . our Course was SE with a view of discovering that extensive Coast which Mr Dalrymple lies down in his Chart in which is the Gulph of St Sebastian, I designed to make the Western point of that Gulph in order to have all the other part before me. Indeed I had some doubts about the existence of such a Coast and this appeared tome to be the best rout to clear it up and to explore the Southern part of this ocean. *January 1775*

FRIDAY *6th* January. At 8 o'Clock in the evening, being then in the Latitude of 58° 9′ S Longitude 53° 14′ West, we close-reefed our Top-sails and hauled to the North with a very strong gale at West attended with a thick haze and sleet. The situation just mentioned is nearly the same as M[r] Dalrymple assigns for the point of the Gulph of S[t] Sebastian, but as we saw neither land nor signs of any, I was the more doubtfull of its existence and was fearfull that by keeping to the South I might miss the land said to be discovered by La Roche in 1675 and by the Ship Lion in 1756 which M[r] Dalrymple places in 54° 30′ Latitude and 45° of Longitude; but on looking over D'Anvill's Chart I found it laid down 9° or 10 ° more to the West, this difference of situation was to me a sign of the uncertainty of both and determined me to get into the Parallel as soon as possible and this was the reason of my hauling to the North at this time.

THURSDAY *12th* January. At day-break bore away and steered East-northerly with a fine fresh breeze at WSW. At Noon observed in Latitude 54° 28′ S, Longitude in 42° 08′ West, which is near 3° E of the situation in which M[r] Dalrymple places the NE point of the Gulph of S[t] Sebastian, but we had no other signs of land than seeing a Seal and a few Penguins; on the contrary we had a Swell from ESE which could hardly have been if any extensive tract of land laid in that direction.

FRIDAY *20th* January. At 2 o'Clock in the morning made sail to SW round Coopers Island, it is a rock of considerable height about 5 miles in circuit and lies one from the main. At this isle which I called Cape Disappointment the Coast takes a SW direction for the space of four or five leagues to a point off which lie three small isles, the Southermost of which is pretty low and flat and lies one league from the Cape. As we advanced to SW land opened of this point in the direction of N 60° West and 9 leagues beyond it. It proved an Island quite detatched from the Main and obtained the name of Pickersgill Island after my third officer. Soon after a point of the main beyond this Island came in sight in the direction of N 55° West which exactly united the Coast at the very point we had seen and set the day we first came in with it and proved to a demonstration that this land which we had taken to be part of a great Continent was no more than an Island of 70 leagues in circuit. Who whould have thought that an Island of no greater extent than this is, situated between the Latitude of 54° and 55° should in the very height of summer be in a manner wholy covered many fathoms deep with frozen snow, but more especially the SW Coast, the very sides and craggy summits of the lofty Mountains were cased with snow and ice, but the quantity which lay in the Vallies is incredable, before all of them the

January 1775 Coast was terminated by a wall of Ice of considerable height. It can hardly be doubted but that a great deal of ice is formed here in the Winter in the Spring is broke off and dispersed over the Sea: but this isle cannot produce the ten thousand part of what we have seen, either there must be more land or else ice is formed without it. These reflections led me to think that the land we had seen the preceeding day might belong to an extensive tract and I still had hopes of discovering a continent. I must confess the disappointment I now met with did not affect me much for to judge of the bulk by the sample it would not be worth the discovery. This land I called the Isle of *Georgia* in honour of H. Majesty. It is situated between the Latitudes of 53° 57′ and 54° 57′ South and between 38° 13′ and 35° 54′ West Longitude, it extends SEBE and NWBW and is 31 leagues long in that direction and its greatest breadth is about 10 Leagues. It seems to abound in Bays and Harbours, the NE Coast especially, but the great quantity of Ice must render them inaccessable the greatest part of the year or at least it must be dangerous lying in them on account of the breaking up of the Ice clifts.

FRIDAY *27th* January. I now reckoned we were in the Latitude 60° and farther I did not intend to go, unless I met with some certain signs of soon meeting with land for it would not have been prudent in me to have spent my time in penetrating to the South when it was, at least as probable, that a large tract of land might be found near Cape Circumcision; besides I was now tired of these high Southern Latitudes where nothing was to be found but ice and thick fogs. We had now along hollow swell from the West a strong indication that there was no land in that direction. I think I may now venture to assert that that extensive Coast laid down in M[r] Dalrymple's Chart of the Ocean between Africa and America, and the Gulph of S[t] Sebastian does not exist. I too doubt if either Le Roche or the Ship Lion ever saw the Isle of Georgia, but this is a point I will not dispute as I neither know where they were bound or from whence they came.

FRIDAY *3rd* February was succeeded by a calm which continued till 8 when we got a breeze at EBS attended with hazy weather. At this time we saw the land we were after and which proved to be two isles; the day on which they were discovered was the occasion of calling them Candlemas Isles (Latitude 57° 11° S Longitude 27° 06′ W). They are of no great extent but have a considerable height and were covered with Snow.

MONDAY *6th* February. We continued to steer to the South and SE till noon at which time we were in the Latitude of 58° 15′ S Longitude 21° 34′ West and seeing neither land nor signs of any, I concluded that what we had seen which I named Sandwich Land was either a group of Isles &c[a] or else a point of the Continent, for I firmly believe that there is a tract of land near the Pole, which is the source of most of the ice which is spread over this vast Southern Ocean:

and I think it is also probable that it extends farthest to the North opposite the Southern Atlantick and Indian Oceans because ice has always been found farther to the North in these Ocean(s) than any where else, which I think could not be if there was no land to the South. I mean a land of some considerable extent, for if we suppose that there is none and that ice may be formed without, it will follow of course that the cold ought to be every where nearly equal round the Pole, as far as 70° or 60° of Latitude, or so far as to be out of the influence of any of the known Continents, consequently we ought to see ice every where under the same Parallel or near it, but the contrary has been found. It is but few ships which have met with ice going round Cape Horn and we saw but little below the sixtieth degree of Latitude in the Southern Pacific Ocean. Whereas in this Ocean between the Meridian of 40° West and 50° or 60° East we have found ice as far North as 51°. Bouvet found some in 48° and others have seen it in a much lower Latitude. It is however true that the greatest part of this Southern Continent (supposing there is one) must lay within the Polar Circle where the Sea is so pestered with ice that the land is thereby inaccessible. The risk one runs in exploaring a Coast in these unknown and Icy Seas is so very great that I can be bold to say that no man will ever venture farther than I have done and that the lands which may lie to the South will never be explored. Thick fogs, snow storms, Intense cold and every other thing that can render Navigation dangerous one has to encounter and these difficulties are greatly heightened by the inexpressable horrid aspect of the Country, a Country doomed by Nature never once to feel the warmth of the Suns rays, but to lie for ever buried under everlasting snow and ice. The Ports which may be on the Coast are in a manner wholy filled up with frozen snow of a vast thickness, but if any should so far be open as to admit a ship in, it is even dangerous to go in for she runs a risk of being fixed there for ever or coming out in an Ice island. The islands and floats of ice on the Coast, the great falls from the ice clifts in the Port, or a heavy snow storm attended with a sharp frost, would prove equally fatal. After such an explanation as this the reader must not expect to find me much farther to the South. It is however not for want of inclination but other reasons. It would have been rashness in me to have risked all which had been done in the voyage in finding out and exploaring a Coast which when done would have answered no end whatever or been of the least use either to Navigation or Geography or indeed any other Science. Bouvet's Discovery was yet before us, the existence of which was to be cleared up and lastly we were now not in a condition to undertake great things, nor indeed was there time had we been ever so well provided. These reasons induced me to alter the Course to East, with a very strong gale at North attended with an exceeding heavy fall of snow. The quantity which fell into our sails was so great that we were obliged every now and then to throw the ship up in the Wind to shake it out of the Sails.

February
1775

February 1775 SATURDAY 18*th* February. At Noon we were in the Latitude of 54° 25′, Longitude 8° 46′ East. I thought this a good Latitude to keep in to look for Cape Circumcision because if the land had ever so little extent in the direction of North and south we could not miss seeing it, as the northern point is said to lie in 54°. We had got a great swell from the South so that I was now well assured it could only be an island and it was of no consequence which side we fell in with.

☾ By late February Cook had sailed so far eastwards in high latitudes that he was convinced, incorrectly, that Cape Circumcision (Bouvet Island) could not exist. The question was however, insignificant, compared with the fact that the *Resolution* had now circumnavigated the globe from west to east in very high latitudes and had proved that, although it was certain that the South Polar Region contained a small continent or islands, these lands were useless for European exploration with the means available at that period. Cook, the *Resolution*, and a courageous crew could do no more, and further action was obviously useless.

TUESDAY 21*st* February. At Day-break made sail and bore away East and at Noon we observed in Latitude 54° 16′ S Longitude 16° 13′ E which was 5° to the East of the Longitude of Cape Circumcision was said to lie in, so that we began to think that no such land ever existed. . . . As we were now no more than 2 degrees of Longitude from our rout to the South after leaving the Cape of Good Hope, it was to no purpose to proceed any fa[r]ther to the East under this parallel knowing no land could be there but as an oppertunity now offered of clearing up some doubts of our having seen land father to the South I steered SE to get into the situation in which it was supposed to lie. . . . Having now run over the place where the land was supposed to lie without seeing the least signs of any it was no longer to be doubted but that the Ice hills had deceived us as well as Mr Bouvet. . . . I had now made the circuit of the Southern Ocean in a high Latitude and traversed it in such a manner as to leave not the least room for the Probabillity of there being a Continent unless near the Pole and out of the reach of Navigation, by twice visiting the Pacific Tropical Sea, I had not only settled the situation of some old discoveries but made there many new ones and left, I conceive, very little more to be done even in that part. Thus I flater myself that the intention of the voyage has in every respect been fully answered, the Southern Hemisphere sufficiently explored and the final end put to the searching after a Southern Continent, which has at times ingrossed the attention of some of the Maritime Powers for near two Centuries past and the Geographers of all ages. That there may be a Continent or large tract of land near the Pole, I will not deny, on the contrary I am of opinion there is, and it is probable that we have seen a part of it. The excessive cold, the many islands and vast floats of ice all tend to prove that there must be land to the South and that this Southern

February 1775

land might lie or extend farthest to the North opposite the Southern Atlantick and Indian Oceans, I have already assigned some reasons to which I may add the greater degree of cold which we have found in these seas, than in the Southern Pacific Ocean under the same parallel of Latitude. In this last Ocean the Mercury in the Thermometer seldom fell so low as the freezing point, till we were in Sixty and upwards, whereas in the others it fell frequently as low in the Latitude of fifty four; this was certainly owing to there being a greater quantity of Ice and extending farther to the North in these two Seas than in the other, and if Ice is first formed at or near land of which I have no doubt, it will follow that the land also extends farther North. The formation or coagulation of Ice Islands has not to my knowledge been thoroughly investigated: some have supposed them to have been formed by the freezing of the Water at the mouth of large Rivers or great Cataracts and so accumulate till they are broke of by their own weight. . . . How are we then to suppose that there are large rivers in these Countries, the Vallies are covered many fathoms deep with everlasting snow and at the sea they terminate in Ice clifts of vast heights. It is here where the Ice islands are formed, not from streames of Water but from consolidated snow which is allmost continually falling or drifting down from the Mountains, especially in Winter where the frost must be intence during that Season, that these Ice clifts must so accumulate as to fill up all the Bays be they ever so large is a fact which cannot be doubted as we have seen it so in summer also during that season the snow may fix and consolidate to ice to most of the other coasts and there also form Ice clifts. These clifts accumulate by continually falls of snow and what drifts from the Mountains till they are no longer able to support their own weight and then large pieces break off which we call Ice islands. . . . If this imperfect account of the formation of these extraordinary floating island of ice, which is written wholy from my own observation, does not convey some usefull hints to some abler pen, it will however convey some Idea of the Lands where they are formed, Lands doomed by Nature to everlasting frigidness and never once to feel the warmth of the suns rays, whose horrible and savage aspect I have no words to describe: such are the lands we have discovered, what may we expect those to be which lie more to the South, for we may reasonably suppose that we have seen the best as lying most to the North, whoever has resolution and perseverance to clear up this point by proceeding farther than I have done, I shall not envy him the honour of the discovery but I will be bold to say that the world will not be benefited by it.

'I had at this time some thought of revisiting the place where the French discovery was said to lie, but when I considered that if they had realy made this discovery the end would be as fully answered as if I had done it my self, we know it can only be an Island and if we may judge from the degree of cold we found in that Latitude it cannot be a fertile one. Besides this would have kept me two

February 1775 months longer at sea and in a tempestuous Latitude which we were not in a condition to support, our sails and rigging were so much worn that some thing was giving way every hour and we had nothing left either to repair or replace them.

'We had been a long time without refreshments, our Provisions were in a state of decay and little more nourishment remained in them than just to keep life and soul together. My people were yet healthy and would cheerfully have gone where ever I thought proper to lead them, but I dreaded the Scurvy laying hold of them at a time when we had nothing left to remove it. Besides it would have been cruel in me to have continued the Fatigues and hardships they were continually exposed to longer than absolutely necessary, their behaviour throughout the whole voyage merited every indulgence which was in my power to give them.

'Animated by the conduct of the officers, they shewed themselves capable of surmounting every difficulty and danger which came in their way and never once looked upon the one or the other to be a bit heightened by being seperated from our companion the Adventure.

℄ On Thursday, 16th March, when nearing the Cape of Good Hope, Cook carried out his instructions and collected the Log Books and Journals which his crew had kept. On 18th March, impatient for news, he sent a boat to a vessel which the *Resolution* sighted, and learned that the *Adventure* had reached the Cape of Good Hope some twelve months earlier, and that Furneaux had had a boat's crew killed and eaten by the Maoris of Queen Charlotte Sound, which accounted for the vague and cautious stories which had reached Cook who wrote the following comment:

SATURDAY 18*th* March. Day break saw the land again bearing NNW Six or seven Leagues distant, depth of Water 48 fms. . . . At 1 PM the boat returned from on board the Bownkerke Polder, Captain Cornelis Bosch, a Dutch Indiaman from Bengal; Captain Bosch very obligingly offered us sugar, Arrack and whatever he had to spare. Our people were told by some English Seamen on board this Ship that the Adventure arrived at the Cape of Good Hope twelve months ago and that one of her boats crew had been murdered and eat by the people of New Zealand, so that the story which we heard in Queen Charlottes Sound was now no longer a mystery . . . (to be doubted, it was to this effect: that a ship or boat had been dashed to pieces on the Coast, but that the crew got safe on shore; on the Natives who were present stealing some of the strangers clothes, they were fired upon till all their ammunition was spent, or as the Natives express'd, till they could fire no longer, after which the Natives fell upon them, knocked them all on the head and treated them as above mentioned: this was the substance of what our people understood from them; when I examined them about it they denied their knowing any thing about the matter or that any thing of the kind had happened and never after would mention it to any one, consequently I thought our people had misunderstood them. I shall make no refu[ta]tions on this Melancholy affair untill I hear more about it. I must however observe in favour of the New Zealands that I have allways found them of a Brave, Noble, Open and benevolent disposition, but they are a people that will never put up with an insult if they have an oppertunity to resent it.) *March 1775*

℄ At the Cape, Cook also received news of several French voyages of Pacific exploration which had met either with disaster or with very little success. Surville and Marion du Fresne had perished, while Crozet and Kerguelen had cleared up only a number of small points such as the extent of the reefs to the south of New Caledonia and the exact location of Kerguelen Island, which Cook had missed.

℄ Arriving at St. Helena on 15th May by direct and accurate course, based on 'Kendal's watch' Cook was extremely annoyed in finding that Hawkesworth's edition of Cook's Journal not only contained inserted material, which insulted the worthy people of St. Helena, but contained an entirely fallacious statement that Cook had approved of Hawkesworth's manuscript. With apparently justified indignation he wrote:

[*Undated*] I am well convinced that the island in many particulars has been misrepresented. It is no wonder that the account which is given of it in the narrative of my former Voyage should have given offence to all the principle Inhabitants. It was not less mortifying to me when I first read it, which was not till I arrived now at the Cape of Good Hope, for I never had the perusal of the Manuscript nor did I ever hear the whole of it read in the mode it was written, notwithstanding what Dr Hawkesworth has said to the Contrary in the Interduction. In the narrative my Country men at St Helena are charged with exercizing a wanton cruelty over their slaves, they are also charged with want of ingenuity in not having Wheel carriages, Wheel Barrows and Porters Knotts to facilitate the task of the labourer. With respect to the first charge, I must say, that perhaps, there is not a European settlement in the world where slaves are better treated and better fed than here, out of the many of whom I asked these questions not one had the least shaddow of complaint. The Second charge, tho' of little consequence is however erronious for I have seen every one of the three Articles that are said not to be on the island; they have Carts which are drawn sometimes by men and sometimes by oxen, and Wheel Barrows have been used in the island from the first settlement and some are sent annually out from England in the store Ship. How these things came to be thus misrepresented I can not say, as they came not from me, but if they had I should have been equally open to conviction and ready to have contridicted any thing, that upon proof like this, appeared to be ill-founded, and I am not a little obliged to some people in the isle for the obligeing manner they pointed out these mistakes.

July 1775 ℂ On Saturday, 29th July 1775 the *Resolution* sighted 'the land about Plymouth' and it was typical that Cook should end his great Journal by a tribute to 'Mr Kendal's Watch', which after a voyage of three years and eighteen days in almost every type of climate was still astonishingly correct.

SATURDAY *29th* July we made the Land about Plymouth, Maker Church, at 5 o'Clock in the afternoon, bore N 10° west distant 7 Leagues, this bearing and distance shew that the error of Mr Kendals Watch in Longitude was only 7′ 45″, which was too far to the West.

Chapter XIV
COOK HONOURED IN ENGLAND

"What wreaths are due to that man, who having himself saved many, perpetuates the means by which Britain may now, on the most distant voyages, preserve numbers of her intrepid Sons, her mariners."

PRESIDENT OF ROYAL SOCIETY, 1776

AS IN THE CASE OF THE FIRST EXPEDITION THE POSITIVE results of Cook's Second Voyage were of great importance, although, on the geographical side, they were overshadowed by the negative outcome, the proof of the non-existence of huge continental land masses in the South Pacific-Antarctic. On the positive side, however, Cook propounded the existence of a relatively small Antarctic continent which he closely circumnavigated. In the apt words of Professor G. Arnold Wood, 'He was the last seeker of the continent which Mercator had drawn, and which Quiros had described. But he was also the first scientific explorer of the South Polar Regions, the precursor of Weddell and Ross, of Shackleton, Amundsen and Scott'. His journal has shown that he was certain that Antarctic lands existed, for the immense icebergs amongst which he had sailed could have been formed only on land. He believed that he himself might have seen it in that frightful world of 'perpetual frigidness'. Cook believed, however, that this new continent would prove useless. South Georgia had presented 'a horrible and savage aspect'. How much more horrible and savage would be a continent still further South! In addition to his Antarctic explorations Cook had supplemented his circumnavigation of the continent by two immense sweeps of the Pacific which had discovered totally unknown islands such as New Caledonia, South Georgia and Norfolk Island, and rediscovered islands such as the Friendly Islands, Easter Island, the Marquesas and the

New Hebrides. He thus created a map of the Central and South Pacific so correct in conception and outline, that, as the famous French explorer La Pérouse justly complained, Cook had left nothing for his successors to do but praise him.

¶ Important as were these geographical results Cook and others gave pride of place to the victories gained in the fields of health and hygiene. We have seen that, with the assistance of Sir Hugh Palliser, the expedition carried the anti-scorbutics, which had effectively combated sea diseases on the *Endeavour*, and we have also seen Cook's constant and successful efforts to enforce the use of these anti-scorbutics, and to keep his ships and personnel dry and clean during a voyage of over three years in circumstances of great hardship and danger and in almost all climatic zones. Of the *Resolution's* company of 112 men the commander had lost three by accidental death and one by a disease which was not scurvy, while it was noticeable that Furneaux on the *Adventure* had been less strict than Cook with the result that he had had one death from scurvy and his crew had suffered far more severely from this disease than had the crew of the *Resolution*. We may today levy some justifiable criticisms at Cook. He gave correct weight to the value of wort and sauerkraut as anti-scorbutics, but modern analysis has shown that his portable broth was valueless, and he has been alleged to have retarded the progress of nautical medicine and hygiene by condemning the invaluable citrus as successful but over expensive for general use. Nevertheless his achievements in the application of anti-scorbutics, including the use of plants obtained on his voyages, together with his rigorous attention to hygiene produced results so striking that he ranks with the greatest pioneers of nautical medicine. The Royal Society to its lasting credit recognised the greatness of his achievement by the award of its highest distinction, the Copley Gold Medal.

¶ Cook never received the medal, which was awarded by the Council of the Society for the best paper of the year, but the President of the Society, Sir John Pringle, told Cook of the proposed recognition. He made the announcement in November 1776, while Cook was engaged on the Third Voyage, and the medal, which was presented to Mrs Cook, is now in the British Museum. In the address which proclaimed the award to the Fellows of the Royal Society, Pringle paid this magnificent tribute to Cook. 'If Rome', he said, 'decreed the Civic Crown to him who saved the life of a single citizen, what wreaths are due to that man, who, having himself saved many, perpetuates in your Transactions the means by which Britain may now, on the most distant voyages, preserve numbers of her intrepid sons, her mariners; who, braving every danger, have so liberally contributed to the fame, to the opulence, and to the Maritime Empire of this country.'

¶ The third important result of the voyage was the proof that a comparatively simple means had at last been devised for the accurate calculation of longitude.

We have seen that, during the voyage of the *Endeavour*, Cook and the astronomer Green, who died during the expedition, had used with considerable success, the tables of lunar distances produced by Maskelyne the Astronomer Royal, Cook's own calculation of the longitude of Port Venus being only 1′, or roughly a mile, incorrect. Nevertheless, it was often difficult to take accurate observations at sea and hence the test of the four chronometers mentioned previously. The Arnold instruments proved useless, but the Harrison watch was only 7′ 45″ slow after three years at sea under many conditions of temperature. Cook had now proved that Harrison had constructed an instrument through which longitude could be easily and rapidly ascertained. It is sad to note that even then King George III had to intervene personally—'By God Harrison I'll see you righted'—to force a mean and reluctant Board of Longitude to disgorge the remainder, or most of the remainder, of the prize.

❡ J. A. Williamson has pointed out that the results of Cook's Second expedition could not have become known at a more opportune time. In the summer of 1775 the British North American colonies were blazing into revolt. France and Spain were crouched ready to spring for their revenge, and it was clear that Britain was likely to stand alone in an embattled world. If Cook had returned with news that the vast and fertile continent of Dalrymple's imagination was awaiting European exploitation the position might well have been embarrassing. Very fortunately Cook showed that no great Pacific continent existed and that the Antarctic continent, which he virtually discovered, offered no inducement for European settlement. At this time there was still little realization that, in his first voyage, Cook had discovered a fertile shoreline of continental dimensions of the East Australian coast, and, although the American revolution led to immediate British settlement in this one of Cook's continents, it was only as a very humble substitute that Australia replaced America as a receptacle for British convicts.

❡ Cook was now a distinguished figure of international repute. He was presented to the King; promoted to post-captain; and appointed Fourth Captain of His Majesty's Royal Hospital for Seamen, at Greenwich. His salary here was £200 a year with perquisites, and the post was a sinecure because lieutenants carried out the active duties. Banks saw that he was elected a Fellow of the Royal Society which, as we have seen, paid him the highest possible tribute. He also sat for his portrait by Nathaniel Dance R.A., which Cook's friends and fellow voyagers, like Samwell, considered an excellent likeness.

❡ The only annoyance after the expedition seems to have been the conduct of the highly objectionable Mr Forster, who, after being a constant nuisance on the voyage, claimed that Lord Sandwich had promised verbally that Forster alone should write the History of the Voyage; receive all the profits and be afforded employment for the rest of his life.

⸿ Although Lord Sandwich totally denied any such promise he arranged a compromise under which Cook was to write the account of the voyage and Forster was to write a second volume containing his observations as a scientist. Cook was to submit his volume to Forster for revision and Forster his to Lord Sandwich.

⸿ Under this arrangement Cook gave Forster much of his manuscript but Forster not only proved impossible to work with but refused to submit his manuscript to Lord Sandwich. It is clear from Cook's letters that he tolerated Forster with exemplary patience, although in the end he wrote with unusual severity, 'What Mr Forster intends to do I have not heard, but I suppose he will publish as soon as possible, and if so he will get the start of me. He has quite deceived me: I never thought he would have separated himself from the Admiralty. but it cannot hurt me, and I am only sorry My Lord Sandwich has taken so much trouble to serve an undeserving man.'

⸿ Cook's suspicions of Forster were fully justified as the Forsters published their unofficial story of the voyage some weeks before the official account which was produced by Cook himself with the assistance of Canon John Douglas, Canon of Windsor and later Bishop of Carlisle. Kitson considers that the Forsters' book 'appears to have been compiled by one person from Cook's work and finished by a second endowed with a facile pen and a smattering of semi-scientific knowledge'.

⸿ Cook unfortunately left on his third voyage before this book appeared and it fell to Wales, the Astronomer, to defend Cook and other members of the expedition from the lies and sneers of these unpleasant people who were totally unaccustomed to sea life and hardships. Fortunately Mr Forster's book had no effect on Cook's official publication which was well received and gave some financial assistance to Mrs Cook.

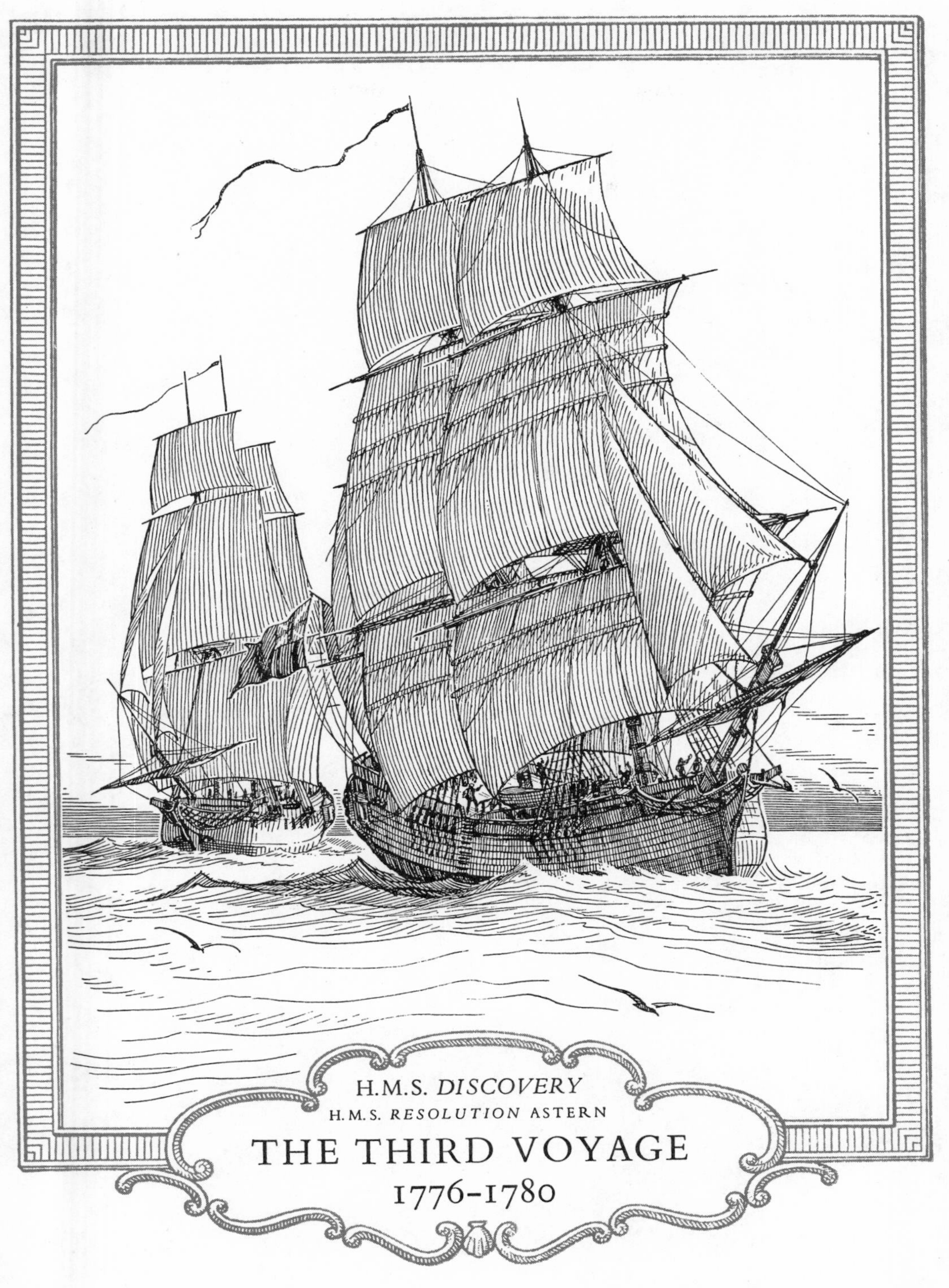

H.M.S. *DISCOVERY*
H.M.S. *RESOLUTION* ASTERN

THE THIRD VOYAGE

1776-1780

Chapter XV

PREPARATIONS AND INSTRUCTIONS

"Search for, and explore, such rivers or inlets as may appear to be of a considerable extent, and pointing towards Hudson's or Baffin's Bays."

INSTRUCTIONS TO COOK, THIRD VOYAGE, 1776

THE FATES WERE NOW CLOSING IN UPON COOK. IT WAS natural that he should lead a third expedition, an expedition which was to solve one of the few remaining ocean mysteries, the geography of the region in which the Pacific and Arctic meet. It was also natural that the Pacific should at least take its toll from the greatest of its adventurers, and ensure that his fame should glow even more brightly when death immediately followed success. The pitcher could in fact go too often to the well and the ocean and its inhabitants which slew, even on their first voyages, so many famous explorers from Magellan to La Pérouse could scarcely permit its most audacious intruder to survive ten years of almost unsullied achievement.

☾ The chief object of the third expedition was the attempt to discover a navigable and commercial sea route from the Pacific to the Atlantic around the north of the American continent. The passage from the Atlantic to Hudson Bay was well known and feasible, but, although Samuel Hearne, and other servants of the Fur companies, had shown that there was no seaway from that Bay to the Pacific, it was still hoped that a passage might be found further North. On the Pacific side geographical knowledge was extremely vague, partly because of the immense difficulties and distances involved, and partly through weak Russian administration. Although by the beginning of the Eighteenth Century Moscow considered Siberia as conquered, there was still, even by that time, no accurate knowledge that Asia and North America were separate continents, while rumours still existed that, to the north of Japan, lay islands, fabulously rich in silver, islands which, even in the Seventeenth Century, Tasman and others had sought without success.

℄ As early as 1655 a Cossack named Deshnev had reported to the governmental authorities at Yakutsk that he had rounded the 'East Cape' of Asia and had sailed southwards from the 'Icy Sea' to the Pacific, thus proving that Asia and North America were separated. Again, in 1713, the Governor of Siberia had sent out Henrich Busch, a Swede or Dutchman, who had crossed from Kamchatka to Alaska or the Aleutians. These reports, and other significant accounts, lay pigeonholed with the Siberian authorities, so that, in order to ascertain the truth and to satisfy European scientific curiosity, Peter the Great designed, and his successors, the Empresses Catherine I and Anna, despatched under the Dane, Vitus Bering, two famous expeditions, which, despite the ultimate break down and death of the leader, discovered Bering Strait between the continents and traced parts of the Arctic shoreline, and parts of the North West American Coast and the islands lying off it. Nevertheless, in spite of Bering's successes, and further Russian penetration, Bering's work was not regarded as conclusive, and, until Cook's third voyage, his reports were, to some extent, disregarded.

℄ When, in 1775, Cook returned to England from his second expedition, the question of a northern passage from the Pacific was becoming of considerable importance. Although the British Canadians were pushing their occupation across the continent, Britain was in the process of losing the future United States; the soils of the rich West Indian sugar islands were becoming exhausted; Clive's successes in India had blazed the trail for further British expansion, and it was becoming evident that the future of the Empire lay, to a large extent, in the Indian Ocean and the East. Also, as Williamson points out, tea, which was bulky and whose transport required an all-sea route, was beginning to replace the Chinese gold, porcelain, silk and lacquer ware, which 'had made the Manila galleons rather treasure ships than ordinary merchantmen'. The only routes possible for such commerce were across the isthmus of Panama, which was a land route in Spanish hands; the impossibly long and dangerous voyage around Cape Horn; and the passage around the Cape of Good Hope, which, although it was the route then utilised, involved the longest voyage undertaken at that time by British merchantmen, and very great expense. A route from India and China, around North America to Britain, would be much shorter and much less vulnerable in time of war than any then existing. The British Parliament had already voted a prize of £20,000 to the first commander of a British merchantman to discover a passage, and this was now made applicable to naval officers, provided that the passage lay North of Latitude 52, probably because this region lay well to the north of the zone of colonization which the Spaniards were at that time extending northwards into California.

(What was now required was a leader who would execute the orders which Byron had disregarded in 1765, and it was soon clear that the task would be entrusted to Cook. He had nearly completed the editing of the Journal of the Second Expedition, and it was apparent that a sinecure post on shore would provide little solace to a spirit that was restless and ambitious in the best sense. He had accepted a Captaincy of the Greenwich Hospital under the assurance of the Admiralty that the position would not prejudice him in any future offer of service, and he had written sadly to Walker, ' "The Resolution" was found to answer even beyond my expectations, and is so little injured by the voyage that she will soon be sent out again. But I shall not command her. My fate drives me from one extreme to another; a few months ago the whole Southern Hemisphere was hardly big enough for me, and now I am going to be confined to the limits of Greenwich Hospital, which are far too small for an active mind like mine. I must confess it is a fine retreat and a pretty income but, whether I can bring myself to like ease and retirement time will show.'

(Time soon showed. Neither ease, nor family, nor comparative affluence could hold Cook. Although the Admiralty did not think it fair to order him to undertake another great voyage after so short an interval, he wrote in January 1776 that he had been given the task of finding a ship to accompany the *Resolution*, and, when in February a dinner party, which included Lord Sandwich, Sir Hugh Palliser and Mr Stephens of the Admiralty, discussed the difficulty of finding a suitable commander, he jumped up and declared that he would go. His formal offer of 10th February was accepted the same day, and he wrote joyfully to Walker, 'I have quitted an easy retirement for an active, perhaps dangerous voyage—I embark on as fair a prospect as I can wish'.

(Unfortunately, Cook had already made the first of a number of miscalculations which contributed to his death. Although the personnel selected for the expedition was excellent, and, although the newly purchased second vessel, the *Discovery*, a 229 ton Whitby Collier, was a fine little ship, the *Resolution*, like the *Endeavour*, should have been replaced by a new vessel. This was particularly the case, because, in spite of Lord Sandwich's interest in the expedition, the corruption and incompetence which then occurred at times in the navy led to the *Resolution's* being so badly refitted at Deptford that she gave, on the voyage, constant trouble, which in the end contributed to Cook's death.

(The excellent personnel selected included as Commander of the *Discovery* Charles Clerke, commissioned after the first voyage but a victim of tuberculosis contracted in the pestiferous 'Rules of Fleet', a slum to which he had been forced to fly owing to his generous efforts to save a brother from the penalties of debt. Clerke's first lieutenant was James Burney who had been a midshipman, and later a second lieutenant, on the first voyage, and was to become a distinguished admiral and writer on ocean exploration. Cook had in the *Resolution* as lieutenant, John Gore, who was with him in the *Endeavour*, and who was to bring the ships home; lieutenant James King, who was to complete the journal of the expedition; lieutenant John Williamson, the much criticised commander of the boats which might have rescued Cook, and William Bligh, the stormy hero, or villain, of the 'Mutiny of the Bounty' and of the 'Rum Rebellion' in New South Wales.

❡ The Board of Longitude left the scientific observations in the *Resolution* to Cook and King to whom it also entrusted the Kendal-Harrison chronometer which had proved so satisfactory on the second voyage. Bayly, who had had charge of the scientific instruments in the *Adventure*, was appointed to the *Discovery*. An excellent choice was that of Webber, a Swiss painter, who succeeded Hodges as artist. At the wish of the crown, the expedition carried, for the well meaning King 'Farmer George', a menagerie of gifts to the islands, which, however, so crowded the ships that Cook described the *Resolution* as 'a Noah's Ark, lacking only a few females of our own species'.

INSTRUCTIONS FOR THE THIRD EXPEDITION

❡ As on the Second Voyage Cook assisted to draft his instructions which he received at Plymouth on 8th July 1776. The Admiralty ordered the Commander to proceed to the Cape of Good Hope via Madeira, Cape Verde or the Canaries, and from the Cape to sail to his old base, New Zealand, searching on the way for islands which the French had discovered in latitude 48°S. and the longitude of Mauritius. From New Zealand Cook was to proceed to Otaheite in the Society Islands in order to return to his home 'Omai', a 'noble savage' whom Furneaux had brought to England in the *Adventure*, and who had intrigued London Society. On leaving Otaheite Cook was to commence his real task by encountering the North American coast in about latitude 45° North, taking care to avoid any Spanish dominions or offending any Spanish inhabitants. He was then to sail rapidly to latitude 65°N. from which point he was to continue northwards, very carefully examining 'such recess or inlets as may appear of considerable extent, and pointing towards Hudson's or Baffin's Bays', either sailing his ships through such passages or completing for the purpose the small vessels whose frames the Admiralty had provided.

❡ If the expedition found no passage before the winter Cook was to visit Kamchatka in Siberia, and, in the spring of 1778, make efforts to discover either a northern passage to the Atlantic or a northern passage around Russia to the European North Sea. According to H. R. Wagner these instructions indicate that the British Admiralty had ample knowledge of the recent Spanish explorations on the North American West Coast. As noted above, the journeys of Samuel Hearne (1769-72) had proved that no passage could exist south of latitude 72° N., while Spanish sea expeditions, despatched in 1769-70 and 1774-5, had reached as far north as latitude 58°, which accounts for Cook's being ordered to sail rapidly from latitude 45° to latitude 65° N. Wagner also thinks that Cook may have had additional secret instructions which have not been published. This may explain the fact that, although he was ordered to take possession, with the consent of the natives, of countries not previously discovered by other nations, he did not fulfil these instructions until he reached Cook's Inlet or River, in Alaska, in latitude 59° north.

By the COMMISSIONERS for executing the Office of Lord High Admiral of GREAT BRITAIN and IRELAND, &c.

SECRET INSTRUCTIONS for Captain JAMES COOK, Commander of his Majesty's Sloop the RESOLUTION.

Whereas the Earl of Sandwich has signified to us his Majesty's pleasure, that an attempt should be made to find out a Northern passage by sea from the Pacific to the Atlantic Ocean; and whereas we have, in pursuance thereof, caused his Majesty's sloops Resolution and Discovery to be fitted, in all respects, proper to proceed upon a voyage for the purpose above-mentioned, and, from the experience we have had of your abilities and good conduct in your late voyages, have thought fit to intrust you with the conduct of the present intended voyage, and with that view appointed you to command the first mentioned sloop, and directed Captain Clerke, who commands the other, to follow your orders for his further proceedings; You are hereby required and directed to proceed with the said two sloops directly to the Cape of Good Hope, unless you shall judge it necessary to stop at Madeira, the Cape de Verd, or Canary Islands, to take in wine for the use of their companies; in which case you are at liberty to do so, taking care to remain there no longer than may be necessary for that purpose.

On your arrival at the Cape of Good Hope, you are to refresh the sloops companies, and to cause the sloops to be supplied with as much provisions and water as they can conveniently stow.

You are, if possible, to leave the Cape of Good Hope by the end of October, or the beginning of November next, and proceed to the Southward in search of some islands said to have been lately seen by the French, in the latitude of 48° 0′ South, and about the meridian of Mauritius. In case you find those islands, you are to examine them thoroughly for a good harbour; and upon discovering one, make the necessary observations to facilitate the finding it again; as a good port, in that situation, may hereafter prove very useful, although it should afford little or nothing more than shelter, wood, and water. You are not, however, to spend too much time in looking out for those islands, or in the examination of them, if found, but proceed to Otaheite, or the Society Isles (touching at New Zealand in your way thither, if you should judge it necessary and convenient), and taking care to arrive there time enough to admit of your giving the sloops companies the refreshment they may stand in need of, before you prosecute the farther object of these instructions.

Upon your arrival at Otaheite, or the Society Isles, you are to land Omiah at such of them as he may choose, and to leave him there.

You are to distribute among the Chiefs of those islands such part of the presents with which you have been supplied, as you shall judge proper, reserving the remainder to distribute among the natives of the countries you may discover in the Northern Hemisphere: And having refreshed the people belonging to the sloops under your command, and taken on board such wood and water as they may respectively stand in need of, you are to leave those islands in the beginning of February, or sooner if you shall judge it necessary, and then proceed in as direct a course as you can to the coast of New Albion, endeavouring to fall in with it in the latitude of 45° 0′ North; and taking care, in your way thither, not to lose any time in search of new lands, or to stop at any you may fall in with, unless you find it necessary to recruit your wood and water.

You are also, in your way thither, strictly enjoined not to touch upon any part of the Spanish dominions on the Western continent of America, unless driven thither by some unavoidable accident; in which case you are to stay no longer there than shall be absolutely necessary, and to be very careful not to give any umbrage or offence to any of the inhabitants or subjects of his Catholic Majesty. And if, in your farther progress to the Northward, as hereafter directed, you find any subjects of any European Prince or State upon any part of the coast you may think proper to visit, you are not to disturb them, or give them any just cause of offence, but, on the contrary, to treat them with civility and friendship.

Upon your arrival on the coast of New Albion, you are to put into the first convenient port to recruit your wood and water, and procure refreshments, and then to proceed Northward along the coast, as far as the latitude of 65°, or farther, if you are not obstructed by lands or ice; taking care not to lose any time in exploring rivers or inlets, or upon any other account, until you get into the before-mentioned latitude of 65°, where we could wish you to arrive in the month of June next. When you get that length, you are very carefully to search for, and to explore, such rivers or inlets as may appear to be of a considerable extent, and pointing towards Hudson's or Baffin's Bays; and if, from your own observations, or from any information you may receive from the natives (who, there is reason to believe, are the same race of people, and speak the same language, of which you are furnished with a Vocabulary, as the Esquimaux), there shall appear to be a certainty, or even a probability, of a water passage into the aforementioned bays, or either of them, you are, in such case, to use your utmost endeavours to pass through with one or both of the sloops, unless you shall be of opinion that the passage may be effected with more certainty, or with greater probability, by smaller vessels; in which case you are to set up the frames of one or both the small vessels with which you are provided, and, when they are put together, and are properly fitted, stored, and victualled, you are to dispatch one or both of them, under the care of proper officers, with a sufficient number of petty officers, men, and boats, in order to attempt the said passage; with such instructions for their rejoining you, if they should fail, or for their farther proceedings, if they should succeed in the attempt, as you shall judge most proper. But, nevertheless, if you shall find it more eligible to pursue any other measures than those above pointed out, in order to make a discovery of the before-mentioned passage (if any such there be), you are at liberty, and we leave it to your discretion, to pursue such measures accordingly.

In case you shall be satisfied that there is no passage through to the above-mentioned bays, sufficient for the purposes of navigation, you are, at the proper season of the year, to repair to the port of St. Peter and St. Paul in Kamtschatka, or wherever else you shall judge more proper, in order to refresh your people and pass the Winter; and, in the Spring of the ensuing year 1778, to proceed from thence to the Northward, as far as, in your prudence, you may think proper, in further search of a North East, or North West passage, from the Pacific Ocean into the Atlantic Ocean, or the North Sea; and if, from your own observation, or any information you may receive, there shall appear to be a probability of such a passage, you are to proceed as above directed: and, having discovered such passage, or failed in the attempt, make the best of your way back to England, by such route as you may think best for the improvement of geography and navigation; repairing to Spithead with both sloops, where they are to remain till further order.

At whatever places you may touch in the course of your voyage, where accurate observations of the nature hereafter mentioned have not already been made, you are, as far as your time will allow, very carefully to observe the true situation of such places, both in latitude and longitude; the variation of the needle; bearings of head-lands; height, direction, and course of the tides and currents; depths and soundings of the sea; shoals, rocks, &c.; and also to survey, make charts, and take views of such bays, harbours, and different parts of the coast, and to make such notations thereon, as may be useful either to navigation or commerce. You are also carefully to observe the nature of the soil, and the produce thereof; the animals and fowls that inhabit or frequent it; the fishes that are to be found in the rivers or upon the coast, and in what plenty; and, in case there are any peculiar to such places, to describe them as minutely, and to make as accurate drawings of them, as you can: and, if you find any metals, minerals, or valuable stones, or any extraneous fossils, you are to bring home specimens of each; as also of the seeds of such trees, shrubs, plants, fruits, and grains, peculiar to those places, as you may be able to collect, and to transmit them to our Secretary, that proper examination and experiments may be made of them. You are likewise to observe the genius, temper, disposition, and number of the natives and inhabitants, where you find any; and to endeavour, by all proper means, to cultivate a friendship with them; making them presents of such trinkets as you may have on board, and they may like best; inviting them to traffic; and shewing them every kind of civility and regard; but taking care, nevertheless, not to suffer yourself to be surprized by them, but to be always on your guard against any accidents.

You are also, with the consent of the natives, to take possession, in the name of the King of Great Britain, of convenient situations in such countries as you may discover, that have not already been discovered or visited by any other European power; and to distribute among the inhabitants such things as will remain as traces and testimonies of your having been there; but if you find the countries so dicovered are uninhabited, you are to take possession of them for his Majesty, by setting up proper marks and inscriptions, as first discoverers and possessors.

But forasmuch as, in undertakings of this nature, several emergencies may arise not to be foreseen, and therefore not particularly to be provided for by instructions before-hand; you are, in all such cases, to proceed as you shall judge most advantageous to the service on which you are employed.

You are, by all opportunities, to send to our Secretary, for our information, accounts of your proceedings, and copies of the surveys and drawings you shall have made; and upon your arrival in England, you are immediately to repair to this office, in order to lay before us a full account of your proceedings in the whole course of your voyage; taking care, before you leave the sloop, to demand from the officers and petty officers, the log-books and journals they may have kept, and to seal them up for our inspection; and enjoining them, and the whole crew, not to divulge where they have been, until they shall have permission so to do: and you are to direct Captain Clerke to do the same, with respect to the officers, petty officers, and crew of the Discovery.

If any accident should happen to the Resolution in the course of the voyage, so as to disable her from proceeding any farther, you are, in such case, to remove yourself and her crew into the Discovery, and to prosecute your voyage in her; her Commander being hereby strictly required to receive you on board, and to obey your orders, the same, in every respect, as when you were actually on board the Resolution: And, in case of your inability, by sickness or otherwise, to carry these Instructions into execution, you are to be careful to leave them with the next officer in command, who is hereby required to execute them in the best manner he can.

Given under our hands the 6th day of July, 1776,

SANDWICH.
C. SPENCER.
H. PALLISER.

By command of their Lordships,
PH. STEPHENS.

Chapter XVI

THE CENTRAL PACIFIC

"They knew that I was fully acquainted with the history of the massacre . . . but expressed surprise at my forbearance."

COOK IN NEW ZEALAND, 1777

PROFESSOR V. T. HARLOW HAS POINTED OUT THAT THE BRITISH sea explorers of the Eighteenth Century attempted to aid rather than exploit the aboriginal peoples. Hence, when Cook sailed in July 1776, he carried an embarrassing quantity of livestock as a gift from King George III to the Pacific islanders as well as Kendall's chronometer, adequate scientific instruments, warm clothing and anti-scorbutics, for not even the American war was allowed to interfere with so important an expedition.

SATURDAY 8*th* June. The Earl of Sandwich, Sr Hugh Palliser and others of the Board of Admiralty, paid us the last mark of the extraordinary attention they had al along paid to this equipment by coming on board to see that every thing was compleated to their desire and to the satisfaction of all who where to embark in the Voyage. They and several other Noblemen and Gentlemen honoured me with their Company at dinner and were saluted with 17 Guns and 3 cheers at their coming on board and also on going a shore.

MONDAY 10*th* June. Took on board a Bull, 2 Cows with their Calves & some sheep to carry to Otaheite with a quantity of Hay and Corn for thier subsistance. These Cattle were put on board at His Majestys Command and expence with a view of stocking Otaheite and the Neighbouring Islands with these usefull animals—nor was this the only attention paid to them; I was furnished by the

June *1776* Admiralty with many other useful articles for those Islands and both Ships were provided with a proper assortment of Iron tools, trinquets &c[a] to traffick and Cultivate a friendship and an alliance with the Inhabitants of such new Countrys as we might meet with. Some additional Cloathing adapted to a cold climate was put on board for the Crews and nothing was wanting that was thought condusive to either conveniency or health, such was the extraordinary care taken by those at the head of the Naval department.

TUESDAY 11*th* June. Received on board several Astronomical & Nautical Instruments which the Board of Longitude intrusted to me and M[r] King my second Lieutenant, we having engaged to that board to make all the necessary Astronomical and Nautical observations that should accrue and to supply the place of an Astronomer which was intended to be sent out in the Ship. They also put on board the same Watch Machine that was out with me last voyage: it was too slow for mean time at Greenwich this day at Noon by 3′ 31″.890 and its Rate of going was losing on mean time 1″.209 per day. Another Watch Machine and the same number and sort of Instruments were put on board the Discovery under the care of M[r] W[m] Baily who was the late voyage with Captain Furneaux, and whom the Board of Longitude engage to go this.

SATURDAY 30*th* November. On the 5th a Squale of Wind carried away the Miz[n] Topm[t] we had another to replace it so that loss was not felt especially as it was a bad stick and had often complained.

℄ Typical of the evolution of the Second British Empire was the fact that Cook was instructed to examine the islands which the Frenchmen Kerguelen, Crozet and Marion du Fresne had recently discovered in the far south of the Indian Ocean as 'A good Port in that situation may hereafter prove very useful, although it should afford little or nothing more than shelter, wood and water'.

℄ After visiting Teneriffe and the Cape of Good Hope, Cook spent the latter part of December 1776 in examining Kerguelen and other islands, but although he found good harbours and ample supplies of water, there was nothing but sea life to recommend a desolate region of naked and barren rocks.

℄ The following entry in the Journal is typical:

MONDAY 30*th* December. The first discoveries with some reason imagined it to be a Cape of a Southern Continent, the English have sence proved that no such Continent exists and that the land in question is an island of no great extent, which from its stirility I shall Call the *Island of Desolation*.

℄ Cook was now in urgent need of wood, and of grass for his stock, and on 24th January 1777 sighted Van Diemen's Land on his way to New Zealand. He gave a favourable account of the island and of the mild Tasmanian negroids whose women surprisingly rejected the advances of some of the English 'gentlemen'. Poor souls, in less than thirty years they were to face extermination at the hands of licentious British soldiers, whalers, and convicts.

January 1777

MONDAY 27*th* January. In the afternoon we were agreably surprised at the place where we were cuting Wood, with a visit from some of the Natives, Eight men and a boy: they came out of the Woods to us without shewing the least mark of fear and with the greatest confidence immaginable, for none of them had any weapons, except one who had in his hand a stick about 2 feet long and pointed at one end. They were quite naked & wore no ornaments, except the large punctures or ridges raised on the skin, some in straight and others in curved lines, might be reckoned as such: they were of the common Stature but rather slender; their skin was black and also their hair, which was as Woolly as any Native of Guinea, but they were not distinguished by remarkable thick lips nor flat Noses, on the contrary their features were far from disagreeable; they had pretty good eyes and their teeth were tolerable even but very dirty; most of them had their hair and beards anointed with red ointment and some had their faces painted with the same composition. They differ in many respects from the Inhabitants of the more northern parts of this Country, nor do they seem to be that miserable people Dampier mentions to have seen on the western coast. They received every thing we gave them without the least appearence of satisfaction; some bread was given them but as soon as they understood it was to eat, they either return'd it or threw it away without so much as tasting it; and the same by fish either dress'd or undressed, but birds they kept, & gave us to understand they would eat them.

WEDNESDAY 29*th* January. After staying about an hour with the Wooding party and the Natives and finding that the latter was not likely to give the former any disturbance, I left them and went over to the party that were cuting grass and found they had met with a fine patch. After lading the boats I left that party and return'd on board to dinner, where Mr King arrived soon after; from whom I learnt that soon after I had left him several Women and Children made there appearance, and were interduced to him by some of the Men; he made them all presents of such trifles as he had about him, and the Men gave them the most of what they had got from me. The Women wore a Kanguroo skin in the same shape as it came from the animal, tied over the shoulder and round the waist, but it was evidently intended for no other purpose than for the conveniency of carrying the child; for in all other respects they [are] as naked as the Men, and as black, with hair of the same Colour & texture. Some had their heads wholy shaved, some only on one side, while others again shaved all the upper part and leaving a circle of hair round the head as is the custom with some Fryers. Many of the Children had fine features and were thought pretty, but the Women especially those advanced in years, were thought otherways; Some of the Gentlemen belonging to the Discovery I was told, paid their addresses and made them large offers which were rejected with great disdain whether from a sence of Verture or for fear of displeasing the Men I shall

January 1777 not pretend to determine. This thing was certainly not very agreeable to the latter; for an elderly man as soon as he observed it, ordered all the Women & Children away, which they obeyed, but not without some of them shewing a little reluctancy. This conduct to Indian Women is highly blameable, as it creates a jealousy in the Men that may be attended with fatal consequences without answering any one purpose whatever, not even that of the lover obtaining the object of his wishes. I believe it has generally been found amongst uncivilized people that where the Women are easy of access, the Men are the first who offer them to strangers, and where this is not the case they are not easily come at, neither large presents nor privacy will induce them to violate the laws of chastity or custom. This observation I am sure will hold good throughout all parts of the South Sea where I have been, why then should men risk their own safety where nothing is to be obtained?

❨ As soon as the crews had collected sufficient grass to last until New Zealand, Cook sailed for Queen Charlotte Sound, again accepting Furneaux's mistaken view that Tasmania was 'the Southern point of New Holland', which was all the more remarkable when he wrote that the Tasmanoids, 'differ in many respects from the Inhabitants of the more northern parts of this Country'.

❨ The Maoris of Queen Charlotte Sound were somewhat disappointed when Cook failed to avenge the slaughtered boat's crew from the *Adventure*.

THURSDAY 13*th* February. The advantage we received by the Natives coming to live by us was not a little, as some of them went out afishing every day when the weather would permit, and we generally got by exchanges a good part of the fruits of their labour: so that whith what we got from them, and with our own nets & lines we seldom wanted fish, and celery, Scurvy grass and Portable soup were boiled with the Pease and Wheat for both ships companys every [day] during our whole stay and they had spruce beer for their drink: so that if any of them had contracted any seeds of the Scurvy these articles soon removed it, but when we arrived here there was only two invalids belonging to the Resolution on the Sick lists in both ships.

'Besides the people who took up their aboad by us, we were occasionally visited by others whose residence was not far off, and other who lived more remote. Thier articles of commerce were Curiosities, Fish and Women the two first always came to a good market, which the latter did not: the Seamen had taken a kind of dislike to these people and were either unwilling or affraid to associate with them; it had a good effect as I never knew a man quit his station to go to their habitations. A connection with Women I allow because I cannot prevent it but never encourage tho many Men are of opinion it is one of the greatest securities amongst Indians, and it may hold good when you intend to settle amongst them but with travelers and strangers it is generally otherwise and more men are betrayed than saved by having connection with their women, and how can it be otherwise sence all their View are selfish without the least mixture of regard or attachment whatever; at least my observations which have been pretty general, have not pointed out to me one instance to the contrary. *February 1777*

'Amongst those occasional Visiters was a Chief named *Kahoura* who headed the party that cut off Captain Furneux's boat and who himself killed the officer that commanded. To judge of the character of this man by what some of his Country said of him, he seemed to be a man more feared than beloved by them: many of them said he was a very bad man and importuned me to kill him and I beleive they were not a little surprised that I did not, for accord[ing] to their ideas of equity this ought to have been done. But if I had followed the advice of all our pretended friends, I might have extirpated the whole race, for the people of each Hamlet or village by turns applyed to me to distroy the other, a very striking proof of the divided state in which they live. We could not misunderstand them as Omai who understood their language perfectly well was our interpreter.

☾ Cook sailed from Queen Charlotte Sound on 25th February 1777, and moving north east made discoveries in various island groups including the group that bears his name. He realised that he must move rapidly if he was to catch the Arctic summer season, but he encountered much bad weather and the securing of water for his animals was a constant anxiety. In the end he realised that refreshment was inevitable so he turned westwards to winter amongst his old favourites, the Friendly Islands where the expedition spent delightful months in feasting and dancing. Before this, however, they found in the small island of Wautieu fair Society Islanders, who had lost their way while crossing from Otaheite to Ulietea twelve years before, an incident which Cook reported in order to show how population must have spread from island to island.

THURSDAY *3rd* April. Omai met with four of his Country men upon this island, who about ten years ago were coming from Otaheite to Ulietea but missing the latter, were after being at sea a long time, cast ashore upon this. There were twenty in the whole Men and Women in the Canoes, but only five survived the hardships they under went, having had neither Victuals nor drink for many days; during some of the last days, the Canoe was oversent and these five men saved themselves by hanging by the side of her, till Providence brought them in sight of the people of this island, who sent out Canoes to bring them a shore, where they were kindly treated, and were now so well satisfied with their situation that they refused the offer which Omai made of giving them a passage with us to their native isle.

'This circumstance very well accounts for the manner the inhabited islands in this Sea have been at first peopled; especially those which lay remote from any Continent and from each other.

April 1777 ⟬ After visiting the small and low Palmerston Group, Cook gave a valuable opinion on the vexed question of how such islands were formed.

THURSDAY 17*th* April. There are different opinions in respect to these low islands, some will have it they are the remains of large islands, that in remote times these little heads or isles, were joined and formed one continued track of land which the Sea in process of time has washed away and left only the higher grounds, and that they will in time share the same fate. Others and I think with far more reason, Mentain that they are formed from Shoals or Coral banks and of consequence increasing: and there are some who think they have been thrown up by Earth quakes. Without mentioning the several arguments made use of in support of the different opinions, I shall only relate such observations as I made when upon them. The foundation is every where a Coral rock the Soil Coral Sand, with which the decayed Vegetables have but in a few places intermixed so as to form any thing like mould, a very strong presumption that they are not of very ancient date nor the remains of large islands, for if either one or the other, more mould must have been formed or some part of the original soil remain. There are far beyond the reach of the Sea even in the most violent Storms, elevated coral rocks perforated by the waves in the same manner as those on the outer edge of the reef, which evidently shews that the Sea has at one time or another reached them. But the strongest proof of their increase is the gentle graduation obser[v]able in the Plants round the skirts of the islands, from within a few inches of high-water mark to the edge of the wood. In many places the divisions of the plants of different grouths were very distinguishable, especially on the lee or West side, this I take to have been effected by extraordinary high tides occasioned by accedental gales from the westward, which has heaped up the sand beyond the reach of common tides; these again throw up the Sand so as to form a barrier to the next extraordinary high tide or Storm, so as to prevent it from reaching as far as the former and distroying the plants that may have Vegetated from Cocoanuts, roots and seed b[r]ought there by the wind, birds, or thrown up by the sea. Perhaps there is a nother thing which if allowed, will accelerate the increase of these islands as much as any other, and will also account for the Sea receeding from those elevated rocks before mentioned. That is the spreading of the Coral bank or reef into the Sea, which in my opinion, is continually though imperceptibly effected, the waves receeding with it leaves a dry rock behind for the reception of broken Coral, sand &c[a].

⟬ Cook reached the Friendly Islands at the end of April and was delighted by their beauty and by their charming inhabitants, who, however, took the usual Polynesian pleasure in theft. Cook made friends with several chiefs and was invited to attend a number of feasts and ceremonies which he described at great length. He also explained his difficulties in deciding where and with whom the gifts of domestic animals and birds could best be placed.

SUNDAY 13*th* July. From this hill we had a full View of the whole island except a part of the South point; the SE side from which the hills are not far distant, rises with very great inequalities directly from the Sea, so that the plains and Medows, of which here are some of great extent, lay all on the NW side; and as they are adorned with tufts of trees and here and there plantations, make a very beautiful Landskip from whatever point they are viewed. Whilst I was viewing these delightfull spots, I could not help flatering my self with the idea that some future Navigator may from the very same station behould these Medows stocked with Cattle, the English have planted at these islands.

¶ In mid July, when Cook sailed, he wrote a very long and interesting account of the Friendly Islands which the Hakluyt Society is publishing in the Third Volume of their Definitive Edition. The islanders were closely akin to the Tahitians both in race and customs, and, as with the Tahitians evil aspects of the white invasion were already at work. Thus Cook wrote:

TUESDAY 15*th* July. *Polygamy*. *Polygamy* is allowed to the Cheifs, and it is no uncommon thing to meet with some who will tell us they have got eight or ten wives, but the most of them are satisfied with one at least many had no more. Some of us were of opinion, that the most of those which they called their wives were only Concubines, and that there was only one that was looked upon as the wife and who always appeared to be the Mistress of the family. As chastity at first sight appeared to be held in no great estimation, we expected to have found frequent breaches of the conjugal fidelity in the Married Women or kept Mistresses, which you please, but it was the very contrary. I do not know that our whole Stay produced one instance; neither are those of the better sort that are unmarr[i]ed more free of their favours, its true there are no want of those of a different stamp, and perhaps they are more numerous in proportion to the number of people than in many other Countries; but it appeared to me that the most, if not all of them, were of the lowest class of people, and such as came to our people were Whores by profession and brought to us in order to make the most of the present time.

'*Diseases*. This commerce has unhappily entailed upon them the Veneral deasease, as we had not long been at Anamocka before some of our people were affected with it, and I had the Mortification to find that all the care I took when I first Visited these islands to prevent this dreadfull desease from being communicated to them, prove enefectual. What is extraordinary the people do not seem to regard it. As we saw no signs of its bad effects, probably their way of living greatly abates it virulency. We observed several who had ulcers upon different parts of their bodies, some of which had a very virulent appearence, particularly those in the face which were shoking to look at; on the other hand some seemed to be cured and others in a fair way, but this was not effected without the loss of the nose or best part of it. But this cannot be the effect of the Veneral as they

July 1777 were subject to it before the English vesited them, unless they had the veneral desease before which they say not.

¶ Cook reached Tahiti in mid August 1777 with the object of leaving at one of the islands Omai and the numerous gifts which he had acquired in Britain. Here, however, Cook faced two difficulties. Directly he reached the islands Omai began to evince a prodigal generosity usually towards flatterers and other unworthy compatriots. Furthermore the inhabitants of Bolabola had invaded Omai's native island of Ulietea and Omai and his supporters soon made it clear that they expected Cook to invade the island and restore Omai's family territories.

¶ Cook also found that during his absence Spanish ships had brought to and removed from Tahiti unsuccessful missionaries leaving behind them a small house and a cross near the grave of a dead commander. The cross carried two inscriptions 'Christus Vincit' and 'Carolus III imperat 1774'. Opposite the latter Cook cut the words Georgius Tertius Rex, Annis 1767, 1769, 1773, 1774 and 1777. A clear indication of Britain's prior claim and greater interest.

¶ Cook, who in 1768 was puzzled when Banks brought valueless plants to the *Endeavour*, was himself becoming a more and more eager and experienced scientist. On the second voyage he had had Maori flesh broiled for Maori consumption, as an ocular and undeniable proof of Maori cannibalism, and he now gained from his friend Chief Otoo of Tahiti permission to attend the ceremonies which followed a human sacrifice, the victim having been knocked on the head to invoke divine assistance on an inter-island expedition which Cook had already refused to help. Cook and his officers told the Tahitians in no uncertain terms that human sacrifices were revolting and that an English chief who slaughtered a servant for such a purpose would bring the gravest results on his own head. One can see, however, from Cook's Journals that the great explorer was already paving the way for the vicious misrepresentation of the Hawaiian missionaries who could not be expected to see that, in participating in ceremonies which to some extent involved him in native adoration, Cook was seeking not his own glory but the opportunity of observing and recording anthropological truth. After describing the somewhat dull ceremony Cook wrote:

TUESDAY *2nd* September. The unhappy sufferer seemed to be a Middle aged man, and as we were told a *Tou tou* but I never understood he had done any crime so as to merit death; it is however certain that they make choise of such for these sacrifices, or else common low fellows who strol about from place to place and island to island without any vesible way of geting an honist livelyhood, of such sort here are enough at these islands. This man was bloody about the head and face, which we attributed to the manner he was killed having been privatly knocked on the head with a Stone, for those who fall a sacrifice to this barbarous custom are never apprised of their fate till the Moment that puts an end to their

September 1777

existence. Whenever any of the Great cheifs thinks a human Sacrifice necessary on any particular occasion, he pitches upon the Victim, sends some of his trusty Servants who fall upon him and kill him; the King is then acquainted with it, whose presence at the Ceremony, as I was told is absolutely necessary, indeed except the Priests he was the only man that had any thing to do in it. From what we could learn these Sacrifices are not very uncommon, there were in the face of the Morai where this man was buried forty nine Sculls, every one of which were those of men who had been sacrificed at this place; and I have seen Sculls at many of the other great Morais, so that it is not confined to this place alone. This is not the only barbarous custom we find amongst these people, we have great reason to beleive there was a time when they were Canibals; however I will not insist upon this but confine my self to such as we have unquestionable authority for. Besides the cuting out the jaw-bones of the enemy that is slain in battle, they in some Measure offer their bodies as a Sacrifice to the Eatua the day after when the Victors collect all the dead that have fallen into their hands and bring them to the Morai, where with a great deal of ceremony they dig a hole and bury them all in it as an offering to the Gods. But the great cheifs who fall in battle and into the hands of their enimies are treated in a different manner. We were told that the late King Tootaha, Tebourai Tamaida, and a nother Chief who fell with them were brought to this Morai, their bowels cut out by the Priests before the great alter, and the bodies afterwards buried in three different places, which were pointed out to us in the great pile of stones which compose the most conspicious part of this Morai. And the Common Men who fell also in this battle were all burried in one hole at the foot of the pile. . . . During the Ceremony we were silent but as soon as it was over we made no scruple in giving out sentments very freely upon it and of Course condemned it. I told the Chief that this Sacrifice was so far from pleasing the Eatua as they intended that he would be angry with them for it and that they would not succeed against Maheine. . . . During this debate most of the people on the spot were present, which were chiefly the Attendants and servants of the Chief, and when Omai began to explaine the punishment that would be enflected upon even the greatest man in England if he killed his Servant, they seemed to listen with attention and were probably of a different opinion with their master.

⦅ On Sunday, 2nd November, Cook and his party said a sorrowful farewell to Omai whom the expedition left on the island of Huaheine with a retinue which included two young Maoris who had accompanied the expedition from New Zealand; in a house which the British built and with firearms and a quantity of other goods. Cook was warmly attached to Omai as his Journal testifies, but he also recognised the grave weaknesses in Omai's character which appeared so strongly after the British sailed that neither Omai nor his possessions long survived.

November *1777* SUNDAY *2nd* November. Whatever faults this Indian had they were more than over ballanced by his great good Nature and docile disposition, during the whole time he was with me I very seldom had reason to find fault with his conduct. His gratifull heart always retained the highest sence of the favours he received in England nor will he ever forget those who honoured him with their protection and friendship during his stay there. He had a tolerable share of understanding, but wanted application and perseverance to exert it, so that his knowledge of things was very general and in many instances imperfect. He was not a man of much observation, there were many little arts as well as amusements amongst the people of the Friendly islands which he might have conveyed to his own, where they probably would have been adopted, as being so much in their own way, but I never found that he used the least endeavours to make himself master of any one. This kind of indifferency is the true Character of his Nation, Europeans have visited them at times for these ten years past, yet we find neither new arts nor improvements in the old, nor have they copied after us in any one thing. We are therefore not to expect that Omai will be able to interduce many of our arts and customs amongst them or much improve those they have got, I think however he will endeavour to bring to perfection the fruits &c[a] we planted which will be no small acquisition. But the greatest benifit these islands will receive from Omais travels will be in the Animals that have been left upon them, which probably they never would have got had he not come to England; when these multiplies of which I think, there is little doubt, they will equal, if not exceed any place in the known World for provisions.

Chapter XVII
THE DISCOVERY OF HAWAII, 1778

"A discovery which, though the last, seemed in many respects to be the most important . . . made by Europeans throughout . . . the Pacific area."
COOK, CONCLUSION OF JOURNAL, 1779

COOK LEFT BORABORA IN THE SOCIETY ISLANDS IN December 1777, after making a complete survey of the stores and provisions in the two vessels. The Society Islanders stated that they knew of no lands to the north, but Cook knew that Mendaña had discovered an island near the Equator and in an appropriate longitude during his voyage of 1568, so that he was not surprised to see land-frequenting birds, and to sight on 24th December, Christmas Island. Here the expedition secured little of value excepting turtle, although Cook noted that the soil was 'light and black, evidently composed of decayed vegetables, the dung of birds and sand'.

❡ Resuming their northward course on 2nd January 1778 the expedition continued to sight evidence of land such as turtles and land birds and on 18th January saw the lofty hills of Hawaii which Cook named the Sandwich Islands. This discovery in the empty waters of the eastern Pacific was of such strategic and commercial importance that we will quote the greater part of Cook's own account.

FRIDAY *2nd* January. We continued to see birds every day of the sorts last mentioned, sometimes in greater numbers than at others: and between the latitude of 10 and a 11 we saw several turtle. All these are looked upon as signs of the vecinity of land; we however saw none till day break in the Morning of the 18th when an island was descovered bearing NEBE and soon after we saw

January 1778 more land bearing North and intirely ditatched from the first; both had the appearence of being high land.

MONDAY 19*th* January. We now had a fine breeze at EBN and I stood for the East end of the second island, which at noon extended from N½E to WNW¼W, the nearest part about two leagues distant. At this time we were in some doubt whether or not the land before was inhabited, this doubt was soon cleared up, by seeing some Canoes coming off from the shore towards the Ships, I immediately brought to to give them time to come up, there were three and four men in each and we were agreeably surprised to find them of the same Nation as the people of Otahiete and the other islands we had lately visited. It required but very little address to get them to come along side, but we could not prevail upon any one to come on board; they exchanged a few fish they had in the Canoes for any thing we offered them, but valued nails, or iron above every other thing; the only weapons they had were a few stones in some of the Canoes and these they threw overboard when they found they were not wanted. Seeing no signs of an anchoring place at this part of the island, I boar up for the lee side, and ranged the SE side at the distance of half a league from the shore. As soon as we made sail the Canoes left us, but others came off from the shore and brought with them roasting pigs and some very fine Potatoes, which they exchanged, as the others had done, for whatever was offered them; several small pigs were got for a sixpeny nail or two apiece, so that we again found our selves in the land of plenty, just as the turtle we had taken on board at the last island was nearly expended. We passed several villages, some seated upon the sea shore and other up in the Country; the inhabitants of all of them crowded to the shore and on the elevated places to view the Ships. The land on this side of the island rises in a gentle slope from the sea shore to the foot of the Mountions that are in the middle of the island, except in one place, near the east end where they rise directly from the sea; here they seemed to be formed of nothing but stone which lay in horizontal stratas; we saw no wood but what was up in the interior part of the island and a few trees about the villages; we observed several plantations of Plantains and sugar canes, and places that seemed to be planted with roots. We continued to Sound without strieking ground with a line of 50 fathoms till we came abreast of a low point which is about the middle of the south side of the island or rather nearer to the NW end; here we met with 12 and 14 fathoms over a rocky bottom; being past this point, from which the coast trended more northerly, we had 20, then 16, 12 and at last 5 fathom over a sandy bottom; the last soundings was about a mile from the shore. Night now put a stop to any further researches and we spent it standing off and on. The next morning we stood in for the land and were met by several Canoes filled with people, some of them took courage and ventured on board. I never saw Indians so much astonished at the entering a ship before, their eyes were continually flying from object to object, the wildness of thier looks and actions fully express'd their surprise and astonishment at the several new objects before them and evinced that they never had been on board of a ship before. However the first man that came on board did not with all his surprise, forget his own intrest, the first moveable thing that came in his way was the lead and line, which he without asking any questions took to put into his Canoe and when we stopped him said "I am only going to put it into my boat" nor would he quit it till some of his countrymen spoke to him. At 9 o'clock being pretty near the shore, I sent three armed boats under the command of Lieutenant Williamson, to look for a landing place and fresh water. I ordered him, that if he found it necessary to land to look for the latter not to suffer more than one man to go out of the boat. As the boats put off an Indian stole the Butcher cleaver, leaped over board with it, got into his canoe and made for the shore, the boats pursued him but to no effect.

January 1778

'As there were some venereal complaints on board both the Ships, in order to prevent its being communicated to these people, I gave orders that no Women, on any account whatever were to be admited on board the Ships, I also forbid all manner of connection with them, and ordered that none who had the veneral upon them should go out of the Ships. But whether these regulations had the desired effect or no time can only discover. It is no more than what I did when I first visited the Friendly Islands yet I afterwards found it did not succeed, and I am much afraid this will always be the case where it is necessary to have a number of people on shore; the oppertunities and inducements to an intercourse between the sex, are there too many to be guarded against. It is also a doubt with me that the most skilfull of the Faculty can tell whether every man who has had the veneral is so far cured as not to communicate it further, I think I could mention some instances to the contrary. It is likewise well known that amongst a number of men, there will be found some who will endeavour to conceal this desorder, and there are some again who care not to whom they communicate it, of this last we had an instance at Tongatabu in the Gunner of the Discovery, who remained a shore to manage the trade for Captain Clerke. After he knew he had contracted this disease he continued to sleep with different women who were supposed not to have contracted it; his companions expostulated with him without effect; till it came to Captain Clerke's knowlidge who ordered him on board.

'While the boats were in shore examining the coast we stood on and off with the Ships, waiting their return, at length, about noon Mr Williamson came on board and reported that he had seen a large pond behind a beach near one of the Villages, which the Natives told him was fresh water and that there was anchorage before it. He also reported that he attempted to land in a nother place but was prevented by the Indians coming down to the boat in great

January 1778

numbers, and were for taking away the oars, muskets and in short every thing they could lay hold upon and pressed so thick upon him that he was obliged to fire, by which one man was killed. But this unhappy circumstance I did not know till after we left the islands, so that all my measures were directed as if nothing of the kind had happened. Mr Williamson told me that after the man fell they took him up, [c]arried him off, and then retired from the boat and made signs for them to land, but this he declined. It did not appear to Mr Williamson that they had any design to kill or even hurt any of the people in the boat but were excited by mere curisoity to get what they had from them, and were at the same time, ready to give in return any thing they had.

'After the boats were on board I sent away one of them to lay in the best anchoring ground, and as soon as she got to her station I bore down with the ships and anchored in 25 fathom water the bottom a fine grey owsey sand. The East point of the road, which was the low point before mentioned, bore S 51° E, the west point N 65° W and the Village where the water was said to be, NEBE distant one mile, but there were breakers little more than a quarter of a mile which I did not see till after we had anchored; The Discovery anchored to the Eastward of us and farther from the shore. As soon as the Ships was anchored I went a shore with three boats, to look at the water and try the disposition of the inhabitants, several hundreds of whom were assembled on a sandy beach before the Village. The very instant I leaped ashore, they all fell flat on their faces, and remained in that humble posture till I made signs to them to rise. They then brought a great many small pigs and gave us without regarding whether they got any thing in return or no indeed the most of them were present[ed] to me with plantain trees, in a ceremonious way as is usual on such like occasions, and I ratified these marks of friendship by presenting them with such things as I had with me. After things were a little settled I left a guard upon the beach and got some of the Indians to shew me the water, which proved to be very good and convenient to come at. Being satisfied with the conveniency of Watering and that we had nothing to fear from the Natives, I returned on board and gave orders for every thing to be in readiness for Watering in the Morning, when I went ashore with the people employed on this service my self, having a party of Marines for a guard which were stationed on the beach. We no sooner landed, that a trade was set on foot for hogs and potatoes, which the people gave us in exchange for nails and pieces of iron formed into some thing like chisels. We met with no obstruction in watering on the contrary the Natives assisted our people to roll the Casks to and from the pond. As soon as every thing was settled to my saitisfaction, I left the command to Mr Williamson who was with me and took a walk up the Vally, accompaned by Dr Anderson and Mr Webber; conducted by one of the Natives and attended by a tolerable train. Our guide proclamed our approach and every one whom we met fell on their faces and remained in that position till we had passed. This as I afterwards understood, is done to their great chiefs. Our road lay in among the Plantations, which were chiefly of Tara, and sunk a little below the common level so as to contain the water necessary to nourish the roots. As we ranged down the coast from the East in the Ships, we observed at every Village one or more elevated objects, like Pyramids and we had seen one in this vally that we were desireous of going to see. Our guide understood us but as this was on the other side of the river, he conducted us to one on the same side we were upon; it proved to be in a Morai which in many respects was like those of Otaheite. The *Pyramid* which they call [Henananoo] was erected at one end, it was 4 feet square at the base and about 20 feet high, the four sides was built of small sticks and branches, in an open manner and the inside of the pyramid was hollow or open from bottom to top. Some part of it was, or had been covered with a very thin light grey cloth which seemed to be consecrated to Religious and ceremonious purposes, as a good deal of it was about this Morai and I had some of it forced upon me on my first landing. On each side and near the Pyrimid, stood erect some rude carved boards, exactly like those in the Morais at Otahiete. At the foot of these were square places, a little sunk below the common level and inclosed with stone, these we understood were graves. About the middle of the Morai were three of these places in a line, where we were told three chiefs had been buried; before them was another that was oblong, this they called Tanga taboo and gave us clearly to understand that three human sacrefices had been buried there, that is one at the burial of each chief. The next thing that fixed out attention, was a house or close shed on one side of the Morai, it was 40 feet long, 10 broad in the middle, each end being narrower, and about 10 feet high. The entrance was at the middle of the side which was in the Morai, fronting it on the other side was a kind of Altar, composed of a piece of carved wood set ere[c]t and on each side the figure of a Woman carved in wood, neither very ill designed nor executed; on the head of one was carved a cap like a helmet worn by the ancient warriors and on the other a round cap, like the head dress at Otaheite called Tomou. These two images, which were about three feet high, they called Eatua no Veheina, Godess's, but that they worship them may be doubted. Before this place and in the middle of the house, was an oblong space, inclosed by a low edging of stone and covered over with the thin cloth; this they told us was the grave of seven chiefs. On one side of the door on the out side of the house was a nother Tanga taboo, or a place where a human secrefise had been buried. On the out side of the Morai was a smal shed no biger than a dog kennel, and before it a grave where, as we were told, the remains of a woman laid. This Morai was inclosed by a wall of Stone about 4 feet high like many of those at Otahiete, to which as I have already observed it bore a very great resemblence, and the several parts that compose it being called by the same names shews, at least,

January 1778 that these people have nearly the same Notions of Religion and that the only material diffeerence is in the disposal of the dead.

'After having seen every thing that was to be seen about this Morai and M[r] Webber had taken a drawing of it, we returned to the beach by a different rout to the one we came. Besides the Tara plantations before mentioned we met with some plantations of plantain, Sugar cane and the Chinese paper Mulbery tree or cloth plant, as it is more generally called by us, there were also a few low cocoanut trees, but we saw but one bread fruit tree and but very few of any other sort.

'At the beach I found a great crowd and a brisk trade for pigs, fowls and roots which was carried on with the greatest good order, though I did not see a man that appeared of more consequince than a nother, if there was they did not shew themselves to us. At Noon I returned on board to dinner and sent M[r] King ashore to command the party; he was to have gone in the Morning, but was detained aboard to make lunar observations. In the after noon I went ashore again accompaned by Captain Clerke, I designed to have taken a walk into the Country, but thinking it too late defered it to another oppertunity and that did not afterwards happen. At sun set I brought every body on board, having got during the day Nine tons of water, and by exchanges chiefly for nails and pieces of iron, about sixty or eighty Pigs, a few Fowls, a quantity of potatoes and a few plantains and Tara roots. No people could trade with more honisty than these people, never once attempting to cheat us, either ashore or along side the ships. Some indeed at first betrayed a thievish disposition, or rather they thought they had a right to any thing they could lay their hands upon but this conduct they soon laid aside.

FRIDAY 30*th* January. On the 30th I sent M[r] Gore ashore again with a guard of Marines and a party to trade with the Natives for refreshments; I intended to have followed soon after and went from the Ship with that design, but the surf had increased so much, that I was fearfull if I got ashore I should not get off again as realy happened to the party that was ashore, the cummunication by our own boats being soon stoped. In the evening the party a shore made the Signal for the boats, sent them accordingly. Not long after they returned with a few yams and salt, a tolerable quantity of both was procured during the day but the greatest part was lost in geting into the boats. The officer with about twenty men were left a shore; thus the very thing happened that I had above all others wished to prevent. Most of what we got to day was brought off by the Natives and purchased along side the ship in exchange for Nails and pieces of iron hopes. About 10 or 11 oclock the wind veered to the South and the sky seemed to foreboad a storm; thinking we were rather too near the shore, took up the Anchor and shoot into 42 fathom and there came to again. This precausion was unnecessary as the wind soon veered to NNE, where it blew a fresh gale with

Squals attended with very heavy showers of rain. This weather continued all the next day and the sea run so high that we had no manner of communication with the people on shore; even the Natives durst not venture out in their canoes. In the evening I sent the master in a boat up to the SE head, or point, to see if a boat could land under it, he returned with a favourable report, but too late to send for the party till the next mor[n]ing, when I sent an order to Mr Gore, that if he could not imbark the people where he was to march them up to the point. As the boat could not land a person swam a shore with the order; on the return of the boat I went my self with a Pinnace and Launch up to the point to bring the party on board, taking with me a Ram goat and two Ewes, a Boar and Sow pig of the English breed, the seeds of Mellons, Pumpkins and Onions. I landed with great ease under the west side of the point, and found the party already there, with a few of the Natives among them. There was one man whom Mr Gore had observed to have some command over the others, to him I gave the Goats, Pigs and seeds. I should have left these things at the other island had we not been so unexpectedly driven from it. While the people were filling four water casks from a small stream occasioned by the late rain, I took a little walk into the island attended by the man above mentioned, and followed by two others carrying the two pigs. As soon as we got upon a rising ground I stoped to look round me, a woman on the other side of the Vally where I landed, called to the men with me, on which the Chief began to mutter something like a prayer and the two men with the pigs continued to walk round me all the time, not less than ten or a dozen times before the other had finished. This ceremony being ended, we proceeded and presently met people coming from all parts, who, on the men with me calling to them laid down till I was out of sight. . . .

January 1778

'These five Islands, *Atoui*, *Enēēhēēoū*, *Orrehoua*, *Otaoora* and *Wouahoo*, names by which they are known to the Natives, I named *Sandwich Islands*, in honour of the Earl of Sandwich. They are situated between the Latitude of 21° 30′ and 22° 15′ N and between the Longitude of 199° 20′ and 201° 30′ East. *Wouahoo*, which is the Eastermost and lies in the Latitude of 21° 36′ we knew no more of than that it is high land and inhabited. *Atoui*, which is the largest, is at least ten leagues in length from East to West. It is, as I have already observed also high land and without wood, except what may be in the Mountains which we had no oppertunity to examine. This island produceth all the sorts of fruit and roots that are found at Otaheite or any other of the South Sea islands, but nothing seemed to be in great plenty, but Potatoes, which are the largest I ever saw, some being as big as a mans head. They have a sweet taste but are not so farinaceous as our best potatoes; perhaps many of those we got were not come to their full perfection. I am told these potatoes are very common in Virginia and other parts of North America and known by the name of spanish potatoes. The Taro or

January 1778 eddy root, is also in tolerable plenty and the best I ever tasted. The tame Animals are hogs, dogs and fowls, all of the same kind as at Otahiete and equally as good. We saw no other wild animals than rats, small lizards and birds; but as we did not penetrate into the country, we neither know in what plenty no[r] variety they may have of the latter. . . . I have already observed that these people are of the same nation as the people of Otaheite and many others of the South sea islands, consequently they differ but little from them in their persons. These have a darker hue than the generality of the Otahietans, which may be owing to their being more exposed to the Sun and wearing less cloathing. How shall we account for this Nation spreading it self so far over this Vast ocean? We find them from New Zealand to the South, to these islands to the North and from Easter Island to the Hebrides; an extent of 60° of latitude or twelve hundred leagues north and south and 83° of longitude or sixteen hundred and sixty leagues east and west, how much farther is not known, but we may safly conclude that they extend to the west beyond the Hebrides.

'These people are scanty in their cloathing, very few of the Men wear any thing more than the Maro, but the women have a piece of cloth wraped round the waist, so as to hang down like a petticoat as low as the knee; all the rest of the body is naked. Thier ornaments are braclets, necklaces and Amulets, which are made of shells, bone or stone; They have also neat Tippets made of red and yellow feathers, and Caps and Cloaks covered with the same or some other feathers; the cloakes, reach to about the middle of the back, and are like the short cloakes worn by the women in England, or like the riding cloaks worn in Spain. The Caps are made so as to fit very close to the head with a semicircular protuberance on the crown exactly like the helmets of old. These and also the cloaks they set so high a Value upon that I could not procure one, some where however got.

'Tattowing or staining the skin is practised here, but not in a high degree, nor does it appear to be directed by any particular mode but rather by fancy. The figures were straight lines, Stars &c[a] and many had the figure of the *Taame* or brea[s]t plate of Otahiete, though we saw it not among them. The hair is in general black were they not to stain it, as at the Friendly islands; it is worn in different forms, some have it long and some short, and some both; but the general fashion, among the women in particular, is to have it long before and short behind. Some of the men had a kind of wig made of human hair twisted together into a number of long tails, each a finger thick that hung down as low as the breach. Some of the men had long beards but the general custom was to have it short. They are an open, candid, active people and the most expert swimmers we had met with; in which they are taught from their very birth: It was very common for women with infants at the breast to come off in Canoes to look at the Ships, and when the surf was so high that they could not land them

January 1778

in the Canoe they used to leap over board with the child in their arms and make their way a shore through a surf that looked dreadfull. It hath been mentioned that I did not see a chief of note, there were however several on *Atoui* and one of them called Tamahano, made Captain Clerke a visit after I had left the island. He came off in a double canoe, and like the King of the Friendly islands, paid no regard to those who happened to lay in his way but ran against or over them without endeavouring in the least to avoide them; nor could they get out of his way as the people in them were obliged to lay down till he had passed. His attendants helped him into the Ship and placed him on the gangway, and were so carefull of him that they stood round him with their hands locked with each other, not suffering any one to come near him but Captain Clerke. He was a young man, cloathed from head to foot and accompaned by a young woman, suppos'd to be his wife. Captain Clerke made him some sutable presents and in return he gave him a large Cava bowl, that was supported by car[v]ed men, neither ill designed nor executed. Cave or Ava Ava, as it is called at Otahiete is prepared and drank here as at the other islands. Captain Clerk could not prevail upon him to go below, nor move from the place he was first fixed in; at length after a short stay he was conducted a shore in the same manner as he came on board. The next day several messages came off to Captain Clerke, desiring him to go ashore, and acquainting him that the Cheif had got a large present for him; but being anxious to get to sea did not go.

'We had good reason to think that all the islands are subject or belong to the great men of *Atoui*, though the people of *Eheeneeou*, told us, they sometimes fought with them. Their weapons are Spears or lances, some barbed at one end and flatened to a point at the other, and a short instrument something like a dagger about a foot and a half long, sharpened at one, or both ends and secured to the hand by a string: the use of this weapon is to stab in close fighting and seems well adapted for the purpose. Such were the weapons they offered to us for sale, they may have other which we did not see. Some of these were made of a redish dark coloured wood not unlike Mahogany.

'Although we saw very few trees except the Cocoanut tree, they must have some of a good size on which they make their Canoes; as they are in general about twenty four feet long and the bottom for the most part formed of one piece, hollowed out to about an inch, or an inch and a half thick, and brought to apoint at each end: the sides consits of three boards, each about an inch thick and neatly fited and lashed to the bottom part. The extremities of both head and stern is a little raised, and both are made sharp, something like a wedge but flatenes more abruptly, so that the two side boards join each other side by side for more than a foot; but the drawing will explain this better than words. As they are not more than fifteen or eighteen inches broad, those that go single have out riggers, which are shaped and fited with more judgement than any I

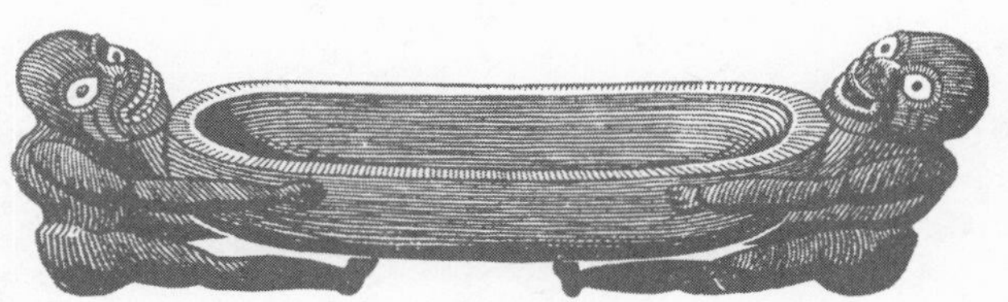

December 1778 had before seen. They are rowed by paddles and some have a light triangler sail, like those of the Friendly islands, extended to a mast and boom.

'Their houses are not unlike oblong corn stacks, they are of various sizes from forty or fifty feet long and twenty or thirty broad to little huts: they have low walls and a high roof consiting of two flat sides inclining to each other, and terminating in a ridge like the thatched houses in England. The framing is of wood, and both walls and roof consits of Course dry grass which is very closely put together so that they appear to afford too warm a retreat for the climate. The door is so low that a man can hardly get in without going upon his hands and knees, and they have no other light except what may come through the crevices in the wall; some of [the] gentlemen observed that when they wanted light they made a hole in the wall and closed it again when they had done with it. The floor is covered with dry hay and upon this they spread Mats to sleep upon. A few gourds and wooden bowls, make up their whole catalouge of household utensils. Their mats are both strong and fine and some are neatly coloured. But what they most excell in colouring is cloth, which, like the cloth of the other islands, is made of bark, none of it is remarkably fine but it is all glazed and prented with different Colours, which are so disposed as to have a pritty and pleasing effect; they have a very great variety of patterns and many of them are extremely beautifull. Of this cloth they have of different degrees of thickness, but no large pieces like what is at the other islands, the thickest sort is in general made in small pieces, several of which are sewed together to make a dress. We had no oppertunity to see how it was Coloured and prented nor did we see any of the instruments with which it is done, by which we might form a judgement.

'*Religion and Government.* As to their Religion, I can add nothing to what has been already mentioned, and we have fewer lights to form a judgement of the Government, but from the subordination that was observed, there is great reason to believe that it is of the same nature as at the other islands. We had no oppertunity to see any of their amusements and the only musical instruments that was seen among them was a hollow vessel of wood like a platter and two sticks, on these one of our gentlemen saw a man play: one of the sticks he held as we do a fiddle and struck it with the other, which was smaller and something like a drum stick and at the same time beat with his foot upon the hollow Vessel and produced a tune that was by no means disagreable. This Musick was accompaned with a song, sung by some women and had a pleasing and tender effect. Another instrument was seen among them, but it can scarcely be called an instrument of music; this was a small gourd with some pebblestones in it, which they shake in the hand like a child's rattle and are used, as they told us, at their dances. They must have some game in which they use bowls as we found among them some which were in the shape of Cheeses, about an inch and a half thick and three and an half in the diameter. Some are made of stone others of clay hardened in the fire and then glazed. But though some of these bowls are made of Clay we did not find they had any Earthen vessels. *January* 1778

'Such of their working instruments or tools which I saw were the same as at the other islands, their hatchets or adzes exactly so, and seemed to be of the same kind of black stone, but they had others that were made of a clay coloured stone. The only iron tools or indeed pieces of iron seen among them, which they were supposed to have before our arrival, was a piece of iron hoop about three inches long, fited into a wooden handle in the same manner as their stone adzes and a nother edge tool which was supposed to have be[en] made of the point of a broad sword. This, and their knowing the use of iron made some immagine that we were not the first Ships that had been at these islands, on the other hand the very great surprise they shewed at the sight of the ships and their total ignorance of fire arms seemed to prove the contrary. There are many ways by which these islands as well as many others, may come by the knowlidge of iron without being visited by shipping; for without mentioning the intercourse which one group may have with another, is there not the whole coast of America to windward, where the Spaniards have been settled for more than two hundred years and where Shipwrecks must and have frequently happened. It therefore cannot be thought an extraordenary thing for part of such wrecks with iron in it, to be now and then cast upon islands, scatered about this vast ocean; the distance is no argument whatever against it; but even if it was, it would not distroy it, as many things containing iron may be thrown out, or lost from ships that have made passages across this ocean, such as the loss of a mast and many other things which must be obvious to every one. But what confirms it one of my people seeing some wood in one of the houses at Wymoa, which he judged to be fir; it had been eat by the worm and the people made him understand that it was driven a shore by the waves of the sea.

'Spain may probably reap some benifit by the discovery of these islands, as they are extremely will situated for the Ships sailing from New Spain to the Philippine Islands to touch and refresh at, being about midway between Acapulco and the Ladrone islands. It is necessary to mention that no dependence can be placed, in the hogs taken on board at these islands, for they will niether thrive nor live on board a ship. This was one great inducement to my leaving of the English breed as the hogs we got at Otaheite, that were of the Spanish breed, thrived and fed on board the Ship as well as our own, at the very time that others were pining away and dying daily.

Chapter XVIII

THE NORTH AMERICAN COAST

"This Point of land which I named Cape Prince of Wales, is the . . . Western extremity of all America hitherto known."

COOK, 1778

IN HIS YEARS OF EXPLORATION COOK NATURALLY MADE A number of blunders, although it is fair to say that these included no major mistakes such as reporting that small islands were continents in the manner of some of his predecessors. He did, however, believe that Tasmania was a peninsula of Australia, and Stewart Island a peninsula of New Zealand and his arrival on the North American coast was darkened by his failure to discover the channel to the south of Vancouver Island, now known as Juan de Fuca's Strait. It must be remembered, however, that Cook was instructed to reach New Albion in the vicinity of latitude 45° north and push rapidly northwards along coasts where no profit to Britain seemed likely to exist. Also Cook made his landfall in weather so threatening that he named a neighbouring point Cape Foul Weather, and was twice blown off the coast between 6th March and 29th March when he had reached latitude 49° 15′ north. Nevertheless he was unwise to write that he had named Cape Flattery in latitude 48° 15′ north because it might have concealed an opening in the 'very latitude' where geographers had placed 'the pretended Strait of Juan de Fuca', but 'we saw nothing like it, nor is there the least probability that iver any such thing exhisted'.

❡ At the end of March Cook regained the coast and entered King George's or Nootka Sound, the northern entrance of the channel which forms Vancouver

Island. He remained there until 26th April, using the abundant supply of local timber to repair the disgraceful condition of his ships and trading with the natives of whom Dr Anderson left interesting descriptions.

March 1778

MONDAY 30*th* March. In the Morning I sent three armed boats under the command of M[r] King to look for a harbour for the Ships and soon after I went my self in a small boat on the same service. On the NW side of the Arm we were in and not far from the Ship, I found a pretty snug Cove, and M[r] King who returned about Noon found one still better on the NW side of the Sound; but as it would have required more time to get to it than the other, it was resolved to make the nearest serve. But being too late in the day to transport the Ships thither before night, I ordered the sails to be unbent, the Topmast to be struck and the Foremast to be unrig'd in order to fix a new bib, one of the old ones being decayed. A great many Canoes filled with the Natives were about the Ships all day, and a trade commenced betwixt us and them, which was carried on with the Strictest honisty on boath sides. Their articles were the Skins of various animals, such as Bears, Wolfs, Foxes, Dear, Rackoons, Polecats, Martins and in particular the Sea Beaver, the same as is found on the coast of Kamtchatka. Cloathing made of these skins and a nother sort made, either of the bark of a tree or some plant like hemp; Weapons, such as Bows and Arrows, Spears &c[a] Fish hooks and Instruments of various kinds, pieces of carved work and even human sculs and hands, and a variety of little articles too tedious to mention. For these things they took in exchange, Knives, chissels, pieces of iron & Tin, Nails, Buttons, or any kind of metal. Beads they were not fond of and cloth of all kinds they rejected.

TUESDAY 31*st* March. The next day the Ships were got into the Cove and their moored head and stern most of the Moorings being fast to the shore. We found on heaving up the anchor that notwithstanding the great depth of water it was let go in, there were rocks at the bottom which had done some considerable damage to the Cable, and the hawsers that were carried out to warp the Ship into the cove got also foul of rocks, so that it appeared that the whole bottom was strewed with them. As we found the Ship again very leaky in her upper works, the Caulkers were set to work to caulk her and repair such other defects as were wanting.

SATURDAY 4*th* April. In the afternoon we resumed our work and the next day rigged the Foremast; the head of which being rather too small for the Cap, the Carpenter went to work to bring, or fix a piece on one side to fill up the Cap. In cuting into the mast head for this purpose, and examining a little farther into it, both Cheeks were found so rotton that there was no possibility of repairing them without geting the mast out and fixing on new ones. It was evedent that one of the Cheeks had been defective at the first, and the defective part had been cut out and a piece put [in], what had not only weakened the mast head, but

April 1778 had in a great measure been the occasion of roting all the other part. Thus when we were almost ready to put to Sea, we had all our work to do over again, and what was worse a job of work to perform that required some time to finish, but as there was no remedy we immidiately set about it. It was lucky these defects were descovered in a place where wood, the principal thing wanting was to be had; for among the drift wood in the Cove where we lay, were some well seasoned trees and very proper for our purpose, one of which was pitched upon and the Carpenters went to work to make out of it two new Cheeks.

MONDAY 13*th* April. In the after noon of the next day, I went into the woods with a party of men and cut down a tree for a Mizen Mast and the next morning it was got to the place where the Carpenters were at work upon the Fore-mast. In the evening the wind which had been for some time westerly, veered to SE and increased to a very hard gale with rain which continued till 8 oclock the next morning when it abated and veered again to the West. On the Morning of the 15th the Foremast being finished got it along side and set the Carpenters to work to make a new Mizen Mast, but the weather was so bad that the Foremast could not be got in till the afternoon. At this time several Indians were about the Ship who looked on with more silent attention than is usual with Indians.

⁅ It is quite possible to follow Cook's course from the statements in his Journal, although some of his names remain on the map and some do not. H. R. Wagner in his *Cartography of the North West Coast of America*, notes that Cook, in all probability, had knowledge of the recent Spanish expeditions, and was very possibly instructed to follow the route taken by Bering the great Danish explorer sent out by the Russians, particularly as Cook followed this route. Leaving Nootka Sound on 26th April 1778, Cook sighted land on 1st May in 55° 20′ north; named Mt. Edgecumbe, Edgecumbe Bay and Cross Sound; saw Mt. St. Elias, which he thought was Bering's mountain, and, following the coast westwards, landed on Keyes Island, which he named after the Royal Chaplain. He then sailed into the inlet which he first named Sandwich, and later King William Sound, spending some days in Snug Corner Cove. On 18th May he named Montague and Green Islands and on 21st May Cape Elizabeth. He later named Point Banks; the Barren Islands, and Cape Douglas, the last in honour of his friend Canon Douglas of Windsor whose editing of the Second Journal had met with Cook's approval. On 28th May he sailed up Cook's Inlet and Cook's River, and landing at Possession Point, in the Southern inlet, took possession of the region for the British Crown.

⁅ Cook then sailed westwards along the Alaskan coast, naming prominent geographical features; sighted Shishaldan Volcano on Unimak Island and was very nearly wrecked on the northern point of Unalaska Island which he named Providence. On the north end of Unalaska he found a harbour which he named

Samganooda and is now known as Samganuda. After this Cook passed through Bering Strait into the Arctic, where, as Christopher Lloyd points out, he spent the last part of August tacking backwards and forwards off the American and Asian Coasts in an effort to break through an impenetrable ice pack. He saw Cape Prince of Wales, the western point of Alaska; Icy Cape in the American Arctic, his farthest north, and North Cape on the north eastern Siberian Coast. It was a magnificent achievement, which not only demonstrated Cook's abilities as an explorer and cartographer, but also the very fair accuracy of Bering's cartography considering the circumstances under which he worked.

April 1778

❨ On 29th August in latitude 69° 17′ north Cook decided that he could do no more that season but must return to the Hawaiian Islands to refit for a second effort. On the way he stopped at Unalaska in the Aleutians as the *Resolution* was leaking badly from her disgraceful caulking, and her masts, rigging and sails were in a sorry plight. Russian traders had tried to contact Cook on his voyage northwards; now they met him at Unalaska and gave him most useful information, from their knowledge, or ignorance, of the geographical features northwards, and were most open and honest in handing him their charts. Wagner asks the pertinent question as to why the British Government behaved so very differently in concealing Cook's achievements in the Arctic, and delaying the publication of his Third Journal after his death. Perhaps, as Wagner suggests, the furs which Cook's crews sold to the Chinese, had already brought a rush of British fur traders to the Pacific, and disputes with Spain and further Anglo-French rivalries were imminent. We return to the Journals.

WEDNESDAY *22nd* April. Here I must observe that I have no were met with Indians who had such high notions of every thing the Country produced being their exclusive property as these; the very wood and water we took on board they at first wanted us to pay for, and we had certainly done it, had I been upon the spot when the demands were made; but as I never happened to be there the workmen took but little notice of their importunities and at last they ceased applying. But made a Merit on necessity and frequently afterwards told us they had given us Wood and Water out of friendship.

SUNDAY *26th* April. The 26th in the Morning every thing being ready, I intended to have sailed, but both wind and Tide being against us was obliged to wait till noon, when the SW Wind was succeeded by a Calm and the tide turning in our favour, we cast off the Moorings and with our boats towed the Ships out of the Cove. . . . *Nautical remarks.* The inlet I honoured with the name of *King Georges Sound*, but its name, with the Natives is *Nook ka.* The entrance is situated in the East corner of *Hope Bay*, in the latitude of 49° 33′ N, Long^{g} 233° 12′ E. . . . The land boardering upon the Sea Coast is of a middling hieght and livel, but about the Sound it consits of high hills and deep Vallies, for the most part cloathed with large timber, such as Spruce fir and white Cedar.

April 1778 The more inland Mountains were covered with Snow, in other respects they seemed to be naked. When ever it rained with us Snow fell on the Neighbouring hills, the Clemate is however infinately milder than on the East coast of America under the same parallel of latitude. The Mercury in the Thermometre never even in the night fell lower than 42 and very often in the day it rose to 60; no such thing as frost was percieved in any of the low ground, on the Contrary Vegetation had made considerable progress, I met with grass that was already above a foot long. . . . *Inhabitants their Persons and Habits.* I can form no estimate of the number of Inhabitants that may be in this Sound, they however appeared to be pretty numerous. And they as also all others who visited us are, both men and Women, of a small Stature, some, Women in particular, very much so and hardly one, even of the younger sort, had the least pretentions to being call'd beauties. Thier face is rather broad and flat, with highish Cheek bones and plump cheeks. Their mouth is little and round, the nose neither flat nor prominent; their eyes are black little and devoid of sparkling fire. But in general they have not a bad shape except in the legs which in the most of them are Crooked and may probably arrise from thier much siting. Their Complextion is swarthy, but this seems not alltogether natural but proceeds partly from smoke dirt and pai[n]t, for they paint with a liberal hand, and are slovenly and dirty to the last degree. . . . The men on some occasions wore Masks of which they have many and of various sorts such as the human face, the head of birds and other Animals, the most of them both well designed and executed. Whether these masks are worn as an Ornament in their public entertainments, or as some thought, to guard the face against the arrows of the enimy, or as decoys in hunting, I shall not pretend to say; probably on all these occasions. The only times however we saw them used was by some of the Chiefs when they made us a ceremonious and in some of thier Songs. . . . *Canoes.* Thier Canoes are 40 feet long, 7 broad and about 3 deep, some greater some less; they are made out of one tree hollowed out to an inch or an inch and a half in the sides, and in shape very much resemble a Norway yawl only longer in proportion to their breadth, and the head and stern is higher. In the upper part of the former, or prow, is a groove or hollow, for the conveniency of laying their Spears, darts, harpoons &c[a]. They are generally without carving or any other ornament except paint and but few have it. The paddles are small and light; the shape in some measure resembling a large leaf, pointed at the bottom, broadest in the middle, and gradually losing it self in the shaft, the whole being about five feet long.

'*Food and Habitations.* As the food of these people seems to consist chiefly of fish and other Sea animals, their houses or dwelings are situated close to the shore. They consist in a long range of buildings, some of which are one hundred and fifty feet in length, twenty four or thirty broad and seven or eight high from the floor to the roof, which in them all is flat and covered with loose boards. The

Walls or sides and ends, are also built up of boards and the framing consits of large trees or logs. . . . *Large Images.* At the upper end of many of the appartments, were two large images, or statues placed abreast of each other and 3 or 4 feet asunder, they bore some resemblance to the human figure, but monsterous large; the best idea will be had of them in a drawing which M[r] Webber made of the inside of one of thir appartments wherein two of them stood. They call them Acweeks which signifies supreme, or Chief; a curtin or mat for the most part hung before them which they were not willing at all times to remove, and when they did shew us them or speak of them, it was in such a Mysterious manner that we could not comprehend their meaning. This made some of our gentlemen think they were their gods, but I am not altogether of that opinion, at least if they were they hild them very cheap, for with a small matters of iron or brass, I could have purchased all the gods in the place, for I did not see one that was not offered me, and two or three of the very smalest sort I got. *April 1778*

SUNDAY *26th* April. Having put to Sea on the evening of the 26th as before related, with strong signs of an aproaching Storm; these signs did not dicieve us: we were hardly out of the Sound before the Wind in a instant shifted from NE to SEBE and increased to a Strong gale with Squals and rain and so dark that we could not see the length of the Ship. Being apprehensive of the wind veering more to the South, as usual, and puting us in danger of a lee shore, got the tacks on board and stretched off to the SW under all the sail the Ships could bear. Fortunatly the Wind veered no farther Southerly than SSE so that at day light the next Morning we were quite clear of the Coast. . . . At this time the Resolution Sprung a leak which at first alarmed us not a little; it was found to be under the Starboard buttock, where from the bread room we could both hear and see the Water rush in. . . . The Weather now began to clear up, so that we could see several leagues round us and I steered more to the Northward. At Noon the Latitude by observation was 50° 01′ N, Longitude 229° 26′ E. I now steered NWBN with a fresh gale at SSE and fair weather, but at 9 PM it began aagin to blow hard, and in squals with rain. With such weather and the wind between SSE and SW I continued the same course till the 30th at 4 AM when I steered NBW in order to make the land, regreting very much that I could not do it sooner, especially as we were passing the place where Geographers have placed the pretended Strait of Admiral de Fonte. For my own part, I give no credet to such vague and improbable stories, that carry their own confutation along with them nevertheless I was very desirous of keeping the Coast aboard in order to clear up this point beyond dispute; but it would have been highly imprudent in me to have ingaged with the land in such exceeding tempestious weather, or to have lost the advantage of a fair wind by waiting for better weather. . . .

FRIDAY *1st* May. Between 11 and 12 oclock we passed a groupe of small islands laying under the Mainland in the latitude of 56° 48′ and off, or rather

May *1778* to the Northward of the south point of a large bay, in the northern part of which an arm of it seemed to extend into the Northward behind a round elevated Mountain that lies between it and the sea. This Mountain I called *Mount Edgcombe* and the point of land that shoots out from it *Cape Edgcombe*; the latter lies in the latitude of 57° 3′ N, longitude 224° 7′ E and at Noon bore N 20° W six leagues distant. . . .

SUNDAY *3rd* May. The 3rd at half past 4 AM Mount Edgecombe bore S 54° E, a large Inlet N 50° E distant 6 leagues and the most advanced point of land to the NW laying under a very high peaked mountain bore N 32° W. The Inlet was named *Cross Sound*, as being first seen on that day; it appeared to branch in several arms, the largest of which turned to the Northward. . . . At 5 PM being in the Latitude of 58° 53′, Long[g] 220° 52′ E the summit of an elevated Mountain which we supposed to be M[t] S[t] Elias appeared above the horizon bearing N 26° W and as was afterwards found, 40 leagues distant. . . .

WEDNESDAY *6th* May. Having but light Winds with some Calms, we advanced but slowly, so that on the 6th at Noon we were only in the latitude of 59° 8, longitude 220° 19′; Mount Fair weather bore S 63° E and Mount S[t] Eleas N 30° W the nearest land about 8 leagues distant. In the direction of N 47° E from this Station, there was the appearence of a bay and an island of the South point of it, that was covered with wood. It is here where I suppose Commodore Behring to have Anchored, the latitude, which is 59° 18′, corresponds pretty well with the Map of his Voyage and the longitude is 221° E. Behind this Bay which I shall dis[t]inguish by the name of its discoverer (*Behrings Bay*) or rather to the South of it, the Chain of Mountains before mentioned is broke by a plain of a few leagues in extent, beyond which the sight was unlimited, so that there is either a level Country or water behind it. . . . We now found the Coast to trend very much to the west inclining hardly any thing to the North, and as we had the Wind mostly from the westward and but little of it, our progress was slow.

MONDAY *11th* May. The 11th at 4 AM the wind which had been mostly at NE shifted to North, this being against us I gave up the design of going within the island or into the bay as neither could be done without loss of time. I therefore bore up for the west end of the island; the wind blew faint and at 10 oclock it fell Calm. Being not far from the island I went in a boat and landed upon it with a view of seeing what lay on the other side, but finding it farther to the hills than I expected and the way steep and woody, I was obliged to drop the design. At the foot of a tree on a little eminency not far from the Shore, I left a bottle in which was an Inscription seting forth the Ships Names, date &c[a] and two Silver penny pieces (date 1772) which with many others were furnished me by the Rev[d] D[r] Kaye. And as a mark of my esteem and regard for that Gentleman I named the island after him. *Keyes Island.*

AN INDIAN VILLAGE
ON THE NORTH WEST COAST
OF AMERICA

TUESDAY 12*th* May. The weather bad as it was did not however hinder three of the Natives from paying us a visit they came off in two Canoes, two men in one and one in the other, being the number each would carry, for they were built and constructed in the same manner as the Esquimauxs, only in the one was two holes for two men to sit in and in the other but one. Each of these men had a stick about 3 feet long with the large feathers or wings of birds tied to it: these they frequently held up to shew us to express their peaceable sentiments. *May 1778*

THURSDAY 14*th* May. It was not long before all the Indians returned to us again, but instead of coming to the Ship they went towards the boat, the officer in her seeing this, returned to the Ship and was followed by all the Canoes. The crew were no sooner out of the boat, all but two to look after her, than Some of the Indians steped into her, some held spears before the two men, others cast loose the rope she was fast to, while others attempted to tow her away. But the instant they saw us preparing to oppose them they let her go steped out of her into their canoes and made signs to us to lay down our arms, and not only seemed but were as perfictly unconcerned as if they had done nothing amiss. This though rather a more daring attempt was hardly equal to what they attempted on board the Discovery. The man who came and carri'd them all from the Resolution to the Discovery, had first been on board of her, where, after looking down all the hatchways, and seeing no body but the officer of the watch and one or two more he no doubt thought they might plunder her with ease, especially as she lay some distance from us: and it was unquestionable with this View they all went to her. Several without any ceremony went on board, drew their knives, made signs to the officer and people on deck to keep off and began to look about them to see what they could find; the first thing they met with was the Rudder of one of the boats which they threw over board to those who remained in the Canoes. Before they had time to through a Second thing over board the Crew were alarmed and began to come on deck armed with cutlasses on which the others sneaked off into their Canoes with as much deliberation as they let go the boat and began to discribe to the others, how much longer knives the people on board the Ship had than them. It was at this time my boat was away Sounding, which they must have seen as they proceeded directly for her after leaving the Discovery. I have no doubt but their visiting us so very early in the Morning was with a view to plunder, thinking they would find every body a sleep. Does not these circumstances shew these people to be strangers to fire arms? for certainly if they had known any thing of their effect they never would have dar'd to take a boat from under a ships guns, in the face of above a hundred men for the most of my people were looking at them at the very time they made the attempt. However after all these tricks, we had the good fortune to leave them as ignorant as we found them, for they neither heard nor saw a musket fired unless at birds. . . .

May 1778 FRIDAY 15*th* May. Early the next morning we gave the ship a good heel to port, in order to come at and stop the leak, on reping off the Sheathing, it was found to be in the Seams which both in and under the wale, were very open and in several places not a bit of Oakam in them. While the Carpenters were making good these defects we filled all our empty water Casks at a stream hard by the Ship. . . . Some both men and women have the under lip slit quite through horizontally, and so large as to admit the tongue which I have seen them thrust through, which happened to be the case when it was first discovered by one of the Seamen, who called out there was a man with two mouths and indeed it does not look unlike it. Though the lips of all were not slit, yet all were bored, espicially the women and even the young girls; to these holes and slits they fix pieces of bone placed side by side in the inside of the lip; a thread is run through them to keep them together, and some goes quite through the lip and fastens, or fore locks on the out side to which they hang other pieces of bones or beads. This Ornament is a very great impediment to the Speach and makes them look as if they had a double row of teeth in the under jaw. . . . Their Weapons, or rather their Instruments for fishing and hunting, are the very same as are made use of by the Esquemaux and Greenlanders. . . .

SUNDAY 17*th* May. The leak being stoped and the Sheathing made good over it, at 4 oclock in the Morning of the 17th we weighed and Steered to the NW with a light breeze at ENE: thinking if their was any passage to the North through this inlet it would be in that direction.

MONDAY 18*th* May. At 3 AM weighed and with a gentle breeze at North proceeded to the Southward down the Inlet, and met with the same broken ground as the preceding day but soon got clear of it and then never struck ground with a line of 40 fathoms. Another passage into this inlet was now discovered to the SW of the one we came in by, which afforded us a shorter cut to Sea, it is separated from the other by an island of 18 leagues in extent in the direction of NE and SW and was called *Montagu Island*. In this SW Channell are several islands, those that lie in the entrance next the Sea are high and rocky whereas those within are low and were intirely free from Snow and covered with wood and Verdure on which account they were called Green islands.

TUESDAY 19*th* May. The Inlet we had now left I name *Sandwich Sound*: to judge of this Sound from what we saw of it, it occupies at least a degree and a half of Latitude and two of longitude, exclusive of the several arms or branches, the extent of which is not known. The direction which they seemed to take, as also the situation and Magnitude of the Several islands in and about it will be best seen in the Chart which is delineated with as much accuracy as the short time and other circumstances would allow.

'After being clear of Sandwich Sound I steered to the SW with a gentle breeze at NNE which at 4 the next morning was succeeded by a Calm and soon after the Calm by a breeze from SW which freshened and veered to NW. So that we still continued to stretch to SW and passed a lofty promontory situated in the Latitude of 59° 10′, Longg 207° 45′ E. As it was first seen on Princess Elizabeth birth day I named it *Cape Elizabeth*, beyond it we could see no land so that we were in hopes it was the western extremity of the Coast, but not long after we got sight of land bearing WSW. *May 1778*

MONDAY 25*th* May. Toward the evening the weather, which had been hazey all day, cleared up, and we got sight of a very lofty promontary whose elevated summit forming two exceeding high Mountains was seen above the Clouds. This promontary I named *Cape Douglas* in honour of my very good friend *Dr Douglas Canon of Windsor* it is situated in the latitude of 58° 56′, longitude 206° 10′ E, ten leagues to the westward of the barren isles and twelve from Smoky Point in the direction of NWBW½W. Between this point and the Cape the Coast seemed to form a very large and deep bay which obtained the Name of [Smokey Bay].

THURSDAY 28*th* May. As it continued Calm all day, I did not move till 8 oclock in the evening when with a light breeze at East we weighed and Stood to the North up the Inlet. We had not been long under sail before the Wind Veered to the North, increased to a fresh gale and blew in Squals with rain; this did not hinder us from plying up so long as the flood continued, which was till near 5 AM the next day. We continued to have Soundings all the way from 35 to 24 fathoms. In this last depth we anchored about two leagues from the Eastern shore in the Latitude of 60° 8 N some low land that we judged to be an island lying under the western Shore, extended from N½W to NWBN distant three or four leagues.

MONDAY 1*st* June. At 2 oclock in the Morning the Master returned and reported that he had found the Inlet or rather river contracted to the breadth of one league by low land on each side, through which it took a northerly direction.... All hopes of a passage was now given up, but as the Ebb was almost spent & we could not return against the flood, I thought I might as well take the advantage of the latter to get a nearer view of the Eastern branch, and finally to determine whether the low land on the East side of the River was an island as we had supposed or not.

'If the discovery of this River should prove of use, either to the present or future ages, the time spent in exploring it ought to be the less regreted, but to us who had a much greater object in View it was an essential loss; the season was advancing apace, we knew not how far we might have to proceed to the South and we were now convinced that the Continent extended farther to the west than from the Modern Charts we had reason to expect and made a passage into Baffin or Hudson bays far less probable, or at least made it of greater extent. But if I had not examined this place it would have been concluded, nay asserted

June that it communicated with the Sea to the North, or with one of these bays to the
1778 East. In the after noon I sent M[r] King again with two armed boats, with orders to land on the northern point of the low land on the SE side of the River, there to desplay the flag, take possession of the Country and River in his Majestys name and to bury in the ground a bottle containing t[w]o pieces of English coin (date 1772) and a paper on which was in[s]cribed the Ships names date &c[a].

THURSDAY 18*th* June. In the after noon we got a light breeze of Wind Southerly which enabled us to steer west for the Channell that appeared between the islands and the Continent, and at day break in the Morning we were no great distance from it, and perceived several other islands within those we had seen before of various extent both in height and circuit. But between these last islands and those we has seen before, there appeared to be a clear channell for which I steered, for I was afraid to keep the coast of the continent aboard, lest we should mistake some point for an island and by that means be drawn into some inlet and loss the advantage of the fair wind which at this time blew. I therefore kept along the Southermost Chain of island[s], and at Noon we were in the latitude of 55° 18′ and in the narrowest part of the channell formed by them and those which lie along the continent, where it is about a league and a half or two leagues over. The largest island in this group was now on our left and is distinguished by the name of *Kodiak*, as we were afterward informed, the rest I left without names; I beleive them to be the same as Behring calls Schumagins islands, or those islands which he called by that name to be a part of them for this group is pretty extensive.

THURSDAY 25*th* June. At 10 oclock hauled the Wind to the Southward till day break then resumed our course to the West. Day light availed us little as the Weather was so thick that we could not see a hundred yards before us, but as the wind was now very moderate I ventured to run. At half past 4 we were alarmed at hearing the Sound of breakers on our larboard bow; on heaving the lead found 28 fathom water and the next cast 25; I immideately brought the ship to with her head to the Northward and anchored in this last depth over a bottom of Coarse Sand, and called to the Discovery who was close by us to anchor also. A few hours after, the fog cleared away a little and it was percieved we had scaped very emminant danger; we found our selves three quarters of a mile from the NE side of an island which extended from SBW½W to NBE½E, each extreme about a league distant, two elevated rocks the one bearing SBE and the other EBS each half a league distant and about the same distance from each other. There were several breakers about them and yet Providence had conducted us through between these rocks where I should not have ventured in a clear day, and to such an anchoring place that I could not have chosen a better.

SATURDAY 27*th* June. We had now land in every direction, that to the South extended to the SW in a ridge of Mountains beyond our sight, but could not till whether it composed one or more islands. It was afterwards found to be only one island and known by the Name of *Oonalaschka*; between it and the land to the North, which had the appearence of being a group of islands, there seemed to be a Channell in the direction of NWBN. On a Point which bore West from the Ship ¾ of a mile distant, were several Indians and their habitations; to this place we saw them tow in two Whales which we supposed they had killed that Morning. A few now and then came off to the Ships and bartered a few trifling things with our people, but never remained above a quarter of an hour at one time on the contrary they rather seemed shy, and yet seemed to be no strangers to Vessels in some degree like ours, and had acquired a degree of politeness uncommon to Indians. *June 1778*

☾ On Sunday, 2nd August, Cook lost his surgeon, Anderson, from tuberculosis, which in the following summer was to kill Cook's successor Captain Clerke. The loss of Anderson was serious, for he seems to have had some knowledge of anthropology and ethnology and some of the long descriptions of native tribes, which Cook included in his Third Journal are thought to have been taken from Anderson's Journal, or written with his help.

SUNDAY *2nd*, MONDAY *3rd* August. The 2nd We had Variable light Winds with Showers of rain. The 3rd in the Morning the Wind fixed in the SE quarter and we resumed our Course to the Northward. At Noon we were by observation in the latitude of 62° 34′ N, Longitude 192° 30′ E and the depth of Water 16 fathoms. Mr Anderson my Surgeon who had been lingering under a Consumption for more than twelve Months, expired between 3 and 4 this after noon. He was a Sensible Young Man, an agreeable companion, well skilld in his profession and had acquired much knowlidge in other Sciences, that had it pleased God to have spar'd his life might have been usefull in the Course of the Voyage. Soon after land was Seen to the Westward, 12 leagues distant, it was supposed to be an Island and to perpetuate the Memory of the deseased for whom I had a very great regard, I named [it] *Andersons Island*. The next day I removed Mr Law the Surgeon of the Discovery into the Resolution and appointed Mr Samuel the Surgeons first mate of the Resolution to be surgeon of the Discovery.

WEDNESDAY *8th* August. The weather at this time was very thick with rain; but at 4 the next Morning it cleared so that we could see the lands about us. A high steep rock or island descovered the preceding evening, bore WBS a Nother island to the North of it and much larger bore WBN, the peaked hill above mentioned SEBE and the point under it S 32° E. Under this hill lies some low land stretching out towards the NW the extreme point of which bore NEBE about 3 Miles distant, over and beyond it some high land was seen supposed to be a continuation of the continent. This Point of land which I named *Cape Prince of Wales*, is the more remarkable by being the Western extremity of all America hitherto known; it is situated in the Latitude of 65° 46′ N, Longitude 191° [45′] E:

August 1778 the observations by which both were determined, altho made in sight of it, were liable to some small error on account of the haziness of the weather.

SATURDAY 15*th* August. At 1 PM the sight of a large field of ice left us in no longer doubt about the cause of the brightness of the Horizon we had observed. At ½ past 2 we tacked close to the edge of it in 22 fathoms Water being then in the latitude of 70° 41′, not being able to stand any fa[r]ther, for the ice was quite impenetrable and extend[ed] from WBS to EBN as far as the eye could reach. Here were abundance of Sea Horses, some in the Water but far more upon the Ice; I had thoughts of hoisting the boats out to kill some, but the Wind freshning I gave up the design and continued to ply to the southward, or rather to the Westward for the Wind was from that quarter; but we gained nothing, For on the 18th at Noon our latitude was 70° 44′ and the Timekeeper shewed that we were near five leagues farther to the Eastward. We were at this time in 20 fathoms Water, close to the edge of the ice which was as compact as a Wall and seemed to be ten or twelve feet high at least, but farther North it appeared much higher, its surface was extremely rugged and here and there were pools of Water.

'We now stood to the Southward and after runing Six leagues shoaled the Water to 7 fathoms, which depth continued for near half a mile and then it deepened to 8 and 9 fathom. At this time the weather which had been very hazey cleared a little and we saw low land extending from South to SEBE about 3 or 4 miles distant. The East extreme form[s] a point which was much incumbered with ice for which Reason it obtained the name of *Icey Cape*, Lat 70° 29′ N, long 198° 20′ E but the other extreme was lost in the horizon, so that there can be no doubt but it was a continuation of the Amirica cont[i]nent. The Discovery being about a mile astern and to leeward found less water than we did and was obliged to tack for it, which obliged me to tack also for fear of being Separated. Our situation was now more and more critical, we were in shoaled water upon a lee shore and the main body of the ice in sight to windward driving down upon us. It was evident, if we remained much longer between it and the land it would force us ashore unless it should happen to take the ground before us; it seemed nearly if not quite to join to the land to leeward and the only direction that was open was to the SW.

WEDNESDAY 19*th* August. At ½ past 1 PM we got close in with the edge of the main ice, it was not so compact as that which we had seen more to the Northward, but it was too close and in too large pieces to force the ships through it. On the ice lay a prodigious number of Sea horses and as we were in want of fresh provisions the boats from each ship were sent to get some. By 7 o'clock in the evening we had got on board the Resolution Nine of these Animals which till now we had supposed to be Sea Cows, so that we were not a little disapointed, especially some of the Seamen who for the Novelty of the thing, had been feasting their eyes for some days past, nor would they have been disapointed now, or known the difference, if we had not happened to have one or two on board who had beęn in Greenland and declared what animals these were, and that no one ever eat of them. But not withstanding this we lived upon them so long as they lasted and there were few on board who did not prefer it to salt meat. The fat at first is as sweet as Marrow but in a few days it grows ransid unless it is salted, then it will keep good much longer, the lean is coarse, black and rather a strong taste, the heart is nearly as well tasted as that of a bullock. The fat when Melted yeilds a good deal of Oil which burns very well in lamps and their hides, which are very thick, were very usefull about our rigging. The teeth or tusks of most of them were at this time very small, even some of the largest and oldest had them not passing Six inches long, from which we conclude that they had lately shed their old teeth. They lay in herds of many hundreds upon the ice, huddling one over the other like swine, and roar or bray very loud, so that in the night or foggy weather they gave us notice of the ice long before we could see it. We never found the Whole herd a sleep, some were always upon the watch, these, on the approach of the boat, would wake those next to them and then the others, so that the whole herd would be awake presently. But they were seldom in a hurry to get away till after they had been once fire[d] at, then they would tumble one over the other into the sea in the utmost confusion, and if we did not at the first discharge kill those we fired at out right we generally lost them tho' mortally wounded. They did not appear to us to be that dangerous animal some Authors have discribed, not even when attacked, they are rather more so to appearence than reality; Vast numbers of them would follow and come close up to the boats, but the flash of a Musket in the pan, or even pointing one at them would send them down in an instant. The feemale will defend the young one to the very last and at the expence of her life whether in the Water or on the ice; nor will the young quit the dam though she be dead so that if you kill one you are sure of the other. The Dam when in the Water holds the young one between her fore fins.

August 1778

'*Pennant* in his *Syn. Quadr.* p. 335, has given a very good discription of this Animal under the Name of Arctick Walrus, but I have no were seen a good drawing of one. Why they should be called Sea horses, is hard to say unless it be a corruption of the Russian name Morse, for it has not the least Similitude to a Horse; It is without doubt the same Animal as is found in the Gulph of S[t] Lawrence and there called Sea Cow, it is certainly more like a Cow than a Horse, but this likeness consits in nothing but the Snout. In short it is an animal like a Seal but incomparably larger.

THURSDAY *20th* August. By such time as we had done with the Sea horses we were in a manner surrounded by the ice and had no way left to clear it but by standing to the Southward which was done till 3 AM of the 20th with a gentle breeze Westerly and for the most part thick foggy weather. The Sounding[s]

August 1778 were from twelve to 15 fathoms. At 2 AM we tacked and stood to the North till 10 when the Wind veering to the Northward we stood West South West and West. At 2 PM we fell in with the Main ice, along the edge of which we kept, being partly directed by the roaring of the Sea Horses, for we had a very thick fog. Thus we continued sailing till ½ past a 11 when we got in amongst the loose ice and heard the surge of the Sea upon the Main ice. The fog being very thick and the Wind easterly I haul'd to the Southward, and at 10 o'clock the next Morning, the fog clearing away we saw the Continent of America extending from SBE to EBS and at Noon from SW½S to East, the nearest part five leagues distant.

THURSDAY 27*th* August. The 27th at 4 AM we tacked and stood to the west and at 7 PM we were close in with the edge of the ice which lay ENE and WSW as far each way as the eye could reach. Having but little wind I went with the boats to examine the state of the ice, and found it consit of loose pieces of various extent, and so close together that I could hardly enter the outer edge with a boat and was as imposible for the Ships to enter it, as if it had been so many rocks. I took Notice that it was all pure transparent ice, except the upper surface which was a little porous. It appeared to be intirely composed of frozen Snow and had been all formed at sea, for setting side the improbability or rather impossibility of such masses floating out of Rivers in which there is hardly Water for a boat, none of the productions of the land was found incorporated, or fixed in it, which must unavoidably have be[en] the case had it been formed in Rivers either great or small. The pieces of ice that formed the outer edge of this feild were from 40 to 50 yards in extent to 4 or 5 and I judged that the larger pi[e]ces reach'd 30 feet or more under the surface of the Water. It appeared to me, very improbable that this ice could be the produce of the preceding Winter alone, but rather that of a great many, or that the little that remained of the summer would distroy the tenth part of what now remained, sence the Sun had already exerted the full influence [of] his rays. . . . A thick fog came on while I was away with the boats hastened me aboard rather sooner than I desired, with one Sea Horse to each Ship, we had killed more but could not wait to bring them aboard: the number of these animals on all the ice we had seen is almost incredable. We spent the night Standing off and on amongst the drift ice and at 9 oclock the next Morning, the fog clearing away a little boats from each Ship were sent for Sea horses, for by this time our people began to relish them and all those we had got before were consumed.

SATURDAY 29*th* August. The season was now so very far advanced and the time when the frost is expected to set in so near at hand, that I did not think it consistant with prudence to make any farther attempts to find a passage this year in any direction so little was the prospect of succeeding. My attention was now directed towards finding out some place where we could Wood and

Water, and in the considering how I should spend the Winter, so as to make some improvement to Geography and Navigation and at the same time be in a condition to return to the North in further search of a Passage the ensuing summer. *August 1778*

MONDAY 31*st* August. At 7 PM Two points of land some distance beyond the Eastern head opened of it in the direction of S 37° E, at this time the head was about two leagues distant. I was now well assured that this was the Coast of Tchuktschi, or the NE Coast of Asia, and that thus far Captain Behring proceeded in 1728, that is to this head which Mr Muller says is called *Serdze Kamen*, on accou[n]t of a rock upon it in the shape of a heart.

WEDNESDAY 2*nd* September. In the evening we passed the Eastern Cape, or the point above mentioned, from which the Coast trends SW. It is the same point of land that we past on the 11 of last Month, thought then to be the East point of the island of Alaschka, but it is no other than the *Eastern Promontory of Asia* and probably the proper *Tchuktschi Noss*. . . . But as I hope to visit these parts again I shall leave the descussion of this point untill then, and untill then I must conclude, as Behring did before me, this Promontary to be the Eastern point of Asia.

THURSDAY 3*rd* September. After passing the Cape I steered SW½W for the northn point of St Lawrence Bay the same as we anchored in on the 10th of last Month. We were the length of it by 8 oclock in the Morning and saw some of the Inhabitants at the place where I had seen them before, as well as several others on the opposite side of the bay, but none attempted to come off to us, which seemed a little extraordinary as the Weather was favourable enough and those we had visited had no reason that I know of to deslike our company. These people must be Tchuktschkians a Nation that at the time Mr Muller wrote the Russians had not be[en] able to conquor, and from the whole of their conduct with us it appears that they have not yet brought them under subjection; though they must have a trade with the Russians either directly or by means of some neighbouring nation or else how came the by then Spontoons we saw in their possession.

FRIDAY 4*th* September. In justice to *Behrings Memory*, I must say he has delene-ated this Coast very well and fixed the latitude and longitude of the points better than could be expected from the Methods he had to go by. This judgement is not formed from Mr *Mullers* accou[n]t of the Voyage or his Chart, but from the account of it in Harris's *Collection of Voyages* and a Map thereto annexed Vol. II. pag which is both more circumstantial and accurate that that of Mr Mullers.

WEDNESDAY 16*th* September. Haveing now fully satisfied myself, that Mr Staehlin's Map must be erroneous and not mine it was high time to think of leaving these Northern parts, and to retire to some place to spend the Winter where I could procure refreshments for the people and a small supply of Pro-

September 1778 visions. *Petropaulowska* in *Kamtschatka*, did not appear to me a place where I could procure either the one or the other for so large a number of men, and besides I had other reasons for not going there at this time, the first and on which all the others depended was the great dislike I had to lay inactive for Six or Seven Months, which must have been the case had I wintered in any of these Northern parts. No place was so conveniently within our reach where we could expect to meet with these necessary articles, as *Sandwich Islands*, to these islands, therefore, I intended to proceed, but before this could be carried into execution it was necessary to have a supply of Water. With this View I resolved to search the America coast for a harbour, by proceeding along it to the Southward and endeavour to Connect the Survey of this Coast with that to the North of Cape Newenham. If I failed of finding a har[b] then to proceed to *Samgoonoodha* which was fixed upon for a Rendezvouse in case of Separ[a]tion.

SATURDAY 3*rd* October. The 3[rd] at 1 PM we anchored in Samgoonoodha and the next Morning the Carpenters belonging to both Ships were set to work to rip off the Sheathing of and under the Wale on the Starboard side abaft, where many of the Seams were found quite open so that it was no wonder that so much water found its way into the Ship. While we lay here we cleared the Fish room, Spirit room and after hold, desposed things in such a manner that if we should happen to have any more leaks of the same Nature the Water might find its way to the pumps. And besides this work compleating our Water we cleared the Fore hold to the very bottom and took in a quantity of ballast.

'The Vegetables we met with when first at this place were now mostly in a state of decay, so that we benifited but little by them; but this loss was more than made up by the great quantity of berries every where found a Shore, and in order that we might benifit as much as possible by them one third of the people by turns, had leave to go and pick them and besides a good quantity were procured from the Natives; so that if there was any seeds of the S[c]urvey in either Ship, these berries and Spruce beer which they had to drink every other day, effectually removed it. We also got plenty of fish, at first from the Inhabitants, mostly Salmon both fresh and dryed; some of the fresh salmon was in high perfection, but there was one sort which we called hook nosed from the figure of its head, that was but indifferent.

THURSDAY 8*th* October. On the 8th I received by the hand of an Indian named *Derramoushk* a very singular present considering the place, it was a rye loaf or rather a pie made in the form of a loaf, for some salmon highly seasoned with peper &c[a] was in it. He had the like present for Captain Clerke and a Note to each of us written in a language none of us could read. We however had no doubt but this present was from some Russians in our Neighbourhood and sent to these our unknown friends by the same ha[n]d a few bottles of Rum, Wine and Porter which we thought would be as acceptable as any thing we had besides, and the event prove[d] we were not misstaken. I also sent along with Derramoushk and his party Corp[l] Ledyard of the Marines, an inteligent man in order to gain some further information, with orders, if he met with any Russians, or others, to endeavour to make them understand that we were English, Friends and Allies. *October 1778*

SATURDAY 10*th* October. The 10th he returned with three Russian Seamen or Furriers, who with some others resided in *Egoochshac* where they had a dweling house some store houses and a Sloop of about thirty Tons burden. One of these Men was either Master or Mate of this Vessel, a nother wrote a very good hand and understood figures; they were all three well behaved intellingent men, and very ready to give me all the information I could disire, but for want of an interpretor we had some difficulty to understand each other. They seemed to have a thorough knowlidge of the attempts that had been made by their Country men to Navigate the Frozen Sea, and the discoveries which had been made in this by *Behring Tchirekoff* and *Spanburg*, but seemed to know no more of Lieutenant Sindo or *Sind* than his name. . . . I laid before them my Chart, and found they were strangers to every part of the America Coast except what lies opposite to them. One of these Men said he was the America Voyage with *Behring*, he must however been very young for he had not now the appearance of an old man. The Memory of few men is held in greater esteem than these Men do *Behrings*, probably from his being the occation of thier fur trade being extended to the Eastward, which was the consequence of that able Navigators missfortunes, for had not chance and his distresses carried him to the island which bears his name, and where he died, its probable the Russians would never have thought of making further discover[ie]s on the America Coast as indeed Government did not for what has been sence done, has been by traders. . . . The 14[th] in the evening, as M[r] Webber and I was at an Indian Village a little way from Samgoonoodha, a Russian landed there who I found was the principal person amongst the Russians in this and the neighbouring islands. His name was *Erasim Gregorioff Sin Ismyloff*, he came in a Canoe carrying three people, attended by twenty or thirty other Canoes each conducted by one man; I took notice that the first thing they did after landing was to make a small tent for Ismyloff of materials which they brought with them, and then they made others for themselves of their Canoes paddles &c[a] which they covered with grass, so that the people of the Village were at no trouble to find them lodging. . . . I found he was very well acquainted with the Geography of these parts and with all the discoveries the Russians had made and at once pointed out the errors of the Modern Maps. He told us he was with Lieutenant *Sindo*, or Sind as he called him, in his expidition to the North, said they were not farther than the *Tchukchi Nos*, or rather the *Bay of S[t] Lawrence*, for he pointed to the very place where I landed. . . . Both M[r] Ismyloff and the others affirmed that they knew nothing of the Con-

October 1778 tinent of America to the Northward; that neither Lieutenant *Sind* or any other Russian had ever seen it of late. They call it by the same name, as *M*[r] *Sind* does his great island, *Alaschka*: *Stachtan Nitada* as it is calld in the Modern maps, is a name quite unknown to these people, Indians as well as Russians, but both know it by the name of America. From what we could gather from M[r] Ismyloff and the others, the Russians have made several attempts to get a footing upon that part of the Continent which lies adjacent to the islands, but have allways been repulsed by the Natives, whom they describe as a very treacherous people; they mentioned too or three Captains or chief men, that had been Murdered by them and some of the Russians here shewed us wounds which they said they received there. . . .

MONDAY 19*th* October. Accordingly on the 19th he made us a nother visit and brought with him the Charts Afore mentioned which he allowed me to Copy. There were two of them both Manuscripts and had every mark of being Authentick. The first comprehended the *Penschinskian Sea*, the Coast of *Tartary* as low as the latitude of 41°, the *Kurilian* Islands and the *Peninsula* of *Kamtschatka*. Sence this map had been made *Wawseetee Irkeechoff* Captain of the Fleet explored in 1758, the coast of *Tartary* between *Okhotsk* and the *River Amur* to *Japon* or 41 degrees of latitude. . . . The Second Chart was to me the most intresting as it comprehended all the discoveries made by the Russians to the Eastward of Kamtschatka towards America, which if we exclude the *Voyage of Behring* and *Tcherikoff*, will amount to little or nothing. . . . It appeared by the Chart as well as by the testimony of Ismyloff and the others that this is as far as the Russians have discovered and extended themselves sence Behrings time, they all said no Russian had been where the Indians gave Capt[n] Clerke the note, which M[r] Ismyloff, to whom I gave it said was written at *Oomanak*. It was however from him we got the name of the Island *Kodiak* the largest of Schumagens islands for it had no name upon the Chart; the names of all the other islands were taken from the Chart and written down as he pronounced them, which he said were all Indian names but if so, some were strangly altered. It is worth observing that no names were put to the islands that were to be struck out of the Chart which is some confirmation that they have not existence. I have already observed that the America Continent is here called by the Russians as well as Indians *Alaska*, which is the proper Indian name for it, and probably means no more than that part adjoining to *Ooneemak*, however the Indians as well as the Russians call the whole by that name and know very well that it is a great land.

'This is all the information I got from these people relating to the Geography of those parts, and which I have reason to beleive is all they were able to give; for they assured me over and over again that they k[n]ew of no other islands but what were laid down on this chart and that no Russian had ever seen any part of the Continent to the northward, excepting that part lying opposite the

Country of the Tchuktschis. If M[r] *Stælin* was not greatly imposed upon what could induce him to publish so erroneous a Map? in which many of these islands are jumbled in in regular confusion, without the least regard to truth and yet he is pleased to call it a very accurate little Map? A Map that the most illiterate of his illiterate Sea-faring men would have been ashamed to put his name to. *October 1778*

WEDNESDAY 21*st* October. M[r] *Ismyloff* remained with us till the 21st in the evening when he took his final leave. To his care I intrusted a letter to the Admiralty in which was inclosed a chart of all the Northern coasts I had Visited, he said their would be an oppertunity to send it to *Kamtschatka* or *Okhotsk* the ensuing Spring and that it would be at Petersburg the following [winter?].

'He was so obliging as to give me a letter to Major *Bairme* Governor of *Kamtschatka*, who resides at *Bolscheretskoi*, and a nother to the Commanding Officer at *Petropaulowska*.

'This M[r] *Ismyloff* seemed to have abilities to intitle him to a higher station in life than that in which he was employed, he was tolerably well versed in Astronomy and other necessary parts of the Mathematicks. I complemented him with an Hadlys Octant and altho it was the first he had perhaps ever seen, yet he made himself acquainted with most of the uses that Instrument is capable of in a very short time.

THURSDAY 22*nd* October. In the Morning of the 22nd we made an attempt to get to Sea with the Wind at SE, which misscarried.

'The following afternoon we were visited by one *Jacob Iwanawitch*, a Russian Chief who Commanded a boat or small Vessel at Oomanak. This man seemed to be the very reverse of all the other Russians, he had a great share of Modesty and would drink no strong liquor, which all the other were immoderatly fond of. . . . After we became acquainted with these Russians some of our gentlemen at different times visited there settlement where they always met with a hearty welcome. This settlement consisted of a dwelling house & two store houses; and besides the Russians, there were a number of Kamtschatkadales and Natives, as Servants or slaves to the former, some others of the Natives, that seemed independent of the Russians lived at the same place. . . . There are Russians on all the principal Islands between this and *Kamtschatka*, for the sole purpose of furing, and the first and great object is the Sea Beaver or Otter; I never heard them enquire after any other Animal, not that they let any other furs Slip through their fingers whin they can get them. I never thought to ask how long it was sence they got a footing upon *Oonalaska* and the neighbouring isles, but to judge from the great subjection the Natives are under, it must have been some time. All these Furriers are releived from time to time by others, those we met with came here from *Okhotsk* in 1776 and are to return in 1781, so that there stay at the island will be four years at least.

October 1778 '*Fishes*, &c[a]. The fishes which are Common to other Northern Seas are found here; as Whales, Grampusses, Porpoises, Sword fish, halibut, Cod, salmon, trout; soals, flat fish, several other sorts of small fish and there may be many more that we had no oppertunity of seeing. Halibut and salmon seem to be in the greatest plenty, of which the inhabitants of the isles chiefly Subsist at least these were the only fish, except a few cod, we found laid up for winter store. They have a great variety of Salmon, but they are not all of equal goodness, nor are any of them so large, especially amongst the isles, as those we have in England. Cod fish seem not to be in plenty on any part of the Coasts. To the North of 60° the sea is in a manner quite barren of small fish of every kind, but then Whales are more numerous, and we some times saw a White fish which blows like a Whale, but it is much smaller. Seals and that whole tribe of Sea Animals are not so numerous as they are in many other seas, nor can this be thought strange sence there is hardly any part of the Coast on either Continent or island that is not inhabited by Indians, who hunt these animals for food and Cloathing. Sea Horses are indeed in prodigious numbers about the ice, and the Sea beaver or otter is I believe no were found but in this Sea. We sometimes saw an Animal with a head like a Seals but blew like a Whale, it was larger than a Seal and its colour was white with some dark spots, probably this was the Sea Cow or Manate.

'They are remarkably cheerfull and friendly amongst each other and always behaved with great civility to our people. The Women grant the last favour without the least scruple; young or old, Married or Single, I have been told, never hisitate a Moment. The Russians told us they never had any connections with the Indian Women, because they were not Christians; our people were not so scruplas, and some were taken in, for the venereal distemper is not unknown to these people; they are also subject to the cancer or a disease like it, which those who have it are very careful to conceal. They do not seem to be long lived, I no where saw a person, man or women, which I could suppose to be sixty years of age and but very few that I thought above fifty, probably thier hard way of living may be the means of shortening thier days.

¶ Cook now sought refreshment in his new and important discovery the Hawaiian (Sandwich) Islands, after which he intended to return to the Arctic via Kamtschatka in May 1779. His ships and their gear were in a serious state as was proved by a fatal accident on the *Discovery*, and for the first and only time Cook spoke disparagingly of his crews who were clearly suffering from their hardships in the Arctic. Some of Cook's biographers have considered his criticisms unduly harsh and have thought that he himself was in a state of mind which produced a tactlessness and lack of judgment that contributed to his death.

'In the Morning of Monday October the 26th, we put to sea and as the Wind was Southerly stood away to the Westward.

'My intention was now to proceed to *Sandwich Islands* to spend a few of the Winter Months provided we met with the necessary refreshments there, and then proceed to *Kamtschatka*, endeavouring to be there by the Middle of May next. In consequence of this resolution I gave Captain Clerke orders how to proceed in case of separation, appointing Sandwich islands for the first place of Rendezvouze and the harbour of *Petropaulowska* in Kamtschatka the second.

October 1778

FRIDAY *6th* November. In the after Noon, there being but little wind, Captain Clerke came on board and informed me of a melancholy accident that happened on board his Ship the second night after we left Samgoonoodha; the Main tack gave way, killed one man out right and wounded the Boatswain and two or three more.

THURSDAY *26th* November. At day-break saw land extending from SSE to West. Made sail and stood for [it]. At 8 it extended from SE½S to West, the nearest part two leagues distant. It was supposed we saw the extent of the land to the East but not to the West. In the country was an elevated saddle hill whose summit appear'd above the Clouds, from this hill the land fell in a gentle Sloap and terminated in a steep rocky coast against which the sea broke in a dreadfull surf. Finding we could not weather the island I bore up and ranged along the coast to the westward. It was not long before we saw people on several parts of the Coast, some houses and plantations, and the Country seemed to be well wooded and Watered, the latter was seen falling into the Sea in several places.

'As it was of the last importance to procure a supply of provisions at these islands, and knowing from experience this could not be done if a free trade was allowed, that is every man allowed to trade for what he pleased and as he pleased, I therefore published an order prohibiting all persons from trading but such as should be apoint'd by me or Captain Clerke and these only for provisions and refreshments. Women were also forbid to be admited into the Ships, but under certain restrections, but the evil I meant to prevent by this I found had already got amongst them.

'At Noon the coast extended from S 81° E to N 56° West, a low flat like an isthmus bore S 42° W the nearest shore 3 or 4 Miles distant. Lat 20° 57′, longi 203° E. Seeing some Canoes coming off to us I brought to; as soon as they got a long side many of the people who conducted them came into the Ships without the least hisitation. They were of the same Nation as those of the leeward islands, and if we did not mistake them they knew of our being there. Indeed it appeared rather too evident as these people had got amongst the Veneral distemper, and I as yet knew of no other way they could come by it.

MONDAY *30th* November. In the after noon of the 30th being off the NE end of the island, several Canoes came off to the Ships, the most of them belonged to a Chief named Terryaboo who came in one; he made me a present of two or three small pigs and we got by barter from the other people a little fruit. After

November 1778 a stay of about two hours they all left us except six or eight who chused to remain, a double sailing canoe came soon after to attend upon them which we towed a stern all night. In the evening we discovered another island to windward which the Natives call [O'why'he] the name of the one we had been off we now learnt was [Mow'ēē].

WEDNESDAY *2nd* December. The 2nd in the Morning we were surprised to see the summits of the highest [mountains] cover[ed] with snow; they did not appear to be of any extraordinary height and yet in some places the snow seemed to be of a considerable depth and to have laid there some time. As we drew near the shore, some of the Natives came off to us; they were a little shy at first, but we soon inticed some on board and at length prevailed upon them to go a shore and bring off what we wanted. Soon after these reached the shore we had company enough, and as few came empty, we got a tolerable supply of small pigs, fruit and roots. We continued tradeing with them till Six in the evening when we made sail and stood off, with a view of plying to windward round the island.

SUNDAY *6th* December. Having procured a quantity of Sugar Cane and had upon trial made but a few days before, found that a strong decoction of it made a very palatable beer, which was esteemed by every one on board, I ordered some more to be brewed, but when the Cask came to be broached not one of my Mutinous crew would even so much as taste it. As I had no montive for doing it but to save our spirit for a Colder climate, I gave my self no trouble either to oblige or persuaid them to drink it, knowing there was no danger of the Scurvy so long as we had plenty of other Vegetables; but that I might not be disapointed in my views I gave orders that no grog Should be served in either Ship. My self and the Officers continued to make use of this beer whenever we could get cane to make it; a few hops, of which we had on board, was a great addition to it: it has the taste of new malt beer, and I beleive no one will d[o]ubt but it must be very wholesom, though my turbulent crew alleged it was injurious to their healths. They had no better reason to support a resolution they took on our first arrival in King Georges Sound, not to drink the spruce beer we made there, but whether from a consideration that this was no new thing or any other reason they did not attempt to carry their risolution into execution and I never heard of it till now. Every innovation whatever tho ever so much to their advantage is sure to meet with the highest disapprobation from Seamen, Portable Soup and Sour Krout were at first both condemned by them as stuff not fit for human being[s] to eat. Few men have introduced into their Ships more novelties in the way of victuals and drink than I have done; indeed few men have had the same oppertunity or been driven to the same necessity. It has however in a great measure been owing to such little innovations that I have always kept my people generally speaking free from that dreadful distemper the Scurvy.

SUNDAY 13*th* December. I kept at some distance from the Coast, till the 13th when I stood in again Six leagues farther to wind ward than we had yet been; and after having some trade with the Natives who visited us, stood out to sea. I should have stood in again on the 15th to procure a supply of fruit or roots, but the wind hapening to be at SEBS and SSE I thought a good time to stretch to the Eastward in order to get round, or at least a sight of the SE end of the island. The Wind continued at SEBS most part of the 16th. The 17th was variable between South and E. And on the 18th it was continually varying from one quarter to a nother: blowing sometimes in hard squals and at other times Calm with thunder lightning and rain. In the after noon we had the wind Westerly for a few hours, but in the evening it shifted to EBS and we stood to the Southward close hauled, under an easy sail as the Discovery was some distance a stern. At this time the SE point of the island bore SWBS about 5 leagues distant and I had not a doubt but we should weather it. But at one oclock in the morning it fell Calm and left us to the Mercy of a North easterly swell which hove us fast towards the land, so that long before day light we saw lights upon the Shore which was not more than a league distant. The night was dark with thunder, lightning and rain. At 3 the calm was succeeded by a breeze from the SEBE blowing in squals with rain; we stood to NE thinking it the best tack to clear the coast but had it been day-light we should have made choice of the other. At day-break the coast was seen extending from NBW to SWBW, a dreadfull surf broke upon the shore which was not more than half a league distant, it was evident we had been in the most eminent danger, nor were we yet out of danger; the wind veering more easterly so that for some time we did but just keep our distance from the coast. What made our situation more alarming was the leach rope of the Main topsail giving way, which was the occasion of the sail being rent in two and the two top-gallant sails gave way in the same manner tho not half worn, by takeing a favourable oppertunity we soon got others to the yards and then we left the land a stern. The Discovery by being some distance to the North was never near the land, nor did we see her till 8 oclock.

December 1778

'On this occasion I cannot hilp observing, that I have always found that the bolt-ropes to our sails have not been of sufficient strength, or substance, to even half wear out the Canvas this at different times has been the occasion of much expence of canvas and infinate trouble and vexation. Nor are the cordage and Canvas or indeed hardly any other stores made use of in the Navy, of equal goodness with those in general used in the Merchant service, of this I had incontestable proof last voyage.

SUNDAY 20*th* December. These people trade with the least suspicion of any Indians I ever met with, it is very common for them to send up into the Ship every thing they bring off to despose of: afterwards come in themselves and make their bargens on the quarter deck. This is more than the people of Otahiete

December 1778 will do even at this day, which shews that these people are more faithfull in their dealings one with another than they are; for if little faith was observed among themselves they would not be so ready to trust strangers. It is also remarkable that they have never once attempted to cheat us in exchanges or once to commit a thieft. They understand tradeing as well as most people and seem to have discovered what we are plying upon the coast for, for tho they bring off things in great plenty, particularly pigs, yet they keep up their price and rather than despose of them for less than they demand will take them a shore again.

TUESDAY *5th* January. The 5th in the Morning we passed the South point of the island which lies in the latitude of [18° 54′] and from which we found the coast to trend N 60 W. On this point stands a pritty large Village, the inhabitants of which thronged off to the Ship with hogs and women. It was not possible to keep the latter out of the Ship and no women I ever met with were more ready to bestow their favours, indeed it appeared to me that they came with no other view.

SATURDAY *9th* January. As soon as the Natives retired ashore we made sail and spent our time standing off and on. It happened that four Men and ten women were left on board, as I did not like the company of the latter I stood in shore towards noon with no other View than to get clear of them.

SUNDAY *10th* January. At 2 PM drawing near the shore a few Canoes Came off and in them we sent away our guests.

SUNDAY *17th* January. Fine pleasent Weather and variable faint breezes of Wind. In the Evening M[r] Bligh returned and reported that he had found a bay in which was good anchorage and fresh water tolerable easy to come at, into this bay I resolved to go to refit the Ships and take in water. . . . At 11 AM anchored in the bay (which is called by the Natives[Karakakooa]) in 13 fathom water over a Sandy bottom and a quarter of a mile from the NE shore. In this situation the South point of the bay bore S$\frac{1}{4}$W and the North point W$\frac{1}{2}$S. Moored with the Stream Anchor and Cable to the Northward, Unbent the sails and struck yards and topmasts. The Ships very much Crouded with Indians and surrounded by a multitude of Canoes. I have no where in this Sea seen such a number of people assembled at one place, besides those in the Canoes all the Shore of the bay was covered with people and hundreds were swiming about the Ships like shoals of fish. We should have found it dfficult to have kept them in order had not a Cheif or Servant of *Terrioboos* named *Parea* now and then [exerted] his authority by turning or rather driving them all out of the Ships. Among our numerous Visiters was a man named *Tou-ah-ah* who we soon found belonged to the Church, he intorduced himself with much ceremony, in the Course of which he presented me with a small pig, two Cocoanuts and a piece of red cloth which he wraped round me: in this manner all or most of the chiefs or people of Note interduce them selves, but this man went farther, he brought with him a large hog and a quant[it]y of fruits and roots all of which he included in the present. In the after noon I went a shore to view the place, accompaned by Touahah, Parea, M[r] King and others; as soon as we landed Touahah took me by the hand and conducted me to a large Morai, the other gentlemen with Parea and four or five more of the Natives followed.

January 1779

⸿ Cook sighted the Hawaiian islands on 26th November 1778, and his journal ends with his landing in Karakakooa Bay, Hawaii, on 17th January 1779. The British were astounded at the vast concourse of islanders and the 'multitude of canoes'. With their ignorance of the language they could not know that the Hawaiians had gathered to celebrate the return of their white God Rono (or Lono), the God of prosperity and peace, who had sailed away from that very island leaving a promise that he would return.

⸿ Students of Hawaiian anthropology have explained what was passing through Hawaiian minds in these interesting events. In 1778 the inhabitants of the islands Cook had visited had reported, often to sceptical compatriots, the arrival of great floating islands with masts like forests. On these islands were white creatures with loose skins fitted with doors from which treasure was brought forth. They also had three cornered heads and long hair and they breathed fire and smoke from their mouths. Now, in less than a year, these floating islands had returned. The God Rono was revisiting his people. What an opportunity was presented to the chiefs and priests, for theocratic ceremonies in honour of a God who probably had no realisation that he was receiving anything more than the unpleasant and embarrassing homage due to a great chief.

⸿ Some forty years later American missionaries—anti-science and anti-British—were to sift the oral traditions of the Hawaiians and publish highly coloured accounts, going so far as to say that Cook 'was left to infatuation and died by the visitation of God'. Bingham wrote for example, 'How vain, rebellious, and at the same time contemptible for a worm to presume to receive homage and sacrifices from the stupid and polluted worshippers of demons and of the vilest visible objects of creation . . . without one note of remonstration of the dishonour cast on the Almighty Creator'. S. D. Porteus points out that by this means the missionaries cast scorn on a great and much admired Englishman, and also condemned the heathen adoration to which he was subjected, although that alleged adoration produced for the expedition peace and ample supplies during the weeks of the first visit to Kealakekua Bay.

⸿ That distinguished historian, the late Professor Sir Holland Rose, vigorously defended Cook, and strongly attacked the bias and inaccuracy which the Rev. S. Dibble showed in his *History of the Sandwich Islands Mission*, 1837, and *A History of the Sandwich Islands*, 1843. After reviewing the evidence for Dibble's accusations that Cook was immoral; that he allowed his sailors to conduct themselves loosely, and that he was responsible for the murder of natives,

January 1778

Holland Rose wrote, 'If while professing to write "faithful history" Dibble had consulted the records left in 1823 by earlier American missionaries viz. Thurston, Bishop and Gooderich, he would have found their impressions of Cook quite favourable. Indeed, the nearer we go back to Cook's time, the more eulogistic is the testimony to him. Also, in all fairness, Dibble should have consulted the written accounts left by Cook and his successor, Captain King. The latter declared that Cook evaded the divine honours as soon as he decently could. . . .

'It is clear then that Dibble's censures on Cook for immorality and allowing loose conduct of his sailors, also for murdering the natives are not only groundless but contrary to fact. The more closely his behaviour to natives is examined the more just and friendly it appears. But he saw great difficulties ahead in dealing with the Pacific Islanders and hoped that no European power would ever annex them.'

❨ The substantial evidence now available makes it clear that Cook himself set a high standard of morality and that when he was unable to prevent his crew from mingling with the islanders he made every possible effort to prevent them introducing disease. It is true that his instructions did result in King's people shooting the unfortunate Kareemo, a tragedy which cost Cook his life, but the Europeans were justified in taking a strong line in order to secure the return of the stolen cutter, and to prevent further violence and thefts.

Chapter XIX

THE DEATH OF JAMES COOK

"His name will live for ever in the remembrance of a people grateful for the services his labours have afforded to mankind in general."

BANKS TO MRS COOK, 1784

THE ACCOUNT OF COOK'S DEATH WHICH FOLLOWS IS THE official rendering by King, who completed the journal of the Third Voyage, and recorded the story of the tragedy as told by Lieutenant Phillips who commanded the Marines. The best and fairest account of the whole series of events is thought to be that of Surgeon Samwell of the *Resolution*, although he and Clerke, who was using a telescope, watched the actual tragedy from the vessel lying about a quarter of a mile from the shore.

¶ It is quite clear, however, that the killing was unpremeditated. Rather it was an unhappy calamity, due to an extraordinary series of events. Cook himself set the train in motion by accepting the *Resolution* for a second immense voyage, although the Deptford dockyard must bear the blame for the disgracefully bad refitting. The storm which sprung the foremast of the *Resolution* was an act of God which unhappily occurred at a time and place that forced Cook back to Kealakekua Bay where he knew that he had already outstayed his welcome. Some authorities consider that the coming of trouble was hastened by the burial ashore of the seaman Watman, whose death ill accorded with the return of immortal Gods.

¶ Cook left Kealakekua Bay on 4th February after an 'enormous consumption of hogs and vegetables', and the consternation of impoverished Hawaiian commoners at the return of these hungry Gods on 11th February may well account for the thieving and other troubles which produced stonethrowing and musket fire within a few hours.

❨ When Cook landed to seize the old King as a hostage for the return of the *Discovery's* cutter he was only repeating a customary and successful practice, but he was clearly in the grip of one of those outbursts of temper, which were possibly becoming more frequent, and his anger may well have affected his judgment and fatally prolonged his efforts to secure the royal hostage. Moreover, he made two very grave mistakes when he underestimated the loyalty of the Hawaiians to their King and overestimated the power of a tiny force of marines, and the psychological effects of one volley from muzzle loading muskets upon an armed and infuriated Hawaiian multitude. Nevertheless Cook would probably have escaped, save for the fact that he had sent King with boats to blockade the other end of the Bay; and the news that King's people had fired on some canoes and had slain the leading and friendly Chief, Kareemo, arrived at the crucial moment and produced immediate and not unjustified retaliation. Accounts of the fracas which followed are naturally confused, but it is clear that, by confronting the mob, Cook reached the waterside, and was not struck down until he turned, first to address Phillips, and then to order the launch and pinnace either to draw in, or to cease fire to save Hawaiian life, an order which would have been typical of Cook's career. It is noteworthy that at this fatal moment the pinnace pulled in and picked up Phillips and other survivors but Williamson stated that he misunderstood the order and took the launch further out. Kitson notes that this Williamson, one of the few failures amongst Cook's officers, was later found, when Captain of the *Agincourt*, guilty of disobedience to signals, and not having done his duty in rendering all assistance possible, 'and was sentenced to be placed at the bottom of the list of Post Captains and be rendered incapable of ever serving on board any of His Majesty's ships'.

❨ However at Kealakekua Bay the criticisms which his companions levelled at Williamson were not that he failed to attempt a rescue, but that neither he, nor anyone else, including of course the new commander Clerke, made an effort to bring off the bodies of Cook and the four marines which seem to have lain deserted on the beach after the guns of the *Resolution* had dispersed the killers. It is easy to dogmatise after the event. Was there time for Clerke to have fired cannon over the threatening mob and would this action have saved Cook? Could energetic action by Williamson have effected a rescue, particularly as Cook actually reached shallow water? Was the fact that Cook could not swim of any importance? Although Clerke's grave ill health and Williamson's timidity may have destroyed any faint chance of a rescue, events moved with great rapidity and hence it is fairest to say that Cook died through a series of misadventures and misunderstandings, culminating in a fracas and a tragedy which filled both sides with regret. This is certainly true in the case of Cook who was slain by friendly Hawaiians, and was probably true in the case of Kareemo who, just as clearly, was slain by friendly whites. The scuffle cost the lives of five Europeans, while some twenty-five Hawaiian commoners and six chiefs, several of whom were particular supporters of the explorers, fell to their cannon or musquets.

⁋ Today a memorial stands, and very rightly stands at Kealakekua, to the memory of a very great, very noble and very merciful Pacific explorer, but as Porteus notes, there is no memorial to the Hawaiians, who, armed only with clubs and stones, bravely defended their old Chieftain against the first wave of those aliens, who, even by then, may have introduced social diseases, and who were to return to bring upon a fine but unfortunate people the conquest and absorption of their race.

⁋ After Cook's death Captain James King, LL.D., F.R.S., took up the task of writing the official journal which, although King omits the details of the shooting of Kareemo that precipitated reprisals, contains a clear account of the tragedy, together with an outline of the preceding and subsequent events.

⁋ In regard to Cook's landing on 17th January 1779, King wrote:

SUNDAY 17*th* January 1779. Soon after the Resolution had got into her station, our two friends, Pareea and Kaneena, brought on board a third chief, named Koah, who, we were told, was a priest, and had been, in his youth, a distinguished warrior. He was a little old man, of an emaciated figure; his eyes exceedingly sore and red, and his body covered with a white leprous scurf, the effects of an immoderate use of the *ava*. Being led into the cabin, he approached Captain Cook with great veneration, and threw over his shoulders a piece of red cloth, which he had brought along with him. Then stepping a few paces back, he made an offering of a small pig, which he held in his hand, whilst he pronounced a discourse that lasted for a considerable time. This ceremony was frequently repeated during our stay at Owhyhee, and appeared to us, from many circumstances, to be a sort of religious adoration. Their idols we found always arrayed with red cloth, in the same manner as was done to Captain Cook; and a small pig was their usual offering to the *Eatooas*. Their speeches, or prayers, were uttered too with a readiness and volubility that indicated them to be according to some formulary.

'When this ceremony was over, Koah dined with Captain Cook, eating plentifully of what was set before him; but, like the rest of the inhabitants of the islands in these Seas, could scarcely be prevailed on to taste a second time our wine or spirits. In the evening, Captain Cook, attended by Mr Bayly and myself, acompanied him on shore. We landed at the beach, and were received by four men, who carried wands tipt with dog's hair, and marched before us, pronouncing with a loud voice a short sentence, in which we could only distinguish the word *Orono*. The crowd, which had been collected on the shore, retired at our approach; and not a person was to be seen, except a few lying prostrate on the ground, near the huts of the adjoining village.

'Before I proceed to relate the adoration that was paid to Captain Cook, and the peculiar ceremonies with which he was received on this fatal island, it will be necessary to describe the *Morai*, situated, as I have already mentioned, at the South side of the beach at *Kakooa*. It was a square solid pile of stones, about forty yards long, twenty broad, and fourteen in height. The top was flat, and well paved, and surrounded by a wooden rail, on which were fixed the sculls of the captives, sacrificed on the death of their chiefs. In the centre of the area, stood a ruinous old building of wood, connected with the rail, on each side, by a stone wall, which divided the whole space into two parts. On the side next the country, were five poles, upward of twenty feet high, supporting an irregular kind of scaffold; on the opposite side, toward the sea, stood two small houses, with a covered communication.

'We were conducted by Koah to the top of this pile by an easy ascent, leading from the beach to the North West corner of the area. At the entrance, we saw two large wooden images, with features violently distorted, and a long piece of carved wood, of a conical form inverted, rising from the top of their heads; the rest was without form, and wrapped round with red cloth. We were here met by a tall young man with a long beard, who presented Captain Cook to the images, and after chanting a kind of hymn, in which he was joined by Koah, they led us to that end of the *Morai*, where the five poles were fixed. At the foot of them were twelve images ranged in a semicircular form, and before the middle figure stood a high stand or table, exactly resembling the *Whatta* of Otaheite, on which lay a putrid hog, and under it pieces of sugar-cane, cocoa-nuts, bread-fruit, plantains, and sweet potatoes. Koah having placed the Captain under this stand, took down the hog, and held it toward him; and after having a second time addressed him in a long speech, pronounced with much vehemence and rapidity, he let it fall on the ground, and led him to the scaffolding, which they began to climb together, not without great risk of falling. At this time we saw, coming in solemn procession, at the entrance of the top of the *Morai*, ten men carrying a live hog, and a large piece of red cloth. Being advanced a few paces, they stopped, and prostrated themselves; and Kaireekeea, the young man above-mentioned, went to them, and receiving the cloth, carried it to Koah, who wrapped it round the Captain, and afterward offered him the hog, which was brought by Kaireekeea with the same ceremony.

'Whilst Captain Cook was aloft, in this awkward situation, swathed round with red cloth, and with difficulty keeping his hold amongst the pieces of rotten scaffolding, Kaireekeea and Koah began their office, chanting sometimes in concert, and sometimes alternately. This lasted a considerable time; at length Koah let the hog drop, when he and the Captain descended together. He then led him to the images before mentioned, and having said something to each in a sneering tone, snapping his fingers at them as he passed, he brought him to that in the centre, which, from its being covered with red cloth, appeared to be in greater estimation than the rest. Before this figure he prostrated himself, and kissed it, desiring Captain Cook to do the same; who suffered himself to be directed by Koah throughout the whole of this ceremony.

'We were now led back into the other division of the *Morai*, where there was a space, ten or twelve feet square, sunk about three feet below the level of the area. Into this we descended, and Captain Cook was seated between two wooden idols, Koah supporting one of his arms, whilst I was desired to support the other. At this time, arrived a second procession of natives, carrying a baked hog, and a pudding, some bread-fruit, cocoa-nuts, and other vegetables. When they approached us, Kaireekeea put himself at their head, and presenting the pig to Captain Cook in the usual manner, began the same kind of chant as before, his companions making regular responses. We observed, that after every response, their parts became gradually shorter, till, toward the close, Kaireekeea's consisted of only two or three words, which the rest answered by the word *Orono*.

'When this offering was concluded, which lasted a quarter of an hour, the natives sat down fronting us, and began to cut up the baked hog, to peel the vegetables, and break the cocoa-nuts; whilst others employed themselves in brewing the *ava*; which is done by chewing it, in the same manner as at the Friendly Islands. Kaireekeea then took part of the kernel of a cocoa-nut, which he chewed, and wrapping it in a piece of cloth, rubbed with it the Captain's face, head, hands, arms, and shoulders. The *ava* was then handed round, and after we had tasted it, Koah and Pareea began to pull the flesh of the hog in pieces, and to put it into our mouths. I had no great objection to being fed by Pareea, who was very cleanly in his person; but Captain Cook, who was served by Koah, recollecting the putrid hog, could not swallow a morsel; and his reluctance, as may be supposed, was not diminished, when the old man, according to his own mode of civility, had chewed it for him.

'When this last ceremony was finished, which Captain Cook put an end to as soon as he decently could, we quitted the *Morai*, after distributing amongst the people some pieces of iron and other trifles, with which they seemed highly gratified. The men with wands conducted us to the boats, repeating the same words as before. The people again retired, and the few that remained, prostrated themselves as we passed along the shore. We immediately went on board, our minds full of what we had seen, and extremely well satisfied with the good disposition of our new friends. The meaning of the various ceremonies, with which we had been received, and which, on account of their novelty and singularity, have been related at length, can only be the subject of conjectures, and those uncertain and partial: they were, however, without doubt, expressive of high respect on the part of the natives; and, as far as related to the person of Captain Cook, they seemed approaching to adoration.

¶ On Tuesday, 26th January, King Terreeo-boo came to the ships with great ceremony and with highly decorated canoes, which also contained further gifts of hogs and vegetables which the islanders were pouring on the whites.

'The next day, about noon, the king, in a large canoe, attended by two others, set out from the village, and paddled toward the ships in great state. Their appearance was grand and magnificent. In the first canoe was Terreeoboo and his chiefs, dressed in their rich feathered cloaks and helmets, and armed with long spears and daggers; in the second, came the venerable Kaoo, the chief of the priests, and his brethren, with their idols displayed on red cloth. These idols were busts of a gigantic size, made of wicker-work, and curiously covered with small feathers of various colours, wrought in the same manner with their cloaks. Their eyes were made of large pearl oysters, with a black nut fixed in the centre; their mouths were set with a double row of the fangs of dogs, and, together with the rest of their features, were strangely distorted. The third canoe was filled with hogs and various sorts of vegetables. As they went along, the priests in the centre canoe sung their hymns with great solemnity; and after paddling round the ships, instead of going on board, as was expected, they made toward the shore at the beach where we were stationed.

'As soon as I saw them approaching, I ordered out our little guard to receive the king; and Captain Cook, perceiving that he was going on shore, followed him, and arrived nearly at the same time. We conducted them into the tent, where they had scarcely been seated, when the king rose up, and in a very graceful manner threw over the Captain's shoulders the cloak he himself wore, put a feathered helmet upon his head, and a curious fan into his hand. He also spread at his feet five or six other cloaks, all exceedingly beautiful, and of the greatest value. His attendants then brought four very large hogs, with sugar-canes, cocoa-nuts, and bread-fruit; and this part of the ceremony was concluded by the king's exchanging names with Captain Cook, which, amongst all the islanders of the Pacific Ocean, is esteemed the strongest pledge of friendship. A procession of priests, with a venerable old personage at their head, now appeared, followed by a long train of men leading large hogs, and others carrying plantains, sweet potatoes, &c. By the looks and gestures of Kaireekeea, I immediately knew the old man to be the chief of the priests before mentioned, on whose bounty we had so long subsisted. He had a piece of red cloth in his hands, which he wrapped round Captain Cook's shoulders, and afterwards presented him with a small pig in the usual form. A seat was then made for him, next to the king, after which, Kaireekeea and his followers began their ceremonies, Kaoo and the chiefs joining in the responses.

'I was surprized to see, in the person of this king, the same infirm and emaciated old man, that came on board the Resolution when we were off the North East side of the island of Mowee; and we soon discovered amongst his attendants most of the persons who at that time had remained with us all night. Of this number were the two younger sons of the king, the eldest of whom was sixteen years of age, and his nephew Maiha-Maiha, whom at first we had some difficulty in recollecting, his hair being plastered over with a dirty brown paste and powder, which was no mean heightening to the most savage face I ever beheld.

'As soon as the formalities of the meeting were over, Captain Cook carried Terreeoboo, and as many chiefs as the pinnace could hold, on board the Resolution. They were received with every mark of respect that could be shewn them; and Captain Cook, in return for the feathered cloak, put a linen shirt on the king, and girt his own hanger round him. The ancient Kaoo, and about half a dozen more old chiefs, remained on shore, and took up their abode at the priests houses. During all this time, not a canoe was seen in the bay, and the natives either kept within their huts, or lay prostrate on the ground. Before the king left the Resolution, Captain Cook obtained leave for the natives to come and trade with the ships as usual; but the women, for what reason we could not learn, still continued under the effects of the *taboo*; that is, were forbidden to stir from home, or to have any communication with us.

¶ As could have been expected, however, reaction soon set in, when the generous gifts which the priests were extracting for the white Gods, began to strain the islanders' resources. Thefts became more frequent; the burial of a sailor, although conducted on shore at the especial wish of the King, seemed to reflect on the immortality of Rono's followers, and even Terreeoboo and his chiefs 'became very inquisitive' as to the time at which these hungry Gods intended to leave both the island, and the Hawaiian women.

'Terreeoboo, and his Chiefs, had for some days past, been very inquisitive about the time of our departure. This circumstance had excited in me a great curiosity to know, what opinion this people had formed of us, and what were their ideas respecting the cause and objects of our voyage. I took some pains to satisfy myself on these points; but could never learn any thing farther, than that they imagined we came from some country where provisions had failed; and that our visit to them was merely for the purpose of filling our bellies. Indeed, the meagre appearance of some of our crew, the hearty appetites with which we sat down to their fresh provisions, and our great anxiety to purchase, and carry off, as much as we were able, led them, naturally enough, to such a conclusion. To these may be added, a circumstance which puzzled them exceedingly, our having no women with us; together with our quiet conduct, and unwarlike appearance. It was ridiculous enough to see them stroking the sides, and patting the bellies of the sailors (who were certainly much improved in the sleekness of their looks, during our short stay in the island), and telling them, partly by signs, and partly by words, that it was time for them to go; but if they would come again the next bread-fruit season, they should be better able to supply their wants. We had now been sixteen days in the bay; and if our enormous consumption of hogs and vegetables be considered, it need not be wondered, that they should wish to see us take our leave. It is very probable, however, that Terreeoboo had no other view, in his inquiries, at present, than a desire of making sufficient preparation for dismissing us with presents, suitable to the respect and kindness with which he had received us. For, on our telling him we should leave the island on the next day but one, we observed, that a sort of proclamation was immediately made, through the villages, to require the people to bring in their hogs, and vegetables, for the king to present to the *Orono*, on his departure.

(On 4th February, when the carpenters had completed their repairs, the ships sailed, although not before the King had made a formal request to Cook to leave the popular James King behind. Unfortunately, however, on the night of 7th February the expedition encountered a gale which sprung the defective foremast of the *Resolution*—the mast which had been repaired with so much difficulty at Nootka Sound. Although he realised that he had outstayed his welcome Cook returned to Karakakooa Bay as the only safe anchorage immediately available. To the surprise of the British, the Hawaiians, hitherto so friendly, immediately began to show hostility, and a series of unhappy incidents led Cook into making a series of miscalculations which resulted in his death. In the final issue the natives seem to have been in the wrong and the theft of the cutter was unprovoked. Nevertheless Cook, in following his usual practice of obtaining hostages, completely underestimated the loyalty of the Hawaiians to their aged King Terreeoboo and their courage in facing the volley fired by the marines' muskets. The question of whether or not the ailing Clerke or the timorous Williamson could have saved their commander is examined in another place. Samwell and others left important accounts of this tragic affair but the text followed here is the official account given by King who, of course, had the views of the only officer actually on the spot, the commander of the marines Lieutenant Molesworth Phillips.

'We were employed the whole of the 11th, and part of the 12th, in getting out the foremast, and sending it, with the carpenters, on shore. Besides the damage which the head of the mast had sustained, we found the heel exceedingly rotten, having a large hole up the middle of it, capable of holding four or five cocoa-nuts. It was not, however, thought necessary to shorten it; and fortunately, the logs of red toa-wood, which had been cut at Eimeo, for anchor-stocks, were found fit to replace the sprung parts of the fishes. As these repairs were likely to take up several days, Mr Bayly and myself got the astronomical apparatus on shore, and pitched our tents on the *Morai*; having with us a guard of a corporal and six marines. We renewed our friendly correspondence with the priests, who, for the greater security of the workmen, and their tools, *tabooed* the place where the mast lay, sticking their wands round it, as before. The sailmakers were also sent on shore, to repair the damages which had taken place in their department, during the late gales. They were lodged in a house adjoining to the *Morai*, that was lent us by the priests. Such were our arrangements on shore. I shall now proceed to the account of those other transactions with the natives, which led, by degrees, to the fatal catastrophe of the 14th.

'Upon our coming to anchor, we were surprized to find our reception very different from what it had been on our first arrival; no shouts, no bustle, no confusion; but a solitary bay, with only here and there a canoe stealing close along the shore. The impulse of curiosity, which had before operated to so great a degree, might now indeed be supposed to have ceased; but the hospitable treatment we had invariably met with, and the friendly footing on which we parted, gave us some reason to expect, that they would again have flocked about us with great joy, on our return.

'We were forming various conjectures, upon the occasion of this extraordinary appearance, when our anxiety was at length relieved by the return of a boat, which had been sent on shore, and brought us word, that Terreeoboo was absent, and had left the bay under the *taboo*. Though this account appeared very satisfactory to most of us; yet others were of opinion, or rather, perhaps, have been led, by subsequent events, to imagine that there was something, at this time, very suspicious in the behaviour of the natives; and that the interdiction of all intercourse with us, on pretence of the king's absence, was only to give him time to consult with his Chiefs, in what manner it might be proper to treat us. Whether these suspicions were well founded, or the account given by the natives was the truth, we were never able to ascertain. For though it is not improbable, that our sudden return, for which they could see no apparent cause, and the necessity of which we afterward found it very difficult to make them comprehend, might occasion some alarm; yet the unsuspicious conduct of Terreeoboo, who, on his supposed arrival, the next morning, came immediately to visit Captain Cook, and the consequent return of the natives to their former friendly intercourse with us, are strong proofs, that they neither meant, nor apprehended, any change of conduct.

'In support of this opinion, I may add the account of another accident, precisely of the same kind, which happened to us on our first visit, the day before the arrival of the king. A native had sold a hog on board the Resolution, and taken the price agreed on, when Pareea, passing by, advised the man not to part with the hog, without an advanced price. For this, he was sharply spoken to, and pushed away; and the *taboo* being soon after laid on the bay, we had at first no doubt, but that it was in consequence of the offence given to the Chief. Both these accidents serve to shew, how very difficult it is to draw any certain conclusion from the actions of people, with whose customs, as well as language, we are so imperfectly acquainted; at the same time, some idea may be formed from them, of the difficulties, at the first view, perhaps, not very apparent, which those have to encounter, who, in all their transactions with these strangers, have to steer their course amidst so much uncertainty, where a trifling error may be attended with even the most fatal consequences. However true or false our conjectures may be, things went on in their usual quiet course, till the afternoon of the 13th.

'Toward the evening of that day, the officer who commanded the watering-party of the Discovery, came to inform me, that several Chiefs had assembled at the well near the beach, driving away the natives, whom he had hired to assist the sailors in rolling down the casks to the shore. He told me, at the same time, that he thought their behaviour extremely suspicious, and that they meant to give him some farther disturbance. At his request, therefore, I sent a marine along with him, but suffered him to take only his side-arms. In a short time the officer returned, and on his acquainting me, that the islanders had armed themselves with stones, and were grown very tumultuous, I went myself to the spot, attended by a marine, with his musquet. Seeing us approach, they threw away their stones, and, on my speaking to some of the Chiefs, the mob were driven away, and those who chose it, were suffered to assist in filling the casks. Having left things quiet here, I went to meet Captain Cook, whom I saw coming on shore, in the pinnace. I related to him what had just passed; and he ordered me, in case of their beginning to throw stones, or behave insolently, immediately to fire a ball at the offenders. I accordingly gave orders to the corporal, to have the pieces of the sentinels loaded with ball, instead of small shot.

'Soon after our return to the tents, we were alarmed by a continued fire of musquets, from the Discovery, which we observed to be directed at a canoe, that we saw paddling toward the shore, in great haste, pursued by one of our small boats. We immediately concluded, that the firing was in consequence of some theft, and Captain Cook ordered me to follow him with a marine armed, and to endeavour to seize the people as they came on shore. Accordingly we ran toward the place where we supposed the canoe would land, but were too late; the people having quitted it, and made their escape into the country before our arrival.

'We were at that time ignorant, that the goods had been already restored; and as we thought it probable, from the circumstances we had at first observed, that they might be of importance, were unwilling to relinquish our hopes of recovering them. Having therefore inquired of the natives, which way the people had fled, we followed them, till it was near dark, when judging ourselves to be about three miles from the tents, and suspecting, that the natives, who frequently encouraged us in the pursuit, were amusing us with false information, we thought it in vain to continue our search any longer, and returned to the beach.

'During our absence, a difference, of a more serious and unpleasant nature, had happened. The officer, who had been sent in the small boat, and was returning on board, with the goods which had been restored, observing Captain Cook and me engaged in the pursuit of the offenders, thought it his duty to seize the canoe, which was left drawn up on the shore. Unfortunately, this canoe belonged to Pareea, who arriving at the same moment, from on board the Discovery, claimed his property, with many protestations of his innocence. The officer refusing to give it up, and being joined by the crew of the pinnace, which was waiting for Captain Cook, a scuffle ensued, in which Pareea was knocked down, by a violent blow on the head, with an oar. The natives, who were collected about the spot, and had hitherto been peaceable spectators, immediately attacked our people with such a shower of stones, as forced them to retreat, with great precipitation, and swim off to a rock, at some distance from the shore. The pinnace was immediately ransacked by the islanders; and, but for the timely interposition of Pareea, who seemed to have recovered from the blow, and forgot it at the same instant, would soon have been entirely demolished. Having driven away the crowd, he made signs to our people, that they might come and take possession of the pinnace, and that he would endeavour to get back the things which had been taken out of it. After their departure, he followed them in his canoe, with a midshipman's cap, and some other trifling articles of the plunder, and, with much apparent concern at what had happened, asked, if the *Orono* would kill him, and whether he would permit him to come on board the next day? On being assured, that he should be well received, he joined noses (as their custom is) with the officers, in token of friendship, and paddled over to the village of Kowrowa.

'When Captain Cook was informed of what had passed, he expressed much uneasiness at it, and as we were returning on board, "I am afraid," said he, "that these people will oblige me to use some violent measures; for," he added, "they must not be left to imagine, that they have gained an advantage over us." However, as it was too late to take any steps this evening, he contented himself with giving orders, that every man and woman on board should be immediately turned out of the ship. As soon as this order was executed, I returned on shore; and our former confidence in the natives being now much abated, by the events of the day, I posted a double guard on the *Morai*, with orders to call me, if they saw any men lurking about the beach. At about eleven o'clock, five islanders were observed creeping round the bottom of the *Morai*; they seemed very cautious in approaching us, and, at last, finding themselves discovered retired out of sight. About midnight, one of them venturing up close to the observatory, the sentinel fired over him; on which the men fled, and we passed the remainder of the night without farther disturbance. Next morning, at day-light, I went on board the Resolution for the time-keeper, and, in my way, was hailed by the

Discovery, and informed, that their cutter had been stolen, during the night, from the buoy where it was moored.

'When I arrived on board, I found the marines arming, and Captain Cook loading his double-barrelled gun. Whilst I was relating to him what had happened to us in the night, he interrupted me, with some eagerness, and acquainted me with the loss of the Discovery's cutter, and with the preparations he was making for its recovery. It had been his usual practice, whenever any thing of consequence was lost, at any of the islands in this ocean, to get the king, or some of the principal *Erees*, on board, and to keep them as hostages, till it was restored. This method, which had been always attended with success, he meant to pursue on the present occasion; and, at the same time, had given orders to stop all the canoes that should attempt to leave the bay, with an intention of seizing and destroying them, if he could not recover the cutter by peaceable means. Accordingly, the boats of both ships, well manned and armed, were stationed across the bay; and, before I left the ship, some great guns had been fired at two large canoes, that were attempting to make their escape.

'It was between seven and eight o'clock when we quitted the ship together; Captain Cook in the pinnace, having Mr Phillips, and nine marines, with him; and myself in the small boat. The last orders I received from him were, to quiet the minds of the natives, on our side of the bay, by assuring them, they should not be hurt; to keep my people together; and to be on my guard. We then parted; the Captain went toward Kowrowa, where the king resided; and I proceeded to the beach. My first care, on going ashore, was to give strict orders to the marines to remain within the tent, to load their pieces with ball, and not to quit their arms. Afterward I took a walk to the huts of old Kaoo, and the priests, and explained to them, as well as I could, the object of the hostile preparations, which had exceedingly alarmed them. I found, that they had already heard of the cutter's being stolen, and I assured them, that though Captain Cook was resolved to recover it, and to punish the authors of the theft, yet that they, and the people of the village on our side, need not be under the smallest apprehension of suffering any evil from us. I desired the priests to explain this to the people, and to tell them not to be alarmed, but to continue peaceable and quiet. Kaoo asked me, with great earnestness, if Terreeoboo was to be hurt? I assured him, he was not; and both he and the rest of his brethren seemed much satisfied with this assurance.

'In the mean time, Captain Cook, having called off the launch, which was stationed at the North point of the bay, and taken it along with him, proceeded to Kowrowa, and landed with the Lieutenant and nine marines. He immediately marched into the village, where he was received with the usual marks of respect; the people prostrating themselves before him, and bringing their accustomed offerings of small hogs. Finding that there was no suspicion of his design, his next step was, to enquire for Terreeoboo, and the two boys, his sons, who had been his constant guests on board the Resolution. In a short time, the boys returned along with the natives, who had been sent in search of them, and immediately led Captain Cook to the house where the king had slept. They found the old man just awoke from sleep; and, after a short conversation about the loss of the cutter, from which Captain Cook was convinced that he was in no wise privy to it, he invited him to return in the boat, and spend the day on board the Resolution. To this proposal the king readily consented, and immediately got up to accompany him.

'Things were in this prosperous train, the two boys being already in the pinnace, and the rest of the party having advanced near the water-side, when an elderly woman called Kanee-kabareea, the mother of the boys, and one of the king's favourite wives, came after him, and with many tears, and entreaties, besought him not to go on board. At the same time, two Chiefs, who came along with her, laid hold of him, and, insisting that he should go no farther, forced him to sit down. The natives, who were collecting in prodigious numbers along the shore, and had probably been alarmed by the firing of the great guns, and the appearances of hostility in the bay, began to throng round Captain Cook and their king. In this situation, the Lieutenant of marines, observing that his men were huddled close together in the crowd, and thus incapable of using their arms, if any occasion should require it, proposed to the Captain, to draw them up along the rocks, close to the water's edge; and the crowd readily making way for them to pass, they were drawn up in a line, at the distance of about thirty yards from the place where the king was sitting.

'All this time, the old king remained on the ground, with the strongest marks of terror and dejection in his countenance; Captain Cook, not willing to abandon the object for which he had come on shore, continuing to urge him, in the most pressing manner, to proceed; whilst, on the other hand, whenever the king appeared inclined to follow him, the Chiefs, who stood round him, interposed, at first with prayers and entreaties, but afterward having recourse to force and violence, and insisted on his staying where he was. Captain Cook therefore finding, that the alarm had spread too generally, and that it was in vain to think any longer of getting him off without bloodshed, at last gave up the point; observing to Mr Phillips, that it would be impossible to compel him to go on board, without the risk of killing a great number of the inhabitants.

'Though the enterprize, which had carried Captain Cook on shore, had now failed, and was abandoned, yet his person did not appear to have been in the least danger, till an accident happened, which gave a fatal turn to the affair. The boats which had been stationed across the bay, having fired at some canoes, that were attempting to get out, unfortunately had killed a Chief of the first rank. The news of his death arrived at the village where Captain Cook was, just as he had left the king, and was walking slowly toward the shore. The ferment it occasioned was very conspicuous; the women and children were immediately sent off; and the men put on their war-mats, and armed themselves with spears and stones. One of the natives, having in his hands a stone, and a long iron spike (which they call a *pahooa*) came up to the Captain, flourishing his weapon, by way of defiance, and threatening to throw the stone. The Captain desired him to desist; but the man persisting in his insolence, he was at length provoked to fire a load of small-shot. The man having his mat on, which the shot were not able to penetrate, this had no other effect than to irritate and encourage them. Several stones were thrown at the marines; and one of the *Erees* attempted to stab Mr Phillips with his *pahooa*; but failed in the attempt, and received from him a blow with the butt end of his musquet. Captain Cook now fired his second barrel, loaded with ball, and killed one of the foremost of the natives. A general attack with stones immediately followed, which was answered by a discharge of musquetry from the marines, and the people in the boats. The islanders, contrary to the expectations of every one, stood the fire with great firmness; and before the marines had time to reload, they broke in upon them with dreadful shouts and yells. What followed was a scene of the utmost horror and confusion.

'Four of the marines were cut off amongst the rocks in their retreat, and fell a sacrifice to the fury of the enemy; three more were dangerously wounded; and the Lieutenant, who had received a stab between the shoulders with a *pahooa*, having fortunately reserved his fire, shot the man who had wounded him just as he was going to repeat his blow. Our unfortunate Commander, the last time he was seen distinctly, was standing at the water's edge, and calling out to the boats to cease firing, and to pull in. If it be true, as some of those who were present have imagined, that the marines and boat-men had fired without his orders, and that he was desirous of preventing any further bloodshed, it is not improbable, that his humanity, on this occasion, proved fatal to him. For it was remarked, that whilst he faced the natives, none of them had offered him any violence, but that having turned about, to give his orders to the boats, he was stabbed in the back, and fell with his face into the water. On seeing him fall, the islanders set up a great shout, and his body was immediately dragged on shore, and surrounded by the enemy, who snatching the dagger out of each other's hands, shewed a savage eagerness to have a share in his destruction.

'Thus fell our great and excellent Commander! After a life of so much distinguished and successful enterprize, his death, as far as regards himself, cannot be reckoned premature; since he lived to finish the great work for which he seems to have been designed; and was rather removed from the enjoyment, than cut off from the acquisition, of glory. How sincerely his loss was felt and lamented, by those who had so long found their general security in his skill and conduct,

THE DEATH OF COOK
FEBRUARY 1779

and every consolation, under their hardships, in his tenderness and humanity, it is neither necessary nor possible for me to describe; much less shall I attempt to paint the horror with which we were struck, and the universal dejection and dismay which followed so dreadful and unexpected a calamity.

⸿ So at the age of fifty fell James Cook, like Magellan covering the retreat of his men. It is pathetic to think that, clinging to a rock in shallow water, he raised his head and looked for rescue to his ineffective boats. Yet, perhaps, his Hawaiian slayers were in reality not unmerciful to a far ranging soul which would have found England, and Greenwich Hospital, intolerably confined after the vast spaces of the Pacific. It is useless to speculate, but Cook's death may have influenced the course of history. That the Crown may have given him a baronetcy is immaterial, what matters is that he might have supplanted another very great and good man, Captain Arthur Phillip, in the foundation of British Australia in 1788. Again, would he have used his very great influence to direct the first fleet from New South Wales to his beloved Queen Charlotte Sound, or Dusky Bay, New Zealand, or would he, like his subordinate Matra, have advocated the establishment of the American 'Loyalists with their negro slaves in the South Pacific'?

⸿ Although the islanders had rejected Cook's divinity they afforded his mutilated body the funeral honours paid only to the highest chiefs. As, however, these honours involved the dismemberment and distribution of the remains, Captain Clerke, who assumed command, had a difficult task in collecting some sad remnants for ocean burial, and was unable to leave the ill-fated island until 8th March. It is, however, to the credit of Clerke and the British, that they realised that the fracas was quite unpremeditated and hence there was no retaliation other than that necessary to cover the retreat, water the ships, and secure portions of Cook's body which had not been burnt.

THE NEWS REACHES ENGLAND

⸿ As early as November 1779 the press began to voice anxiety owing to the fact that Cook had not been reported from Canton where, it was believed, he had intended to winter. In January 1780 the blow fell when the 'London Gazette' announced that Captain Clerke had reached the harbour of St. Peter and St. Paul, Kamtschatka, and had reported to the Admiralty the sad news of Cook's death. Amongst many tributes the 'Gazette' stated that 'His Majesty, who had always the highest opinion of Captain Cook, shed tears, when Lord Sandwich informed him of his death and immediately ordered a pension of £300 (actually £200) for his widow.' As the Admiralty also gave Mrs Cook half the proceeds of the 'Journal of the Third Voyage' she was, considering the current purchasing power of money, treated justly. The posthumous honours that fell on Cook included the King's action in granting to the Cook family a coat of arms (possibly the last ever bestowed 'in recognition of service'), and the striking by the Royal Society of a special gold medal in honour of Cook and his many services to science—a medal which Banks forwarded to Mrs Cook in 1784. It is interesting to note that Cook also made two contributions to the Royal Society on the tides of the Pacific, and that the Society published these in its journal.

⸿ Unfortunately, with the exception of his widow, no member of Cook's family long survived to enjoy the honours gained by their celebrated relative, for Cook's tragic death was followed by an extraordinary succession of family disasters. Of the six Cook children, the only daughter, Elizabeth, died in childhood during the voyage of the *Endeavour*, and two sons died in 1768 and 1772, in infancy. Of the three sons remaining, one, Nathaniel, gained commissioned rank in the navy but perished at the age of sixteen in the *Thunderer* which was lost in a hurricane off the coast of Jamaica in 1780, just before his mother knew that she was a widow. Another son, Hugh, named after Sir Hugh Palliser, and born in 1776, remained at home with Mrs Cook, but died of scarlet fever in 1793 two months after entering Christ's College, Cambridge. The last remaining child, the eldest son, James, rose to be a commander in the Navy, but perished by drowning or violence while taking a boat to join his ship in stormy weather at Portsmouth early in 1794. This series of blows prostrated, and nearly killed the unfortunate Mrs Cook, but, recovering, she lived with her cousin Admiral Isaac Smith and did not die until 1835 when she reached the age of 93 years.

⸿ With her pension, legacies and the profits from her husband's writings, Mrs Cook lived in moderate affluence in a house filled with relics of the voyages. According to Kitson, some of these were presented on her death to the British Museum, but some, like Cook's holograph account of the first voyage, passed, at any rate for a time, into private hands, while any personal correspondence between Cook and his wife disappeared, possibly destroyed by the very reserved Mrs Cook as too sacred for public view.

⸿ Kitson says that Canon Bennett, who knew Mrs Cook very well, described her as follows:

'A handsome, venerable lady, her white hair rolled back in ancient fashion, always dressed in black satin; with an oval face, an aquiline nose, and a good mouth. She wore a ring with her husband's hair in it; and she entertained the highest respect for his memory, measuring everything by his standard of honour and morality. Her keenest expression of disapprobation was that "Mr Cook"—to her he was always Mr Cook, not Captain—"would never have done so". Like many widows of sailors, she could never sleep in high wind for thinking of the men at sea, and she kept four days in the year of solemn fasting, during which she came not out of her own room: they were the days of her bereavements: the days when she had lost her husband and her three boys. She passed those days in prayer and meditation with her husband's Bible; and for her husband's sake she befriended the nephews and grandnephews and nieces and grandnieces of his whom she never saw; they were not suffered to want.'

THE END OF THE EXPEDITION

☾ King gave a long account of the negotiations which followed Cook's death, a time of considerable danger to the British, for the expedition seemed completely demoralised without its great leader, a fact which King openly confessed.

'It has already been related, that four of the marines, who attended Captain Cook, were killed by the islanders on the spot. The rest, with Mr Phillips, their Lieutenant, threw themselves into the water, and escaped, under cover of a smart fire from the boats. On this occasion, a remarkable instance of gallant behaviour, and of affection for his men, was shewn by that officer. For he had scarcely got into the boat, when, seeing one of the marines, who was a bad swimmer, struggling in the water, and in danger of being taken by the enemy, he immediately jumped into the sea to his assistance, though much wounded himself; and after receiving a blow on the head from a stone, which had nearly sent him to the bottom, he caught the man by the hair, and brought him safe off.

'Our people continued for some time to keep up a constant fire from the boats (which, during the whole transaction, were not more than twenty yards from the land), in order to afford their unfortunate companions, if any of them should still remain alive, an opportunity of escaping. These efforts, seconded by a few guns, that were fired at the same time, from the Resolution, having forced the natives at last to retire, a small boat, manned by five of our young midshipmen, pulled toward the shore, where they saw the bodies, without any signs of life, lying on the ground; but judging it dangerous to attempt to bring them off, with so small a force, and their ammunition being nearly expended, they returned to the ships, leaving them in possession of the islanders, together with ten stands of arms.

'As soon as the general consternation, which the news of this calamity occasioned throughout both crews, had a little subsided, their attention was called to our party at the *Morai*, where the mast and sails were on shore, with a guard of only six marines. It is impossible for me to describe the emotions of my own mind, during the time these transactions had been carrying on, at the other side of the bay. Being at the distance only of a short mile from the village of Kowrowa, we could see distinctly an immense crowd collected on the spot where Captain Cook had just before landed. We heard the firing of the musquetry, and could perceive some extraordinary bustle and agitation in the multitude. We afterward saw the natives flying, the boats retire from the shore, and passing and repassing, in great stillness, between the ships. I must confess, that my heart soon misgave me. Where a life so dear and valuable was concerned, it was impossible not to be alarmed, by appearances both new and threatening. But, besides this, I knew, that a long and uninterrupted course of success, in his transactions with the natives of these seas, had given the Captain a degree of confidence, that I was always fearful might, at some unlucky moment, put him too much off his guard; and I now saw all the dangers to which that confidence might lead, without receiving much consolation from considering the experience that had given rise to it.

'My first care, on hearing the musquets fired, was, to assure the people, who were assembled in considerable numbers, round the wall of our consecrated field, and seemed equally at a loss with ourselves how to account for what they had seen and heard, that they should not be molested; and that, at all events, I was desirous of continuing on peaceable terms with them. We remained in this posture, till the boats had returned on board, when Captain Clerke, observing, through his telescope, that we were surrounded by the natives, and apprehending they meant to attack us, ordered two four-pounders to be fired at them. Fortunately these guns, though well aimed, did no mischief, and yet gave the natives a convincing proof of their power. One of the balls broke a cocoa-nut tree in the middle, under which a party of them were sitting; and the other shivered a rock, that stood in an exact line with them. As I had, just before, given them the strongest assurances of their safety, I was exceedingly mortified at this act of hostility; and, to prevent a repetition of it, immediately dispatched a boat to acquaint Captain Clerke, that, at present, I was on the most friendly terms with the natives; and that, if occasion should hereafter arise for altering my conduct toward them, I would hoist a jack, as a signal for him to afford us all the assistance in his power.

'We expected the return of the boat with the utmost impatience; and after remaining a quarter of an hour, under the most torturing anxiety and suspense, our fears were at length confirmed, by the arrival of Mr Bligh, with orders to strike the tents as quickly as possible, and to send the sails, that were repairing, on board. Just at the same moment, our friend Kaireekeea having also received intelligence of the death of Captain Cook, from a native, who had arrived from the other side of the bay, came to me, with great sorrow and dejection in his countenance, to inquire, if it was true?

'Our situation was, at this time, extremely critical and important. Not only our own lives, but the event of the expedition, and the return of at least one of the ships, being involved in the same common danger. We had the mast of the Resolution, and the greatest part of our sails, on shore, under the protection of only six marines: their loss would have been irreparable; and though the natives had not as yet shewn the smallest disposition to molest us, yet it was impossible to answer for the alteration, which the news of the transaction at Kowrowa might produce. I therefore thought it prudent to dissemble my belief of the death of Captain Cook, and to desire Kaireekeea to discourage the report; lest either the fear of our resentment, or the successful example of their countrymen, might lead them to seize the favourable opportunity, which at this time offered itself, of giving us a second blow. At the same time, I advised him to bring old Kaoo, and the rest of the priests, into a large house that was close to the *Morai*; partly out of regard to their safety, in case it should have been found necessary to proceed to extremities; and partly to have him near us, in order to make use of his authority with the people, if it could be instrumental in preserving peace.

'Having placed the marines on the top of the *Morai*, which formed a strong and advantageous post, and left the command with Mr Bligh, giving him the most positive directions to act entirely on the defensive, I went on board the Discovery, in order to represent to Captain Clerke the dangerous situation of our affairs. As soon as I quitted the spot, the natives began to annoy our people with stones; and I had scarcely reached the ship, before I heard the firing of the marines. I therefore returned instantly on shore, where I found things growing every moment more alarming. The natives were arming, and putting on their mats; and their numbers increased very fast. I could also perceive several large bodies marching toward us, along the cliff which separates the village of Kakooa from the North side of the bay, where the village of Kowrowa is situated.

'They began, at first, to attack us with stones, from behind the walls of their inclosures, and finding no resistance on our part, they soon grew more daring. A few resolute fellows, having crept along the beach, under cover of the rocks, suddenly made their appearance at the foot of the *Morai*, with a design, as it seemed, of storming it on the side next the sea, which was its only accessible part; and were not dislodged, till after they had stood a considerable number of shot, and seen one of their party fall.

'The bravery of one of these assailants well deserves to be particularly mentioned. For having returned to carry off his companion, amidst the fire of our whole party, a wound, which he received, made him quit the body and retire; but, in a few minutes, he again appeared, and being again wounded, he was obliged a second time to retreat. At this moment I arrived at the *Morai*, and saw him return the third time, bleeding and faint; and being informed of what had happened, I forbad the soldiers to fire, and he was suffered to carry off his friend; which he was just able to perform, and then fell down himself, and expired.

'About this time, a strong reinforcement from both ships having landed, the natives retreated behind their walls; which giving me access to our friendly priests, I sent one of them to endeavour to bring their countrymen to some terms, and to propose to them, that if they would desist from throwing stones, I would not permit our men to fire. This truce was agreed to, and we were suffered to launch the mast, and carry off the sails, and our astronomical *apparatus*, unmolested. As soon as we had quitted the *Morai*, they took possession of it, and some of them threw a few stones; but without doing us any mischief.

'It was half an hour past eleven o'clock, when I got on board the Discovery, where I found no decisive plan had been adopted for our future proceedings. The restitution of the boat, and the recovery of the body of Captain Cook, were the objects, which, on all hands, we agreed to insist on; and it was my opinion, that some vigorous steps should be taken, in case the demand of them was not immediately complied with.

'In favour of more conciliatory measures, it was justly urged, that the mischief was done, and irreparable; that the natives had a strong claim to our regard, on account of their former friendship and kindness; and the more especially, as the late melancholy accident did not appear to have arisen from any premeditated design: that, on the part of Terreeoboo, his ignorance of the theft, his readiness to accompany Captain Cook on board, and his having actually sent his two sons into the boat, must free him from the smallest degree of suspicion: that the conduct of his women, and the *Erees*, might easily be accounted for, from the apprehensions occasioned by the armed force with which Captain Cook came on shore, and the hostile preparations in the bay; appearances so different from the terms of friendship and confidence, in which both parties had hitherto lived, that the arming of the natives was evidently with a design to resist the attempt, which they had some reason to imagine would be made, to carry off their king by force, and was naturally to be expected from a people full of affection and attachment to their Chiefs.

'To these motives of humanity, others of a prudential nature were added; that we were in want of water, and other refreshments: that our foremast would require six or eight days work, before it could be stepped: that the spring was advancing apace; and that the speedy prosecution of our next Northern expedition ought now to be our sole object: that therefore to engage in a vindictive contest with the inhabitants, might not only lay us under the imputation of unnecessary cruelty, but would occasion an unavoidable delay in the equipment of the ships. In this latter opinion Captain Clerke concurred. . . .

'In pursuance of this plan, it was determined that I should proceed toward the shore, with the boats of both ships, well manned and armed, with a view to bring the natives to a parley, and, if possible, to obtain a conference with some of the Chiefs.'

❨ With great difficulty and danger Captain King, who proceeded ashore, secured a promise that the Hawaiians would return the bodies of the slain but this was not honoured.

'The breach of their engagement to restore the bodies of the slain, and the warlike posture, in which they, at this time, appeared, occasioned fresh debates amongst us concerning the measures next to be pursued. It was, at last, determined, that nothing should be suffered to interfere with the repair of the mast, and the preparations for our departure; but that we should, nevertheless, continue our negociations for the recovery of the bodies.

'The greatest part of the day was taken up in getting the fore-mast into a proper situation on deck, for the carpenters to work upon it; and in making the necessary alterations in the commissions of the officers. The command of the expedition having devolved on Captain Clerke, he removed on board the Resolution, appointed Lieutenant Gore to be Captain of the Discovery, and promoted Mr Harvey, a midshipman, who had been with Captain Cook in his last two voyages, to the vacant Lieutenancy. During the whole day, we met with no interruption from the natives; and, at night, the launch was again moored with a top-chain; and guard-boats stationed round both ships as before.

'About eight o'clock, it being very dark, a canoe was heard paddling toward the ship; and as soon as it was seen, both the sentinels on deck fired into it. There were two persons in the canoe, and they immediately roared out "*Tinnee*," (which was the way in which they pronounced my name), and said they were friends, and had something for me belonging to Captain Cook. When they came on board, they threw themselves at our feet, and appeared exceedingly frightened. Luckily neither of them was hurt, notwithstanding the balls of both pieces had gone through the canoe. One of them was the person, whom I have before mentioned under the name of the *Taboo* man, who constantly attended Captain Cook with the circumstances of ceremony I have already described; and who, though a man of rank in the island, could scarcely be hindered from performing for him the lowest offices of a menial servant. After lamenting, with abundance of tears, the loss of the *Orono*, he told us, that he had brought us a part of his body. He then presented to us a small bundle wrapped up in cloth, which he brought under his arm; and it is impossible to describe the horror which seized us, on finding in it a piece of human flesh, about nine or ten pounds weight. This, he said, was all that remained of the body; that the rest was cut to pieces, and burnt; but that the head and all the bones, except what belonged to the trunk, were in the possession of Terreeoboo, and the other *Erees*; that what we saw had been allotted to Kaoo, the chief of the priests, to be made use of in some religious ceremony; and that he had sent it as a proof of his innocence and attachment to us.

'This afforded an opportunity of informing ourselves whether they were cannibals; and we did not neglect it. We first tried, by many indirect questions, put to each of them, to learn in what manner the rest of the bodies had been disposed of; and finding them very constant in one story, that, after the flesh had been cut off, it was all burnt; we at last put the direct question, Whether they had not eat some of it? They immediately shewed as much horror at the idea, as any

European would have done; and asked, very naturally, if that was the custom amongst us? They afterward asked us, with great earnestness and apparent apprehension, "When the *Orono* would come again? and what he would do to them on his return?" The same inquiry was frequently made afterward by others; and this idea agrees with the general tenour of their conduct toward him, which shewed, that they considered him as being of a superior nature.'

(As the natives interfered with the watering of the ships, which was essential, the British retaliated with justified severity and unfortunately destroyed some of the houses of their good friends the priests.

'In this exposed situation, our people were so taken up in attending to their own safety, that they employed the whole forenoon in filling only one ton of water. As it was therefore impossible to perform this service, till their assailants were driven to a greater distance, the Discovery was ordered to dislodge them with her great guns; which being effected by a few discharges, the men landed without molestation. However, the natives soon after made their appearance again, in their usual mode of attack; and it was now found absolutely necessary to burn down some straggling houses, near the well, behind which they had taken shelter. In executing these orders, I am sorry to add, that our people were hurried into acts of unnecessary cruelty and devastation. Something ought certainly to be allowed to their resentment of the repeated insults, and contemptuous behaviour, of the islanders, and to the natural desire of revenging the loss of their Commander. But, at the same time, their conduct served strongly to convince me, that the utmost precaution is necessary in trusting, though but for a moment, the discretionary use of arms, in the hands of private seamen, or soldiers, on such occasions. The rigour of discipline, and the habits of obedience, by which their force is kept directed to its proper objects, lead them naturally enough to conceive, that whatever they have the power, they have also the right, to do. Actual disobedience being almost the only crime for which they are accustomed to expect punishment, they learn to consider it as the only measure of right and wrong; and hence are apt to conclude, that what they can do with impunity, they may do with justice and honour. So that the feelings of humanity, which are inseparable from us all, and that generosity toward an unresisting enemy, which, at other times, is the distinguishing mark of brave men, become but weak restraints to the exercise of violence, when opposed to the desire they naturally have of shewing their own independence and power.

'I have already mentioned, that orders, had been given to burn only a few straggling huts, which afforded shelter to the natives. We were therefore a good deal surprized to see the whole village on fire; and before a boat, that was sent to stop the progress of the mischief, could reach the shore, the houses of our old and constant friends, the priests, were all in flames. I cannot enough lament the illness, that confined me on board this day. The priests had always been under my protection; and, unluckily, the officers who were then on duty, having been seldom on shore at the *Morai*, were not much acquainted with the circumstances of the place. Had I been present myself, I might probably have been the means of saving their little society from destruction.'

(The vigorous retaliation made by the British immediately took effect as portions of Cook's body were restored two days later.

'The natives, being at last convinced that it was not the want of ability to punish them, which had hitherto made us tolerate their provocations, desisted from giving us any farther molestation; and, in the evening, a Chief called Eappo, who has seldom visited us, but whom we knew to be a man of the very first consequence, came with presents from Terreeoboo to sue for peace. These presents were received, and he was dismissed with the same answer which had before been given, that, until the remains of Captain Cook should be restored, no peace would be granted. We learned from this person, that the flesh of all the bodies of our people, together with the bones of the trunks, had been burnt; that the limb bones of the marines had been divided amongst the inferior Chiefs; and that those of Captain Cook had been disposed of in the following manner: the head, to a great Chief, called Kahoo-opeon; the hair to Maihamaiha; and the legs, thighs, and arms to Terreeoboo. After it was dark, many of the inhabitants came off with roots and other vegetables; and we also received two large presents of the same articles from Kaireekeea.

'The 19th was chiefly taken up in sending and receiving the messages which passed between Captain Clerke and Terreeoboo. Eappo was very pressing, that one of our officers should go on shore; and, in the mean time, offered to remain as an hostage on board. This request, however, it was not thought proper to comply with; and he left us with a promise of bringing the bones the next day. At the beach, the waterers did not meet with the least opposition from the natives; who, notwithstanding our cautious behaviour, came amongst us again, without the smallest appearance of diffidence or apprehension.

'Early in the morning of the 20th, we had the satisfaction of getting the fore-mast stepped. It was an operation attended with great difficulty, and some danger; our ropes being so exceedingly rotten, that the purchase gave way several times.

'Between ten and eleven o'clock, we saw a great number of people descending the hill, which is over the beach, in a kind of procession, each man carrying a sugar-cane or two on his shoulders, and bread-fruit, *taro*, and plantains in his hand. They were preceded by two drummers; who, when they came to the water-side, sat down by a white flag, and began to beat their drums, while those who had followed them, advanced, one by one; and, having deposited the presents, retired in the same order. Soon after, Eappo came in sight, in his long feathered cloak, bearing something with great solemnity in his hands; and having placed himself on a rock, he made signs for a boat to be sent him.

'Captain Clerke, conjecturing that he had brought the bones of Captain Cook, which proved to be the fact, went himself in the pinnace to receive them; and ordered me to attend him in the cutter. When we arrived at the beach, Eappo came into the pinnace, and delivered to the Captain the bones wrapped up in a large quantity of fine new cloth, and covered with a spotted cloak of black and white feathers. He afterward attended us to the Resolution; but could not be prevailed upon to go on board; probably not choosing, from a sense of decency, to be present at the opening of the bundle. We found in it both the hands of Captain Cook entire, which were well known from a remarkable scar on one of them, that divided the thumb from the fore-finger, the whole length of the metacarpal bone; the skull, but with the scalp separated from it, and the bones that form the face wanting; the scalp, with the hair upon it cut short, and the ears adhering to it; the bones of both arms, with the skin of the fore-arms hanging to them; the thigh and leg-bones joined together, but without the feet. The ligaments of the joints were entire; and the whole bore evident marks of having been in the fire, except the hands, which had the flesh left upon them, and were cut in several places, and crammed with salt, apparently with an intention of preserving them. The scalp had a cut in the back part of it, but the scull was free from any fracture. The lower jaw and feet, which were wanting, Eappo told us, had been seized by different Chiefs, and that Terreeoboo was using every means to recover them.'

'The next morning, Eappo, and the king's son, came on board, and brought with them the remaining bones of Captain Cook; the barrels of his gun, his shoes, and some other trifles that belonged to him. Eappo took great pains to convince us, that Terreeoboo, Maiha-maiha, and himself were most heartily desirous of peace; that they had given us the most convincing proof of it in their power; and that they had been prevented from giving it sooner by the other Chiefs, many of whom were still our enemies. He lamented, with the greatest sorrow, the death of six Chiefs we had killed, some of whom, he said, were amongst our best friends. The cutter, he told us, was taken away by Pareea's people; very probably in revenge for the blow that had been given him; and that it had been broken up the next day. The arms of the marines, which we had also demanded, he assured us, had been carried off by the common people, and were irrecoverable; the bones of the Chief alone having been preserved, as belonging to Terreeoboo and the *Erees*.

'Nothing now remained, but to perform the last offices to our great and unfortunate commander. Eappo was dismissed with orders to *taboo* all the bay; and, in the afternoon, the bones having been put into a coffin, and the service read over them, they were committed to the deep with the usual military honours. What our feelings were on this occasion, I leave the world to conceive; those who were present know, that it is not in my power to express them.'

❨ When he had committed the fragments of Cook's body to the deep Clerke could do nothing more in the Hawaiian Islands so sailed on 22nd February 1779, to continue his leader's work in the Arctic. Before leaving, however, the expedition encountered serious trouble at another Hawaiian island, Atooi, where a landing was made to secure water, the trouble being due partly to the absence of the local chiefs, and partly to native quarrels over the ownership of goats left by Captain Cook in the previous year. King's good temper and tact prevented a second massacre of whites, although one Hawaiian was seriously wounded by musket fire.

❨ The ships reached Kamchatka on 23rd April, where, after some difficulties, the Russians supplied provisions, the British in return effecting 'a surprising alteration' in the health of the local inhabitants and soldiers who were suffering from an attack of scurvy. From June until August, Clerke, who was dying of tuberculosis, and whose ships and gear were dangerously rotten, passed through Bering Strait and again attempted unsuccessfully, to find passages around America and Asia to the East and West. Although Clerke failed to reach, by some five leagues, Cook's furthest North (Latitude 70° 33′) his heroic efforts deserve recording. King writes:

'In the morning of the 23d, the clear water, in which we continued to stand to and fro, did not exceed a mile and a half, and was every instant lessening. At length, after using our utmost endeavours to clear the loose ice, we were driven to the necessity of forcing a passage to the Southward, which, at half past seven, we accomplished, but not without subjecting the ship to some very severe shocks. The Discovery was less successful. For, at eleven, when they had nigh got clear out, she became so entangled by several large pieces, that her way was stopped, and immediately dropping bodily to leeward, she fell, broadside foremost, on the edge of a considerable body of ice; and having, at the same time, an open sea to windward, the surf caused her to strike violently upon it. This mass at length either so far broke, or moved, as to set them at liberty to make another trial to escape; but, unfortunately, before the ship gathered way enough to be under command, she again fell to leeward on another fragment; and the swell making it unsafe to lie to windward, and finding no chance of getting clear, they pushed into a small opening, furled their sails, and made fast with ice-hooks.

'In this dangerous situation we saw them at noon, about three miles from us, bearing North West, a fresh gale from the South East driving more ice to the North West, and increasing the body that lay between us. Our latitude, by account, was 69° 8′, the longitude 187°, and the depth of water twenty-eight fathoms. To add to the gloomy apprehensions which began to force themselves on us, at half past four in the afternoon, the weather becoming thick and hazy, we lost sight of the Discovery; but, that we might be in a situation to afford her every assistance in our power, we kept standing on close by the edge of the ice. At six, the wind happily coming round to the North, gave us some hopes, that the ice might drift away and release her; and in that case, as it was uncertain in what condition she might come out, we kept firing a gun every half hour, in order to prevent a separation. Our apprehensions for her safety did not cease till nine, when we heard her guns in answer to ours; and soon after, being hailed be her, were informed, that upon the change of wind, the ice began to separate; and that, setting all their sails, they forced a passage through it. We learned farther, that whilst they were encompassed by it, they found the ship drift, with the main body, to the North East, at the rate of half a mile an hour. We were sorry to find, that the Discovery had rubbed off a great deal of the sheathing from the bows, and was become very leaky, from the strokes she had received when she fell upon the edge of the ice.'

℄ In such circumstances Clerke made the only possible decision—that to return home.

'Thus, finding a farther advance to the Northward, as well as a nearer approach to either continent, obstructed by a sea blocked up with ice, we judged it both injurious to the service, by endangering the safety of the ships, as well as fruitless, with respect to the design of our voyage, to make any farther attempts toward a passage. This, therefore, added to the representations of Captain Gore, determined Captain Clerke not to lose more time in what he concluded to be an unattainable object, but to sail for Awatska Bay, to repair our damages there; and, before the winter should set in, and render all other efforts toward discovery impracticable to explore the coast of Japan.

'I will not endeavour to conceal the joy that brightened the countenance of every individual, as soon as Captain Clerke's resolutions were made known. We were all heartily sick of a navigation full of danger, and in which the utmost perseverance had not been repaid with the smallest probability of success. We therefore turned our faces toward home, after an absence of three years, with a delight and satisfaction, which, notwithstanding the tedious voyage we had still to make, and the immense distance we had to run, were as freely entertained, and perhaps as fully enjoyed, as if we had been already in sight of the Land's-end.'

℄ By early August it was clear that Clerke was on the point of death, and, as no more could be effected in the Arctic that season, the commander turned south to die of consumption at the early age of thirty-eight on 22nd August when the ships were in sight of St. Peter and St. Paul. Gore took over the command and buried the most trusted of Cook's lieutenants under a tree in or near a ruined church. The officers then decided to return home via Macao near Canton where the sailors sold to the Chinese for over £2,000 the furs which they had collected in the North Pacific. Hearing that, in spite of war, both France and the United States had granted free passage to the ships of the famous Cook, Gore returned home by the Cape of Good Hope without escort and reached the Nore after an absence of four years two months and twenty-two days.

⁋ Very properly King concludes his journal with another glowing tribute to Cook's success in the use of anti-scorbutics. The *Resolution* had lost only five men by sickness, three of whom were in a precarious state of health when they left England. The *Discovery* had not lost a man. Cook had indeed trained a magnificent school of officers. In spite of fogs and accidents the *Resolution* and *Discovery* had lost sight of one another on only two occasions.

THE RESULTS OF THE THIRD EXPEDITION

⁋ Cook and Clerke secured during the third voyage the negative information that there were no northern passages, navigable by sailing ships, from the North Pacific to the Atlantic either by east or west. Cook, however, obtained highly important positive results by proving that Bering had accurately reported and located his Strait and other discoveries; by examining long sections of the North West American and the Arctic coastlines (where his crews secured valuable furs), and by the discovery of the Hawaiian (Sandwich) Islands. Although Cook was wrong in regarding these islands as his most important discovery, they were to prove of considerable economic significance and of immense strategic value. In future years the group was in grave danger of passing into the hands of Russia, and it was a matter of major importance to the free world that the discovery of the islands and the infant contacts were made by British and American people.

⁋ While the return of the expedition attracted great interest that interest was clouded by war and by the death of the famous leader. Also for a variety of reasons there was considerable delay in the publication of the results of the voyage. Despite the fact that under his instructions Gore collected near Macao the private journals of the personnel, some unofficial accounts appeared, but the journals of Cook and King were not published until 1784.

⁋ One of the most noteworthy results of the voyage was the fact that once again anti-scorbutics, whether applied by Cook or by his subordinate commander or by his successors, dealt effectively with sea diseases. Nevertheless, a four years voyage in tropical and arctic climates, and endangered by frequent landings amongst primitive peoples, wrought havoc amongst the leading officers. Cook was murdered; Clerke and Surgeon Anderson died of tuberculosis on the voyage; Gore barely survived to bring the vessels home, and the very able King, who concluded Cook's journal, died in 1784, largely as a result of the hardships encountered.

⁋ Of those who survived Burney attained distinction and Bligh notoriety. The most famous of all, Vancouver, continued Cook's work by charting the North West American coast. Once again it may be emphasised that in the opinion of some authorities Cook's hydrography was one of his greatest contributions to science in the help that it afforded seamen.

(It was on the coast of North West America that Cook's third voyage brought developments in exploration and commerce. Although Mackenzie showed Peter Pont of the Hudson Bay Company to be wrong in believing that the Mackenzie reached the Pacific at Cook's inlet, the publication of Cook's explorations of the Pacific and Arctic shores promoted North American discovery, while the successful sale of furs by members of the expedition greatly stimulated that fur trade through which the British, Americans and Russians opened up much of the Northern Pacific and Arctic. Even the Spaniards were sufficiently aroused to continue their explorations northwards and by 1802 the Spanish explorer Martin Fernandez de Navarrette admitted that the existence of a northern passage, alleged to have been discovered in 1592 by a 'priceless liar' named Juan da Fuca, was, like every other legend of a then navigable passage, a complete myth.

Chapter XX
THE MAN AND HIS ACHIEVEMENTS

"Cook figura éternellement à la tête des navigateurs de tous les Siècles et de toutes les nations."

DURMONT D'URVILLE, 1836

THE JOURNALS HAVE SHOWN THAT COOK, WITH HIS PASSION for complete accuracy, tended to overemphasise the negative results of his explorations and to underestimate the importance of the positive side of his discoveries. It seems, therefore, that Cook himself has been partly responsible for the fact that some of his biographers have overemphasised his failures to discover non-existent continents and ocean passages, and have underemphasised some of his great positive achievements. On this positive side his outstanding contributions to geographical knowledge were the completion of the outline map of the Pacific by the discovery of the long eastern shoreline of Australia, the delineation of New Zealand, the examination of long sections of the coast of North America; the discovery of entirely new islands, such as Hawaii and New Caledonia; and the rediscovery and accurate placing of other island groups.

℄ Cook stands as the navigator who virtually discovered, possibly saw, and certainly set close limits to the Antarctic continent, while in the Arctic he confirmed Bering's discovery of his Strait, and the then impossibility of commercial sea routes from this passage either east or west to the Atlantic. No previous navigator had contributed voyages of such length; remained at sea for such long periods, or brought back so much accurate knowledge of such an immense extent of the Earth. While the practical consequences of Cook's work were less than those which followed Columbus' discovery of America or the pioneering of the sea route around Africa, they were consequences of immense importance. Cook's discoveries were responsible for the English-speaking occupation of Australia and New Zealand, together with the acquisition of islands, which later, like Hawaii, became of great strategic and commercial importance. Cook's third voyage also caused rapid developments in exploration, in fur trading, and in the occupation of the North American Pacific coast.

In addition to his contributions to geographical science Cook made gifts to nautical medicine, to navigation and to cartography, which are so evident in his journals that it is unnecessary to emphasise them. Clearly the author of such achievements must have been a man of outstanding character and genius.

Here the biographer encounters the inevitable problem of the hen and the egg. Did the times produce the man or did the man produce the times by his efforts? The conclusion is almost always a compromise between the alternatives, and this is certainly so in the case of Cook, for Cook was the child of a period of scientific revolution, yet in the field of ocean exploration he himself sired the most revolutionary progress. Cook in fact holds in his field a similar eminence to the eminence achieved by Newton and Darwin in other branches of science, and the span of his life lay between theirs for Newton died in 1727 and Darwin was born in 1809. Cook 'arrived' at a moment when the British Government had become officially interested in sea exploration and could and did provide adequate personnel and adequate ships whose design and equipment included the devices for sailing, steering, navigation and so forth which did so much to make possible the European conquest of the Pacific. Then again the Royal Society, founded in 1660, had reached the status and strength to seek overseas observations and data, and to provide important scientific instruments. In the spheres of medicine and astronomy Lind, Pelham and others had paved the way for Cook's defeat of sea diseases, while the astronomer Masklyn and the clock-maker Harrison had devised two methods which Cook was to show could solve, even at sea, the age-old problem of accurately calculating longitude. Yet the magnitude of Cook no more suffers from these advantages than does the greatness of Darwin because evidence existed upon which he could build so brilliantly the doctrine of evolution. For generations men had known that Australia must possess an eastern shoreline, just as they had long known of the existence of certain anti-scorbutics. Now, however, at long last, the existing knowledge in several fields passed to a man of such ability and strength that he could rise from the humblest of beginnings to become one of the very greatest of sea explorers and scientists, and one whose discoveries are in the first rank in fruitful results.

Two of Cook's officers left important estimates of his character, while a third estimate of considerable importance was contributed to the *Morning Chronicle* at the time of the death announcement by an anonymous friend who signed himself 'Columbus', but who Kitson believed from one or two terms of expression was possibly Joseph Banks. King wrote that Cook—'appears to have been most eminently and peculiarly qualified for this species of enterprise (discovery). The earliest habits of his life, the course of his services, and the constant application of his mind, all conspired to fit him for it, and gave him a degree of professional knowledge which can fall to the lot of very few. The constitution of his body was robust, inured to labour, and capable of undergoing the severest hardships. His stomach bore, without difficulty, the coarsest and most ungrateful food. Indeed, temperance in him was scarcely a virtue; so great was the indifference with which he submitted to every kind of self denial. The qualities of his mind were of the same hardy, vigorous kind with those of his body. His understanding was strong and perspicacious; his judgment, in whatever related to the services he was engaged in, quick and sure. His designs were bold and manly, and both in conception, and in the mode of execution, bore evident marks of original genius. His carriage was cool and determined, and accompanied with an admirable presence of mind in the moment of danger. His manners were plain and unaffected. His temper might perhaps have been justly blamed as subject to hastiness and passion, had not these been disarmed by a disposition the most benevolent and humane.'

'Such were the outlines of Captain Cook's character, but its most distinguishing feature was that unremitting perseverance in the pursuit of his object, which was not only superior in the opposition of dangers, and the pressure of hardships, but even exempt from the want of ordinary relaxation. During the long and tedious voyages in which he was engaged, his eagerness and activity were never in the least abated. No incidental temptation could detain him for a moment; even those intervals of recreation, which sometimes unavoidably occurred, and were looked for by us with a longing that people who have experienced the fatigues of service will readily excuse, were submitted to by him with a certain impatience, whenever they could not be employed in making further provision for the more effectual prosecution of his designs'. . . . 'With respect to his professional abilities I shall leave them to the judgment of those who are best acquainted with the nature of the services in which he was engaged. They will readily acknowledge, that, to have conducted three expeditions of so much danger and difficulty, of so unusual a length, and in such a variety of situation with uniform and invariable success, must have required not only a thorough and accurate knowledge of his business, but a powerful and comprehensive genius, fruitful in resources, and equally ready in the application of whatever the higher and inferior calls of the service required.'

⁅ King's estimate of Cook's character should be read in conjunction with the opinion of Samwell, Surgeon's Mate on the *Resolution* until the death of Surgeon Anderson when he was promoted to Surgeon of the *Discovery*. Samwell wrote of Cook, 'Nature had endowed him with a mind vigorous and comprehensive, which in his riper years he had cultivated with care and industry. His general knowledge was extensive and various; in that of his profession he was unequalled. With a clear judgment, strong masculine sense, and the most determined resolution; with a genius peculiarly tuned for enterprise, he pursued his object with unshaken perseverance:—vigilant and active in an eminent degree: cool and intrepid among dangers: patient and firm under difficulties and distress: fertile in expedients: great and original in all his designs, active and resolved in carrying them into execution. These qualities rendered him the animating spirit of the expedition; in every situation he stood unrivalled and alone: on him all eyes were turned: he was our leading star, which at its setting left us involved in darkness and despair. His consitution was strong, his mode of living temperate: why Captain King should not suppose temperance as great a virtue in him as in any other man I am unable to guess. He had no repugnance to good living; he always kept a good table, though he could bear the reverse without murmuring. He was a modest man, and rather bashful; of an agreeable lively conversation, sensible and intelligent. In his temper he was somewhat hasty, but of a disposition the most friendly, benevolent and humane. His person was above six feet high, and though a good looking man, he was plain both in address and appearance. His head was small; his hair which was dark brown, he wore tied behind. His face was full of expression, his nose exceedingly well shaped, his eyes, which were small and of a brown cast, were quick and piercing: his eyebrows prominent, which gave his countenance altogether an air of austerity. He was beloved by his people, who looked up to him as a father, and obeyed his commands with alacrity. The confidence we placed in him was unremitting: our admiration for his great talents unbounded; our esteem for his good qualities affectionate and sincere.

'In exploring unknown countries, the dangers he had to encounter were various and uncommon. On such occasions he always displayed great presence of mind, and steady perseverance in pursuit of his object. The acquisition he has made to our knowledge of the globe is immense, besides improving the art of navigation and enriching the science of natural philosophy. He was remarkably distinguished for the activity of his mind; it was that which enabled him to pay an unwearied attention to every object of the service. The strict economy be observed in the expenditure of the ships stores, and the unremitting care he employed for the preservation of the health of his people, were the causes that enabled him to prosecute discoveries in remote parts of the globe for such a length of time as had been deemed impracticable by former navigators. The method he discovered of preserving the health of seamen in long voyages will transmit his name to posterity as the friend and benefactor of mankind; the success which attended it afforded this truly great man more satisfaction than the distinguished fame that attended his discoveries.'

❡ The tribute paid by 'Columbus', or Joseph Banks, to Cook runs as follows— 'I desire to call to your memory that, beside the merit of having by a series of public services raised himself to a situation eminently above his most sanguine expectations, his genius broke forth, and enabled him to emerge from obscurity, by giving proofs of the most shining capacity in every qualification that could be required in a discoverer of unknown countries.

'Taught by his early education to sail always near the shore, and by frequent practice deeply versed in all manoeuvres necessary to preserve ships from the dangers to which the vicinity of land exposes them, he was never afraid of approaching an unknown coast, and would for weeks and months together persevere to sail amongst sands and shoals, the very appearance of which would have been thought by most seamen a sufficient reason for leaving them; which fact, by comparing the accounts of his voyages with those of some other late discoverers, will be truly verified. He trusted in most cases to the lead, but in some, sent boats to sound ahead of his ship.

'His paternal courage was undaunted. His patience and perseverance not to be fatigued. His knowledge in the art of practical surveying inferior to no man's. His skill in mathematics and astronomy was compleat, as far as those sciences are necessary to a seaman.

'His great attention to the cleanliness of his people, and other minutiae discipline (nothing of which he trusted to anyone but himself) were the great causes of that wonderful health which his ships' company always enjoyed.

'The humanity with which he treated the natives of all places, where he had occasion to touch, had carried him safe through a variety of nations, among whom were many different tribes of warlike and barbarous people; but his attention to the safety of those under his command, and his fixed resolution that no-one should incur more danger than himself, made it his constant measure never to trust any man ashore without him in unknown country till a good understanding with the natives had taken place; but, alas! it is to this humane and laudable disposition that the loss of his life is most probably to be attributed, as he seems to have fallen a sacrifice to his having put himself foremost in attempting to procure redress for the insults his companions had received from the Indians, and to his having placed too much confidence in the return of benevolence which uncivilized people so generally make to those who treat them like fellow-creatures, and which he so frequently experienced.

'His diligence and application were beyond example; for by that alone, even amidst his various occupations, he so far supplied the want of education as to be able, on his return from his second voyage, to write a book, the very style of which was approved, I had almost said admired, by the publick.

'His economy was very uncommon, and made him personally attend with the strictest care to the expenditure of stores, by which means alone he was enabled to make his materials hold out in the long voyages which he made, without a possibility of supply. His manner of living was calculated not for his own comfort, but for what he thought would be most beneficial to the people under his care; for he eat constantly at his own table the usual food of the inhabitants of the country he was in, except when he was amongst the cannibals of New Zealand; which example he contrived to have followed by far the greater part of his crew, lengthening out by this means his European provisions which alone could be kept for any length of time.

'In short, if being a most able and distinguished character in the line of life he had taken and to the summit of which he had raised himself by his merits only, entitles him to the approbation of mankind in general, surely a tear is due to his untimely fate, when he was on the point of returning to his native country to enjoy the applause which would have been bestowed on him by every scientific man, and the comfort that awaited him in domestic life, and in an honourable retirement for the rest of his days.'

¶ This letter seems to come from the pen of one who knew Cook extremely well, admired him greatly and had in all probability sailed with him. It is a very shrewd and revealing document.

¶ Of later, and in some cases striking estimates by Dr J. C. Beaglehole and others we will quote the charming and penetrating tribute paid to Cook by the late Professor G. Arnold Wood, whose *Discovery of Australia* is in the first rank of Australasian literature. Professor Wood wrote—

'The sense of Cook's greatness grows in the student's mind. He does not storm our admiration as, for example, does Drake or Wolfe. There is a certain quietness and reticence in his life, as in his conversation, and as in his writings. He was, we are told, a good talker, yet none of his talk has lived. He wrote accounts of his own voyages in admirable English, but his object was to get the story told, and, as we read, we think rather of the story than of the man. In no one moment does Cook shine forth the evident hero. His character in some way reminds one of that of his greatest contemporary, George Washington—he who won a great war without winning a battle. His greatness appears as we think, not of one moment, but of the whole life. Heroism was so wrought into the texture of character, that he tells a heroic story in a way that makes one imagine it a matter-of-course affair. We think that the story lacks interest, when the fact is that it lacks egotism. Cook solves the riddle of the Pacific, and he tells you that he has done his duty, and has made "a complete voyage". We have to find for ourselves that none but Cook could have done this duty, or could have completed this voyage; that the reason of victory was greatness of mind, of will, and of spirit.

'Cook possessed a marvellous combination of qualities. His physique was splendid; he could do anything, endure anything, eat anything, and digest almost anything; he was only once seriously ill, and was then cured by eating the ship's dog in the way of soup. His activity of mind, both in speculation and in affairs was amazing. He had the full scientific temperament, alike enthusiastic—though he would have hated the word—and sceptical; eager to know, and to know nought save the truth. And he had wonderful judgment in the drawing of inferences, and in the balancing of argument. His eye for scientific problems was as keen as that of a professional student. He observed, for example, the curious problem of the precise relation of the peoples of New Holland and of New Guinea, and he discussed, a century before Darwin, the probable origin and growth of the coral islands.

'And he applied the same vigour of mind to the solution of practical questions. In the story of exploration he is the great organiser of victories. His was the policy of thorough. He first thought out in full and exact ways all the matters of necescary detail:—the choice of ships, the instruments of navigation, the methods of coastal survey, and, above all, the means of preserving health. And, having thought things out, he got things done. He not only did things himself, he persuaded others to do them. He was a Scotchman's son, and therefore a philosopher. Very remarkable are his quiet studies of psychology:—the psychology, for example, of affectionate South Sea island thieves, and of drinking, cursing, courageous, faithful British seamen. He understood them, and he knew how to persuade them to do what he wanted them to do, or as much of it as it was in any way possible that they should do; for, like Burke, he believed that a large part of wisdom is to know how much of the corruption of human nature it is wise to tolerate.

'And dominant in the centre of things was character. Those who sailed with him said that his nature was very passionate. There are facts that illustrate this judgment; and on his last voyage he was guilty of actions which one would like to forget. But the witness who records these actions was himself amazed by them;—amazed, because they stood in inexplicable contrast to his usual conduct. In general, he ruled his passions with such apparent ease that one is tempted to wish that he had been a trifle less virtuous. British seamen in those days were still famous for what Mr Forster, one of the scientific gentlemen on the "Resolution", called the dreadful "energy of their language". Yet I do not remember that Cook ever used a phrase above the average. And he had his opportunities. What, for example, did he say when he found that the islanders had stolen his stockings from under his head while he was wide awake? The carnal man would like to know, but there is silence. We look eagerly into his virtuous life for some small redeeming vice. "Temperance in him," wrote Captain King, who sailed in the last voyage, "was scarcely a virtue; so great was the indifference with which he submitted to every kind of self-denial." Surgeon Samwell quarrels with this statement. Cook, he says "had no repugnance to good living; he always kept a good table, though he could bear the reverse without murmuring"; a statement which makes his virtue exceed the measure attributed by King. His "austerity" was due, not to lack of capacity for pleasure, but to perfection of moral self-control.

'Cook, to use Cromwell's phrase, was a man of a spirit, and his spirit was the spirit of the gentleman. In his intercourse with men of high rank and great wealth, he was always courteous, always dignified, not claiming equality but assuming it. He was their equal and more than their equal, not because he was a great British navigator, but because he was a British gentleman. And he was a farmer's son, self-educated and self-made, and his pay when he named Port Jackson was five shillings a day. As a child cannot be too careful in choosing his grandfather, so a country cannot be too careful in choosing its discoverer; and a country with the ideals of New South Wales could have made no more happy choice.'

⟬ Other leading historians have added their praises. Beaglehole said that the map of the Pacific is 'Cook's ample panegyric'. Christopher Lloyd wrote that Cook's character was summed up in the names of his ships *Resolution* and *Endeavour*, *Adventure* and *Discovery*. Cook, himself, might have appreciated most the words written by his old friend Joseph Banks in consolation to Mrs Cook. 'His name will live for ever in the remembrance of a people grateful for the services his labours have afforded to mankind in general.'

⟬ Few as are the existing memorials, and slight as may be public gratitude today, the fact remains that, throughout vast stretches of the Pacific basin, millions of English speaking people, including many in United States territory, can attribute the foundation of their homes and prosperity to the pioneering discoveries of James Cook.